Force of Words

The Northern World

NORTH EUROPE AND THE BALTIC C.400–1700 AD
PEOPLES, ECONOMIES AND CULTURES

Editors

Jón Viðar Sigurðsson (*Oslo*)
Piotr Gorecki (*University of California at Riverside*)
Steve Murdoch (*St. Andrews*)
Cordelia Heß (*Greifswald*)
Anne Pedersen (*National Museum of Denmark*)

VOLUME 90

The titles published in this series are listed at *brill.com/nw*

Force of Words

A Cultural History of Christianity and Politics in Medieval Iceland (11th-13th Centuries)

By

Haraldur Hreinsson

BRILL

LEIDEN | BOSTON

Cover illustration: A fragment of the boards from Flatatunga. It depicts two figures with halos, possibly Christ and an apostle. National Museum of Iceland.

Library of Congress Cataloging-in-Publication Data

Names: Haraldur Hreinsson, 1985- author.
Title: Force of words : a cultural history of Christianity and politics in Medieval Iceland (11th-13th centuries) / by Haraldur Hreinsson.
Description: Leiden ; Boston : Brill, [2021] | Series: The Northern world, 1569-1462 ; volume 90 | Revision of the author's thesis (doctoral)–University of Münster, 2019. | Includes bibliographical references and index.
Identifiers: LCCN 2020054325 (print) | LCCN 2020054326 (ebook) | ISBN 9789004444966 (hardback) | ISBN 9789004449572 (ebook)
Subjects: LCSH: Christianity and culture–Iceland–History. | Christianity and politics–Iceland–History. | Iceland–Church history.
Classification: LCC BR115.C8 H378 2021 (print) | LCC BR115.C8 (ebook) | DDC 322/.109491209021–dc23
LC record available at https://lccn.loc.gov/2020054325
LC ebook record available at https://lccn.loc.gov/2020054326

Typeface for the Latin, Greek, and Cyrillic scripts: "Brill". See and download: brill.com/brill-typeface.

ISSN 1569-1462
ISBN 978-90-04-44496-6 (hardback)
ISBN 978-90-04-44957-2 (e-book)

Copyright 2021 by Koninklijke Brill NV, Leiden, The Netherlands.
Koninklijke Brill NV incorporates the imprints Brill, Brill Hes & De Graaf, Brill Nijhoff, Brill Rodopi, Brill Sense, Hotei Publishing, mentis Verlag, Verlag Ferdinand Schöningh and Wilhelm Fink Verlag.
All rights reserved. No part of this publication may be reproduced, translated, stored in a retrieval system, or transmitted in any form or by any means, electronic, mechanical, photocopying, recording or otherwise, without prior written permission from the publisher. Requests for re-use and/or translations must be addressed to Koninklijke Brill NV via brill.com or copyright.com.

This book is printed on acid-free paper and produced in a sustainable manner.

Contents

Acknowledgments IX
Abbreviations XI
List of Figures XIII

1 Introduction 1
  1.1 Historiographical Context 4
    1.1.1 *History of Medieval Christianity in Iceland: A Fragmented Field* 4
    1.1.2 *Church and Society in Medieval Iceland* 11
  1.2 Theoretical Considerations 17
    1.2.1 *Ecclesiastical Discourse* 17
      1.2.1.1 Discourse 18
      1.2.1.2 Discourse: Religious and Ecclesiastical 22
    1.2.2 *Perspective of Empire* 24
      1.2.2.1 The Roman Church as an Empire in Medieval Iceland 25
      1.2.2.2 The Perspective of Empire: A Text Oriented Approach 27
  1.3 Source Material 31
    1.3.1 *Textual Sources* 31
    1.3.2 *Material Sources* 34

2 The Roman Church in Free State Iceland 36
  2.1 Christianization of Iceland 37
    2.1.1 *The Roman Ecclesiastical Empire* 37
      2.1.1.1 The Rise of the Papal Center 39
      2.1.1.2 From Center to the Periphery 42
      2.1.1.3 On the Outskirts 46
    2.1.2 *Expanding Boundaries: Christianization of Scandinavia* 48
    2.1.3 *Christianization of Iceland* 53
    2.1.4 *Conclusion: Becoming Christian* 59
  2.2 Christianization and the Production of Religious Texts 60
    2.2.1 *Background: The Roman Church as a Cultural Hegemon* 61
    2.2.2 *Iceland's Earliest Religious Manuscripts* 66
      2.2.2.1 Collections of Hagiographic Material 67
      2.2.2.2 Collections of Sermonic Material 74
      2.2.2.3 Manuscripts with Mixed Content 78

- 2.2.3 *Beyond the Manuscripts: The Materiality of Religious Discourse* 82
- 2.2.4 *Conclusion: Texts in Motion* 87
- 2.3 Icelandic Ecclesiastics and Their Audiences 89
  - 2.3.1 *Representing Rome: Ecclesiastics in Iceland* 89
    - 2.3.1.1 Clerics in the Free State: Socially Diverse or Homogenous? 90
    - 2.3.1.2 Clerical Education: Practical but International 95
    - 2.3.1.3 In Whose Authority? 101
  - 2.2.2 *Audiences of All Kinds* 103
    - 2.2.2.1 Audience according to Religious Source Material 104
    - 2.2.2.2 Audience According to Contemporary Narrative Sources 108
  - 2.3.3 *Pastor and Flock: Points of Encounter* 114
    - 2.3.3.1 *Translatio Ecclesiae:* A Medieval Icelandic Textual Community 114
    - 2.3.3.2 Social Significance of the Church: Panopticon or a Heterotopia 117
  - 2.3.4 *Conclusion: Conflicts of Interests* 119
- 2.4 Ecclesiastical Imagination 120
  - 2.4.1 *Icelanders in the Sixth Age* 120
  - 2.4.2 *Typological Thought* 124
  - 2.4.3 *Typological Thought in Medieval Icelandic Literature* 127
  - 2.4.4 *Conclusion: Beyond the Written Word* 130

3 **Force of Words: Constructing a Christian Society** 132
- 3.1 Authority 133
  - 3.1.1 *Teaching* 134
    - 3.1.1.1 The Original Teaching 135
    - 3.1.1.2 Teaching in the Icelandic Free State 139
  - 3.1.2 *Apostolic Authority* 144
    - 3.1.2.1 Apostolic Mandate 145
    - 3.1.2.2 Apostolic Domination 150
  - 3.1.3 *Hierarchy* 159
    - 3.1.3.1 Primatus Petri 160
    - 3.1.3.2 Church Hierarchy 166
  - 3.1.4 *Conclusion: Powering Over* 170

CONTENTS   VII

- 3.2 The 'Other'   171
  - 3.2.1 *Enemies of the Church*   172
    - 3.2.1.1 Heretics   174
    - 3.2.1.2 Heathens   177
    - 3.2.1.3 Jews   185
  - 3.2.2 *Encountering the 'Other'*   188
    - 3.2.2.1 Expansion of Error   189
    - 3.2.2.2 Becoming Other   192
  - 3.2.3 *Conclusion: Making Enemies*   196
- 3.3 Perish or Prosper   197
  - 3.3.1 *Peace or Unrest?*   198
    - 3.3.1.1 Performing Peace   199
    - 3.3.1.2 Peace of the Church   201
    - 3.3.1.3 Fighting for Peace   204
    - 3.3.1.4 The Danger of Unrest   206
  - 3.3.2 *Heaven or Hell?*   209
    - 3.3.2.1 War   209
    - 3.3.2.2 Anger of God   214
    - 3.3.2.3 Justice   217
    - 3.3.2.4 Punishment   222
    - 3.3.2.5 Rewards   225
  - 3.3.3 *Conclusion: The Only Way*   228

4 Rome Goes North   230

- 4.1 In the Beginning   231
  - 4.1.1 *Chaotic Beginnings*   231
  - 4.1.2 *Echoes from Rome*   236
  - 4.1.3 *Gizurr's Age of Peace*   242
  - 4.1.4 *Conclusion: The Chieftain Church Rises*   246
- 4.2 The Reform of Bishop Þorlákr   247
  - 4.2.1 *Libertas Ecclesiae in Iceland*   248
    - 4.2.1.1 *Backdrop:* Libertas Ecclesiae in Norway   248
    - 4.2.1.2 The First Clash of Church and Chieftains   251
  - 4.2.2 *The Authority of the Archbishop*   254
  - 4.2.3 *Enemies of the Church*   257
  - 4.2.4 *Conclusion: On the Other Side*   263
- 4.3 Reform and Violence: The Rule of Bishop Guðmundr   264
  - 4.3.1 *Guðmundr's Rise to the Episcopacy*   264
  - 4.3.2 *Religious Fervour and Armed Battles*   268

4.3.3   *Iceland's Salvation*   273
   4.3.4   *Conclusion: Framing Violence*   275

5 Conclusion   277

   Appendix   Manuscript Sources   281
   Bibliography   294
   Index of Biblical References   317
   General Index   319

Acknowledgments

This book is a revised version of my doctoral dissertation which I submitted and defended at the University of Münster in Westfalen, Germany, in 2019. In the process of writing the dissertation and, at a later stage, when preparing its publication, I received encouragement, assistance, and support without which this book would never have seen the light of day.

First, I wish to thank my supervisors in my doctoral studies, Wolfram Drews and Agnes S. Arnórsdóttir, for accompanying me along the way. Through their supervision, I am grateful for having come to know the two academic traditions they represent each in their own way, the German on the one hand and the Scandinavian on the other. In Münster, Wolfram Drews provided me with much freedom to work on my research which challenged me at times but also contributed to my independence as a scholar. In Aarhus, Agnes offered me invaluable support through her active engagement with my work, detailed readings of my text, astute remarks, and constructive criticisms, but last but not least for her encouragement and moral support in the moments when it was needed the most.

I carried out the research for this book within the confines of the Graduate School of the Cluster of Excellence: Religion and Politics at the University of Münster which supplied it with a constructive institutional and academic context and financial support which I am highly grateful for. In the course of my studies in Münster, in lectures, colloquia, research groups and regular meetings with other doctoral students, I came across new ideas and perspectives which contributed to my work in various ways. Most of this book was written in the office in Johannisstraße 1 in Münster, where I was fortunate enough to share working space with people who became my friends: Elke Spiessens and, at a later stage, Nadeem Khan. I am particularly grateful for the special support I received in the Cluster from Rüdiger Schmitt, who was always willing to meet and discuss my concerns, whether they were of academic or practical nature. Special thanks are also due to the administrative staff of the Cluster, especially the coordinators of the Graduate School, Julia Simoleit and Vít Kortus, for their advice and kind support throughout the process.

I am indebted to the Arnamagnæan Commission which funded a three months stay at the Arnamagnæan Institute at the University of Copenhagen, in the early stages of my research. These few months were fruitful and in many ways decisive for the direction my research would later take.

Thanks to the editorial board of Brill's Northern World series for accepting this volume into their series as well as to Marcella Mulder and Theo Joppe, editors at Brill, for their kind but professional management of the publication process. Further, I want to thank Philip Roughton for allowing me to use his translation of the hagiographic material from AM 652/630 4to and AM 645 4to and Camilla Basset for her permission to use her translation of *Hungrvaka*. I am also grateful to the Árni Magnússon Insitute for Icelandic Studies in Reykjavík for the permission to use their manuscript pictures as well as the children of Hörður Ágústsson for allowing me to use their father's illustrative drawings from the book, *Dómsdagur og helgir menn á Hólum*.

At all stages of the project, I have benefited from conversations and exchange with friends and colleagues who have generously given me their time with special thanks going out to Ralf Ahlers, Andra Alexiu, Ólafur Haukur Árnason, Richard Cole, Markus Dreßler, Mitchell Duffy, Ásdís Egilsdóttir, Sigurjón Árni Eyjólfsson, Pétur Hreinsson, Hjalti Hugason, Gottskálk Þór Jensson, Steinunn Kristjánsdóttir, Jón Viðar Sigurðsson, Stefán Einar Stefánsson, and Orri Vésteinsson. My father, Hreinn S. Hákonarson, read through the whole manuscript before I submitted it for defense and Tiffany Nicole White read proofs before publication. For all this help I am very grateful while, naturally, all mistakes the book may contain remain my own.

Since I began my doctoral studies, I have been supported by my family and friends who have made everything easier. My parents, Sigríður and Hreinn, my siblings, Dóra, Jóhanna, and Pétur, my grandmother, Halldóra, my friends, Hermann, Hlöðver, and Sigurður; my heartfelt thanks go out to all of these and many other relatives and friends for their care and steadfast support. Last but not least, I thank Silke for the friendship, for the love, and, of course, for going through all of this with me.

    Leipzig, October 10, 2020
    Haraldur Hreinsson

Abbreviations

AM	Manuscripts from the collection of Árni Magnússon.
BHL	*Bibliotheca Hagiographica Latina.*
Cleasby-Vigfusson	Richard Cleasby, Gudbrand Vigfusson. *An Icelandic-English Dictionary.* Oxford: Clarendon, 1874. Accessible on: http://www.ling.upenn.edu/~kurisuto/germanic/oi_cleasbyvigfusson_about.html
DI	*Diplomatarium Islandicum. Íslenzkt fornbréfasafn,* 16 vols (Copenhagen and Reykjavík: Möller and Hið íslenzka bókmenntafélag, 1857–1952).
Fritzner	Online version of Johan Fritzner's *Ordbog over det gamle norske Sprog.* Accessible on http://www.edd.uio.no/perl/search/search.cgi?appid=86&tabid=1275
HMS I and II	*Heilagra manna søgur. Fortællinger og legender om hellige mænd og kvinder.* Vols. I and II. Ed. by C. R. Unger. Christiania [Oslo]: B. M. Bentzen, 1877.
IHB	*Icelandic Homily Book: Perg. 15 4to in The Royal Library, Stockholm.* Ed. by Andrea de Leeuw van Weenen. Icelandic Manuscripts: Series in Quarto 3. Reykjavík: Stofnun Árna Magnússonar á Íslandi, 1993.
ÍB I	*Íslensk bókmenntasaga* I. Ed. by Guðrún Nordal, Sverrir Tómasson, and Vésteinn Ólason. Vol I. Reykjavík: Mál og menning, 1992.
ÍB II	*Íslensk bókmenntasaga* II. Ed. by Böðvar Guðmundsson, Sverrir Tómasson, Torfi H. Tulinius, and Vésteinn Ólason. Vol II. Reykjavík: Mál og menning, 1993.
ÍF	*Íslenzk fornrit*
ÍH	*Íslensk hómilíubók: Fornar stólræður.* Ed. by Sigurbjörn Einarsson, Guðrún Kvaran, and Gunnlaugur Ingólfsson. Reykjavík: Hið íslenska bókmenntafélag, 1993.
KÍ I	Hjalti Hugason. *Frumkristni og upphaf kirkju.* Vol. I of *Kristni á Íslandi.* Reykjavík: Alþingi, 2000.
KÍ II	Gunnar F. Guðmundsson. *Íslenskt samfélag og Rómakirkja.* Vol. II of *Kristni á Íslandi.* Reykjavík. Alþingi, 2000.
KLNM	*Kulturhistorisk lexikon for nordisk middelalder fra vikingetid til reformationstid,* 22 vols. Copenhagen: Rosenkilde og Bagger, 1956–1978.
Leifar	*Leifar fornra kristinna fræða íslenzkra: Codex Arna-Magnæanus 677 4to auk annara enna elztu brota af íslenzkum guðfræðisritum.* Ed. by Þorvaldur Bjarnarson. Copenhagen: Hagerup, 1878.

Mombritius	Boninus Mombritius. *Sanctuarium Seu Vitae Sanctorum*, I-II. Paris: apud Albertum Fontemoing, 1910.
PL	*Patrologia cursus completus, sive bibliotheca universalis, integra, uniformis, commoda, oeconomica, omnium ss. Patrum, doctorum scriptorumque ecclesiasticorum, sive latinorum, sive graecorum. Series Latina.* 217 vols. Ed. J. P. Migne. Paris: Frères Garnier, 1841–1855.
Post	*Postola sögur: Legendariske fortællinger om apostlernes liv deres kamp for kristendommens udbredelse samt deres martyrdød.* Ed. by C. R. Unger. Christiania [Oslo]: B. M. Bentzen, 1874.
Roughton I	Study part (Part I and II) of Philip G. Roughton's *AM 645 4to and AM 652/630 4to: Study and Translation of Two Thirteenth-Century Icelandic Collections of Apostles' and Saints' Lives.* Unpublished Doctoral Dissertation. University of Colorado, Boulder, 2002.
Roughton II	Translation part (Part III.) of Philip G. Roughton's *AM 645 4to and AM 652/630 4to: Study and Translation of Two Thirteenth-Century Icelandic Collections of Apostles' and Saints' Lives.* Unpublished Doctoral Dissertation. University of Colorado, Boulder, 2002.
Sturlunga I and II	*Sturlunga saga. Árna Saga biskups. Hrafns saga Sveinbjarnarsonar hin sérstaka.* Vols. I and II. Ed. by Örnólfur Thorsson. Reykjavík: Mál og menning, 2010 [1988].
Vg.	*Biblia Sacra Iuxta Vulgatam Versionem.* 5th ed. Stuttgart: Deutsche Bibelgesellschaft, 2007.

List of Figures

1. The map shows the locations of the two episcopal sees, the monasteries known to have been established in the course of the Middle Ages and two of the most important centers of clerical education. 2
2. The archbishopric of Niðarós consisted of Norway's five episcopal sees as well as those of Orkney (Kirkwall), the Faroes (Kirkjubø), the Isle of Man, Iceland (Skálholt and Hólar), and Greenland (Garðar). 26
3. The image shows the movement of the Christian religion between Iceland, Scandinavia, the British isles and the continent. Irish influence in Iceland remains a controversial issue and is marked with a dotted line 50
4. Among the earliest and best preserved medieval ecclesiastical artefacts is the Door of Valþjófsstaður. The upper circle shows a knight fighting a lion. The lower circle shows four winged dragons. The door has been dated to the late 12th century. National Museum of Iceland 84
5. The image shows one fragment of the boards from Flatatunga. It depicts two figures with halos, possibly Christ and an apostle. National Museum of Iceland 85
6. Part of an amice. Depicts Christ, sitting on a throne surrounded by the symbols of the evangelists and apostles to his side. It is believed to have been made around 1200 and used at the cathedral of Hólar in Hjaltadalur. National Museum of Iceland 88
7. Icelandic Homily Book, Stock. Perg. 15 4to, 93r. The Árni Magnússon Institute for Icelandic Studies 140
8. Icelandic Homily Book, Stock. Perg. 15 4to, 68r. The Árni Magnússon Institute for Icelandic Studies 142
9. An image showing the crucifixion of the apostle Andrew dating to the 13th century. Andrew's X shaped cross is missing. The statue belonged to the church at Teigur in Fljótshllíð. National Museum of Iceland 156
10. God as King. Illustration from a mid 14th century manuscript AM 227 fol. containing a Norse translation of the Old Testament. Árni Magnússon Institute for Icelandic Studies 211
11. Demon. Illustration from a mid 14th century manuscript AM 227 fol. containing a Norse translation of the Old Testament. Árni Magnússon Institute for Icelandic Studies 212
12. A drawing by Hörður Ágústsson of the images preserved on the panels from Bjarnastaðahlíð. Image: Hörður Ágústsson, Dómsdagur og helgir menn á Hólum, 15 219

13 The Crozier's head shows a gaping creature. It was discovered in Bishop Páll's grave in 1954. National Museum of Iceland   220
14 A creature from a panel from Bjarnastaðahlíð, believed to repesent a serpent surrounding Satan's throne. National Museum of Iceland   222
15 Hörður Ágústsson's reconstruction of the Judgment picture. Unpaginated picture sheets between pages 62 and 63 in Hörður Ágústsson, *Dómsdagur og helgir menn á Hólum*   226

CHAPTER 1

Introduction

The period between 1000 and 1300 stands out as particularly significant in the religious history of Iceland.[1] During these centuries, the people living on the island abandoned the Old Norse religion practiced in Scandinavia for centuries and adopted another one, Christianity, which since then has played a central role in the formation of Icelandic society. As the Icelanders[2] were getting accustomed to the new Christian religious ideas and practices, they also witnessed the introduction of a phenomenon which was to become the wealthiest and most powerful institution in medieval Icelandic society: The Roman Church.[3] Many aspects of the rise of the Church in Iceland have been thoroughly studied by historians. Its growth as an institution has, for example, been investigated down to the smallest preserved details. It has been shown how the Church slowly grew from being a side project of the most powerful families in the country into an autonomous and self-sustaining institution, thoroughly integrated into the institutional hierarchy led by the bishop of Rome. This process brought with it some wide-ranging changes: All around the country, small churches rose close to farmsteads. The country was divided into two dioceses: that of Skálholt in the South, and Hólar in the North. Monasteries were established, the earliest one in 1133 (see figure. 1). In 1097, Icelanders agreed to pay a tithe in order to maintain churches and sustain priests. With time, through a series of political and sometimes armed conflicts, the Church gradually managed to gain more control of its own affairs. These changes, administrative and economical in nature, have been the subject of numerous historical

---

1 In the historiography of medieval Iceland, these centuries fall mostly within a period which in English speaking scholarship is either termed the Commonwealth Period or the Free State Period (*þjóðveldisöld*) during which time there existed no centralized, executive authority in the country. It is taken to begin with the foundation of the general legislative and judicial assembly (*Alþingi*) in 930 and ends with a pledge of allegiance made by the Icelandic chieftains to King Hákon Hákonarson of Norway (r. 1217–1263).
2 The term 'Icelanders' will be used in the socio-geographic sense of the people living on the island with no claim made to the problematic idea of an existing collective (national) identity of that group. For a discussion of the different group-identities among medieval Icelanders, see Sverrir Jakobsson, *Við og veröldin: Heimsmynd Íslendinga 1100–1400* (Reykjavík, 2005), pp. 328–352.
3 When capitalized, the word 'Church' refers to the medieval Roman Church and the manifestation it took in Iceland after its introduction in the course of the 10th and 11th centuries.

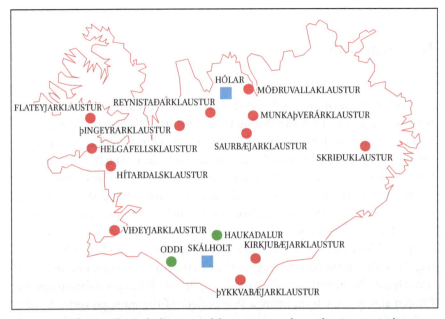

FIGURE 1   The map shows the locations of the two episcopal sees, the monasteries known to have been established in the course of the Middle Ages and two of the most important centers of clerical education.

studies and figure more prominently in the scholarly literature on the medieval Church in Iceland than any other topic in the field.

Although such structural changes made the Church's presence clearly apparent, there were other features of its operation which, in the long run, were to have more impact on people's everyday-life. While bishops and chieftains were debating over matters like church property, all around the country the Church's ordained servants continued to provide their flocks with spiritual nourishment and edification. That was, after all, the divinely sanctioned purpose of the Church as the channel of salvation in the world and the mystical body of Christ. In churches, chapels, and monasteries, medieval Icelanders were taught what to believe and how to behave as good Christians. Through hymns and prayers, preaching and readings, they soon came to learn about their place in the world and the sacred history of the Church. Much information can be gained about how Christianity was practiced in Iceland during these centuries through the preserved source material, such as religious texts, artefacts, and archaeological remains, all of which will be included in the present study. Of most significance, however, is a group of religious texts consisting primarily of sermons containing theological reflections and scriptural interpretations and hagiographic narratives telling of the lives of the saints. It is the contention of the present research, central to its argumentation, that this body of texts what was being mediated to Christian Icelanders of all social standings. The study further argues that these texts contain layers of meaning, of much significance for understanding the social and political developments Icelandic society went through after the arrival of the Church.

No historian of medieval Iceland would deny the importance of religious ideas and practices for the institutional growth of the Church in Iceland. This is, however, not reflected in scholarship. In fact, it often appears as if important decisions regarding church politics and finances were made in isolation from the religious ideas and practices lying at the center of the Church's activities. Along such lines, scholarship has existed in two distinct sides or spheres: an outer one concerned with the Church as a political entity, protecting its interests, striving to increase its wealth and power, and an inner one dealing with the religious ideas and practices. Whilst much is known about each sphere respectively, much has been assumed and less systematically investigated about the ways in which these two spheres may have come together, crossed, clashed, and overlapped. The present study locates itself in this area of intersection. Central to its reasoning is the notion, often overlooked in the historiography of medieval Iceland, that when it comes to matters of medieval Christianity and the Church, the political is religious and the religious is political. As the Church was emerging, growing, and establishing itself in Iceland, its political dealings– conflicts, losses, and victories – had a highly significant religious side. Similarly, the religious message mediated by clerics in churches and elsewhere had a strong political layer which consistently came into play in other fields of society.

As this study proceeds, its course of inquiry centers around the following thesis: The religious message the Church was mediating before and during its institutional consolidation, accessible through sermonic and hagiographic sources from the period, played an important role as the Church was gaining ground in Iceland. This message served as a religious framework for the Church's advance, providing a firm basis for its authority, supporting its institutional structures and legitimizing the ways in which it encountered opposition. In other words, it provided the Church and its representatives with a discursively constructed position of power, of which it made ample use in any dispute or conflict. For describing this neglected aspect of the Christianization process, instructive parallels can be found in how other large-scale political entities have legitimized their imperial expansion and maintained control over distant territories. The following introduction is intended to further prepare and substantiate this central claim by exploring the study's research-historical context, explaining its theoretical premises and introducing the most important source material.

1.1 Historiographical Context

Compared to the scholarship on many other regions of medieval Europe, the political aspects of Christian religious thought have received limited attention in the context of medieval Iceland. Questions pertaining to how religious ideas (as they are reflected in religious texts and images) came into play in the social and cultural changes taking place after the introduction of Christianity, have remained in the shadow of analyses of institutional structures and economic developments. To further explain the research environment that shapes the main thesis of this study, two research trajectories will be explored, each with its own set of challenges and knowledge gaps. These are, on the one hand, the broader scholarly tradition of the history of medieval Christianity in Iceland, and, on the other hand, the more narrow scholarly debate concerning the relationship of the Christian religion to Icelandic society, in which it established itself during the period between 1000 and 1300.

1.1.1 *History of Medieval Christianity in Iceland: A Fragmented Field*

The reasons behind the lack of interest in the social and political significance of religious discourses and practices in Free State Iceland are complex. First of all, the history of medieval Christianity in Iceland has been, and to a certain extent still is, in a somewhat fragmentary state. This means that the attention given to the subject has, more often than not, been limited and short-spanned, driven by goals other than the ones attributed to the field of history of Christianity.[4]

---

4 As it is carried out in this book as a scholarly field of inquiry, 'History of Christianity' is primarily indebted to two scholarly traditions. First, it shares the goals of the history of the Christian religion as it is practiced within the field 'history of religions.' As such, it aims to analyse and explain a particular historical manifestation of the Christian religion as any other sociohistorical phenomenon deserving the label 'religious,' which is much the same as "discussing the temporal, contextual, situated, interested, human, and material dimensions of those discourses, practices, communities, and institutions that characteristically represent themselves as eternal, transcendent, spiritual, and divine." Bruce Lincoln, "Theses on Method," in *Gods and Demons, Priests and Scholars: Critical Explorations in the History of Religions* (Chicago, 2012), p. 1. Second, this study also identifies with the directions taken by the discipline of church history as carried out within academic theological faculties in recent decades. As described by church historian Albrecht Beutel, the discipline's object of research has been expanded to include any historical phenomenon making a claim (*Inanspruchnahme*) – whether explicit or implicit – to represent the Christian

Concentrated efforts of bringing together the research done by scholars in different corners in order to construct a comprehensive view of the Christian religion in Iceland during the Middle Ages are few and far between, although important attempts have been made in the last two decades.[5]

The reasons for this development are found in the fact that the scholars shaping the discourse and research agenda of the field of medieval Icelandic society and culture had other main interests than the Christian religion. Most important of these were, on the one hand, scholars oriented towards literary studies (historians of literature, literary analysts, philologists, linguists, and codicologists (material philologists)) collectively grouped together under the umbrella term Nordic studies (*Norrœn frœði*) and, on the other hand, historians of the Middle Ages. Although these two fields overlapped and supplemented each other, their division of labour could be roughly described in the following way: While scholars of Nordic studies were exploring the history, nature, and context of the indigenous saga literature, medieval historians were preoccupying themselves with topics of political, constitutional, and economic history, primarily during the period before and leading up to the incorporation of Iceland into the Norwegian kingdom in 1262–1264. Of course, granted the central role it played in medieval European societies, the Christian religion and the Church were topics frequently addressed and studied in both fields. It is nonetheless safe to say that the Christian religion was more often treated as a background element; certainly an important background element but only to the extent that it was capable of throwing light on the field specific questions being dealt with each time.[6] By the same token, fields that did not serve such purposes, for

---

religion. According to such an understanding, the concept 'church' refers broadly to any historical materialization of Christian religiosity. Albrecht Beutel, "Vom Nutzen und Nachteil der Kirchengeschichte: Begriff und Funktion einer theologischen Kerndisziplin," in *Protestantische Konkretionen* (Tübingen, 1998), p. 5.

5 Symptomatic of the fragmentary state of the field, the most important contributions to the history of the Christian religion dating to the 20th century can be found as subchapters in overview writings on Icelandic history and Icelandic literature, in introductions to critical editions of medieval sagas and journal articles. Arguably, a large part of the most original research done during this period on medieval Christianity in Iceland is dispersed around the 22 volumes of the *Kulturhistorisk lexikon for nordisk middelalder*, published between 1956 and 1978. *Kulturhistorisk leksikon for nordisk middelalder fra vikingetid til reformationstid*, 22 vols. (Copenhagen, 1956–1978).

6 Exceptions include the work of the French literary scholar Régis Boyer, *La vie religieuse en Islande (1116–1264) d'après la Sturlunga Saga et les Sagas des Évêques* (Paris, 1979) and Arnved Nedkvitne, *Lay Belief in Norse Society 1000–1350* (Copenhagen, 2009). See also Peter Hallberg, "Imagery in Religious Old Norse Prose Literature: An Outline." *Arkiv för nor disk filologi* 102 (1987), 120–170.

example the content of the religion remained largely an unploughed field until a few decades ago, with the exception of the ground research done by art historians and archaeologists. Elsewhere, such concerns would be attended to by theologians and historians of religion, but apart from the important work done by Magnús Már Lárusson[7] and Jón Hnefill Aðalsteinsson[8] (and a number of final theses and articles in journals, magazines, and newspapers) theologians were practically absent from the discussion.[9]

The last two decades have witnessed a marked interest in medieval Christianity in Iceland. On the occasion of the thousand year anniversary of Christianity in the country, a four volume overview work was published in the year 2000.[10] Of the four volumes, two are devoted to the Middle Ages: The first one dealt with the conversion period and the earliest phase of Christianity, written by the main editor Hjalti Hugason and the second volume on the Church in the High and Late Middle Ages was written by the historian Gunnar

---

7 The most important work done by Lárusson, professor of history and theology at different points during his career, was his participation in the editing of the *Kulturhistorisk lexikon* and the numerous entries he wrote for it on various topics relating to the medieval Christianity in Iceland. See also Lárusson's collection of articles *Fróðleiksþættir og sögubrot* (Hafnarfjörður, 1967).

8 The research of Aðalsteinsson, who pursued his academic career within the disciplines of ethnology and anthropology, was to a large extent directed at the conversion from paganism to Christianity. Well-known is his theory, set forth in his doctoral dissertation *Under the Cloak*, on the shamanic role of the lawspeaker Þorgeirr when deciding for Christianity over the pagan religion during the law-assembly at Þingvellir in the year 999. Jón Hnefill Aðalsteinsson, *Under the Cloak: The Acceptance of Christianity in Iceland with Particular Reference to the Religious Attitudes Prevailing at the Time* (Uppsala, 1978).

9 The reasons are of both cultural and practical nature. In the predominantly protestant cultural and religious Icelandic environment, the scholars holding the only professorship endowed for church history at the University of Iceland, have concentrated on those periods of history of most interest and use for the students of the theological faculty of the University of Iceland, whose primary aim has been and still is to educate pastors for the Icelandic national church (Evangelical Lutheran Church of Iceland). Consequently, they have focused on Early Christianity and Post-Reformation Iceland, leaving the medieval period to scholars of other fields.

10 Hjalti Hugason, ed. *Kristni á Íslandi* I-IV (Reykjavík, 2000). The last overview work on Icelandic Christianity was that of bishop Jón Helgason (1866–1942), published in 1925 and 1927 and the one before that bishop Finnur Jónsson's (1704–1789) *Historia Ecclesiastica Islandiæ*, 4 vols., (Copenhagen, 1772–1778). Interestingly, already after the publishing of Jón Helgason's *Islands Kirke fra dens Grundlæggelse til Reformationen*, in 1925, the historiography of the Church in medieval Iceland was being criticized for being fragmentary. In a review of the work, the renowned (and later notorious for his support of the NSDAP) protestant theologian Emanuel Hirsch criticized it for being to a large extent simply "Bischofsgeschichte," in which "das Licht wird stärker gesehen als der Schatten." *Theologische Literaturzeitung* 23 (1927), 541.

F. Guðmundsson.[11] The two volumes provide a good overview of the state of knowledge in the field at the time. From a historiographical point of view, the novelty is to be found in their focus on cultural historical aspects which had until then not received much attention, including chapters on religious ideas and practices. Such an emphasis is apparent in the last part of Hugason's volume and still more visible throughout Guðmundsson's second volume, simply because the source material is richer for the period under inspection.[12] Despite the attention given to cultural historical concerns, the two volumes can rather be said to reproduce the fragmentation of the field instead of working towards its unification. Illustrative of this tendency is the organization of Hugason's volume where the discussion on 'religious life and society" (*trúarlíf og samfélag*) is kept separate from the much more extensive parts on the conversion and the history of the Church as an institution – the rise of the parish system, the episcopacy, the tithe – which happen to be the topics most discussed by medieval historians and literary scholars through the years. Apart from short interludes between the volume's different sections, it does not make an attempt to give a holistic view of the period, primarily because it is not allowed by previous research. It is, as Orri Vésteinsson put it in his overall positive review, a fragmentary history (*brotasaga*), a narrative woven together to the extent possible out of the fragments available.[13]

Along similar lines, the research done in the last two decades – which has been considerably vigorous – has been carried out along the traditional

---

11   The work received generally positive reviews. It was hailed as an "epoch-making work" and coming equal to bishop Finnur Jónsson's *Historia Ecclesiastica Islandiæ*. Sigurjón Árni Eyjólfsson, "Kristni á Íslandi: umfjöllun um tímamótaverk," *Kirkjuritið* 68/2 (2001), 38–48; Gunnar Karlsson, "Verkið sem tókst að vinna: Um Kristni á Íslandi I-IV," *Ný saga* 12 (2000), 28.

12   Jón Viðar Sigurðsson pointed out that the work "directed its attention more towards the religion itself and its many sides than done in previous work on church history," adding that more work was needed. Jón Viðar Sigurðsson, "Allir sem sjá líta þó ekki jafnt á: sagnaritun um íslenskar miðaldir fram um 1300," in *Íslensk sagnfræði á 20. öld*, eds. Guðmundur J. Guðmundsson, Guðmundur Jónsson and Sigurður Ragnarsson (Reykjavík: Sögufélag, 2009), 51–52. Hubert Seelow described it as "tatsächlich eine Darstellung der Kulturgeschichte Islands unter besonderer Berücksichtigung der christlichen Religion." Hubert Seelow, "Hjalti Hugason et al. (Hg.): *Kristni á Íslandi*," *Skandinavistik* 23/1 (2002), 58. Orri Vésteinsson also expressed his appreciation of these features of the work but stressed at the same time that it first and foremost exposes the research gaps existing in the field which could not be filled in an overview work such as Hugason's volume. Orri Vésteinsson, "Brotasaga: Um fyrsta bindi Kristni á Íslandi" in *Kristni á Íslandi: Útgáfumálþing á Akureyri 15. apríl 2000 og í Reykjavík 23. október 2000*, ed. Ágústa Þorbergsdóttir (Reykjavík, 2001), pp. 114–115.

13   Orri Vésteinsson, "Brotasaga," p. 115.

disciplinary trajectories described above. Literary scholars have paid increased attention to religious literature, particularly hagiography.¹⁴ The literary activity surrounding the bishops Þorlákr Þórhallsson and Guðmundr Arason – the two Icelandic bishops who were venerated as saints – has been thoroughly studied, and in Þorlákr's case with careful attention to the Latin literary context in which it took place.¹⁵ Old Icelandic sermonic literature has attracted the attention of philologists (mostly those working in North America and Italy) who continue to publish critical editions of fragments of sermons not published before or only partly in dated editions.¹⁶ These texts have, however, not been subject to much historical contextualization. One of the most fruitful fields of research for medieval Christianity is that of archaeology, but recent excavations of medieval monasteries, churches, and cemeteries have brought out much new material relating to medieval Christianity.¹⁷ In fact, largely fuelled

---

14 See for example Ásdís Egilsdóttir's numerous articles on the subject, for example those collected in a recent *Festschrift* published on the occasion of her 70th birthday: *Frœðimœmi: Greinar gefnar út í tilefni 70 ára afmælis Ásdísar Egilsdóttur* (Reykjavík, 2016).

15 For a general discussion on bishop Þorlákr, see Ásdís Egilsdóttir's introduction to her critical edition of *Þorláks saga* in *íF* XVI. On the Latin literary context, see Gottskálk Jensson, "Nokkrar athugasemdir um latínubrotin úr *Vita sancti Thorlaci episcopi et confessoris*," in *Pulvis Olympicus. Afmælisrit tileinkað Sigurði Péturssyni*, eds. Jón Ma. Ásgeirsson, Kristinn Ólason and Svavar Hrafn Svavarsson (Háskólaútgáfan, 2009), pp. 97–109; Susanne Miriam Fahn and Gottskálk Jensson, "The Forgotten Poem: A Latin Panegyric for Saint Þorlákr in AM 382 4to," *Gripla* 21 (2010), 19–60; Gottskálk Jensson, "*Revelaciones Thorlaci Episcopi* – Enn eitt glatað latínurit eftir Gunnlaug Leifsson munk á Þingeyrum," *Gripla* 23 (2012), 133–175. Bishop Guðmundr has been the subject of two doctoral dissertations in recent years, Joanna A. Skórzewska, *Constructing a Cult: The Life and Veneration of Guðmundr Arason (1161–1237)* in the Icelandic Written Sources (Leiden, 2011) and Gunnvör S. Karlsdóttir, *Guðmundar sögur biskups: Þróun og ritunarsamhengi* unpublished doctoral dissertation (University of Iceland, 2017). A critical edition of the different versions of the saga of bishop Guðmundr is also expected in the series *Íslenzk fornrit*.

16 Examples being the following articles: Carla Cucina, "En kjǫlrinn jarteinir trú rétta. Incidenza di tropi classici e cristiani sulle tradizioni anglosassone e scandinava." *Rivista Italiana di Linguistica e di Dialettologia* XII (2010), 25–93; Stephen Pelle, "Twelfth-Century Sources for Old Norse Homilies: New Evidence from AM 655 XXVII 4to," *Gripla* XXIV (2013), 45–75 and Dario Bullitta, "The Story of Joseph of Arimathea in AM 655 XXVII 4to," *Arkiv för nordisk filologi* 131 (2016), 47–740.

17 Churches and cemeteries have been excavated in the region of Skagafjörður, see Guðný Zoëga, "Early Church Organization in Skagafjörður, North Iceland. The Results of the Skagafjörður Church Project," *Collegium Medievale* 27 (2014), 21–60; Guðný Zoëga 2015, "A Family Revisited: The Medieval Household Cemetery of Keldudalur, North Iceland." *Norwegian Archaeological Review* 48 (2015),105–28; Guðný Zoëga and Douglas Bolender, "An Archaeology of Moments: Christian Conversion and Practice in a Medieval Household Cemetery," *Journal of Social Archaeology* 17 (2017), 69–91. See also Steinunn

by recent excavations of monasteries, the sphere of medieval Christianity which has enjoyed the largest share of attention is that of the Benedictine and Augustinian monasteries founded in Iceland during the medieval period (see figure. 1). As for historical scholarship, strictly defined, apart from the studies of Orri Vésteinsson and Agnes S. Arnórsdóttir, which will be discussed in more detail shortly, few major works have been published dealing specifically with medieval Christianity in Iceland during this period.[18] Scholars of religion have only partaken in the discussion of medieval Christianity in Iceland to a limited degree.[19] The most prolific religion scholar in the field is the medievalist Margaret Cormack, who has done much work on the historical development of the cult of the saints in Iceland. In her doctoral dissertation, for example *The Saints in Iceland*, she has done important groundwork for any cultural historical work in the field by providing an extensive survey of the material and literary items related to every saint recorded to have been known in Iceland during the Middle Ages.[20]

The tendency to keep within the traditional disciplinary boundaries has resulted in many questions relating to the relationship between religion and society being left unattended. In some cases, this has led to overly static and one-sided view of the socio-political capabilities of the Christian religion as

---

    Kristjánsdóttir numerous publications on monasteries in Iceland, the most recent of which is Steinunn Kristjánsdóttir, *Leitin að klaustrunum: Klausturhald á Íslandi í fimm aldir* (Reykjavík: Sögufélag, 2017).

18   Two extensive studies are concerned with medieval Christianity in the late Middle Ages: Lára Magnúsardóttir's 2007 dissertation on excommunication and ecclesiastical power in the late Middle Ages, *Bannfæring og kirkjuvald á Íslandi 1275–1550: Lög og rannsóknarforsendur* (Reykjavík, 2007) and Erika Sigurdsson's 2011 dissertation on the institutional organization of the Church in Iceland in the 14th century, *The Church in Fourteenth-Century Iceland: The Formation of an Elite Clerical Identity*, The Northern World 72 (Leiden, 2016).

19   After the publishing of *Kristni á Íslandi* in 2000, Hjalti Hugason has been primarily concerned with early modern and modern church history, although he has regularly published articles on matters concerning bishop Guðmundr Arason of Hólar. For the present study, his most important recent publication is "Áfök um samband ríkis og kirkju: Deilur Guðmundar Arasonar og Kolbeins Tumasonar í kirkjupólitísku ljósi," *Saga* XLVII (2009), 122–148.

20   See Margaret Cormack, *The Saints in Iceland: Their Veneration from the Conversion to 1400*, Subsidia hagiographica 78 (Brussels,1994). Among other work done by Cormack valuable for the present research, in addition to her many articles, are her edited volumes *Saints and their Cults in the Atlantic World* (Columbia, 2007) and *Muslims and Others in Sacred Space* (Oxford, 2012). In recent years, Cormack has been working on developing an interactive geographical database on churches and veneration of saints in the diocese of Hólar. See *Saints and Geography Portal*, accessible on http://www.saintsgeog.net/.

it manifested itself in the Icelandic Free State.[21] An example of such would be the contradiction between the Church's proclamation of peace on the one hand and the participation of its ordained servants in various conflicts, reproduced time and again by scholars of medieval Icelandic culture and society. Along such lines, the Church's program has been described in terms of establishing "the ideals of unselfish behaviour, abnegation of worldly desires, love of others and duty to God" which were supposed to "undermine the codes of vengeance" characterizing Icelandic society in the 11th, 12th, and 13th centuries.[22] Clerics of all ranks are portrayed as men of peace who should not participate in conflict unless for the purpose of mediating between warring parties.[23] According to such views, putting down one's weapon is seen "as a testimony of a living Christian faith," while doing the opposite is rendered problematic.[24] Surely, as will be discussed later on, peace was a prominent theme in the proclamation of the Church in Commonwealth Iceland but that does not mean that the attitude of the Icelandic clergy and Christian laymen towards disputes or conflict should be reduced to unquestioning pacifism. Neither does it entail that the notion of peace, as it is constructed in the earliest Christian source material, is under all circumstances nonconfrontational and nonviolent.

The preserved source material from medieval Iceland gives access to a rich array of religious ideas and interpretations, which came into play in diverse ways. Religion is, from this point of view, an essentially boundary-crossing phenomenon, thoroughly enmeshed in the social, cultural, political, and economic lives of religious individuals. Applying such an understanding to the significance of religious thought in Free State Iceland, this research seeks to illuminate the great social changes taking place in the course of the Christianization process as well as the disputes, altercations, and armed conflicts accompanying it.

---

21   Certainly, there exist exceptions, Torfi H. Tulinius' *Skáldið í skriftinni: Snorri Sturluson og Egils saga*, Íslensk menning (Reykjavík, 2004) being a particularly impressive example. For a revised version in English, see Torfi H. Tulinius, *The Enigma of Egill: The Saga, the Viking Poet, and Snorri Sturluson*, Islandica LVII, trans. Victoria Cribb (Ithaca, 2014).
22   Guðrún Nordal, *Ethics and Action in Thirteenth-Century Iceland* (Odense, 1998), pp. 20 and 47.
23   Sverrir Jakobsson, *Auðnaróðal: Baráttan um Ísland 1096–1281* (Reykjavík, 2016), p. 29; Ármann Jakobsson, "Hinn fullkomni karlmaður: Ímyndarsköpun fyrir biskupa á 13. öld," *Studia theologica islandica* 25 (2007), 124; Orri Vésteinsson, *Christianization of Iceland: Priests, Power, and Social Change 1000–1300* (Oxford, 2000), p. 211.
24   Guðrún Nordal, *Ethics and Action*, p. 186.

1.1.2 Church and Society in Medieval Iceland

Although scholars of medieval Iceland have been rather reluctant to address concrete examples of the social and political significance of Christian thought and discourses, there has not been a lack of large-scope, all-encompassing paradigms to describe the relationship of the Christian religion to the circumstances – social, cultural, and political – in which it was taking root. Between around 1940 and 1970, an influential group of scholars formulated the view that medieval Icelandic society was marked by a clear division between a clerical, European cultural sphere on the one hand and an indigenous, national, and secular sphere on the other. An example of how such a division was constructed is found in the *Age of the Sturlungs* by Einar Ólafur Sveinsson, one of the proponents of the group which came to be known as the 'Icelandic school' in Nordic scholarship.[25] Opposed to the political arena where the chieftains of the most powerful families fought for domination of the island in the thirteenth century, was the 'world' of the Church and Christian religion: "In cloisters, in churches, and on the episcopal sees there is a different world, a world with its own contrasts and its own struggles, but very different from the other."[26] Not to say that scholars influenced by the Icelandic school disregarded the role of the Church entirely; rather, the Christian Church and its representatives were considered as guests, external to an Icelandic culture and political system which constituted something unique when compared to the rest of Christian Europe.[27] According to this view, which the Swedish literary scholar Lars Lönnroth, an adamant critic of the Icelandic school, called the 'theory of the two cultures' (*Sw.* Tesen om de två kulturerna), Icelandic culture reached its zenith with the production of the saga

---

25 The Icelandic school was primarily known for its *Buchprosatheorie*, i.e. its strict emphasis on the Icelandic sagas as works of literature, opposed to the *Freiprosalehre* which preceded it, according to which the writing of the sagas is considered as a final point of a long development of oral mediation of the sagas content, reaching as far back as the 9th century when the events they describe took place. Notable proponents of this school were the literary scholars Sigurður Nordal (1886–1974) and Einar Ól. Sveinsson (1899–1984) and the historian Jón Jóhannesson (1909–1957).

26 Einar Ól. Sveinsson, *The Age of the Sturlungs: Icelandic Civilization in the Thirteenth Century*, Islandica XXXVI, trans. Jóhann S. Hannesson (Ithaca, 1953), p. 5.

27 For an overview of this discussion, see Jesse L. Byock, "History and the Sagas: The Effect of Nationalism," in *From Sagas to Society: Comparative Approaches to Early Iceland* (Enfield Lock, 1992), pp. 43–59 and Guðmundur Hálfdanarson, "Interpreting the Nordic Past: Icelandic Medieval Manuscripts and the Construction of a Modern Nation," in *The Uses of the Middle Ages in Modern European States: History, Nationhood, and the Search for Origins* (Basingstoke, 2011), pp. 52–71.

literature, representing a pure manifestation of Germanic culture, unaffected by Latin Christendom.[28]

According to this view, the rise of the Church and its most important institutional structures had to be reconciled with the economic and political interests of the ruling class. Along these lines, the Icelandic chieftains were depicted as autonomous representatives of the indigenous Icelandic culture and the Church portrayed accordingly as a vehicle for bolstering their power. Sigurður Nordal, arguably the most influential scholar of medieval Icelandic culture in the first half of the 20th century, coined the term 'Chieftain Church' (*goðakirkja*) to describe the church order in the 11th and 12th centuries. Nordal was first to point out how the imposition of the Tithe Law of 1097 increased the wealth of church owning chieftains explaining how swiftly and smoothly it seems to have been accepted by the Icelandic ruling class.[29] Björn Þorsteinsson probed further into the specifics of the emerging system and used the term 'church chieftains' (*kirkjugoðar*) and the term 'church chieftain supremacy' (*kirkjugoðaveldi*) to describe the political and religious affairs between 1118 (the death of Bishop Gizurr Ísleifsson) and the beginning of the Age of the Sturlungar (usually dated to the year 1220).[30] According to Þorsteinsson, the church chieftains constituted a new 'class of magnates' who grew in wealth and influence through the system engendered by the tithe law. Having bequeathed their land and property to their church, which they continued to handle as if it were their own, they received half of the tithe as well as other profits, which were exempt from taxation. This led to an increase in wealth which the church chieftain families used to buy more land. Gradually, this led to the power consolidation and social differentiation that characterized the thirteenth century. Even though few still adhere to Þorsteinsson's Marxist historiographical paradigm, his findings that the political developments of the 13th century should be explained in view of the tithe and the social and economic consequences it entailed is still widely accepted today.

Much of the scholarship immediately following the era of the Icelandic school came as a reaction to its view of the relationship between Church

---

28   Sigurður Nordal's essay "Samhengið í íslenzkum bókmenntum," in *Íslenzk lestrarbók 1400–1900* (Reykjavík: Bókaverzlun Sigfúsar Eymundssonar, 1924), pp. ix-xxxii, is often cited as representing such a view. For criticisms (of which there are plenty), see for example Torfi H. Tulinius, "The Self as Other: Iceland and the Culture of Southern Europe in the Middle Ages," *Gripla* XX (2009). 199–215.
29   Sigurður Nordal, *Íslensk menning* I, p. 296.
30   For the translations of technical terms from Icelandic medieval history, I rely on Orri Vésteinsson's list of terms at the end of his *Christianization of Iceland*, pp. 287–296.

and society, calling for a reconsideration of the limited role ascribed to the Christian religion in the shaping of society and, primarily perhaps, culture, as it is represented by the production of saga literature. Already in 1964, Lönnroth called for a farewell "to the image of the Icelandic farmer, who afar from the European culture of clerics and courtiers, entertains himself by writing down old accounts from his home."[31] Another scholar objecting to this view was Hermann Pálsson, who in his work on the medieval writing *Hrafnkels saga* insisted that the Icelandic medieval literature was, first and foremost, an offspring of "the Christian tradition of medieval Europe," and that the content of the Icelandic family sagas "is seen through Christian eyes and intended for Christian ears."[32] Inevitably, the tension between the two views extended itself to the field of history, crystallizing in Sveinbjörn Rafnsson's reviews of the second and third volumes of the overview work *Saga Íslands* (*E. History of Iceland*), published in 1975 and 1978. Particularly notable was Rafnsson's harsh criticism of the volumes' chapters on the Church in Iceland, written by Magnús Stefánsson, professor of medieval history in Bergen. Among other things, Rafnsson found fault in Stefánsson's espousal to an outdated historical paradigm in his overemphasis on the national traits of the Church in Iceland during the Free State period. Rafnsson's criticism of the second volume was directed towards the "old nineteenth-century-perspectives" characteristic of the volume including its lack of comparison with other regions of Europe.[33] Throughout his career, Rafnsson has been untiring in his attempts at illustrating the cogency of viewing Icelandic society and literary culture as an integrated part of Latin Christendom. His main field of research has been medieval Icelandic codes of law, more specifically the law code of the Free State, *Grágás*,

---

31 "Tiden är inne att vinka farväl åt bilden av den isländska bonden, som fjärran från klerkers och hovmäns europeiska kultur roar sig med att skriva ned gamla berättelser från hembygden." Lars Lönnroth, "Tesen om de två kulturerna: Kritiska studier i den isländska sagaskrivningens sociala förutsättningar," *Scripta islandica* 15 (1964), 97.
32 Hermann Pálsson, *Art and Ethics in Hrafnkel's saga* (Copenhagen, 1971), p. 10.
33 Sveinbjörn Rafnsson, "Saga Íslands III," *Skírnir* 153 (1979), 208. Sveinbjörn Rafnsson, "Saga Íslands I-II," *Skírnir* 149 (1975): 220. It should be noted that not all historians expressed as sharp criticisms towards Stefánsson's chapter. As late as in his 2007 introductory writing to Icelandic medieval history, Gunnar Karlsson singled out Stefánsson's essays as a "great and in parts a completely new church history" which at the time made itself clearly felt from a historiographical point of view. Gunnar Karlsson, *Inngangur að miðöldum: Handbók í íslenskri miðaldasögu* (Reykjavík, 2007), 37. For a discussion on the theoretical differences between Karlsson and Rafnsson, see Arngrímur Vídalín, "Ný bókfestukenning? Spjall um aðferðir," *Saga* LIII (2015), 124–138.

which he has argued, by way of a number of test cases, to have been influenced by European law.³⁴

The last decades have seen a growing tendency to strike a balance between these two views, portraying Icelandic society as not purely 'Icelandic' nor entirely 'Christian,' but both.³⁵ Such a perspective is evident in several studies on medieval Christianity, emphasizing how Christianity came to be slowly incorporated into Icelandic society. From a strict sociohistorical and socioeconomic perspective, this development has been described most thoroughly by Orri Vésteinsson. While being a proponent of the Chieftain Church-paradigm – emphasizing strongly how the interests of the Icelandic aristocracy shape the rise of the Church – he takes issue with the notion that the Christian Church arrived in Iceland with a fully-fledged 'corporate identity' which shaped the way in which its representatives behaved and organized themselves.³⁶ According to Vésteinsson, it took decades and centuries for the Church to form into the autonomous institution it was to become in the Late Middle ages "with its own jurisdiction, its own property, and an institutionalized influence over the governance of the State."³⁷ Instead, the Christian religion and the Church constituted only "one aspect of life" among many as the political elite carried out its affairs. From such a perspective, Vésteinsson describes in detail the socioeconomic and sociopolitical circumstances under which important ecclesiastical institutions and features took shape, the most important ones being the tithe, regulations on church property, the priesthood and the episcopacy. Central to Vésteinsson's thesis is his argument that Icelandic aristocratic families viewed it as both politically and financially advantageous to affiliate themselves with the Church and the Christian religion. At different stages during the process, it was the economic and political interests of the ruling elite which weighed heavy on the decision-making.³⁸ Despite the sweeping scope and the strong

---

34 Such conclusions cast doubt on the basis of much research done on the constitutional history of Iceland but for many historians, *Grágás* has served as a central source for the reconstruction of the political and constitutional system of the tenth and eleventh centuries. See Gunnar Karlsson, *Goðamenning: Staða og áhrif goðorðsmanna í þjóðveldi Íslendinga* (Reykjavík, 2004), pp. 28–59.

35 Although it is of marginal significance for the current research project, the most vivid discussion on the topic over the last decades has taken place in the field of saga studies after the rise of the so-called 'anthropological school.' For an overview, discussion, and bibliography of that influential body of writings see Gísli Pálsson's edited volume, *From Sagas to Society: Comparative Approaches to Early Iceland* (Enfield Lock, 1992).

36 Orri Vésteinsson, *Christianization of Iceland*, 4.

37 Ibid.

38 Although of a broader geographical scale, a similar kind of argumentation is found in Anders Winroth's interpretation of the conversion of Scandinavia, emphasizing that

explanatory capabilities of Vésteinsson's study, it tends to overestimate the significance of political and economic factors on the expense of cultural and religious elements.

In her *Property and Virginity*, a study of marriage in medieval Iceland (1200–1600), Agnes. S. Arnórsdóttir explores and explains the changes of the practice and understanding of marriage after the advent of Christianity in the country. Throughout her study, she portrays how a non-Christian institution of marriage – marked by its economic and political concerns within a kinship social system – gradually merged into a variation of a Christian marriage, in which notions like mutual consent, individual decision-making based on love and affection, as well as virginity and purity had gained a notable significance. For the present purposes, Arnórsdóttir's study is of particular significance as regards its attention to how the Christian religion, its ideas and norms, came to influence Icelandic society through the institution of marriage. In her inquiry, Arnórsdóttir directs her attention far beyond the traditional historiographical topics of medieval Iceland – institutional and constitutional history – and in the spirit of cultural history, asks "how change in the symbolic meaning of marriage affected the wider understanding of marriage."[39] Thus, in addition to reconstructing the development of the legal and ritual representation of marriage in medieval Iceland, she shows how the Christianization of marriage came to influence gender identity and, further still, the social structures of medieval Iceland. Significantly, she shows that this process was not a one way street but a slow-moving, complex and dynamic development, characterized by compromises between the 'old,' traditional practices and the 'new' Christian ones. Central to this development was the influence of canon law and changes in ritual practices, but in line with scholars like Peter Landau and Sveinbjörn Rafnsson, Arnórsdóttir emphasizes the early influence of canon law on Icelandic law-making and society.

As noted, the studies of Vésteinsson and Arnórsdóttir highlight the ways in which Christianity slowly seeped into Icelandic society. Neither Christianity

---

Christianity was not brought to Scandinavia "as the result of conquest, colonization, and mission" but, assuming for more autonomy on behalf of the kings and magnates of Scandinavia, they chose to accept Christianity primarily because it was advantageous for them economically and politically. Christianity was not forced upon them; they accepted it because it was profitable for them to gain access to "prestigious gift-giving capital of Christianity" and be able to frame their leadership in terms of divine kingship. Anders Winroth, *Conversion of Scandinavia: Vikings, Merchants, and Missionaries in the Remaking of Northern Europe* (New Haven, 2012), pp. 161–163.

39 Agnes S. Arnórsdóttir, *Property and Virginity: The Christianization of Marriage in Medieval Iceland 1200–1600* (Aarhus, 2009), 29.

nor the Icelandic culture in which the Christian religion was becoming infiltrated are considered as fixed, clear-cut entities. The meeting, merging and interaction of the two is viewed as a matter of adaptation and negotiation for which there is no predetermined formula. Along the lines of how transcultural history has been carried out in recent decades, they emphasize the active and creative role of both the arriving culture and the receiving one. This study shares this understanding of the sociocultural situation in Iceland as being in flux or, to use a much-debated term, in a process of acculturation. However, while the studies by Vésteinsson and Arnórsdóttir focus on the processes and the outcome of the cultural negotiation, the concern of the present study leans decisively towards the Roman Church as a participant in such a cultural interaction and the content of what it brought to the negotiating table. In more technical terms, it focuses on the ways in which the agents of the Church constructed their position as they participated in sociopolitical encounters and confrontations and the discursive framework within which they did so. In most recent years, such a position has become increasingly visible, most prominently in Steinunn Kristjánsdóttir's extensive study on the monasteries established in Iceland in the course of the Middle Ages. In addition to the wealth of new information gained through the archaeological investigations and excavations carried out by Kristjánsdóttir and her team around the country, she provides her readers with a useful model for reconstructing the historical development under inspection and the role played by the medieval Church in it.[40]

As shown above, previous studies have thoroughly explored the wide-ranging social changes caused by the introduction of Christianity in Iceland. The present study wishes to investigate the sociopolitical significance of the religious source material by asking how the discourses it preserves and represents comes into play in these social changes, in particular in the conflicts to which they led between individuals, groups, and institutions. In doing so, the study is indebted to the theoretical approach frequently termed 'the new cultural history.'[41] When applied to the topic of political and social conflicts, such an approach focuses on reconstructing the discourses and practices which

---

[40] Steinunn Kristjánsdóttir, *Leitin að klaustrunum*, see esp. pp. 454–465. A similar emphasis can be seen in Gottskálk Þór Jensson's convincing attempt to contextualize the founding of monasteries in Iceland in the church political landscape of North Western Europe. Gottskálk Þór Jensson, "Íslenskar klausturreglur og libertas ecclesie á ofanverðri 12. öld," in *Íslensk klausturmenning á miðöldum,* ed. Haraldur Bernharðsson (Reykjavík, 2016), pp. 9–57.

[41] A well-known collection of articles setting the agenda for the new cultural history is *The New Cultural History: Essays*, ed. Lynn Hunt (Berkeley, 1989). For a more recent overview, see Peter Burke, *What is Cultural History?* (Cambridge, 2008), pp. 51–76.

give access to the structures of meaning employed by the political actors each time.[42] It stresses that decisions taken and actions made in society's different spheres cannot be understood in isolation from the cultural context in which they take place.[43] From such a point of view, this study seeks to contextualize and analyse the religious source material preserved from the first centuries of Christianity in Iceland, arguing that it constitutes an important component of the cultural context in which chieftains and churchmen of the Icelandic Free state communicated, made their deals, and came into conflict.

1.2   Theoretical Considerations

In his *History and Cultural Theory,* historian Simon Gunn defines culture "as made up of complex networks of interacting discourses, socially located and permeated by forces of conflict and power."[44] This citation brings together two important theoretical vantage points for this study. First, its indebtedness to the theorizing taking place within the field of cultural studies and cultural history. Second, the critical perspective from which society is seen – in its entirety down to its smallest constituents – as a *locus* of conflict and power politics. The following discussion will center on two theoretical components enjoying particular prominence in this study: First, the concept of discourse, but the religious source material under analysis is here viewed as source material for the religious discourse being disseminated across Iceland since early in the process of Christanization. Second, it is necessary to outline the critical hermeneutical framework underlying the historical analysis, or what in the present research is called the 'imperial perspective.'

1.2.1   *Ecclesiastical Discourse*

The following discussion is intended to explain in more detail the theoretical background behind the phrase 'ecclesiastical discourse.' With the use of such a phrase, it is emphasized that the discourse under inspection was always both religious and socio-political at the same time. The adjective 'ecclesiastical' has been defined as describing that which is "of or relating to a church especially as an established institution."[45] Given that this study preoccupies itself with how

---

42   Barbara Stollberg-Rilinger, "Was heißt Kulturgeschichte des Politischen? Einleitung" in *Was heißt Kulturgeschichte des Politischen?*, ed. Barbara Stollberg-Rilinger (Berlin, 2005), p. 13.
43   Ibid., p. 11.
44   Simon Gunn, *History and Cultural Theory* (London, 2006), p. 81.
45   *Webster's Third New International Dictionary*, s.v. "Ecclesiastical."

the early Christian religious discourse contributed to the consolidation of the Church as an institution it seems as if the word 'ecclesiastical' encompasses both the religious dimension of the discourse under inspection and the institutional framework out of which it emerged and sustained.

1.2.1.1 Discourse

The concept 'discourse' and the theoretical background on which it rests, aptly offers itself for any research focusing on the relationship between the source-material (mostly but not exclusively texts) under inspection and the society to which it belongs. The term has been used and defined in various ways through the centuries and has frequently been applied to a formal, reasoned discussion on a particular topic, a well known example being René Descartes' (1596–1650) treatise *Discours de la méthode* from 1637. Since the second half of the 20th century, however, it has come to be inextricably linked to the works of the French structuralists and within the field of history to the work of Michel Foucault (1926–1984) in particular.[46] While Foucault employed the term 'discourse' in several different ways in his own writings, his major contribution consisted of viewing discourses as historically situated social practices and not as trajectories of thought isolated from their social surroundings. From such a perspective, all discourse is viewed as a practical, social, and cultural phenomenon and every discursive action must be inspected in view of its interaction with the context for which it was intended and out of which it sprung. No document, statement or utterance – not even the phenomenon of language itself – exists in isolation but are social processes.[47]

Following recent theorizing within the field of discourse studies, this study adopts what can be termed a discursive research perspective.[48] In so doing,

---

[46] See especially Michel Foucault, *The Archaeology of Knowledge. And the Discourse on Language*, trans. A. M. Sheridan Smith (New York, 2010 [1972]).

[47] An influential articulation of this premise is that of Mikhail Bakhtin stating that "[t]he living utterance, having taken meaning and shape at a particular historical moment in a socially specific environment, cannot fail to brush up against thousands of living dialogic threads, woven by socio-ideological consciousness around the given object of an utterance; it cannot fail to become an active participant in social dialogue." Mikhail M. Bakhtin, "Discourse in the Novel," in *The Dialogic Imagination: Four Essays by M. M. Bakhtin*, ed. Michael Holquist, trans. Caryl Emerson and Michael Holquist, University of Texas Press Slavic Series 1 (Austin, 1981), p. 276.

[48] Scholars have also proposed terms such as a 'research style,' 'resarch programme,' and 'thought style' (*Denkstil*). See Kocku von Stuckrad, "Discourse" in *Vocabulary for the Study of Religion* 1 A-E, eds. Robert A. Segal and Kocku von Stuckrad (Leiden, 2015), 433 and Reiner Keller, "The Sociology of Knowledge Approach to Discourse (SKAD)," *Human Studies* 34 (2011), 51.

it aligns itself with approaches which are broadly concerned with the ways in which discourses shape the socio-historical contexts within which subjects construct meaning and produce knowledge and how discourses are shaped by the socio-historical contexts as well. Within such a theoretical framework, scholars have defined the concept of discourse in various ways. What the definitions always share, however, is the principle that reality is constructed through a socially shared use of language and that discourses provide access to the processes through which that takes place. Thus, building on both Foucault and the sociology of knowledge tradition (*Wissenssoziologie*) for his development of what he calls the 'Sociology of Knowledge Approach do Discourse (SKAD), Reiner Keller defines discourse as a "regulated, structured practices of sign usage" which he further understands as "a social practice" reflecting "the (re)-production/transformation of social orders of knowledge."[49] In a similar way, historian of religion Kocku von Stuckrad has defined discourse as "a communicative structure that organizes knowledge in a given community" which "establishes, stabilizes, and legitimizes systems of meaning and provides collectively shared orders of knowledge in an institutionalized social ensemble."[50] Discourses are usually seen to consist of 'statements' or 'utterances' and even 'opinion' about a given topic which together form "relatively stable – but changing and changeable – meaning systems."[51] Through the examination of a selected corpus of sources a historical analysis of discourse aims to throw light on the discursive conditions within which knowledge is produced and meaning made at a given time and place in the past.

It should be noted that a 'discursive research perspective' does not necessarily mean the employment of discourse analysis as a method.[52] A discursive research perspective allows for a broad variety of methods of both qualitative and quantitative nature depending on the research questions and source material each time. Methods which traditionally have been referred to as 'discourse analysis' aiming at analyzing in detail the linguistic features of a text

---

49   Keller, "The Sociology of Knowledge Approach to Discourse," p. 51.
50   von Stuckrad, "Discourse," p. 433. It should be noted at this point, however, that this study does not entirely share the epistemological premises of von Stuckrad's theoretical framework which have been described as "radical constructicvist." Markus Dressler, "*The Social Construction of Reality* (1966) Revisited: Epistemology and Theorizing in the Study of Religion,"*Method and Theory in the Study of Religion* (2018), 12–13.
51   Teemu Taira, "Discourse on 'Religion' in Organizing Social Practices: Theoretical and Practical Considerations," in *Making Religion: Theory and Practice in the Discursive Study of Religion*, eds. Frans Wijsen and Kocku von Stuckrad (Leiden, 2016), p. 126.
52   Achim Landwehr, *Historische Diskursanalyse*, 2nd ed., Historische Einführungen 4 (Frankfurt a. M., 2009), p. 100.

are useful for in-depth study of individual discursive moments but remain difficult to apply for the study of long-term developments through a large corpus of source material. Thus, while insights of such linguistic or textual leaning methods will not be completely absent from the analysis carried out in the present study, it has more in common with approaches which are indebted to both Foucauldian historiography and the sociology of knowledge tradition (*Wissenssoziologie*) which have been termed cultural studies approaches or historically-leaning approaches.[53] With regard to method, this study will be applying a combination of historical-criticism, content analysis and textual interpretation inspired by postcolonial/imperial hermeneutics.

A frequently addressed topic in the study of discourse relates to the role of particular discourses for social power dynamics. Power, to quote von Stuckrad, has been described as an "an element of discourse that plays a role in any form of analysis."[54] Discourses are seen to represent and maintain structures of power and questions as to how they produce and reproduce such structures plays a prominent role in the research of discourse. How prominent a place such questions should be given, however, and the way in which they are formulated, remains a dividing issue among discourse theorists. Scholars such as Norman Fairclough, one of the founders of critical discourse analysis (CDA) and Titus Hjelm, who in a recent article has outlined a framework for what he calls a critical discursive study of religion (CDSR), see it as an inherent and necessary part of the work of the discourse analyst to take a normative stance towards uncovering social injustice and inequalities.[55] While acknowledging the relevance of power as an element of discourse, critics of such claims allow for the possibility that discursive research does not always have to deal with critical questions of social injustice and domination.[56]

---

[53] Teemu Taira, "Discourse on 'Religion' in Organizing Social Practices: Theoretical and Practical Considerations," in *Making Religion: Theory and Practice in the Discursive Study of Religion*, eds. Frans Wijsen and Kocku von Stuckrad (Leiden, 2016), pp. 126–129.

[54] von Stuckrad, "Discourse," p. 430.

[55] Among Norman Fairclough's extensive writing on the topic, see esp. his *Language and Power*, 3rd ed. (Abingdon, 2015). Titus Hjelm, "Theory and Method in Critical Discursive Study of Religion: An Outline," in *Making Religion: Theory and Practice in the Discursive Study of Religion*, eds. Frans Wijsen and Kocku von Stuckrad (Leiden, 2016), 15–34. See also Ernesto Laclau and Chantal Mouffe, *Hegemony and Socialist Strategy: Towards a Radical Democratic Politics*, 2nd ed. (London, 2001) who see the main goal of the analysis of discourse as the reformation of modern democracies. For a thorough discussion the discouse theory of of Laclau and Mouffe, see Marianne W. J Jørgensen and Louise J. Phillips, *Discourse Analysis as Theory and Method* (Los Angeles, 2010), pp. 24–59.

[56] Kocku von Stuckrad, "Religion and Science in Transformation: On Discourse Communities, the Double-Bind of Discourse Research, and Theoretical Controversies," in

The main concern of the present study is the role of Christian religious discourses in the social, cultural, and political process through which the Roman Church became a dominant institution in Icelandic medieval society. Granted the nature of the research topic and the questions posed, issues of critical nature relating to power and domination are bound to figure prominently. A more detailed discussion on how these issues will be formulated – for example through insights gained from postcolonial/imperial hermeneutics – is found in the next section of this introduction. As for how the role of discourse is understood in this process, an informative account is provided by historian of religion Bruce Lincoln in his *Discourse and the Construction of Society* who grounds his theorizing in the works of Antonio Gramsci (1891–1937) and Pierre Bourdieu (1930–2002) and to a certain extent Foucault as well. According to Lincoln, discourse is conceived of as one of two principal means of social construction, the other being the use of (or threat thereof) physical force.[57] While force is a temporary measure – in many cases an effective one – for moving society in a particular direction, it can never hold in the long run and must always be supplemented by discourse. "Together, discourse and force are the chief means whereby social borders, hierarchies, institutional formations, and habituated patterns of behavior are both maintained and modified."[58] According to this view, discourse serves the role of *persuading* people of the value of ideas and practices on the one hand and *invoking sentiments* of affinity and estrangement on the other, both of which are imperative for a particular social change to remain effective.[59] For the present purposes, an illustrative example is that of an empire forging on into new territories. Whereas imperial potentates may find it necessary to apply force while initially assuming control over new territories, a successful incorporation of people into an empire

---

Making Religion: Theory and Practice in the Discursive Study of Religion, eds. Frans Wijsen and Kocku von Stuckrad (Leiden, 2016), pp. 218–219.

[57] Much of the following relies on the work of Bruce Lincoln, an important theorist for the conceptualization of religious discourse and religious texts as discourse, see Bruce Lincoln, *Discourse and the Construction of Society: Comparative Studies of Myth, Ritual, and Classification* (Oxford, 1989); Bruce Lincoln, *Authority: Construction and Corrosion* (Chicago, 1994), and Bruce Lincoln, *Gods and Demons, Priests and Scholars: Critical Explorations in the History of Religions* (Chicago, 2012).

[58] Lincoln, *Discourse and the Construction of Society*, p. 3.

[59] Lincoln defines the sentiments out of which social borders are constructed in the following way: "These I refer to as affinity and estrangement, meaning to include under the general rubric of these terms, on the one hand, all feelings of likeness, common belonging, mutual attachment, and solidarity – whatever their intensity, affective tone, and degree of consciousness – and, on the other hand, those corresponding feelings of distance, separation, otherness and alienation." *Discourse and the Construction of Society*, p. 10.

depends on the slow process of persuasion and identity formation as the new imperial subjects gradually come to see themselves as such. Whether or not such discourses work relies on a variety of factors such as how widely it can be propagated, how persuasive it actually is – both in terms of content but also the receptive context – and how successful it is in calling forth a following.[60]

1.2.1.2 Discourse: Religious and Ecclesiastical

The discourse under inspection can be defined as both religious and ecclesiastical. It can be termed religious on account of characteristics distinguishing it from other kind of discourse in several ways.[61] First of all, a central feature is its claim to a supernatural authority.[62] Its claim of a divine and eternal origin, particularly if it is accepted by a significant number of people, brings it to a status surpassing that of other discursive practices produced in the same society. As will be thoroughly discussed at a later stage in this study, these discourses are primarily found in texts which differ from other texts in that they enter society as a part of a program or a package of a religious system which upholds, compliments, and boosts the religious discourses they contain.[63] They enter, for instance, as a part of a ritual integral to the operation of the Church which further secured the perpetual broadcasting to the people around the country. It is thus very likely that the earliest Christian religious texts in Iceland possessed

---

60 Lincoln, *Discourse and the Construction of Society*, p. 8.
61 In this regard, the present study aligns itself with Lincoln and other scholars who adhere to analytical definitions of 'religion' and therefore 'religious discourse' as well. For a critique of such definitions, see for instance Timothy Fitzgerald, *The Ideology of Religious Studies* (New York: Oxford University Press, 2000) and William Arnal and Russell T. McCutcheon, *The Sacred is the Profane: The Political Nature of "Religion"* (Oxford: Oxford University Press, 2013). With regard to this particular theoretical debate, it suffices for the purposes of this research to subscribe to Markus Dressler's position as he maintains that the theoretical concern with the 'existence' of religion is not productive for empirical research. "Productive is," Dressler states, "to ask whether a particular notion of religion as an analytical category is helpful in deciphering – that is, making legible – social and historical contexts." Dressler, "Epistemology and Theorizing," 10.
62 Bruce Lincoln, "Theses on Method," (repr.) in *Gods and Demons, Priests and Scholars: Critical Explorations in the History of Religions* (Chicago, 2012), 1. Cf. Tim Fitzgerald, "Bruce Lincoln's "Theses on Method": Antitheses," *Method and Theory in the Study of Religion* 18 (2006): 402. See also Bruce Lincoln, "How to Read a Religious Text," in *Gods and Demons*, pp. 5–15.
63 An example of the liturgy of the medieval Church referred to as a 'package,' see Åslaug Ommundsen, "The Word of God and the Stories of Saints: Medieval Liturgy and its Reception in Norway," in *The Performance of Christian and Pagan Storyworlds*, eds. Lars Boje Mortensen and Tuomas M. S. Lehtonen, Medieval Identities: Socio-Cultural Spaces 3 (Turnhout, 2013), p. 50.

a greater authority in their historical context than the renowned saga writings even though the vast reception history of the latter might suggest otherwise.

Early Icelandic Christians were shaped by the spaces of medieval Iceland in which they lived, moved and existed. And these spaces, especially ecclesiastical spaces, such as the interiors and surroundings of churches, monasteries and so on, were filled with statues, images, ornaments and objects which were an important part of the ongoing religious discourses and conversations of the time. In the historical sciences, the concept of discourse has been extended beyond the level of texts to include all kinds of social practices and phenomena, material manifestations included. In the words of Laura Salah Nasrallah, a scholar of Early Christianity, "religious discourse emerges not in some abstract zone, but in lived experiences and practices in the spaces of the world" and the same remains true for 11th-13th century Iceland.[64] From this perspective, it is tempting to view the rapid rise of churches around Iceland during the 11th and 12th centuries as reinforcing, supplementing and amplifying the religious discourse encountered in sermonic and hagiographic sources. It should also be taken into account that most of the textual material was also performative. It was heard by an audience when read aloud or retold in churches, monasteries and elsewhere and so its content extended beyond the group of the few literates to those who could neither read nor write.

The discourse being explored in this study is not only 'religious' but also 'ecclesiastical,' which means for the present purposes relating to the Roman Church as an institution. As will be thoroughly explained in more detail at a later point in this study, this discourse is understood as an inherent part of how the Roman Church operated as an institution. It was produced and diffused by ecclesiastics through ecclesiastical media.

Even though much of the discussion is based on sermonic and hagiographical texts, the same discursive themes can be expressed by different means, for instance through liturgical texts and material objects. The concept thus includes several modes of religious discourse ranging from texts to objects to spoken utterances related to the ecclesiastical realm in one way or another. However, despite the fact that the scope of the concept sweeps diverse kinds of sources under its hat, it is texts which enjoy a central place (quantitatively speaking) in the source material. Ecclesiastical texts might be defined as texts produced and primarily used within the confines of an ecclesiastical or monastic setting. The ecclesiastical texts represent something new, at least something

---

64 Laura Salah Nasrallah, *Christian Responses to Roman Art and Architecture: The Second-Century Church Amid the Spaces of Empire* (Cambridge, 2010), p. 1.

recent in Icelandic society. What constitutes the largest part of the corpus is not in the strictest sense 'original' material but translations, copies, and reproductions of material that had been imported from elsewhere, much of which dates far back into late antiquity and the early middle ages.[65] However, even though the corpus of early Icelandic ecclesiastical literature consists mostly of translations, it should not be considered as something foreign or alien to the native Icelanders but as a discursive reservoir they came to make use of and respond to according to their own understanding and for their own purposes in the socio-cultural context in which they lived.

1.2.2 Perspective of Empire

The postcolonial hermeneutic optic is based on the concept of 'colonialism' broadly referring to "a practice of domination, which involves the subjugation of one people to another."[66] In similarly broad terms, the concept of postcolonialism can be defined as a wide range of responses to the legacy of colonialism. As a theoretical system, however, postcolonial studies rest upon a bulk of writings of differing nature, ranging from elaborate works of literary theory to shorter and simpler works more resembling revolutionary pamphlets than anything else.[67] Closely related to postcolonial hermeneutics is the imperial

---

65 A fact which, among others, certainly accounts for Icelandic scholars' longstanding lack of interest in them, especially during the period of romantic nationalism and independence struggle with an almost exclusive focus on all that was truly and originally Icelandic at the expense of imported material. A clear indicator towards such a propensity is that the majority of scholars carrying out the most important research on Icelandic ecclesiastical literature through the years are non-Icelanders, e.g. Ole Widding, Hans Bekker Nielsen, L. K. Shook, Lucy Grace Collings, Margaret Cormack, Phillip Roughton, Simonetta Battista, and Kirsten Wolf.

66 Margaret Kohn, "Post-colonial theory," in *Ethics and World Politics*, ed. Duncan Bell (Oxford, 2010), pp. 202–203. Historically, terms such as postcolonialism trace their roots to the European practice of subjugating non-European areas beginning in the 15th and continuing through the 19th century. The present research addresses an era well outside this time frame. That fact, however, does not exempt the sources from the critical perspective which has been in development within postcolonial scholarly circles over the last decades. Broadly understood as a critical perspective aimed at disclosing structures of subjugation and domination, postcolonialism has been applied to a variety of sources throughout all periods of history.

67 Among works of central importance for postcolonial theory are the following (in order of appearance): Frantz Fanon, *Black Skin, White Masks* (London, 1986 [1952]; Edward Said, *Orientalism* (New York, [1978]); Gayatri Chakravorty Spivak "Can the Subaltern Speak" in *Marxism and the Interpretation of Culture*, eds. Cary Nelson and Lawrence Grossberg (Champaign, [1985]), pp. 271–313; Homi K. Bhabha, *The Location of Culture* (London, 1994); Dipesh Chakrabarty, *Provincializing Europe: Postcolonial Thought and Historical Difference* (Princeton, 2000).

framework which has a stronger focus on the phenomenon of empire and how it exercises its power through its networks and strategies of expansion. In this section, it will be explained how and why this perspective is relevant for the present analysis of the earliest Icelandic ecclesiastical source material and the historical context in which it emerged.

1.2.2.1 The Roman Church as an Empire in Medieval Iceland

It is not entirely unproblematic to apply the perspective of empire to the historical context of the earliest Icelandic ecclesiastical texts. The political situation was complex. Risking simplification, three political streams were shaping their courses in Icelandic society at the time. First, there were the Icelandic chieftains representing the Icelandic commonwealth while many were also striving to increase their own power and property. As discussed above, the Church was on the rise but still not in the position of power it later was to attain. Far across the sea - but not too far - the Norwegian king loomed, building up his power through his emissaries and Icelandic attachés. While this might appear simple, the Icelandic political landscape was not so well defined. Representatives of each stream often acted in the interest of multiple parties simultaneously, with ordained chieftains being a case in point. It should also be kept in mind that despite the, at times stormy, relationship between king and Church during this period, they had a common interest in the growing influence of each party in Iceland with the eventual political incorporation of Iceland into the Norwegian kingdom in 1262–4.[68]

Despite the complexities of the political context of 11th, 12th, and 13th century Iceland the question of empire leads directly to the Roman Church. This fact will become increasingly clear in the following pages. The position of the medieval Western Church as an empire is a central premise for the hermeneutical framework of this study and warrants an examination of a number of important characteristics of historical empires at this point.[69] The geographic extent alone shows that other political entities in the Scandinavian realm,

---

68 See Magnús Stefánsson, "Kirkjuvald eflist," p. 59.
69 It should be noted that the present understanding of the Church as an empire has little to do with "the imperial church system" or the *Reichskirchensystem* in the sense of how the Church, its offices and property, was employed as an instrument of royal government, most famously under Ottonian and Salian rulers. Rudolf Schieffer, "Reichskirche", in *Lexikon des Mittelalters* 7, cols. 626–628, in *Brepolis Medieval Encyclopaedias - Lexikon des Mittelalters Online*). See also Timothy Reuter, "The 'Imperial Church System' of the Ottonian and Salian Rulers: A Reconsideration," *Journal of Ecclesiastical History* 33 (1982), pp. 347–374.

FIGURE 2   The archbishopric of Niðarós consisted of Norway's five episcopal sees as well as those of Orkney (Kirkwall), the Faroes (Kirkjubø), the Isle of Man, Iceland (Skálholt and Hólar), and Greenland (Garðar).

such as the Norwegian kingdom, pale in comparison to the geographical reach of the papal regime, covering around a million square kilometers, amounting to the scope of the Persian and Roman empires of antiquity.[70] In a recent work on historical Empires, Alejandro Colás identifies three characteristics of an empire, i.e. expansion, hierarchy, and order.[71] All of them can be applied to the Roman Church with relative ease. It is a well-established fact that the Roman Church was an organized, large-scale network of political and cultural expansion under the head of a single monarch, the pope, with authority over archbishops, bishops, clerics and other ecclesiastics. This hierarchical infrastructure had been present in Iceland in an embryonic state since the arrival of the first missionaries at the end of the 10th century but did not reach full maturity until 1153 with the establishment of the Archbishopric of Niðarós (medieval name of Trondheim) (see figure. 2).

It should be noted that the medieval Roman Church was not an empire in the strict sense as sometimes employed by political scientists working with a definition shaped within the context of international politics. According to such conceptualizations, empires have to be defined in contrast to institutional

---

70   Michael Mann, *The Sources of Social Power*, vol. 1, *A History of Power from the Beginning to A.D. 1760* (Cambridge, Eng., 1986), p. 379.
71   Alejandro Colás, *Empire* (Cambridge, Eng., 2007), p. 9.

territorial states as well as hegemonic structures of dominance.⁷² Even though the medieval Western Church surely made itself felt in the realm of international power politics, it was not an empire in the same right as the Roman empire or the British empire. As a religious institution it did not make the same claims to power over people and territories as rulers of a more secular sort. But even though, for this reason, categories of international politics do not apply to the medieval Church, it did operate and expand by power structures comparable to other empires, as will be further explored in view of recent developments in the field of the historical study of empires.

1.2.2.2   The Perspective of Empire: A Text Oriented Approach

Recent decades have seen a renewed interest in the historical phenomenon and concept of empire producing a range of scholarly works distinguishing themselves in several ways from previous historical scholarship on the subject. The classic approach to writing the history of an empire would be the diachronic approach, following the historical trajectory of one of history's empires through its ups and downs, victories and losses, expansions and contractions.⁷³ Traditionally, such scholarly enterprises pay a great deal of attention to the imperial center and decisions made by authorities located there, inspired by a conscious imperialistic will to rule.⁷⁴ Recent studies of empire have moved away from such diachronic accounts of an empire's history from its birth to its wake in directions significant for the present project in at least three ways.

Firstly, in line with much postcolonial scholarly literature focusing on the power relationships between imperial ruling classes and subjected and even subaltern groups of people, scholars of empire have come to view the concept of an 'empire' not only as a particular form of political arrangement manifesting itself in history's many examples of empires, but also as a broad, inclusive concept referring to various means of maneuvering power within a structure of power and/or domination shaped by a movement between an imperial center

---

72 Herfried Münkler, *Empires: The Logic of World Domination from Ancient Rome to the United States*, trans. Patrick Camiller (Cambridge, Eng. 2007), pp. 4–8.

73 For classical examples of the traditional approach of writing empire history, see Otto Franke, *Geschichte des chinesischen Reiches: Eine Darstellung seiner Entstehung, seines Wesens und seiner Entwicklung bis zur neuesten Zeit*, 5 vols (Berlin, 1939–1952) and Edward Gibbon, *The History of the Decline and Fall of the Roman Empire*, 8 vols (London, 1984–1990).

74 Münkler, *Empires*, p. 8.

and its peripheries.[75] Instructive for such viewpoints are comparative works taking numerous empires and imperial formations into consideration with the intention of identifying and analyzing structures and processes common to their operation. Two examples of such comparative projects are Herfried Münkler's *Imperien*, published in German in 2005 and translated into English with the title *Empires* in 2007, and Alejandro Colás' *Empire*, also published in 2007. Although both of these authors ground their discussion in cases of empires as traditionally defined, such as the Roman Empire, the Chinese Han Empire, the Ottoman Empire or the European Colonial Empires of the 19th and 20th centuries, their analysis of what Münkler calls the 'action logic' of empires and Colás might call 'imperial experience,' consisting of characteristics common to various imperial formations, makes it possible to move beyond the 'traditional' or 'commonplace' empires of history and discuss the medieval Western Church and its mode of operation within the hermeneutic parameters of empire studies. Even though the Roman Church of the Middle Ages is not included in treatments of empire like Münkler's and Colás', it bore enough imperial traits to be considered an empire in the broad sense of the term and it is into such imperial tendencies which this study intends to inquire.

Secondly, as stressed by Münkler and others, even though the imperial center must receive its due attention, traditional historical accounts of imperial operations, "must be supplemented with a focus on the periphery – on power vacuums and economic dynamics, request for intervention by losers in regional conflicts and decisions made by local authorities."[76] Empires are not created single-handedly by imperial monarchs by virtue of their brilliant strategies and decisions taken from their throne located at the power center of the empire. In many cases, they are more rightly described as moderators in – and in some cases even as simply spectators to – the course of events taking place at the extremes of the empire. Such points of emphasis are particularly relevant for the present project since Iceland, *Ultima Thule* as historians and cartographers both ancient and medieval sometimes called it, lay at the outskirts of the known world and the papal authorities in Rome could intervene only indirectly in what was taking place there, especially during the period before the establishing of the archbishopric of Niðarós in the mid-12th century.[77] As

---

75 The movement between center and periphery is emphasized e.g. in Herfried Münkler and Grit Straßenberger, *Politische Theorie und Ideengeschichte: Eine Einführung* (München, 2016), p. 378.
76 Münkler, *Empires*, p. 8.
77 Such an emphasis on peripheries and regional differences goes hand in hand with the increased emphasis on the cultural diversity characterizing medieval Europe. See Michael

pointed out by Münkler, when it comes to the relations between imperial center and periphery, each case has to be investigated in its own right.[78] What makes the Icelandic case interesting is that church buildings and religious texts seem to have predated the institutional consolidation of the Church. The fact that the Church in Iceland gradually moved from isolation and 'independence' towards integration into the international Church provides an interesting context for the emergence of the ecclesiastical textual world in the vernacular. Inevitably, hagiographical discourse and tropes had a part to play in such a development as they progressively seeped into society. Thus, it could be said that through the diffusion of the ecclesiastical discourse under analysis here, the ground had been made ripe when the Church started strengthening its position in Icelandic society as a formal part of the Roman Catholic ecclesiastical empire. To continue with Münkler's terminology, turning to his discussion of different parts of the imperial elite, it might be said that the interpretative elite – in this case text-producing clerics – had begun their work before the decision-making elite had done so, keeping in mind that in many other cases it is the other way around.[79]

Thirdly, coinciding with the move away from approaches restricted to a top-down, chronicle-like perspective is the increased awareness among scholars of a need for a 'multilayered' and 'multidisciplinary' approach in order to grasp the complexities of individual imperial formations. Such approaches usually require the narrowing of the scope to a single or few events or aspects – political, legal, economic, cultural – in the relationship between large imperial polities and the various objects of their expansion. As might be clear already from previous discussion on discourse and religious texts, the present study locates itself at the ideological, or in broader terms, the cultural level of imperial expansion.[80] It views texts as the carriers of ideas employed by imperial potentates and their various envoys to increase their influence and control over assets and resources. This is much in line with the imperial reading of biblical texts as it has been developed within the field of biblical studies. On the basis of the broad sense of the empire-concept as a particular sort of power

---

Borgolte, *Europa endeckt seine Vielfalt 1050–1250*, Handbuch der Geschichte Europas 3 (Stuttgart, 2002).

78 Münkler, *Empires*, p. 8.
79 Ibid., p. 85.
80 See ibid., pp. 80–107, esp. pp. 84–96. On several occasions, Münkler resorts to sociologist Michael Mann's theorizing, e.g. Münkler, *Empires*, p. 47. For Mann's discussion of ideological power in the context of his notion of the four sources of power, see his *Sources of Social Power* 1, pp. 22–24. See also Colás' informative discussion of empire as culture in his *Empire*, pp. 116–157.

relationship, there has been an increased interest among biblical scholars in how biblical texts promote "the power of empire, which as "power over" demands submission, subordination, and subjection."[81] Considering that the majority of texts under inspection are either biblical, apocryphal offshoots complementing a biblical narrative or linked to canonical texts in some other way, there is no reason not to read them in the same way.[82] An important task for the present research, therefore, would be to address the questions: who were employing the texts and derivative discourses, in what kind of circumstances were they doing so and and to what end? – which is much the same as repeating feminist biblical scholar Elisabeth Schüssler Fiorenza's statement that "the crucial question for interpretation is not so much what do these texts mean but what do these texts do to those who submit to their world of vision and power of imagination in various contexts that also determine the meaning of the text?"[83] In the troublesome political situation of the 12th and 13th centuries it can be assumed that all kinds of people had availed themselves of the kind of discourses produced by the emerging ecclesiastical textual world for purposes submissive or violent. It does, nevertheless, stand to reason that the more strongly a person was linked to the Church, more likely it seems for him (rarely her) to have made use of its discourse.

The significance of the source material must not, however, be reduced to its interpretive framework since clinging too stringently to a particular hermeneutical position, may produce forced readings of the source material. Thus, it should be avoided by all means to automatically view the texts under inspection and related sources as 'weapons' from the Church's 'arsenal' to be used in whatever conflict its 'troops' found themselves. Similarly, one should not jump to the conclusion that they were being consciously or strategically produced and wielded for reaching particular ends in the Christianization process. As will be discussed at length later on, they were an essential, even intrinsic, part of the operation and appearance of the Roman Church as it was settling into this new territory. It should be clear from the outset, that the material is in full agreement with the theological currents and aesthetics of the medieval Western Church and does not offer anything radically 'unexpected.'

---

81   Elisabeth Schüssler Fiorenza, *The Power of the Word: Scripture and the Rhetoric of Empire* (Minneapolis, 2007), 59.
82   "While this pattern of submissiveness functions differently in different early Christian documents and their social-ecclesial-historical contexts, the imperial pattern of submission seems to be characteristic throughout." Schüssler Fiorenza, *Power of the Word*, p. 155.
83   Ibid., p. 60.

'Not radically unexpected,' however, does not equal being 'socially void.' One of the main concerns of this study is to investigate how the emerging ecclesiastical discourse shaped the social reality of medieval Iceland. It recognizes and wishes to actively accentuate the social potentials and ultimately the political dimension of the sources under inspection and the discourses they produced and sustained. Furthermore, it seeks to specifically inquire into the reciprocal relationship between the ecclesiastical discourse and the historical agents in 11-13th century Iceland; it wishes to ask how it came into contact with medieval Icelanders and shaped the way in which they perceived the world, their place in it, other people and the events taking place there. As already touched upon, there has been a longstanding emphasis on the 'master topic' of political history as well as the developments of the most important institutions of society such as the Church, the most influential families, powerful chieftains, and eventually, the Norwegian king. While the this study will not be directly concerned, at least to begin with, with questions regarding economic systems and political institutions, it is by no means indifferent to it.

1.3 Source Material

The sources for the earliest ecclesiastical discourse are both textual and material and will be thoroughly discussed in part 2.2 of this study. As noted, the bulk of the source material consists of religious texts. It has to be kept in mind, that the material world in which the textual production of the Church took place, belonged to the same discursive framework as the texts under analysis, telling the same stories, promoting the same ideas. Although most of the discussion will be based on the analysis of texts, it is important to resort to the material remains available, including archaeological sites, artifacts and other physical remains.

1.3.1 *Textual Sources*

Manuscripts containing religious material intended for wider dispersion among both ordained and laypeople, that is sermons and hagiographical texts, constitute the most important parts of the corpus under analysis.[84] Manuscripts more likely to have been used exclusively for private study or meditation of ecclesiastics – for example those containing theological, liturgical or computistical material – will keep a supplementary status and only

---

84   For an exhaustive list of the manuscripts belonging to the corpus, see the Appendix.

included in the analysis when able to clarify or contextualize the analysis of the hagiographic and sermonic texts. Hagiographic and sermonic texts constitute a sizeable portion of the Icelandic manuscript tradition. As an example, the number of extant manuscripts of saints' lives alone amounts to the sum total of manuscripts of family and kings' sagas and in view of the number of Catholic religious texts lost during the Protestant reformation they probably further outnumbered them originally.[85]

Apart from the manuscripts' content, several features they have in common should be mentioned, relating to their provenance, time of production and their outward appearance. All of the manuscripts were made and presumably used in Iceland before the end of the thirteenth century and most of them are in quarto format without major ornamentation. Still another common aspect is the fact that all of the manuscripts contain text which has been copied at least once from an original. Regarding the manuscripts' state of preservation, the corpus is characterized by a considerable degree of diversity, ranging from single leafs to relatively intact codices.

Since it is practically impossible to date the earliest translations of hagiographic literature on the basis of their content, it is necessary to rely on the dating of the earliest manuscripts and external references in order to estimate the date of their earliest appearance. The earliest manuscript dates to around 1150 and it is safe to assume that the production of comparable texts began earlier. A mentioning of 'holy expositions' (*þýðingar helgar*) in *The First Grammatical Treatise*, a writing on orthographics dating to the mid-12th century, strongly supports that such texts were in existence at least around the same time the historiographer Ari Þorgilsson was composing his works (*The Book of Icelanders* is considered to have been composed between 1122 and 1133).[86] What sort of expositions this particular author had in mind is not known with certainty. Jónas Kristjánsson assumes that "the Grammarian was presumably referring in a general way to works of religious edification."[87] Lars Boje Mortensen contends that it may refer to patristic biblical commentaries, translations of biblical material (the Psalter for instance) and possibly translations of hagiographical texts.[88] On such grounds, the emergence of ecclesiastical literature in the

---

85 Roughton I, pp. 18–19.
86 Hreinn Benediktsson, *The First Grammatical Treatise: Introduction, text, notes, translation, vocabulary, facsimiles*, University of Iceland publications in linguistics (Reykjavík, 1972), p. 209.
87 Jónas Kristjánsson, *Eddas and Sagas: Iceland's Medieval Literature* (Reykjavík, 1988), p. 127.
88 Lars Boje Mortensen, "Den formative dialog mellem latinsk og folkesproglig litteratur ca 600–1250," in *Reykholt som makt- og lærdomssenter i den islandske og nordiske kontekst*, ed. Else Mundal (Reykholt, 2006), p. 257.

vernacular could be dated to the early 12th century at the latest. Important centers for such early translation endeavors were the relatively young episcopal sees, the schools in the South at Oddi and Haukadalur and certainly, after its establishing in 1133, the first monastery in Iceland, the Benedictine monastery of Þingeyrar in Vesturhóp (see Figure 1).

It is a well-known fact that the preserved manuscript material dating to the 12th and 13th centuries is only a fragment of what actually existed at the time. Sermons had to be available to churchmen and a collection of sermons must have been a standard property of clergymen. Hagiography, on the other hand, can be assumed to have been a sizable part of libraries of cathedrals, cloisters and, major churches. Based on what is known about the dedication of Icelandic churches it can be assumed that the *vitae* of the respective patron saints were available even though they are not among the material preserved from the period under inspection. In this regard, the analysis will be restricted to material dated throughout the 13th century and to texts that are known with certainty to have existed at the time. From a literary historical point of view this period ends around the time when hagiographical material starts to be written in a more elaborate style than the *sermo humilis* which had marked the writing of the hagiography preserved from the 12th and 13th centuries.[89] This demarcation entails that even though 14th and 15th century versions of texts that likely existed at the time are accessible (for example lives of saints to whom churches had been dedicated in the course of the 11th, 12th, 13th centuries) they will not be included in the analysis.

As noted, most of the scholarly work on the earliest ecclesiastical literature of Iceland in the vernacular has been carried out by literary scholars with a decisive source critical and philological focus. This body of scholarly literature – especially the works dating to the second half of last century – is marked by its preoccupation with the relationship between the translated hagiographic material and original and indigenous works of literature such as family sagas and kings' sagas.[90] Even works exclusively concerned with literary

---

89 Jónas Kristjánsson, "Learned Style or Saga Style?" in *Speculum Norroenum: Norse Studies in Memory of Gabrielle Turville-Petre*, ed. Ursula Dronke et al. (Odense, 1981), pp. 260–292. For a more recent discussion, see Jonas Wellendorf, "Ecclesiastical Literature and Hagiography," in *The Routledge Research Companion to the Medieval Icelandic Sagas*, eds. Ármann Jakobsson and Sverrir Jakobsson (London and New York, 2017), pp. 50–51.

90 See for instance Gabriel Turville-Petre, *Origins of Icelandic Literature* (Oxford, 1953) Jónas Kristjánsson, "Sagas and Saints' Lives," in *Cultura classica e cultura germanica settentrionale: atti del Convegno internazionale di studi, Università di Macerata, Facoltà di lettre e filosofia: Macerata-S. Severino Marche, 2–4 maggio 1985*, eds. Pietro Janni, Diego Poli and Carlo Santini, Quaderni linguistici e filologici 3 (Macerate, 1988), pp. 125–143.

analysis of hagiographic material, such as the works of Lucy Grace Collings and Phillip Roughton, openly express a certain unease about the secondary status to which vernacular hagiography is frequently relegated when compared to the original saga literature.[91] While the question as to whether and in which ways the ecclesiastical literature may have influenced the composition of Icelandic saga writing is certainly an intriguing one it is not a concern of the present study. Only when the saga literature can be perceived to contribute to the primary objective of eliciting the religious context and dynamics of early Icelandic Christianity will they be consulted.

1.3.2 Material Sources

Material remains, church inventories and various narrative sources from the period under inspection suggest that like elsewhere in Western Europe, religious motifs figured prominently in ecclesiastical art and ornamentation in Free State Iceland. It can be assumed that churches in Iceland offered their visitors a visual experience in which they could encounter the same ecclesiastical discourses found in the textual material described above.[92] What separates Iceland from other regions in Western Europe, however, is the limited extent to which material remains have survived from the medieval period. This is particularly applicable for the church buildings themselves. Churches in medieval Iceland were not made of stone but of less durable building material like wood and turf.

However regrettable it is, this scarcity makes it possible to include material culture in this analysis, whereas it would have otherwise exceeded the scope of this study. Instead, the number of artefacts and other material sources remains considerably limited. Of the few surviving material remains from church buildings – both interior and exterior – is a small number of wooden boards used for wall panelling in three different churches in northern Iceland, all of which

---

91   Thus, Collings, in her discussion about such comparisons says that the sagas have "been accepted as normative and the terms used in [their] description, such as objective, laconic, restrained, have become imbued with an aura of excellence, any work to which they do not apply assuming a position of inferiority" Lucy Grace Collings, *The Codex Scardensis: Studies in Icelandic Hagiography* (doctoral dissertation, Cornell University, 1969), pp. 147 and similarly Roughton states that his findings are meant to vindicate the status of the Norse apostolic lives, which are in his opinion "undeserving of the common and at best lukewarm literary appraisal of medieval hagiographical narrative." Roughton II, p. 930.

92   Guðbjörg Kristjánsdóttir, "Messuföng og kirkjulist: Búnaður kirkna í kaþólskum sið," in *Hlutavelta tímans: menningararfur á Þjóðminjasafni*, eds. Árni Björnsson and Hrefna Róbertsdóttir (Reykjavík, 2004), pp. 246–259.

have been dated to the mid 11th century. Apart from these panels and a small number of other objects, remains of medieval churches giving direct access to religious discourses are not available. A number of statues and other ornamentation also survive from the period including crucifixes and statues of saints, in addition to various types of objects used for the celebration of the Eucharist such as chalices and patens.

CHAPTER 2

The Roman Church in Free State Iceland

All religious discourse is situated in a particular social context which determines how it is received and, in turn, impacts its surroundings. From such a point of view, the notion of context has been defined by Teun A. van Dijk as "the structure of those properties of the social situation that are systematically (that is, not incidentally) *relevant* for discourse."[1] Following such definitions, in order to gain a sufficient understanding of how the earliest Christian discourse in Iceland came into play in its social enviroment, several contextual factors will be explored.[2] First, an overview will be provided of the historical and institutional context in which the sources of discourse were produced and the discourse was carried out. Such a survey is of particular importance for explaining how the historical developments taking place in the religious sphere during the eleventh, twelfth and thirteenth centuries warrant an imperial reading of the source material. Central to this discussion is the expansion and institutional organization of the Roman Church, reaching its peak with the papal reign of Innocent III (1198–1216) and the related topic of the Christianization of the North. Second, a detailed study of the source material itself will give a clearer picture of how and where the religious content was mediated. The exploration of the medial context will lead directly into a discussion of a third contextual factor focusing primarily on the participants, that is the mediating agents, their audience and the physical setting in which the religious discourses are being mediated, addressing the question posed in the following way by historian and discourse theorist Achim Landwehr: "where and when who is doing what".[3] Given the importance of ordained servants of

---

1   Van Dijk, "Discourse as Interaction in Society," p. 11. Italics original.
2   The division of the discursive landscape into different contextual components is loosely based on Achim Landwehr's discussion in his *Historische Diskursanalyse*, pp. 105–110. Working with a similar understanding of context as Van Dijk, Landwehr suggests four steps of context analysis: situational context, medial context, institutional context, and historical context. Here, this scheme has been adapted to the needs of the project by merging the historical and institutional context – which seemed fitting in view of its preoccupation with the Church as an institution and a main actor in the religious developments taking place in High Medieval Iceland. Also, in view of how radically different it is from the modern one, Landwehr's scheme has been complemented with a section on the medieval Christian hermeneutical and theological framework as a contextual factor.
3   Landwehr, *Historische Diskursanalyse*, p. 107.

the Church for the mediation of the discourse, this part will direct its attention especially towards the figure and role of clerics and their audiences in medieval Icelandic society. In view of the religious nature of the discourse under inspection, it is important to consider the socially shared religious knowledge influencing how the discourse was received and understood. Central to Medieval Christian religiosity was its strong hermeneutical tradition, shaped by the Christian theological world view which will be the topic of the fourth and last section of the discursive context of the earliest Christian religious discourse in Free State Iceland.

2.1 Christianization of Iceland

Central to this research is the relationship between the earliest Christian discourse in Iceland and the sociopolitical context in which it emerged. A reasonable first step is therefore to throw light on the sociopolitical context itself, with a particular focus on the most important developments in the religious sphere. In that regard, it is the process of Christianization which immediately offers itself as the most significant event taking place. In the following, the Christianization will be discussed from two sides. First, it is important to acknowledge that the introduction of Christianity meant the introduction of the Roman Church, a religious institution which strove to increase its power through its distinctive ways of operating and organizing itself. Therefore, it meant the introduction of a particular power structure which would gradually develop as the Christian religion gained ground around the island. The first part of this chapter will discuss the main characteristics of the power structure of the Roman Church, which in many respects resembles that of an empire. However, such power structures cannot be applied *in abstracto* to the environment in which they were being established. They were not adopted wholesale overnight but slowly grew via adaptation and negotiation. Therefore, it is also necessary to provide an overview of the Christianization process in Scandinavia and, most significantly, the events for how the process played out in Iceland. Both of these sides are important to keep in mind when considering the significance of the emerging religious discourse under inspection.

2.1.1 *The Roman Ecclesiastical Empire*
In his now classic book, *Western Society and the Church in the Middle Ages*, Richard Southern brings out the strong similarities between the medieval papacy and the ancient Roman empire in the following way:

If for Roman law we read canon law, if we replace the frontier legions of Rome by Crusaders, if we look on medieval kings as tributary dynasties under the general supervision of the Roman pope, and if we think of Dante as the Virgil of the new Rome, we shall begin to see that the attempt to keep the Roman Empire alive was not entirely chimerical. Looked on in this perspective it is not absurd to say that the Roman Empire achieved its fullest development in the thirteenth century with Innocent IV playing Caesar to Frederick II's Pompey.[4]

For obvious historical reasons, Southern chooses the Roman empire for his comparison, but the points which he highlights – legal and administrative apparatus, military expansion, centralized authority, and cultural propaganda – are all frequently mentioned when discussing the commonalities of imperial formations in general. Resorting to concepts introduced in the first part of this study, such circumstances are ideal for producing what has been termed an 'imperial experience' or an imperial 'action logic.'[5] In what follows, these elements will be explored and applied to the case of the Christianization of Iceland and the rise of the Roman Church in the northernmost parts of the Christian world.

Although medievalists do not frequently apply such categories to the medieval Church, the resemblances do not have to come as a surprise, given how strongly papal government was influenced by classical Roman ideas of government and legislation.[6] Nevertheless, it should be emphasized at the outset of this discussion, that the medieval Roman Church was not an empire in any traditional sense of the term.[7] Such a literal comparison would always offer itself as problematic, if only because of the consistent efforts in Christian thought to separate between secular and spiritual power, one of the most debated topic in medieval political theory.[8] Apart from the so-called Papal States on the Italian peninsula, over which the pope ruled as a secular prince, the Church did not

---

4 Richard Southern, *Western Society and the Church in the Middle Ages*, The Pelican History of the Church II (Harmondsworth, 1970), p. 25.
5 See section 1.2.2 above.
6 Canning, *History of Medieval Political Thought 300–1450* (London, 2005 [1996]), pp. 29–30. See also *Lexikon des Mittelalters*, s.v. "Bischof, -samt, III. Merowinger- und Karolingerzeit,", cols. 230–231. See also Peter Landau, "Kirchenverfassungen," in *Theologische Realenzyklopädie* 18, eds. Gerhard Müller, Horst Balz, and Gerhard Krause, 36 vols. (Berlin, 1976–2004), pp. 114–116.
7 For definition, see section 1.2.2.
8 See Canning, *History of Medieval Political Thought*, pp. 84–110. See also Brian Tierney, *The Crisis of Church and State 1050–1300: With Selected Documents* (Englewood Cliffs, 1964), pp. 7–15 and pp. 24–73.

make comparable claims to power over people as other secular rulers in the Middle Ages. That, however, does not mean that they did not make any claims to power over people. It was, after all, a visible body of believers (*corpus fidelium*) which found itself in the world and as any other group of people in need of organization and governance. Despite the limitations of the Church's power, which was the subject of long-standing debates throughout the Middle Ages, its structure of governance bore enough resemblances to imperial structures of ruling to validate a comparison with the empires of history, providing an important background for how this study perceives and approaches the religious discourse it sets out to analyse.

2.1.1.1 The Rise of the Papal Center

Around the middle of the 11th century the Roman Church began to make bolder claims than before to wide-ranging authority and leadership in the Christian World, marking the beginning of what the German historian Rudolf Schieffer has called the papal-historical turn (*Papstgeschichtliche Wende*) closely linked to the grand topic of reform in the high medieval Church.[9] This development had begun in the 10th century, as monastics and other churchpeople increasingly came to view the situation in the Church, particularly its relationship to secular authorities, as severely faulty.[10] It was marked by "a general transgression against the right order of things – namely, the subordination of the sacred to the profane and the ecclesiastical to the regal."[11] As scholars have repeatedly explained, an important background to understand this general dissatisfaction

---

9   See Rudolf Schieffer, "Motu Propriu. Über die Papstgeschichtliche Wende im 11. Jahrhundert," *Historisches Jahrbuch* 122 (2002), 27–42.

10 It is often traced back to 10th century monastic reforms most importantly the one led by the Burgundian house of Cluny, established in 910. The founding charter of Cluny expresses a decisive turn away from the common practices of the time, that is lay power over churches and other ecclesiastical property: "I hand over from my own rule [the founder Duke William I of Aquitane's] to the holy apostles, Peter, namely and Paul, the possessions over which I hold sway [...] And let the monks themselves, together with all the aforesaid possessions, be under the power and dominion of the abbot Berno [...] but after his death, those same monks shall have power and permission to elect any one of their order whom they please as abbot and rector [...] in such wise that neither by intervention of our own or of any other power may they be impeded from making a purely canonical election." Citation from Tierney, *Crisis of Church and State*, pp. 28–29. Other monastic movements of note include the short-lived Lower-Lotharingian Brogny-movement, also what has been called the Gorzian reform after the monastery of Gorz as well as roughly corresponding developments in England and Italy. Werner Goez, *Kirchenreform und Investiturstreit 910–1122*, 2nd ed. (Stuttgart, 2008), pp. 26–33 and pp. 41–56.

11 Kevin Madigan, *Medieval Christianity: A New History* (New Haven, 2015), p. 120.

within the Church was the chaotic situation in Europe caused by the dissolution of Emperor Charlemagne's empire in the 9th century. The precarious political conditions characterizing the wake of Charlemagne's reign, intensified by outside threats (Muslims, Scandinavians, and, to a lesser degree, Magyars) had spawned a situation in which lay lords and national monarchs had taken it upon themselves to protect churches and ecclesiastical property with the cost that they came to regard it as their own possession. It should be noted that what has been called the reform movement of the High Middle Ages was not a unified movement organized to reach a single goal but the reactions of multiple groups and individuals to a cluster of topics which they found unsatisfactory regarding the Church as well as its interaction to non-ecclesiastical authorities. At the same time, however, these developments lead to the growth and centralization of the papacy as an institution, while it continued to extend its claims to authority and influence in the Christian world.

These topics were forcefully put on the agenda during the pontificate of Leo IX (r. 1049–1054), the first reforming pope of the period, who gathered to the cardinalate important advisors – including Humbert, Peter Damian and Hildebrand (later Gregory VII) – vigorously championing for reform within the Church by all means possible. Pope Leo IX is credited with changing the papacy in significant ways, expanding its reach from Italian local politics to the wider scope of a leading force of the entire Western Church.[12] During his travels and at councils, Pope Leo promoted and enforced his program of reform, calling for the obedience of other bishops and ecclesiastics as he attempted to improve the morals of the Church by purifying it of endemic sins like simony and clerical marriage. Thereby, he set in motion a development aiming for the hierarchical centralization of the Latin Church under the leadership of the pope. Such claims had been well-known and acknowledged for centuries but now they were carried out with an unseen decisiveness and would reach their height during the investiture controversy (*lis investiturarum*) with both pope and emperor claiming authority over the other. After Emperor Henry IV's famous rejection of Gregory VII as pope, Gregory excommunicated the emperor and more importantly deposed him with an authority which is most explicitly set forth in the papal document *Dictatus papae*.[13]

Through reform initiatives in the field of papal organization and communication, the Christian world grew "larger and thicker," as described by Ernst-Dieter Hehl.[14] The papal sphere of influence was growing and so did also the

---

12   Ibid., pp. 126–130.
13   Ibid., pp. 137–138.
14   Ernst-Dieter Hehl, "Das Papsttum in der Welt des 12. Jahrhunderts. Einleitend Bemerkungen zu Anforderungen und Leistungen," in *Das Papsttum in der Welt des 12.*

papacy's "compulsion to intervene," as Herfried Münkler chooses to describe the reluctance of a central imperial power to remain neutral towards competing powers in its reach.[15] Two factors were of particular importance for this development: First, the theoretical body concerning the unique position of Rome and its bishop grew significantly. Second, as will be explained in the next section of this chapter, the administrative apparatus of the Roman Church was expanded.

As regards the first factor, throughout the era of reform, the authority of the bishop of Rome within the Christian Church was being consistently elaborated on in the overlapping and mutually reinforcing fields of ecclesiology and canon law. In letters and other writings of theological nature, the Roman bishop, successor and vicar of the apostle Peter, was claimed to be the exclusive holder of the *plenitudo potestatis* – the fullness of power – and the Roman Church was interchangeably referred to as the heart (*cardo*) of the Church, its head (*caput*), fountain (*fons*), foundation (*fundamentum*), and mother (*mater*).[16] Such ideas received its best-known manifestation in the aforementioned document *Dictatus papae*, which contained dictates like "[t]hat the Roman pontiff alone can with right be called universal," "[t]hat it may be permitted to him to depose emperors," and "[t]hat he who is not at peace with the Roman Church shall not be considered Catholic."[17] This development was also reflected in papal imagery and propaganda for Roman primacy which had been underway since the fifth century but reached its zenith at this point. The episcopal residence at the Lateran was turned into a palace – called a *patriarchium* since the 7th century and a *palatium* since the 9th – where the architecture, iconography and even furniture underlined the heightened authority of the pope and the primacy of Rome.[18] The papal seal (*bulla*) was changed from being exclusively verbal to containing images, inspired by imperial seals. Often they showed images related to the topic of Petrine primacy (keys and pastor) and during

---

    Jahrhunderts, Mittelalter-Forschungen 6, eds. Ernst D. Hehl and Ingrid H. Ringel (Stuttgart, 2002), p. 9.

15 Münkler, *Empires*, pp. 14–17.

16 Yves M.-J. Congar, "Der Platz des Papsttums in der Kirchenfrömmigkeit der Reformer des 11. Jahrhunderts," in *Sentire Ecclesiam: Das Bewusstsein von der Kirche als gestaltende Kraft der Frömmigkeit*, eds. Jean Daniélou and Herbert Vorgrimer (Freiburg i. B., 1963), pp. 199–200.

17 Madigan, *Medieval Christianity*, pp. 137–138.

18 See for example Francesca Pomarici's discussion on papal cathedrae and chairs in "Papal Imagery and Propaganda: Art, Architecture, and Liturgy," in *A Companion to the Medieval Papacy: Growth of an Ideology and an Institution*, eds. Keith Sisson and Atria A. Larson, Brill's Companions to the Christian Tradition 70 (Leiden, 2016), pp. 94–96.

the reign of Gregory the VII, they would show the figures of the apostles Peter and Paul.[19] During the period of reform, popes seem to have begun wearing a pointed hat, a predecessor of the papal tiara which would become a central symbol for the pope's earthly power. In this light, it is not without significance that the Roman *episcopatus* came during this period to be interchanged with the word *papatus*, thereby adding a layer to the ecclesiastical hierarchy above the episcopacy.

Another important outlet for these ideas was in the field of canon law, which was flourishing at the time. Since the Early Middle Ages, it was acknowledged that the pope had a special position of authority when it came to making law and ecclesiastical regulations. Until the time of the papal reform, however, his authority did not amount to "a universally active force as supreme law-giver or law maker."[20] From the reign of Leo IX and especially after Gregory VII and the *Dictatus papae,* it becomes clear that the reform movement was determined to increase the active involvement of the pope in legislation and law interpretation. Vitally important for the success of these efforts was Gratian's *Decretum* (Concordia discordantium canonum) around the mid-12th century and subsequent works of canon law which have been described as a cornerstone in the development towards a more homogenous Church.[21] As an example, the process of aligning the position of the pope to that of the Roman emperor as constructed in Roman law began with Gratian's work. At the beginning of his *Tractatus de legibus*, Gratian equated papal and imperial power and established the foundation for how the Church's "earthly and juridical quality" should be treated – while of course not disregarding the Church's unique spiritual essence. As set out by Gratian, the pope, as Peter's successor, the 'highest priest' (*summus pontifex*) was the head of the Roman Church. He had the "power to rule and command" (*potestas regendi et iubendi*) and enjoyed a position from which he "judges all and is judged by no one" (*cunctos ipse iudicaturus a nemine iudicandus*).[22]

2.1.1.2   From Center to the Periphery

Another factor particularly instrumental for the growth of the papal sphere of influence was the institutional expansion of the Church. Through the

---

19   Pomarici, "Papal Imagery and Propaganda," p. 90.
20   Atria A. Larson, "Popes and Canon Law," in *A Companion to the Medieval Papacy: Growth of an Ideology and an Institution*, eds. Keith Sisson and Atria A. Larson, Brill's Companions to the Christian Tradition 70 (Leiden, 2016), p. 147.
21   Johrendt and Müller, "Zentrum und Peripherie," p. 10.
22   Larson, "Popes and Canon Law," p. 147–148.

consolidation of its administrative apparatus manned by an elite of ordained servants, the theoretical formulation of the position of the pope in ecclesiology and canonical legislation could be carried out in practice. The expansion of administrative organization and the bolstering of its bureaucratic infrastructure, its 'tools of government' as termed by Southern, constituted an important way in which the papal center was able to maintain control and authority over distant territories.[23] The most significant tools of government were papal decretals, papal legates, judges-delegate (*iudices delegati*), and church councils. As the Church was establishing itself at the Northern margins of the Christian world, these measures were regularly put into use.

A papal decretal or a decretal letter (*epistola decretalis*) can refer to a wide spectrum of papal communication. Defined broadly, it refers to any papal communication of importance for canon law but more narrowly, it refers to a written response to a question or plea sent by an ecclesiastic or even a lay person on issues regarding canon law.[24] During the era of reform, but in particular after the mid-12th century, the number of papal decretals increased radically.[25] At this time, the significance of decretals as source of law also increased significantly, as they came to be understood to belong to a consistent and continuing body of decretals, contributing to the canonical tradition.[26] Scholars have interpreted this increase as indicating the intensifying relationship between the Roman center and the periphery of the Church.[27] In the words of Charles Duggan, "the weapon of decretal legislation" made popes capable of making their authority felt "throughout the length and breadth of Western Christendom."[28] The rise in the number of decretals is closely linked to the implementation of Roman primacy and in particular with the pope being widely acknowledged as the *iudex ordinarius ominum*, the judge ordinary of all

---

23 Southern, *Western Society and the Church*, p. 106.
24 Atria A. Larson and Keith Sisson, "Papal Decretals," in *A Companion to the Medieval Papacy: Growth of an Ideology and an Institution*, eds. Keith Sisson and Atria A. Larson, Brill's Companions to the Christian Tradition 70 (Leiden, 2016), p. 158.
25 Scholars have dated around 7000 decretals to the period between 1159 and 1198, amounting to 1750 decretals on average per decade. In the preceding millennium, the number of decretals was much lower, amounting to around 1000 per century. Larson and Sisson, "Papal Decretals," p. 164. See also Southern, *Western Society and the Church*, p. 108.
26 Larson and Sisson, "Papal Decretals," p. 163.
27 Lotte Kéry, "Dekretalenrecht zwischen Zentrale und Peripherie," in *Römisches Zentrum und kirchliche Peripherie: Das universale Papsttum als Bezugspunkt der Kirchen von den Reformpäpsten bis zu Innozenz III*, eds. Jochen Johrendt and Harald Müller (Berlin, 2008), p. 22.
28 Charles Duggan, *Twelfth-Century Decretal Collections and Their Importance in English History*, University of London Historical Studies 12 (London, 1963), pp. 24–25.

men. In that light, a papal decree possessed a heightened authority and in local parishes all around the Christian world, clerics and other ecclesiastics began to turn rather to the papal curia than their episcopal courts.[29]

In occasions of heightened importance, sending a letter was not always a sufficient resource and a more influential type of representation needed. For such instances, the Church made use of the papal legates – the pope's eyes and *alter ego* – who made the one they represented, the pope, fully and virtually present with their own physical appearance. In legal matters and political affairs, the legates represented the bishop of Rome as they ran his errands around the Christian world. Harald Müller ascribes immense significance to the legates, particularly the cardinal legates, for the developing and stabilizing of Roman authority taking place at the time.[30] There were three types of *legati*: perpetual legates (*legati nati*), nuncios (*nuntii, legati missi*), and legates sent directly by the pope (*legati a latere*).[31] Among these, the *legati a latere* could be described as an elite group among the legates, commissioned for projects of particular importance and were understood to have a special share in the pope's fullness of power. The *nuntii* seem to have generally been assigned to more specific tasks and the *legati nati* served as the pope's representatives in specific regions and their power was territorially limited. These were the archbishops of Salzburg, Prague, Cologne, Gniezno, and Esztergom-Budapest.[32] Apart from the duties specifically ascribed to the legates, the legates' role was highly important in that they "formed a flexible bond of communication between the curia and regional churches of Latin Christendom" which corresponds quite accurately to how the role of administrative elites in imperial formations and large-scale political entities has been defined.[33] As distinguished

---

29 Lotte Kéry, "Dekretalenrecht zwischen Zentrale und Peripherie," pp. 24–25.
30 Harald Müller, "The Omnipresent Pope," in *A Companion to the Medieval Papacy: Growth of an Ideology and an Institution*, eds. Keith Sisson and Atria A. Larson, Brill's Companions to the Christian Tradition 70 (Leiden, 2016), p. 209.
31 In addition, there were all sorts of expressions in play: 'the apostolic vicar' who represented the pope in discipline and teaching, the *apocrisiarius*, representing the pope in Constantinople, the *defensor ecclesiae*, had the project of safe-guarding papal property, and *legati vagantes* who were primarily missionaries. Ibid., pp. 205–206.
32 Ibid., p. 205.
33 Ibid., p. 208. For a discussion of pre-modern elites and the elite concept, see for example Jeroen Duindam, "Pre-modern Power Elites: Princes, Courts, Intermediaries," in *The Palgrave Handbook of Political Elites*, eds. Heinrich Nest and John Higley (London, 2018), pp. 161–179. For a more theoretically oriented treatment of the elite concept see Richard Lachmann, "Hegemons, Empires, and Their Elites," *Sociologia, Problemas e Práticas* 75 (2014), 9–38 and John Higely, "Continuities and Discontinuities in Elite Theory," in *The Palgrave Handbook of Political Elites*, eds. Heinrich Nest and John Higley (London, 2018), pp. 25–39.

from the role of messengers, they had powers to involve themselves in disputes and other matters in order to bring about an acceptable solution – for Rome, most importantly. These could be issues of discipline, church organization, doctrinal and legal issues and did not even have to be restricted to the ecclesiastical sphere but could also directly concern the more secular authorities. The increased use of papal emissaries happened in the High Middle Ages and was directly caused by the extended claims of the Roman bishop to a universal papacy.[34] This is clearly evident from the postulations of Gregory VII, who made ample use of legates for staying on top of things in distant regions and make sure that his policies were being enforced.[35] If sent by the pope, Gregory VII maintained, legates who had been granted full powers superseded other bishops and could even depose them. Such ideas reflect the absolute supremacy and preeminence of the bishop of Rome. And they did not come without problems. The notion that the pope could involve himself in local affairs was bound to produce problems with bishops and churches used to govern their own matters to a significant degree. Also, it was also not entirely clear how it was to be practically carried out that a legate could represent the pope in such literal ways.

Still another way in which the power of the pope was being outsourced during this period was through the judges-delegate whose main role was to solve legal disputes. In the High Middle Ages the number of appeals to Rome grew rapidly and the pope and the cardinals could in no way deal with all of them. The judges-delegate were assigned particular cases and were supposed to reach findings on behalf of the pope. Their verdicts had the status of a papal decision, a binding conclusion which only the pope could turn. The judges acted as *vices* and stressed their position as representatives of the pope, possessing apostolic authority (*apostolica auctoritas*). It was not self-evident that the Roman bishop could involve himself in judicial matters far away from the regular jurisdictional bounds and would sometimes cause resistance. Although not without difficulties, the entitlement to a universal jurisdictional primacy as the *iudex ordinarius omnium* was of high importance for papal reform. The possibility of appealing to Rome strengthened the papacy and the primary position of the papal tribunal over against regional courts and hierarchies and bound to further strengthen the homogenization of Latin Christendom under papal leadership.[36]

---

34 Müller, "The Omnipresent Pope," p. 203.
35 Ibid.
36 Ibid., p. 216.

Finally, conciliar gatherings were a significant component of papal government in the High Middle Ages. The size and scope of the councils differed radically, but most important for the present discussion are the general councils – *generalia concilia* – which were summoned and presided over by the pope.[37] The period between the mid-eleventh century and the thirteenth has been described as momentous in the conciliar history of the Western Church because of the high number of such councils and ecclesiastical assemblies.[38] The precise nature of their significance, however, is debated. During the reform period, councils summoned by the pope were intended as legislative assemblies and their decrees were supposed to have a bearing on canon law. By such means, the reforming popes of course attempted to promote and enforce their policies while simultaneously illustrating papal authority and prestige through various means. At the same time, particular cases could be addressed and processed. In that way, the councils also served as a supreme tribunal of the Church. It has, however, been pointed out that the value of conciliar decrees depended to a great extent on their reception and application, both in the law schools and, no less important, their local dissemination. In this regard, the fate of conciliar decrees differed considerably. As an example, it was only in the case of the Third Lateran Council of 1179 that all the conciliar decrees ended up in authoritative canonical collections.[39] It has been shown that at the local level, bishops and archbishops could be relatively selective when it came to the application of conciliar decrees, and in some cases, it seems as if they were understood rather as suggestions than binding prescriptions.[40]

2.1.1.3 On the Outskirts

Any comparison of the medieval papacy to an empire is meaningless without considering how it managed to permanently stay in power in the different regions of Western Christendom. For such purposes, of course, the papal court did not only rely on decretals and legates or other short-termed interventions. Theoretically, the papal center in Rome secured its influence through both the ecclesiastical hierarchy and the organizational system of dioceses and parishes. The notion of ecclesiastical hierarchy has since the Middle Ages referred

---

[37] Danica Summerlin, "Papal Councils," in *A Companion to the Medieval Papacy: Growth of an Ideology and an Institution*, eds. Keith Sisson and Atria A. Larson, Brill's Companions to the Christian Tradidion 70 (Leiden, 2016), p. 189.

[38] Ian S. Robinson, *The Papacy, 1073–1198: Continuity and Innovation* (Cambridge, Eng., 1990), p. 121.

[39] Summerlin, "Papal Councils," p. 194.

[40] Ibid., pp. 194–195.

THE ROMAN CHURCH IN FREE STATE ICELAND 47

to, in the words of Siegfried Widenhofer, "the legally ordered, layered clerical authority over consecration and jurisdiction."[41] In the course of the Middle Ages, the power of the Roman bishop over archbishops and bishops around the Christian West gradually increased and bishops lost the great amount of autonomy and authority they had enjoyed since the 4th century. In that regard, the papacy of Pope Leo IX is seen as a dividing line when subordination to the pope became an unquestionable obligation.

Outside Rome, the highest-ranking members of the hierarchy were the metropolitan bishops or the archbishops as they came to be called in the sixth century, although their power would only decrease in the course of the High Middle Ages.[42] Their absolute subordination to the pope was symbolized with the *pallium* which since the time of Pope Gregory VII had to be acquired personally from the pope. The archbishops' role was to provide leadership within their diocese, supervise their suffragan bishops and visit their dioceses. Moreover, they were allowed to summon provincial councils, confirm the election of new bishops before they ordained them, carry out judgments in cases which had been appealed to their court and involve themselves in various other administrative affairs of their suffragan bishops under particular circumstances.[43]

Each archbishopric was divided into smaller dioceses, each with its own bishop. Since the 4th century, bishops had ruled over specifically delineated areas called dioceses or bishoprics, originally the centers of the late Roman *civitates*. The power of the bishop in both spiritual and more secular affairs rose to its heights during the Carolingian period while bishops and kings still enjoyed the mutual benefits of their cooperation.[44] In the course of the 10th and 11th centuries, with the decline of royal power, much of the bishops' independence was transferred to the Church's center in Rome. As time passed, a central role of the bishop came to be "to assist the pope in exercising his plenitude of power."[45] It was indeed a period of a wide-ranging transition of the episcopal office which at this point can only be treated superficially. Tasks related to the bishops' position as a local magnate, highly involved in the business and politics of his region were transformed into bureaucratic

---

41 Siegfried Wiedenhofer, s.v. "Hierarchie", in *Religion in Geschichte und Gegenwart*, 4th ed.
42 There existed the honorary title of a *primas* among the archbishops of a given region, enjoyed for example by the archbishops of Bourges, Canterbury, and Salzburg. Since the establishing of the archbishopric of Uppsala, the archbishop of Lund had the status of a *primas* among the three Scandinavian archbishoprics.
43 Landau, "Kirchenverfassungen," pp. 133–134; Jarl Gallén, "Biskop," *KLNM* I, col. 611–612.
44 Southern, *Western Society and the Church*, p. 176.
45 Ibid., p. 188.

duties. Their administrative and judicial obligations grew significantly as the highest ranking officials of the ecclesiatical hierarchy in their dioceses. Slowly, the loyalty of the local bishop came to be directed to the center at Rome. Bishops were to follow orders as they were delivered through papal letters and his representatives. At the same time, they were responsible for their parish priests and by extention the salvation of their parishioners. At the end of the 13th century, the bishops had lost much of their independence although their local influence was not greatly diminished. They were still landowners and important players in local politics and at the same time they enjoyed a great deal of authority through their place in the ecclesiastical hierarchy and the papal administrative apparatus. As described by Robert Swanson, the role of bishops and priests was critical within medieval Western societies since they served as "the point of contact both between people and institution, and (in many ways) between people and God."[46] They were not only responsible for pastoral care and providing the people with the means to salvation, but were also the people on whom the papacy relied when something came up in their dioceses.

2.1.2 Expanding Boundaries: Christianization of Scandinavia

Christianity had been known in Scandinavia as long as there had been interaction between the region with the rest of Christian Europe, perhaps since the reign of emperor Constantine.[47] Although the Christian religion had not been formally introduced as a comprehensive set of religious ideas and practices it had reached Scandinavia by various means before, during, and after the arrival of missionaries in the early 9th century. It had, therefore, at least since then been present among other world views in a porous religious landscape.[48] As shown in a recent study, archaeological evidence indicates that through trade and gift giving, travels and raids, various components of the Christian religion became slowly infiltrated into the area.[49] During the centuries-long period of Christianization, it seems as if the Christian religion was not as fixed, clear-cut and immediately victorious as many medieval chroniclers would have it, but fluid and ambiguous.[50]

---

46   Robert N. Swanson, "Manning the Church: Priests and Bishops," in *The Routledge History of Medieval Christianity 1050–1500*, The Routledge Histories (London, 2015), p. 32.
47   Winroth, *Conversion of Scandinavia*, p. 129.
48   Winroth, *Conversion of Scandinavia*, pp. 128–135. See also Steinunn Kristjánsdóttir, "Kristnitakan. Áhrif tilviljanakennds og skipulegs trúboðs," *Saga* XLV/1 (2007), 118 and 123.
49   Winroth, *Conversion of Scandinavia*, p. 129.
50   Ibid., p. 133.

A decisive factor in the Christianization of Scandinavia was the cultural exchange between Scandinavia and the British Isles which had begun during the Viking Age. It was then largely increased after Haraldr Sigurðarson's defeat at Stamford Bridge in 1066 which lead to many Scandinavians retreating overseas to their original homelands. It was, for instance, on English ground that Norway's first Christian kings, including the famous missionary kings Ólafr Tryggvason and Ólafr Haraldsson, came into contact with Christianity.[51] Christianity in Scandinavia was thus influenced by Christian currents in the British Isles but also by ecclesiastical centers on the continent, most importantly in Saxony.[52] In the case of Norway, the Western Part (the Atlantic Coast of Southern Norway) was more influenced by Anglo-Saxon Christianity, while Viken (the area surrounding the Oslofjord and Skagerrak) came into contact with the new religion as it protruted out of the diocese of Bremen through Denmark (see figure. 3).

The conception of Christianization as a prolonged process, beginning with a slow infiltration leading to institutional corroboration, is much in line with the research done on the topic over the past half a century.[53] Before, scholars had rather tended to emphasize the importance of particular individuals and events and thereby depicting a scenario much like the one set forth in the medieval writings themselves in which missionaries and missionary kings fought the devilry of their pagan enemies and converted entire regions through battles or contracts. However, even though stories of missionaries can inform about significant figures in the early progress of Christianity in Scandinavia, it

---

51 As has been pointed out by Nora Berend and others, Christianity/Christendom in the Middle Ages is not an unproblematic concept. In this discussion, it refers to Latin Christianity and in the case of local variations, the broader concept of Christianity is qualified with reference to the region in question, e.g. Anglo-Saxon Christianity, as is customary in the field of Scandinavian medieval history. For a further discussion of the concept, see Nora Berend, "The Concept of Christendom: A Rhetoric of Integration or Disintegration?" in *Hybride Kulturen in mittelalterlichen Europa/ Hybrid Cultures in Medieval Europe*, ed. Michael Borgolte, Europa im Mittelalter 16 (Berlin, 2010), pp. 51–61.
52 For more detailed discussion, see *KÍ* I, pp. 18–37.
53 The earliest and most influential attempt to outline the Christianization process of Scandinavia is that of Fridtjov Birkeli, *Norske steinkors i tidlig middelalder: Et bidrag til belysning av overgangen fra norrøn religion til kristendom* (Oslo, 1973). Other important works are Jan Arvid Hellström, *Vägar till Sveriges kristnande* (Stockholm, 1996); Jón Viðar Sigurðsson, *Kristninga i Norden 750–1200* (Oslo, 2003), pp. 12–13; Orri Vésteinsson, *Christianization of Iceland*; *KÍ* I, pp. 7–11; Winroth, *Conversion of Scandinavia*; and Stefan Brink, "Early Ecclesiastical Organization of Scandinavia, Especially Sweden," in *Medieval Christianity in the North*, eds. Kirsi Salonen, Kurt Villads Jensen and Torstein Jørgensen, Acta Scandinavica 1 (Brepols, 2013), pp. 24–25.

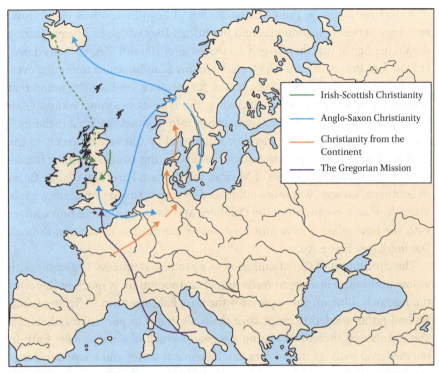

FIGURE 3 The image shows the movement of the Christian religion between Iceland, Scandinavia, the British isles and the continent. Irish influence in Iceland remains a controversial issue and is marked with a dotted line

remains true, as historian Anders Winroth puts it that "[i]n real life, conversion is a much messier business than how our medieval narrators portray it, with many shades of gray."[54]

Although the tendency in recent decades has rather been to downplay the role of the indiviudals carrying out the mission work in the Christianization process, Scandinavia boasts of a long history of missionary activity which should not be entirely overlooked. There exist several narratives of hagiographic nature about the first missionaries in Scandinavia. Among the first missionaries venturing into Scandinavian territories was Archbishop Ebo of Rheims (775–851) who went to Denmark in 823.[55] The most important figure

---

54 Winroth, *Conversion of Scandinavia*, p. 128.
55 Traditionally, the first missionary in Scandinavia was Willibrord of Utrecht (658–739) but the historical value of Alcuin of York's *Vita Willibrordi* for Willibrord's travels into Denmark has been called into questioning. Ibid., p. 15.

for the missionary history of Scandinavia, however, and the one who is traditionally regarded as 'the apostle of Scandinavia' is the monk Ansgar (801–865). Although the information preserved about Ansgar through Rimbert's *Vita Anskari* is considerable, it should be kept in mind that his biography was composed primarily in order to promote him as a saint and might have lead historians to overestimate his significance for the Northern mission and underestimate the contributions of others. As recent research has shown, it probably also led scholars – ever since Adam of Bremen's *Gesta Hammaburgensis Ecclesiae Pontificum* – to exaggerate the alleged downswing of Christianity after the time of Ansgar, simply because there are no extant textual sources for the period.[56] According to Anders Winroth, it was not missionaries who brought the Christian religion to Scandinavia.[57] Missionaries were first and foremost responsible for introducing the 'idea of conversion' to the Scandinavians, by which Winroth refers to a particular way, well-known from various hagiographic writings, of constructing the historical reality of conversion periods as a clear-cut event in which Christianity overcomes the formidable forces of the pagan religions.[58]

Recently, the role of kings and other magnates of a more secular sort has been stressed by Anders Winroth. Christian kings and chieftains provided political protection, securing a favorable environment for the Church to stabilize itself as an institution. When Scandinavian kings, beginning with Haraldr *Bluetooth* Gormsson, realized the political advantages of adopting Christianity, they made use of the religion in order to strengten their own power position. As Winroth explains, the Christian religion was better suited than the Old Norse pagan religion to maintain control over the large political entities emerging in the North. Not only did it provide them with a way to counter potential opposition, with an ideology of divine kingship legitimizing their position of sole authority over their kingdoms, but as they were in control over the clerical caste they could monopolize religious services and distribute them as goods or gifts to their subjects.[59] In addition, Christianity was affiliated with much prestige, as it was adhered to by the most powerful kings of Europe. Seen in this light, the decision to convert to Christianity was first and foremost of a political nature, a point repeatedly stressed by Winroth throughout his book.[60]

---

56   Ibid., pp. 105 and 194.
57   Ibid., p. 146.
58   Ibid., pp. 121–137 and 162.
59   Ibid., pp. 152–160.
60   See esp. ibid., pp. 145–168.

Thus, it was in the tenth century when Scandinavian kings became interested in Christianity and thereafter converted and before the formation of structures of elaborate administration, that the Christian religion settled itself for good in the North. This happened first in Denmark with the conversion of King Haraldr *Bluetooth* (r. 958–986) in the 960s. In Norway, a series of Christian kings (Hákon *the Good*, Haraldr *Greycloak*, Ólafr Tryggvason) attempted to convert Norway but failed because of the opposition of powerful pagan magnates. It was not until the reign of Ólafr Haraldsson, the martyr king and patron saint of Norway, that Norway was ultimately Christianized. As for Sweden, accounts exist saying that the Swedish King Erik had been baptized in Denmark and his son Olof had striven to Christianize the region; but these sources are highly problematic.[61] Having accepted Christianity as the official religion of their kingdoms, themselves becoming the heads of their 'national churches,' the Scandinavian kings accepted at the same time the administrative structures of the Roman Church as an inherent part of their kingdoms. The first bishoprics were founded in Denmark in the mid-tenth century. At the synod of Ingelheim in 948, three bishoprics – Schleswig (Hedeby), Ribe, and Aarhus – were established in Jutland and subordinated to the archbishop of Hamburg-Bremen.[62] Around 1060, the diocesan structure had reached a stable form in Denmark, which is around the same time the first bishoprics were set a foot in Iceland and Norway. Around 1070, three bishoprics were established in Norway – Niðarós, Bergen, and Oslo – to which two more, Stavanger and Hamar, were added in the twelfth century. In Sweden, the formation of a stable diocesan structure took longer than elsewhere in the North, with the first bishopric established in 1020 and the last in 1170, which according to Jón Viðar Sigurðsson was due to Sweden having weaker royal power than Denmark and Norway. The opposition against Christianity was also heavier in Sweden than elsewhere in the North.[63]

The first archbishopric in Scandinavia was that of Lund in Denmark, founded in 1104 after a long-standing tension between the archbishop of Hamburg-Bremen and the Scandinavian kings. Already during the papacy of Leo IX, the Danish king, Sweyn II (1047–1076), had appealed to the pope

---

61 Ibid., p. 117. See also a concise yet informative overview in Lutz E. von Padberg, *Die Christianisierung Europas im Mittelalter*, 2nd ed. (Stuttgart, 2009), pp. 115–136.

62 So-called because the archbishop of Hamburg had to flee to Bremen in the 830s because of the raids of Vikings and others. When the bishop of Bremen died in 845, the boundaries of Hamburg were expanded to include Bremen, which had before belonged to the archdiocese of Cologne. The seat of the archbishop stayed in Bremen and the archbishopric was consequently named after both cities.

63 Jón Viðar Sigurðsson, *Kristninga i Norden*, p. 64.

to found an archepiscopal see. The archbishops of Hamburg-Bremen had actively opposed the founding of new archbishoprics in the North, which would decrease their sphere of influence. The Scandinavian kings were aware of the political implications of the subordination to a German archbishopric which placed them in an uncomfortable position over against the German rulers. This tension was solved when the existence of the archbishopric of Lund, comprising entire Scandinavia and the islands in the West, was confirmed by Pope Paschal II (r. 1099–1118). Within a relatively short time span, the archdiocese of Lund was divided into three smaller archdioceses with the upgrade of the two dioceses furthest North: Niðarós in 1152/1153 and Uppsala in 1164. In addition to the five Norwegian bishoprics, the bishoprics on the Isle of Man, the Hebrides, the Faroe Islands, Greenland, and Hólar and Skálholt in Iceland belonged to Niðarós. Six bishoprics were subordinated to the Uppsala-archdiocese: Uppsala, Västerås, Strängnäs, Linköping, Skara, and Växjö. Eight bishoprics belonged to Lund: Lund, Roskilde, Odense, Slesvig, Ribe, Aarhus, Viborg, and Børglum. This diocesan structure, which had begun in the mid-10th century, was to last throughout the Middle Ages.

2.1.3   *Christianization of Iceland*

Similar to the larger region of Scandinavia, the Christianization of Iceland should be conceived of in terms of a slow process, beginning with informal cultural exchange well before the official conversion in 999 and ending in a fully fledged institutional Church in the 14th century.[64] Due to the extensive reception history of Ari Þorgilsson's account of the events taking place at the law giving synod at Þingvellir in the summer of 999, according to which Icelandic magnates, Christian and pagan, agreed on accepting Christianity through the mediation of the pagan law-speaker Þorgeirr, Iceland's Christianization has very commonly been reduced to that particular conversion event.[65] But even though scholars generally agree that the broad strokes of Ari's account hold, they amount to nothing more and nothing less than that. When painting his picture of the early Christian landscape, Ari's brush strokes come closer to a sketch, as it were, of a single episode (albeit an important one) in a long and complex process than a source for the Christian religion in 11th

---

64   Traditionally, the event of the Christianization of Iceland on Alþingi is dated to the year 1000 but after a closer inspection into the chronological reasoning of Ari *the Wise*, a date of the summer of 999 seems more precise. See Ólafía Einarsdóttir, *Studier i kronologisk metode i tidlig islandsk historieskrivning*, Bibliotheca historica Lundensis 13 (Stockholm, 1964). Cf. Jakob Benediktsson, in *ÍF* I, pp. XXIX–XLII.
65   *ÍF* I, pp. 14–18.

century Iceland. As scholars have increasingly pointed out in recent years, there are other accounts of the arrival of the Christian religion in the country. Summarizing the available sources for how Christianity was introduced, Sverrir Jakobsson adds two narrative strings to the one found in Ari's *Book of Icelanders*. First, there is the view found in *Gesta Hammaburgensis ecclesiae pontificum* composed by Adam of Bremen between 1073 and 1076, according to which Icelanders did not become Christian until Ísleifr Gizurarson had been ordained by Adalbert, archbishop of Hamburg and bishop of Bremen. Another version is found in the *Book of Settlements*, which assumes that Christianity existed in the country since the settlement given that some of the first settlers were Christians.[66]

None of these narratives can sufficiently account for how Christianity arrived and established itself in Iceland on its own. Read together, however, they provide a relatively comprehensive picture of the Christianization process as it has been explained by recent scholarship. Each narrative can thus be understood as representative for the most important components of the process respectively. First, representing what could be called the classical view of the Christianization, is the account found in Ari's *Book of Icelanders*, emphasizing the agency of the Icelandic political elite and the ways in which the upper layers of Icelandic society made it possible for Christianity to develop in the country as one vehicle among many with which they could preserve and employ their social and political power. An obvious representative for this view in recent scholarship is Orri Vésteinsson who in his research of the early development of Christianity in Iceland has argued that the Church in Iceland had not developed an independent institutional identity until after 1200 and not fully until the end of the 13th century.[67] At the same time, it was becoming increasingly integrated into the international Church, adopting and applying its hierarchy and other power mechanisms to the Icelandic context. It should be noted that Vésteinsson's framework is largely based on economic and political changes accompanying the Christianization process and the institutional development of the Church. In order to throw light on the "main threads and thresholds in a long and complex develoment," Vésteinsson has suggested a periodization in which he divides the development into a tripartite framework of conversion (990–1090), formation (1090–1140) and consolidation (1140–1240).[68]

---

66   Sverrir Jakobsson, *Auðnaróðal*, p. 25.
67   Orri Vésteinsson, *Christianization of Iceland*, pp. 4–5, 167–178, and 238–246.
68   Orri Vésteinsson, "The Formative Phase of the Icelandic Church ca 990–1240 AD," in *Church Centres: Church Centres in Iceland from the 11th to the 13th Century and Their*

The conversion period began with the arrival of foreign missionaries, decades before the official acceptance of Christianity by the general assembly at Þingvellir, an event which Vésteinsson appropriately terms a 'political conversion' given that it was a decision made by the holders of political power at the time. The conversion period ends according to Vésteinsson when Gizurr Ísleifsson (r. 1082–1118) succeeds his father as the bishop of Skálholt, formally establishing Skálholt as an episcopal see by donating parts of his family estate to the cathedral. Landowners and aristocracy were involved in the matters of the Church, which is evident from how easily ecclesiastical taxation was introduced in 1097. Many chieftains owned churches and served as priests which made them entitled to a substantial share of the tax revenues.[69] In the beginning of the 12th century the people of Northern Iceland are said to have asked for their own see, which they received in 1106 at Hólar along with their own bishop, Jón Ögmundarson. At the end of the formation-phase, "all the principal elements of an institutional Church are in evidence."[70] In Vésteinsson's view, it was the establishment of Þingeyrar-monastery in 1133 (see Figure 1) that ushered in the consolidation-stage in the development of earliest Christianity.[71] During the years between 1140 and 1240, the proponents of the nascent Church were busy putting order to the operations of the ecclesiastical network in the country. Around 1200 there were around 360 churches with priests attached to them, 6 monasteries and over a 1000 lesser churches and chapels, which called for increased organization and bureaucracy; this set its mark on the

---

Parallels in Other Countries, ed. Helgi Þorláksson, Snorrastofa: Rit 2 (Reykholt, 2005), pp. 73–74.

69 See part 2.2.1 above.
70 Orri Vésteinsson, "Formative Phase of the Icelandic Church," p. 79.
71 The role of monasteries in the Christianization process is the subject of ongoing research both for the Icelandic context but also for the broader Scandinavian one. Until 1200 there were around 100 monasteries established in the North of which by far the highest number, around 60, was in Denmark. Denmark was also the country where the earliest monasteries were established in the end of the eleventh century. Beginning in the early twelfth century, nineteen monasteries were founded in Norway, twelve in Sweden, and six in Iceland between 1130 and 1150. The high number of monasteries in Denmark is explained by the fact that the country had the highest population at the time. In the North, it was usually kings and bishops who established monasteries and not the aristocracy like in other parts of Latin Christendom. In Denmark, Norway, and Iceland, the earliest monasteries belonged to the Benedictine order and were located close to an episcopal seat, which they supported in various ways. The bishop served as the leader of the abbots and the monks often supported the administrative efforts of the bishop. Later in the 12th century, monasteries of the Augustinian and Cistercian orders were founded in Norway and Denmark and in Sweden, the Cistercians remained the dominant order. See Jón Viðar Sigurðsson, *Kristninga í Norden*, pp. 72–74 and Padberg, *Christianisierung Europas*, pp. 115–136.

first half of the period in question. According to Vésteinsson, it is not until the 13th century that he detects a significantly increased influence of the international Catholic Church. This did not result in any significant changes right away but lead to the Icelandic clergy's increasing awareness of their Church, in the words of Vésteinsson, being "too insular, too non-professional and too awkwardly entwined in secular interests."[72] That this was the opinion of the new archiepiscopal Niðarós-authorities as well, was confirmed in 1237 when the episcopal candidates chosen by the Icelanders and sent for ordination in Niðarós were rejected and non-Icelandic priests ordained as bishops in Hólar and Skálholt.[73]

The second perspective on the Christianization of Iceland places more emphasis on the institutional expansion of the Roman Church and the intiatives of ecclesiastical authorities. As noted, such a view is reflected in Adam of Bremen's *Gesta* where Icelanders are first said to have become Christian with the ordination of their first bishop Ísleifr. This perspective has been gathering support among modern scholars in recent years but is perhaps set forth most clearly in a 2017 article by literary scholar Gottskálk Þór Jensson. According to his reading, the most significant events of the Christianization process came about through the influence of powerful ecclesiastics carrying out the policies of the Church administration. The growth of Christianity in Iceland should primarily be read over against the expanding jurisdictional claims of the Church's centralized government and only secondarily in view of local interests and initiatives. Even in the very beginning, Jensson implies, there was a stronger relationship between the archbishopric of Bremen and the first Icelandic bishops and the establishing of the first bishoprics than the medieval sources have been taken to suggest.[74] Moreover, significant events like the founding of Hólar bishopric, the establishing of the monastery of Þingeyrar, and even the confirmation of the tithe should be viewed as indicators of an increased interest of the papacy in the North and the wide-ranging strengthening of ecclesiastical governmental structures accompanying it. A milestone in that development was the founding of the archdiocese of Lund in 1104 and the administrative reorganization undertaken during the episcopacy of the first archbishop, Özurr (r. 1104–1137). In his time, new bishoprics were founded in the Faroe

---

72 Orri Vésteinsson, "Formative Phase of the Icelandic Church," p. 80.
73 For a detailed discussion, see Heidi Anett Øvergård Beistad, "An Almost Fanatical Devotion to the Pope? Power and Priorities in the Integration of the Niðarós Province c. 1152–1300," (Doctoral thesis, Norwegian University of Science and Technology, 2016), pp. 59–80.
74 Gottskálk Jensson, "Íslenskar klausturreglur og libertas ecclesie," p. 20.

Islands and Greenland and the establishing of Hólar should be seen as part of these changes. Thus, contrary to what the *vita* of Bishop Jón Ögmundarson suggests, it was not the 'people of the North' who had the biggest say in the establishing of Hólar bishopric. The earliest Christian law was introduced in Iceland between 1122 and 1133 on the initiative of Archbishop Özurr which among other things confirmed the tithe law which had been put into use in 1097. Jensson also suggests that the establishment of the Benedictine monastery of Þingeyrar was carried out according to the directives of Archbishop Özurr as well seeing that in the first decades of the 12th century, Benedictine monasteries were being set up all around Scandinavia.[75]

Jensson highlights the great significance of the visits of papal legates to the North.[76] Each of the four legatine visits during the Middle Ages, he contends, brought about changes in the realms of church politics, administration and theology. After the second Lateran council in 1139, the papal legate and cardinal Theodwin (d. 1153), bishop of Porto and Santa Rufina, presided over an ecclesiastical synod in the North the main purpose of which was to establish the independence of the archbishopric of Lund over the archbishop of Hamburg and Bremen. Of no less significance was Nicholas Breakspear's (later Pope Hadrian IV (r. 1154–1159)) legatine visit in the years 1152–1154. Breakspear had been commissioned by Pope Eugene III (r. 1145–1153) to found two new archbishoprics in the North in order to strengthen the ecclesiastical administration and more specifically to secure papal influence in the region in the conflict against the German emperor. During this visit, Breakspear only founded one new archbishopric, that of Niðarós but the founding of the archbishopric of Uppsala had to wait until 1164. No less important for the ensuing developments in the church political realm was Breakspear's instigation of cathedral canons who, through their education in France and England, most importantly at the St. Victor Monastery in Paris, would bring about the influence of Augustinian canons who flocked to the North in the following years. Among the promising and aspiring churchmen sent to Paris were men like Eysteinn Erlendsson and Eiríkr Ívarsson, later archbishops of Niðarós, and Þorlákr Þórhallsson, later bishop of Skálholt, who were to become important proponents of the reform movement in Scandinavia as will be discussed at greater length below. During this period, most new monasteries belonged to the order of the Augustinian canons.[77] In Iceland, the first Augustinian monastery was set afoot by Þorlákr

---

75 Ibid., p. 24.
76 Ibid., pp. 24–29.
77 Ibid., pp. 33–34. In the case of at least two monasteries, those of Þykkvibær and Helgafell, there can be established plausible links to the Abbey of Saint Victor in Paris. Gunnar

Þórhallsson in Þykkvibær in Southern Iceland in the year 1168. As pointed out by Jensson, soon after the establishing of these monasteries, the influence of the Norwegian Archbishop seems to increase significantly.

The emphasis on the institutional expansion of the centralized Roman Church as a driving force in the Christianization process has also been adopted by Steinunn Kristjánsdóttir who has applied that perspective to the rise of monasteries in the country. In her comprehensive survey, she discusses the establishing of the seven monasteries founded in the 12th century under the heading "The Roman Church Settles Itself in Iceland" ("Rómarkirkja hreiðrar um sig á Íslandi") which already suggests an increased emphasis on the role of the centralized Church in that time compared to more traditional Christianization paradigms. She emphasizes, contrary to much previous research, that both in regard to their organization as well as their architectural design, monasteries in Iceland were in all main respects comparable to monasteries elsewhere in Europe.[78] The model came from Rome, she states, and as for the role they played in the development for Icelandic religion and society, the same should be assumed.[79] The establishing of the first, large monasteries of the country – for example those of Þingeyrar, Munkaþverá, Þykkvibær, and Hítardalur – were "without doubt the direct result of the expansion of the Roman Church and the Rule of Benedict in the 12th century."[80] In the beginning, a primary objective of the monasteries was to provide the people with religious knowledge. Furthermore, as time passed, they came to provide the most important support in the Church's struggle for power and independence.[81]

The third perspective on the Christianization process could be described as the 'bottom up' point of view in contrast to the 'top down' emphasis on the decision-making of either the Icelandic aristocracy or ecclesiastical authorities. Such a perspective, which in the Icelandic context has been promoted by the aforementioned Steinunn Kristjánsdóttir, emphasizes how before and during the institutional consolidation of the Church, Christianity was being accepted and appropriated in diverse ways as it spread unsystematically and randomly between people, even as early as the settlement period as suggested

---

Harðarson, "Viktorsklaustrið í París og norrænar miðaldir," in *Íslensk klausturmenning á miðöldum*, ed. Haraldur Bernharðsson (Reykjavík: Miðaldastofa Háskóla Íslands, 2016), pp. 136–142. See also Guðmundur J. Guðmundsson, "Tíu páfabréf frá 15. öld," *Saga* XLVI:1 (2008), 69.

78 See discussion in Steinunn Kristjánsdóttir, *Leitin að klaustrunum*, pp. 49–53.
79 Ibid., p. 456.
80 Ibid., p. 457.
81 Ibid., p. 454.

by the *Book of Settlements*.⁸² In a 2015 article, Kristjánsdóttir develops these ideas further, defining Christianization as a "long-term transformation organized through everyday resistance, reactions, negotiations and compromises" involving all members of society as they made sense of the tension between the traditional and the post-traditional, new and old, which are not understood as fixed opposites but as coexisting and overlapping elements.⁸³ Such a process does not have a fixed beginning nor an end but is in a constant process of 'becoming,' a concept she adopts from postcolonial historiography. In that sense, the process of 'becoming' refers to "transforming processes in which new forces and struggles are produced through continuous communication."⁸⁴ Relying on Foucault's theorizing on the operation of power in society, she highlights how the process of Christianization was not only carried out by the official holders of authority in medieval Icelandic society – chieftains and the Church – but also, she emphasizes, everyday communication between less distinguished individuals and groups. In fact, adhering to a broad understanding of the postcolonial, every cultural form or identity has come into being through a cultural encounter which can be defined as colonial, in which values, habits, and identities are being renegotiated between the meeting forces. Through a variety of examples of Christian material – ranging from stone crosses to architectural developments – reflecting such a colonizing moment, Kristjánsdóttir suggests that "the Icelanders became Christian by dealing with new knowledge in their everyday practices that were coloured by memories of old habits."⁸⁵

2.1.4 *Conclusion: Becoming Christian*

The Christianization of Iceland was a complex process leading to multifarious changes in all spheres of society. As should be clear from the above discussion, any attempt to provide an all-encompassing narrative of how these changes took place is fraught with difficulties. The history of the Christianization is better conceived of as a compilation of separate yet interconnected stories complementing each other. The present study chooses to bring the Roman Church into the spotlight, highlighting its capacities as an institution built around hierarchical administrative structures with which it strove to maintain and expand its powers around its spheres of influence. As Iceland and other regions

---

82 Steinunn Kristjánsdóttir, "Kristnitakan. Áhrif tilviljanakennds og skipulegs trúboðs," pp. 113–130.
83 Steinunn Kristjánsdóttir, "Becoming Christian: A Matter of Everyday Resistance and Negotiation," *Norwegian Archaeological Review* 48 (2015), 28.
84 Ibid., p. 29.
85 Ibid., p. 42.

of the North were becoming Christian, these structures gained relevance, but they did not do so in a vacuum. As has been thoroughly explained by scholars such as Anders Winroth and Orri Vésteinsson, they were given relevance by local kings and magnates who allowed them to be used to the extent they found agreeable and compatible with the existing political situation. Receiving less attention – Steinunn Kristjánsdóttir's discussion of Iceland's 'becoming Christian' as a noteworthy exception – is the way in which ordinary people of all standings were being introduced to religious ideas which directly and indirectly supported such power structures. At the same time that the Church was gathering support and building its infrastructure, there was an ongoing cultural negotiation where people were summoned to position themselves for or against these new ideas and developments. Through its diverse operations and especially its production of religious texts and imagery, which will be the subject of the following sections, the Church assumed the role of a *primus motor* in the dialogue. Gradually, as the present study contends, it became clear that this dialogue did not take place on the level of equals and that deciding against the Church would have dire consequences.

2.2 Christianization and the Production of Religious Texts

At the same time that imperial powers and other expansive political formations were developing their administrative and economic infrastructure, they produced conceptual frameworks or, as one scholar put it, "enduring hierarchies of subjects and knowledges" explaining, legitimizing and maintaining a desirable order of the world.[86] The sources under analysis give access to religious discourses which sustained and legitimized the position of the Church as a dominating power in Icelandic society. This section is intended to illuminate the media in which these discourses are found, that is the forms of discourse, and how they can be understood in the context of the cultural hegemony the Church was gradually establishing in the Icelandic Free State. The most prominent form of media under analysis are manuscripts written in the Icelandic vernacular. The largest part of the following section will therefore be devoted to throwing light on the nature of the corpus of manuscripts under inspection, addressing questions relating to the content, purpose, and context of the different types of manuscripts. It is, nonetheless, also important to recognize the

---

86 Gyan Prakash, "Introduction," in *After Colonialism: Imperial Histories and Postcolonial Displacements*, Princeton Studies in Culture/Power/History, ed. Gyan Prakash (Princeton, 1994), p. 3.

plurality of media at play. Even though the most important source material consists of manuscripts, the dispersion of the early Christian discourse should not be limited to the communicative radius of manuscripts. The Christian message was also mediated visually, through illustrations and art work which medieval Icelanders were confronted with in and around churches and other religious buildings. For this reason, at the end of this section, the possibilities for the visual dispursement of religious discourse in the church space will also be explored.

2.2.1 Background: The Roman Church as a Cultural Hegemon

The cultural developments set in motion by the introduction of the Church in Icelandic society supported its growth in several interlocking ways which have received considerable attention by scholars in recent years. A highly significant component of the process was the introduction of literacy and Latin learning.[87] How literacy, introduced and maintained by the Church, came to succeed a predominantly oral culture as the accepted form of preserving and producing knowledge is a thoroughly studied topic.[88] The Church's introduction of literacy as a new form of knowledge production is by no means insignificant for the present study given the role it played in securing its position of authority in Icelandic medieval society.[89] Scribal modes of communication and preserving knowledge came to supplement, and to an important degree, replace the oral culture which had predominated before the arrival of the Christian religion.[90] Religious knowledge was imported from abroad, stored

---

87   Gísli Sigurðsson, *Túlkun Íslendingasagna í ljósi munnlegrar hefðar: Tilgáta um aðferð* (Reykjavík, 2002), pp. 22–23; Ásdís Egilsdóttir, "From Orality to Literacy: Remembering the Past and the Present in *Jóns saga helga*" in *Fræðinæmi: Greinar gefnar út í tilefni 70 ára afmælis Ásdísar Egilsdóttur* (Reykjavík, 2016), p. 235.
88   Two classical books on the topic in the context of the Middle Ages are the collection of articles edited by Rosamund McKitterick, *The Uses of Literacy* (Cambridge, Eng., 1990) and Michael T. Clanchy's study, *From Memory to Wrtten Record: England 1066–1307*, 2nd ed. (Oxford, 1993). For the Scandinavian realm, see for example Arnved Nedkvitne, *The Social Consequences of Literacy in Medieval Scandinavia*, Utrecht Studies in Medieval Literacy 11 (Turnhout, 2004) and a volume edited by Pernille Hermann, *Literacy in Medieval and Early Modern Scandinavian Culture* (Odense, 2005). Among those who have studied the topic of orality and literacy in the Icelandic context, although primarily with regard to its implications for interpreting Icelandic saga literature is Gísli Sigurðsson, see for example his *The Medieval Icelandic Saga and Oral Tradition: A Discourse on Method*, Publications of the Milman Parry Collection of Oral Literature 2 (Cambridge, Mass., 2004).
89   Gísli Sigurðsson, *Túlkun Íslendingasagna í ljósi munnlegrar hefðar*, pp. 58–71.
90   See Pernille Hermann, "Literacy," in *Routledge Research Companion to the Medieval Icelandic Sagas*, eds. Ármann Jakobsson and Sverrir Jakobsson (London and New York:

and mediated through the medium of the book which came to enjoy a central position for the introduction of Christianity. The item of the book was not only theologically and practically indispensable for the operation of the Christian religion but also, as will be addressed later, a source of authority. Thus, literary and scribal culture became the primary although not the only trajectory through which Christian religious ideas, or 'Christian ideology' as some scholars have put it, were mediated to the people.[91]

Of ultimate importance for this development were ecclesiastical institutions where books were collected, produced, copied, and used and where people – most importantly those aspiring to a clerical career – received education in how to keep such activities running. Most significant was the cultural activity taking place at the episcopal seats and larger churches – the so-called church centers as some scholars have called them – but also and no less importantly, the monasteries established in the course of the 12th century.[92] These places were centers for religious and intellectual life where ideas were discussed, books read and copied, literary works composed and art works produced. Literary activities outside the confines of ecclesiastical institutions, for example at larger farmsteads, are believed to have been strongly shaped by ecclesiastical practices.[93] The episcopal seats and larger monasteries were also the main points of contact with the wider Christian world where new currents arrived and made their first mark. Since the late 11th century, the episcopal seats were part of the Church's diocesan system, which made them an obvious destination for people coming from abroad; likewise, the monasteries belonged to international monastic orders and maintained contact with religious houses abroad. These places were also centers for education and scholarly activities. The top layer of the Icelandic clergy, upper class clerics and bishops-to-be were sent abroad to study at religious and cultural centers on the continent and

---

Routledge, 2018), pp. 34–47. For a more general description of the development, see Sverrir Jakobsson, *Auðnaróðal*, pp. 19–36.

91   For an explicit discussion of the establishing of the Christian religion in Iceland in terms of ideological hegemony, see Sverrir Jakobsson, *Við og veröldin*, p. 65. See also Steinunn Kristjánsdóttir, *Leitin að klaustrunum*, p. 128 and Hermann, "Literacy," p. 35. One of the better known formulations of the Christian religion in the medieval West as a powerful ideology shaping the medieval *mentalité* can be found in the writings of Jacques Le Goff, for an explicit discussion see Jacques Le Goff, *The Medieval Imagination*, trans. Arthur Goldhammer (Chicago, 1992), pp. 2–5.

92   See discussion in *Church Centres: Church Centres in Iceland from the 11th to the 13th Century and their Parallels in Other Countries*, ed. Helgi Þorláksson, Rit/ Snorrastofa 2 (Reykholt, 2005).

93   Haraldur Bernharðsson, "Kirkja, klaustur og norskublandið ritmálsviðmið," in *Íslensk klausturmenning á miðöldum*, ed. Haraldur Bernharðsson (Reykjavík, 2016), p. 164.

in England.⁹⁴ If prospective priests did not go abroad for their studies, which must have been the case most of the time, they received their education at such places.

The most important educational centers in medieval Iceland remained at or in strong relation to the two episcopal seats, Skálholt in Biskupstungur and Hólar in Hjaltadalur. Thus, Ari Þorgilsson tells in his *Book of Icelanders* that after his return from his studies in Saxony, people sent their sons to Bishop Ísleifr in Skálholt because of his excellent learning.⁹⁵ These educational efforts of Ísleifr's and later his son and successor Gizurr's in the second half of the 11th century might have amounted to a cathedral school, but the information available is admittedly very limited.⁹⁶ It is also well possible that the descriptions of the earliest educational activity rather reflect the cultural situation when texts such as the *Book of Icelanders* and the Bishops' sagas were composed at least several decades later.⁹⁷ Not very far from Skálholt episcopal see at Haukadalur in Biskupstungur, and a little bit further to the south at Oddi in Rangárvellir, promising candidates for the clergy were housed and tutored by individuals renowned for their learning. Some scholars have speculated that Teitr Ísleifsson in Haukadalur, Ari's mentor and Bishop Gizurr's brother, might have overseen clerical education for his brother as Skálholt cathedral's *scholasticus*.⁹⁸ In Oddi, on the side to his scholarly endeavors, the famous Sæmundr Sigfússon received students and apparently was succeeded by his son Eyjólfr who taught Bishop Þorlákr before he left Iceland for studying in Paris and Lincoln.⁹⁹ These may not have been schools in any formal sense but since an educational process operating on the base of private mentoring amounted to

---

94 Well known examples include the following: According to *Hungrvaka*, Ísleifr Gizurarson, the first Icelander ordained as bishop, studied at the nunnery of Herford in Saxony. *ÍF* XVI, p. 6. Ísleifr's son, Gizurr, also studied in Saxony, in Herford as his father if *Jóns saga Helga* is to be believed, *ÍF* XV₂, p. 182. In his *Book of Icelanders*, Ari claims that Sæmundr *the Wise* studied in France [Frakkland] but where exactly remains an open question, *ÍF* I, pp. 20–21. See discussion in *KÍ* I, p. 229. Bishop Þorlákr studied in Paris and Lincoln, *ÍF* XVI, pp. 52 and 147. See discussion in Sverrir Tómasson, *Formálar íslenskra sagnaritara á miðöldum: Rannsókn bókmenntahefðar*, Stofnun Árna Magnússonar, Rit 33 (Reykjavík, 1988), p. 23. Þorlákr's successor, bishop Páll Jónsson studied in England, *ÍF* XVI, pp. 297–298.

95 Ari claims that two of his students became bishops, the first bishop in the North, Jón and Kolr who became bishop in Norway (Viken). *ÍF* I, p. 20.

96 Orri Vésteinsson, *Christianization of Iceland*, p. 5.

97 *KÍ* I, p. 226.

98 *ÍF* I, 4. See e.g. Gunnar Ágúst Harðarson, "Inngangur," in *Þrjár þýðingar lærðar frá miðöldum* (Reykjavík: Hið íslenska bókmenntafélag, 1989), p. 11.

99 *ÍF* XVI, p. 49.

a school in the Middle Ages, in that sense it can be said that there were several 'schools' active in Iceland since very early on.[100] The first institution mentioned in the sources that might have resembled a school in the more formal sense is that of Hólar episcopal seat, that is to say a cathedral school founded by the first bishop of Northern Iceland, Jón Ögmundarson, shortly after his ascension to the episcopal throne in 1106. For the activities he hired learned teachers and even talented musicians from abroad.[101]

Monasteries became centers for book production and in that regard gathered funds by providing service for other ecclesiastical institutions, individuals and even for export (see Figure 1).[102] Well-known is the literary activity of the monks of Þingeyrar-monastery around 1200 which would have needed a sizable library.[103] Although the evidence for the cultural and educational role of monasteries is scarce and circumstantial, most scholars seem to find it more likely than not that they had a role to play in the education of clerical candidates.[104] Scholars have suggested that such a role was particularly prominent in the operation of the Augustinian monasteries which had scholarly activities and the education of clerics as a main objective. It has been pointed out that after the founding of the monastery of Þykkvibær in Álftaver in 1168, the largest share of the most influential churchmen in the ensuing centuries seem to have received their education there.[105] It has furthermore been suggested that the monastery of Helgafell, founded in 1184, a daughter house of St. Victor monastery, served as an educational center for Skálholt diocese.[106] The monasteries founded in the course of the 12th century and later were located close

---

100   KÍ II, pp. 171–172.
101   ÍF XV$_2$, pp. 204–205, 217, and 231–232.
102   For a thorough discussion of the book production taking place in Icelandic monasteries, see Guðvarður Már Gunnlaugsson, "Voru scriptoria í íslenskum klaustrum?" in *Íslensk klausturmenning á miðöldum*, ed. Haraldur Bernharðsson (Reykjavík, 2016), pp. 173–199. See also Ásdís Egilsdóttir, "Að kunna vort mál að ráða," in *Frœðinæmi: Greinar gefnar út í tilefni 70 ára afmælis Ásdísar Egilsdóttur* (Reykjavík, 2016), p. 251 and Steinunn Kristjánsdóttir, *Leitin að klaustrunum*, p. 128. On the export of Icelandic manuscripts, see Stefán Karlsson, "Islandsk bogeksport til Norge i middelalderen," in *Stafkrókar: Ritgerðir eftir Stefán Karlsson gefnar út í tilefni sjötugsafmælis hans 2. desember 1998*, ed. Guðvarður Már Gunnlaugsson (Reykjavík, 2000), pp. 188–205.
103   Ásdís Egilsdóttir, "Klausturreglur og bókmenntir," in KÍ II, p. 241.
104   Sverrir Tómasson, *Formálar íslenskra sagnaritara*, p. 28. Gunnar Ágúst Harðarson states that schooling was mostly restricted to monasteries and cathedrals, "Inngangur," p. 11. Cf. KÍ I, p. 231, emphasising the role of home schooling of clerical candidates up until the 19th century.
105   Steinunn Kristjánsdóttir, *Leitin að klaustrunum*, pp. 196–197.
106   Ibid., p. 233.

to the most important travel routes around the country.¹⁰⁷ Thus, they were not isolated from the rest of society. In fact, monasteries did not only serve exclusively as residences for monks and nuns but also poor people as well as laypeople who had donated their earthly possessions to the monastery and were allowed to reside at the monastery instead. The number of people residing at monasteries could therefore have amounted to several dozens, although the number of the actual monastic people was not necessarily very high, only around 12 on average.¹⁰⁸

Such an account of how the Church came into the position of a hegemonic cultural force is widely accepted among scholars of medieval Iceland although it is usually not framed in such critical terms. The concept of hegemony is widely used in order to describe forms of domination more subtle than the use of brute force, for example through the production of dominating discourses (constitutive of myths or ideologies) or through control of cultural institutions for example those in charge of education.¹⁰⁹ From such a standpoint, hegemony is a prerequisite for a a successful consolidation of a foreign power and, ultimately, the formation of a subject assenting to the hegemonic representation of reality. Whether applied to imperial expansion and colonization – as it is most frequently employed – or the process of religious conversion, the concept seems equally fitting. The cultural and literary activity taking place at episcopal seats and monasteries and the ways in which it was mediated around the country by the clergy provides an interesting example of the relationship between the production of knowledge – in this case religious knowledge – and sociopolitical power, and how that shaped medieval Icelandic society. The Church was in control of both

---

107   Ibid., p. 59. For a thorough discussion of the most frequented travel routes at the time, see Helgi Þorláksson, *Gamlar götur og goðavald: Um fornar leiðir og völd Oddaverja í Rangárþingi*, Ritsafn Sagnfræðistofnunar 25 (Reykjavík, 1989). See also Helgi Þorlákssons "Sauðafell: Um leiðir og völd í Dölum við lok þjóðveldis," in *Yfir Íslandsála: Afmælisrit til heiðurs Magnúsi Stefánssyni sextugum 25. Desember 1991*, ed. Gunnar Karlsson and Helgi Þorláksson (Reykjavík: Sögufræðslusjóður, 1992), pp. 95–109 and Orri Vésteinsson, *Christianization of Iceland*, pp. 243–245. The significance of the major travel routes for the monasteries was the topic of Guðrún Helga Jónsdóttir's master thesis: "Þjóðleiðir viðklaustrin á kaþólskum tíma: Hvað geta leiðir sagt um stöðu miðaldaklaustranna í samfélaginu?" (Master's Thesis, University of Iceland, 2016).
108   Steinunn Kristjánsdóttir, *Leitin að klaustrunum*, pp. 120–121, 206–207, and 256–257.
109   The concept of hegemony was originally coined by Antonio Gramsci who famously defined it as "the 'spontaneous' consent given by the great masses of the population to the general direction imposed on social life by the dominant fundamental group." Antonio Gramsci, *Selection from the Prison Notebooks*, eds. and trans. Quentin Hoare and Geoffrey Nowell Smith (New York, 1971), p. 2.

the resources and technology through which it managed to become a leading actor in medieval Icelandic culture. From such a point of view, all religious products produced by ecclesiastics at this time can be seen as contributing to the cultural and religious hegemony of the Church, including the source material under inspection.

2.2.2 Iceland's Earliest Religious Manuscripts

Of the 69 manuscripts which have been dated to the earliest period of manuscript production in Iceland, that is before 1300, the great majority is of religious or ecclesiastical nature.[110] As noted, manuscripts containing religious material intended for wider dispersion among both ordained and laypeople, that is sermons and hagiographical texts, constitute the most important part of the corpus under analysis.[111] Manuscripts more likely to have been used exclusively for private study or meditation of ecclesiastics – for example those containing theological, liturgical or computistical material – will keep a supplementary status and only included in the analysis when able to clarify or contextualize the analysis of the hagioraphic and sermonic texts. Apart from the manuscripts' content, important features which they have in common are their provenance, time of production and their outward appearance. All of the manuscripts were made and presumably used in Iceland before the end of the thirteenth century and most of them are in quarto format without major ornamentation. Still another common aspect is the fact that all of the manuscripts contain text which has been copied at least once from an original. In terms of the manuscripts' state of preservation, the corpus is characterized by a considerable degree of diversity in size and preservation, ranging from single leafs to relatively unimpaired codices.

On grounds of the manuscripts' content, they can be divided into three groups: First, there are manuscripts containing only hagiographic narratives, that is, narrative accounts revolving around the lives, deaths, and miracles of the saints. Second, there is a small group of manuscript fragments containing only sermons and homilies, and third, there is a group of miscellaneous manuscripts containing mixed material, that is both hagiographic, sermonic/homiletic, and sometimes also theological and liturgical material as well.

---

110   Hreinn Benediktsson, *Early Icelandic Script As Illustrated in Vernacular Texts from the Twelfth and Thirteenth Centuries*, Icelandic manuscripts (series in folio) 2 (Reykjavík, 1965), pp. 13–18; Stefán Karlsson, "Íslensk bókagerð á miðöldum," in *Stafkrókar: Ritgerðir eftir Stefán Karlsson gefnar út í tilefni sjötugsafmælis hans 2. desember 1998*, ed. Guðvarður Már Gunnlaugsson (Reykjavík, 2000), p. 225.

111   For an exhaustive list of the manuscripts belonging to the corpus, see the Appendix.

It should be noted that the manuscripts' state of preservation poses problems for such a grouping. Most of the manuscripts consist only of few sheets making it difficult to say anything with certainty about what sort of book it originally belonged to.[112] In some cases, codicological and palaeographic information have been used to speculate on the original context of manuscripts preserved only fragmentarily, sometimes only single leaves. In many cases, as pointed out by the philologian Hreinn Benediktsson, "the original manuscripts may have been anything from a booklet of a few leaves to a codex containing even some dozens of leaves."[113] This situation will inevitably lead to the most intact manuscripts receiving the most attention in the following discussion. Such attention is also warranted by the significance of these manuscripts for this study, seeing that these are the manuscripts by far the most cited in the upcoming analysis of the manuscripts' content.[114] In other instances it will be necessary to hypothesize on less concrete grounds, often with recourse to what is known about practices elsewhere in Medieval North Western Europe.

2.2.2.1 Collections of Hagiographic Material

The most important manuscripts in this group are large collections of hagiographic lives like those found in AM 645 4to and AM 652/630 4to. As for such sizeable hagiographic compendia, it is more likely that they belonged to the libraries of episcopal seats or monasteries than individual churches which would not have needed other texts than the lives of their patron saints and not entire collections. It has been argued that AM 645 4to was composed at Skálholt episcopal seat while less can be established about the provenance of AM 652 4to. It is, nonetheless, generally assumed that it was based on the same 12th century original as AM 645 4to.[115] Assuming that the codices belonged to a library of an episcopal seat or a monastery, they would have been accessible there for private study, communal reading or preparation for the celebration of the feast day of the saints in the book. If they belonged to a church, they would have been available for the priest there and possibly other literate people living at the farmstead, perhaps for private devotion or communal reading.

This group also contains the biggest number of manuscript fragments, containing parts of saints' lives which in many cases survive in younger versions.[116] That does not mean, of course, that all of these fragments were

---

112   Hreinn Benediktsson, *Early Icelandic Script*, p. 15.
113   Ibid., p. 15.
114   See Part 3 below.
115   ÍB I, pp. 424–425; Roughton I, p. 2.
116   Most of these belong to the manuscript compound AM 655 4to.

originally parts of collections exclusively containing hagiographic material since they could also have been part of mixed manuscripts like those belonging to the third category discussed below.

The little information available about the book supplies of churches indicates that churches do not seem to have been in possession of a large number of books and, if so, they were usually of direct practical use for the celebration of the mass.[117] According to medieval church charters, two churches are recorded to have been in the possession of collections of hagiographic *vitae*. According to a charter from the church at Húsafell in Hvítársíða, the oldest part of which dates to 1170, there was a book containing eight sagas of holy men ("bok er å eru viij heilagra manna sogur").[118] When exactly the church came into the possession of this book is difficult to say since this particular clause is most likely a later addition to the charter. Another charter, made in the summer of 1170 mentions a "passionalem Apostolorum" belonging to the church at Vallanes in Vellir.[119]

It is not entirely clear for which purposes text collections like those found in AM 645 4to and AM 652/630 4to were made. An important starting point for establishing that is to ask how comparable text collections, containing the same or similar texts, were used elsewhere in Europe. As previous scholarship on the topic frequently mentions – Carl Richard Unger already does so in his foreword to the first (and to this day the only comprehensive) edition of the old Icelandic accounts of the apostles – there can be no doubt that the texts found in AM 652/630 4to and AM 645 4to rely to a significant degree on texts known since the early modern period under the heading 'Collection of Pseudo-Abdias.'[120] According to Christian hagiographic tradition, Abdias was a follower of Simon and Jude whom the two apostles ordained as the first bishop of Babylon and the purported author of a group of *vitae* of the apostles, as will be addressed shortly.

To this day, the most important source critical study of the Icelandic manuscripts is Philip Roughton's doctoral dissertation in which he states that "[t]he majority of the texts in AM 645 4to and AM 652/630 4to are translations of apostles' lives as found in the *Apostolic History of Pseudo-Abdias*, a sixth-century

---

117 Orri Vésteinsson, "Bókaeign íslenskra kirkna á miðöldum" (BA thesis, University of Iceland, 1990), 212–225.
118 *DI* VII, p. 2.
119 *DI* II, p. 84.
120 Unger, "Forord," in *Post*, p. I. See also Collings, "Codex Scardensis," pp. 7–8; Ólafur Halldórsson, "Inngangur," in *Mattheus saga postula*, ed. Ólafur Halldórsson, Rit 41 (Reykjavík, 1994) p. v; Roughton I, p. 4.

work."[121] From this vantage point, Roughton divides the texts of the two manuscripts into three categories, depending on the degree in which they make use of what he calls Pseudo-Abdian texts.[122] The first group (A) contains accounts which are "strictly translations of Pseudo-Abdian texts."[123] The narratives of the second group (B) are "based primarily on the Pseudo-Abdian accounts" but with additions from other works or original prologues or epilogues.[124] The third and last group (C) contains only material "from sources other than Pseudo-Abdias."[125] For deciding whether or not texts should be considered Pseudo-Abdian or not, Roughton relies on previous scholarly work on the topic, most notably that of the German theologian Richard Adalbert Lipsius (1830–1892) who in his major work *Die Apokryphen Apostelgeschichten und Apostellegenden* catalogues manuscripts containing narratives on the apostles, distinguishing between "Abdias-texte" and other texts.[126] This approach is in line with a comparable source critical project on the fourteenth century compilation of accounts on the apostles found in the *Codex Scardensis* (SÁM 1), undertaken by Lucy Grace Collings in her 1969 doctoral dissertation.[127]

Recent research of the transmission of the *vitae*, *passiones*, and *miracula* previously termed Pseudo-Abdian has shown the premises for previous source-critical work to be problematic. This is of course not to say that the studies of Collings and Roughton have been rendered faulty. Working according to the *Stand der Forschung* at the time, they managed to identify the existing sources behind the Icelandic versions and remain as such invaluable for the research of Icelandic hagiography. Their studies are nonetheless in need of important

---

121   Roughton I, p. 4.
122   Ibid., p. 7.
123   These include the accounts of Andrew, Bartholomew and James the Greater in AM 645 4to, the accounts of Matthew as found in AM 645 4to and AM 652 4to, and the accounts of Thomas and that of Simon and Jude which are only found in AM 652 4to. Roughton I, p. 7.
124   These include the accounts of Andrew, Bartholomew, James the Greater, John, Philip and James the Less as they are found in AM 652/630 4to. Roughton I, p. 11.
125   This includes the accounts of Clement, Martin, Paul as found in AM 652/630 4to, the accounts of Peter as it is found in AM 645 4to and AM 652/630 4to. In this category fall also *Niðrstigningar saga* and Þorlákr's miracle book in AM 645 4to. Roughton I, p. 13.
126   Richard Adalbert Lipsius, *Die Apokryphen Apostelgeschichten und Apostellegenden: Ein Beitrag zur Altchristlichen Literaturgeschichte* I (Braunschweig, 1893), pp. 124–149.
127   Even though Collings describes the *Bibliotheca Hagiographica Latina* (BHL) as the "point of departure" for what she describes as her "source hunting," the significance of Lipsius' *Apokryphen Apostelgeschichten und Apostellegenden* is evident as it is the first work cited in the majority of the chapters in the source critical part of her dissertation. Lucy Grace Collings, "The Codex Scardensis: Studies in Icelandic Hagiography," (Doctoral thesis, Cornell University 1969), pp. 6–7.

qualifications in view of recent findings. First, the nomenclature 'the Pseudo-Abdian Collection' and other derived titles should be abandoned altogether since it appears to be an early modern construction. The 'Pseudo-Abdian collection' has for long been taken to be, as described by Lipsius, "eine Sammlung apokrypher Apostelgeschichten" which in its early modern printed versions received the title "historia certaminis apostolici" or in short "historia apostolica." This title is, however, not found in any of the medieval manuscripts and appears first in one of the earliest and most consequential printed editions of this collection, Wolfgang Lazius' 1552 edition.[128] Lazius (1514–1565) composed a *praefatio* to the entire collection according to his interpretation of certain passages found in the texts themselves on their authorship, attributing the entire series to Abdias, the first bishop of Babylon. Apart from the liberty Lazius took in constructing such a prologue, the attribution itself remains highly problematic and is universally rejected by scholars in the field. In fact, the core of the prologue to his entire edition comes from an epilogue which some manuscripts add to the account of Simon and Jude and did never apply to the entire collection but only to the section on Simon and Jude.[129] Already by the end of the nineteenth century, Lipsius called it "ein einfaches Misverständnis" but was still comfortable with assuming that there was a fixed collection of texts circulating in the Middle Ages falsely attributed to Abdias. Recent research, pioneered by the Dutch medievalist Els Rose, has borne a more skeptical attitude towards the existence of such a collection and Rose herself goes as far as stating that by constructing the prologue, Lazius "actually created 'the Collection of Pseudo-Abdias.' "[130]

In the broader historical context, the simple issue of nomenclature might come across as somewhat insignificant but it links into another necessary point of qualification. The attribution of a 'collection' to a certain individual, 'Pseudo-Abdias' conveys the notion of a literary construct characterized by a significant degree of consistency which, however, is not backed up by the manuscript evidence.[131] Certainly, there were collections of narratives about the

---

128 Lipsius, *Die Apokryphen apostelgeschichten und apostellegenden* I, pp. 124 and 130.
129 According to that same epilogue, the work was translated into Greek by a disciple of Abdias, Eutropus, and later into ten books in Latin by the historian Julius Africanus. Lipsius, *Die Apokryphen apostelgeschichten und apostellegenden* I, pp. 120–121.
130 Lipsius, *Die Apokryphen apostelgeschichten und apostellegenden* I, p. 120; Els Rose "*Abdias Scriptor Vitarum Sanctorum Apostolorum*? The "Collection of Pseudo-Abdias" Reconsidered," *Revue d'histoire des textes* VIII (2013), 241.
131 As noted by Els Rose, the term collection has to be qualified in so far that it indicates more consistency and stability than the manuscript evidence allows granted how much diversity there is between manuscripts, geographical regions, and the order in which the

apostles circulating since the eighth century and accounts of separate apostles since much earlier. The reasons for why some manuscripts should be termed Pseudo-Abdian and others not have become increasingly vague as it has been shown how the criteria for establishing which manuscripts contained Pseudo-Abdian texts are also not always clear and different between scholars, leading to a relatively high level of confusion in the scholarly discussion on the topic.[132] Instead of thinking of what previously was called "the Pseudo-Abdian collection," as a fixed collection circulating in the Middle Ages, it has led many scholars to abandon the term, replacing it with the title *Virtutes Apostolorum* which refers to a transmission of a series of narratives on the apostles, characterized by, in the words of the Old Norse philologist Matthew James Driscoll, "textual instability (variance, mouvance, unfixedness)."[133] According to a definition of the phenomenon formulated by Els Rose, the *Virtutes apostolorum* consist of a "more or less coherent series" of separate Latin narratives on individual apostles, containing partly rewritten apocryphal accounts from antiquity, and partly original compositions. The series should be uninterrupted by other accounts in between narratives on apostles, and should contain an account of every one of the twelve apostles. Geographically, Rose also restricts her definition to the transalpine regions of Bavaria and Francia, excluding thereby collections of accounts of apostles which circulated in Rome and Italy quite independently from the tradition of the *Virtutes Apostolorum* north of the Alps.[134] Chronologically, the transmission is restricted to the earliest appearance of a manuscript in the late eighth century until the late thirteenth century when large hagiographic compilations like the *Legenda aurea* start to emerge.[135] In

---

apostles are presented. Moreover, the word collection might also suggest that it was collected by a certain individual, which was not the case even though they were for long attributed to the legendary bishop of Babylon, Abdias. Els Rose, "The Apocryphal Acts of the Apostles in the Latin Middle Ages: Contexts of Transmission and Use," in *The Apocryphal Acts of the Apostles in Latin Christianity*, Proceedings of the International Summer School on Christian Apocryphal Literature (ISCAL), Strasbourg, 24–27 June 2012, ed. Els Rose (Turnhout, 2014 [E-book Only]), p. 36.

132 Rose points out inconsistencies in selection criteria in major works on the topic such as Lipsius' *Die apokryphen Apostelgeschichten und Apostellegenden* and Junod and Kaestli's edition of the *Acta Iohannis*, see Rose, "*Abdias Scriptor Vitarum Sanctorum Apostolorum?*" pp. 233 and 235.

133 Matthew Driscoll, "The Words on the Page: Thoughts on Philology Old and New," in *Creating the Medieval Saga: Versions, Variability, and Editorial Interpretations of Old Norse Saga Literature*, eds. Judy Quinn and Emily Lethbridge, The Viking Collection 18 (Odense, 2010), p. 90.

134 Els Rose, "*Abdias Scriptor Vitarum Sanctorum Apostolorum?*" p. 229.

135 Els Rose, "*Virtutes apostolorum*: Editorial Problems and Principles," *Apocrypha* 23 (2012), 15–18. In the poem *De virginitate* by Venantius Fortunatus (530–609), a poet from

order to respond to the high degree of variance, scholars have, instead of categorizing particular versions as belonging to a Pseudo-Abdian collection or not, resorted to distinguishing between different traditions of transmission of the *Virtutes Apostolorum*.[136]

The question as for how manuscripts containing *Virtutes Apostolorum* were put into practical use has been addressed in recent years. For answering such questions, scholars have looked to three factors: place of origin, manuscript context, and scribal additions and corrections.[137] On the basis of her survey of manuscripts containing such collections from Francia and Bavaria, ranging in time from the late eighth century to the thirteenth century, Els Rose has shown that most of the manuscripts have a monastic background and are primarily found in hagiographic compilations called legendaries or passionaries. This has lead Rose to describe the most likely context in which these texts were transmitted to have been a "hagiographic context presumably with a practice of reading in mind."[138] Elsewhere she has described it as a "performative context of reading out loud in a communal setting."[139] Additions of corrections and glosses, both in Latin and the vernacular, suggest that these codices were in regular use and that their users read them actively.[140] Many of them also contain stress accents, roman numerals and reading divisions which

---

Merovingian Gaul, one encounters a list of the twelve apostles also containing their missionary regions and places of martyrdom, closely corresponding to the narrative versions of the *Virtutes Apostolorum*. Another indicator to an origin in sixth century Gaul is the alleged authorship of bishop Gregory of Tours of the text *Liber de miraculis beati Andreae* which constitutes parts of the section of Andrew of the *Virtutes Apostolorum*. Neither of these points suffices as a proof for the existence of a comprehensive and consistent series of narratives on the apostles circulating in Gaul at the time. It is more likely that such a series might have been known in the Anglo-Saxon world. Aldhelm, abbot of Melmesbury and bishop of Sherborne (639–709), wrote poems which reflect influence from narratives about the apostles, although they depart in some aspects – for example in treating Simon and Jude in separate accounts – from the *Virtutes apostolorum*. Although Aldhelm's poems do not provide strong grounds for the existence of a series of apostolic *Virtutes*, it seems clear that Bede the Venerable made use of such collection for his composition of *Retractatio in Actus apostolorum* around 730. Nonetheless, one should not hasten to conclusions in view of these facts, since, in the words of Els Rose "the series that Aldhelm and Bede knew is not perforce equal to the continental transmission – which in itself is characterized by variety." Rose, "*Virtutes Apostolorum*: Origin, Aim, and Use," *Traditio* 68 (2013), 71.

136 See detailed discussion in Rose, "Editorial Problems and Principles."
137 Rose, "*Virtutes Apostolorum*: Origin, Aim, and Use," 81.
138 Ibid., 83.
139 Rose, "Contexts of Transmission and Use," 41.
140 Rose, "*Virtutes Apostolorum*: Origin, Aim, and Use," 85.

indicate a reading in a performative context.[141] In view of such information, several contexts of use offer themselves as more likely than others, one of the most likely being the liturgical practice of the monastic or cathedral office. The commemoration of the saints was notable in the office but particularly in the night office (Matins) during which readings from hagiographic narratives played a large role. Usually, the readings of the hours were taken from the Bible or patristic writings of religious instruction, but during the night office, a large part and sometimes the majority of readings could consist of hagiographic material.[142] In this regard, one should also assume for a considerable amount of variation between monastic houses.

In addition to the liturgical context of the office, other locations in which these manuscripts were brought into use were the refectories of the monasteries during mealtime according to prescriptions of monastic rules, the best-known being the one found in chapter 38 of *Regula Benedicti*: "Reading will always accompany the meals of the brothers. ... Let there be complete silence. No whispering, no speaking – only the reader's voice should be heard there."[143] A *Liber ordinis* of the Augustinians of St. Victor in Paris, dating to the mid-twelfth century which is around the time Þorlákr Þórhallsson, later prior of the first Augustinian monastery in Iceland (Þykkvibær) and bishop of Skálholt, who probably resided in Paris, contains the chapter *De lectione mensae* (no. 48). The chapter contains an entire annual cycle of readings for the refectory consisting of readings from the Bible accompanied by commentaries and gospel homilies. As for hagiographical readings it only contains the general statement that on saint's days the lives and passions of the saint in question may be read.[144] Although reading during meal times was a standard

---

141 Ibid., 85–86.
142 The composition of the night office, Matins (*Matutinum* or *Matutinae*), also called Vigils (*Vigiliae*), could vary according to whether it was carried out in a monastery or a secular context (most often in a cathedral). One should also assume for considerable variation between monastic houses. In both monastic and secular contexts, Matins is divided into three parts, so-called nocturns, consisting of the reciting of psalms and lessons and a varying number of chants, i.e. antiphones and responsories. The number of lessons varied according to feast days and seasons (they were fewer in summer). In a monastic setting, the lessons were twelve and in a secular setting they were at least three and at most nine. See Eric Palazzo, *A History of Liturgical Books from the Beginning to the Thirteenth Century*, trans. Madeleine Beaumont (Collegeville, 1998), p. 87; see also Els Rose, "*Virtutes Apostolorum*: Origin, Aim, and Use," 87.
143 *RB 1980: The Rule of St Benedict in Latin and English with Notes*, ed. Timothy Fry (Collegeville, 1981), pp. 236–7.
144 *Liber ordinis Sancti Victoris Parisiensis*, eds. Ludovicus Milis and Lucas Jocqué, CCCM 61 (Turnhout, 1984), pp. 211–215.

practice in monasteries since the early Middle Ages, it was not until the twelfth century that it had developed into a cycle of readings corresponding to the liturgical calendar and readings of the office.[145] These readings could be used to either finish a lesson that was not concluded during Matins, further elaborate on the lessons of Mass or Office through patristic or sermonic writings, or, importantly for the present discussion, to supplement the celebration of a saint's feast with readings from hagiographic material. This would also include the commemoration of a saint at mealtime even though that particular saint was not formally celebrated in the liturgy of the community in question.[146]

A third context in which such texts might have been used was in private devotion. Certainly, Icelandic ecclesiastics, especially monastic people, read books on their own for devotional and scholarly purposes. However, it is the practical use of books in a social situation, when a group of people had gathered for participating in a ceremony, which should be taken as characteristic for the use of the source literature of this study.[147] It is important to keep in mind that even though the modern reader's access to the medieval text is most often bound to the private reading of manuscripts or published editions, the mediation of text was by no means restricted to such practices during the Middle Ages. On the contrary, as Dennis Howard Green has shown in his study of the reception and mediation of German literature between 800 and 1300, an exclusive reading of texts in silence was rare and primarily restricted to specific literary genres, such as medical texts. The majority of the literature he surveys, ranging from legal material to lyric poetry, was in all likelihood going to be either listened to or both heard and read.[148]

2.2.2.2 Collections of Sermonic Material

The smallest group of manuscripts consists of manuscript fragments containing only sermons.[149] This group includes for example one of the earliest

---

145 Teresa Webber, "Reading in the Refectory: Monastic Practice in England," London University Annual John Coffin Memorial Palaeography Lecture, revised text 2013, p. 18.
146 Webber, "Reading in the Refectory," p. 18.
147 An exhortation to reading, presumably in private in a monastic setting, can be seen in the *Icelandic Homily Book*, in a section called "In Capite Jejunii," where the audience or readership of the homily is encouraged to frequently read books (*oft á bækur sjá*) in order to enjoy fellowship with God. *íH*, p. 91.
148 Dennis Howard Green, *Medieval Listening and Reading: The Primary Reception of German Literature 800–1300* (Cambridge, Eng., 1994), p. 232.
149 This study will refer to all preaching material as sermons. The modern distinction between sermon as "a catechetical or admonitory discourse built upon a theme or topic not necessarily grounded in Scripture" and homily as "a systematic exposition of a pericope (a liturgically designated passage of Scripture, usually from a Gospel or Epistle) that proceeds

Icelandic manuscripts, AM 237 fol., which, however, contains only two folios but it has been suggested, on account of its folio format and division of the text into two columns, that it belonged to a considerably large collection of sermons.[150] Unfortunately, none of these fragments are preserved intact – larger manuscripts like the *Icelandic Homily Book* contain other material than the sermonic as well and fall into the category of mixed manuscripts – making it problematic to state anything with certainty about the original manuscript context. There is, however, no reason to assume that sermons were grouped together much differently than elsewhere in North Western Europe, that is to say, arranged into a particular order depending on the primary use they were intended for, most frequently according to the liturgical year. Thus, there was a distinction made between *sermones de tempore*, a series of sermons for Sundays and feasts of the Lord, and *sermones de sanctis*, intended for saints' feasts and arranged accordingly. Another way of organizing sermonic material was by distinguishing between Sunday sermons (*dominicales*), feast days (*festiui*), sometimes with the category of Lent weekdays (*sermones quadragesimales*) and even that of *sermones de communi sanctorum*.[151] In addition to collections arranged according to the

---

according to a pattern of *lectio continua*, commenting on a given passage verse by verse or phrase by phrase" does not conform well to the Icelandic preaching material preserved from the Free State era (definition according to Thomas N. Hall, "The Early Medieval Sermon," in *The Sermon*, ed. Beverly Mayne Kienzle, Typologie des Sources du Moyen Âge Occidental (Turnhout, 2000), p. 205). Such a distinction was also not clear among medieval authors who often equated *sermo*, *tractatus*, and *homilia*. Aidan Conti points out that it is a frequent practice among English speaking scholars to refer to both homilies and sermons as homilies. Aidan Conti, "Gammelt og nytt i Homiliebokens Prekenunivers," in *Vår eldste bok: Skrift, miljø og biletbruk i den norske homilieboka*, Bibliotheca Nordica 3, eds. Odd Einar Haugen and Åslaug Ommundsen (Oslo, 2010), p. 167. Much of recent scholarly literature on medieval preaching, however, including major works like Beverly Kienzle's edited volume, *The Sermon*, tends to use the word sermon as a general term connoting both sermons and homilies, as previously defined. The word used most often in the Icelandic manuscripts themselves designating the preaching material is "mál" which in such contexts refers an oral expression on a particular subject matter (In Norwegian: "Ord hvori man udtaler sig i eller om en Sag") or a speech (In Norwegian: "tale, hvad siges"). Fritzner, s.v. "mál.". In the *Icelandic Homily Book*, whose title is not found in the manuscript itself, the word *homilia* never occurs but the word *sermon* twice, in both instances in sermon headings. *íH*, pp. 71 and 217.

150 Hreinn Benediktsson, *Early Icelandic Script*, p. 15; David McDougall, "Homilies (West Norse)" in *Medieval Scandinavia: An Encyclopedia*, ed. Phillip Pulsiano (New York, 1993), p. 290.
151 Louis J. Bataillon, "Approaches to the Study of Medieval Sermons," *Leeds Studies in English* 11 (1980), p. 20.

liturgical year, a few collections exist which are aimed at specific audiences or occasions, *sermones ad status*.[152]

The above categories are particularly applicable for sermons in Latin but there is nothing excluding the possibility that vernacular sermons as the ones represented by the Icelandic fragments might have been grouped together in such collections. Nonetheless, in order to find out how the Icelandic sermon manuscripts were being used, it should be addressed how collections of vernacular sermons from the regions of North Western Europe most influential for the shaping of Christianity in Iceland during its early stages, that is Germany, England, and Norway, were being collected into manuscript form. Manuscripts containing sermonic material surviving from these regions are of various sorts. In her introduction to a comprehensive handbook on German sermons dating to the 12th and early 13th centuries, Regina D. Schiewer divides manuscripts containing early German preaching in the vernacular (G. frühe deutsche Predigten) into two groups. The first contains collections which do not portray any consistency as regards the nature and the order of the sermons they contain while the second group contains collections in which a unifying principle or structure can be discerned. The majority of the German sermons belong to the second group and show some unifying characteristics although they can vary considerably.[153] Most of the manuscripts belong to collections of sermons which could be categorized as *de tempore* or *de sanctorale*, although there are exceptions. The so-called Mettener Collection I, containing two hortatory texts and an explanation of the Lord's Prayer, was not transmitted in a collection of sermons but in a compilatory manuscript, containing both German and Latin material, intended for preparation of preaching.[154] On such grounds, Schiewer argues that most of the sermon manuscripts were intended for pastoral use, which she further supports with codicological information. The manuscript material is of rather low quality, often with holes and other damages. The codices are usually in quarto or even octavo format without grandiose ornamentation.[155]

On the basis of numerous textual examples from sermons, Schiewer asserts that the main location for vernacular preaching was in a church during mass

---

152   See Carolyn Muessig, "Audience and Preacher: *Ad status* Sermons and Social Classification," in *Preacher, Sermon and Audience in the Middle Ages*, ed. Carolyn Muessig (Leiden, 2002), pp. 255–276. See also Bataillon, "Approaches to the Study of Medieval Sermons," p. 20.
153   Regina D. Schiewer, *Die Deutsche Predigt um 1200: Ein Handbuch* (Berlin, 2008), p. 41.
154   Regina D. Schiewer, "Predigten und Predigtsammlungen," in *Die deutsche Literatur des Mittelalters. Verfasserlexikon* 11, 2nd and rev. edition, (Berlin, 2004) cols. 1264–1265.
155   Schiewer, *Deutsche Predigt um 1200*, pp. 70–71.

on Sundays and other feast days, where the audience could have varied considerably. When exactly the preaching took place during the mass is not as clear, but many sermons make references to the scriptural texts read shortly before the delivery of the sermon. Schiewer also mentions that several sermons, many of which are located at the beginning of a sermon collection, include an exhortation to the present congregation to begin what is termed 'communal calling' (*gemeine Ruf*), which could either refer to a hymn or a song in the vernacular or a communal recitation of the *credo*. Other sermons end with an exhortation to renounce the Devil (*abrenuntiatio diaboli*) which in all probability refers to the beginning words of a confessional formula. On these grounds, Schiewer maintains that the vernacular preaching took place at the end of the liturgy of the word, before the recitation of the creed, which would lead into the liturgy of the Eucharist.[156]

In her discussion of preaching in Anglo-Saxon England, Mary Clayton assumes for more variety when it comes to the use of sermonic material. Emphasizing the public use of such texts, she states that sermons in the vernacular offer "an unparalleled insight into how English people were instructed from the pulpits in the tenth and later centuries," providing their readers with a "vivid sense of what the Anglo-Saxon Church considered important for people to hear and read."[157] The Old English homiliaries contain scriptural exegesis, moral exhortations, Saint's lives, accounts from the Old Testament and non-canonical apocrypha.[158] Homiliaries in the vernacular could also contain various other material written in Old English like prayers, material relating to confessions and penance, poetry as well as computistical and astronomical texts.[159] Clayton assumes that as in Carolingian times, it is most likely that collections of sermons were used in one of the following three ways: preaching to the laity, in the liturgy of the night office, or in private devotional readings.[160]

Central to her discussion are collections of sermons like the Vercelli Book, the *Blickling Homilies,* and abbot Ælfric's *Catholic Homilies*, which were composed much earlier than the earliest sermons preserved from Iceland, that is in

---

156 Ibid., pp. 25–26.
157 Mary Clayton, "Preaching and Teaching," in *The Cambridge Companion to Old English Literature*, eds. Malcolm Godden and Michael Lapidge (Cambridge, Eng., 2013), p. 159.
158 The apocryphal material includes apocryphal gospels like the *Gospel of Pseudo-Matthew* and the *Gospel of Nicodemus*, apocalypses like the *Apocalypse of Paul* and the *Apocalypse of Thomas*, apocryphal acts like the *Acts of Matthew* and *Andrew*, epistles like Christ's Sunday letter, and *transitus*-texts on the death and assumption of the Virgin Mary. Clayton, "Preaching and Teaching," pp. 165–166.
159 Clayton, "Preaching and Teaching," p. 166.
160 Ibid., pp. 162–163.

the second half of the tenth century, but were used well into the twelfth century. The earliest collection of sermons in the vernacular is the Vercelli Book which dates to around 975 which many think was intended for devotional reading in private while others believe that it was used for public preaching, presumably by a bishop. The sermons are, however, not written by a single author and different sermons could have been intended for use on different occasions. Some sermons point to a mixed lay audience, including both males and females.[161] The *Blickling Homilies* contain eighteen texts arranged, more or less, according to the liturgical calendar, both *de tempore* and *de sanctorale*. The collection was probably intended for a lay audience.[162] While the Vercelli Book and the *Blickling Homilies* are both anonymous, the so-called *Catholic Homilies* were composed by the Benedictine monk and abbot Ælfric of Eynsham (955–1010), which he wrote specifically for delivery at mass for a mixed congregation. There are, however, indications that Ælfric's homilies may have served several purposes, as it was read privately, for example by non-Latinate monastics or pious laypeople like Ælfric's patron, the ealdorman Æthelweard (d. c. 1000).

2.2.2.3 Manuscripts with Mixed Content

Compared to other regions in Europe, the preserved sermonic material from Norway and Iceland in the Middle Ages is scarce, especially with regard to texts written in Latin.[163] As noted, there are many fragments of sermons about the use of which nothing can be said with certainty because of their fragmentary state.[164] They could have belonged to a similar sort of collection already mentioned to have existed in the neighbouring regions of Germany and England. For answering the question as to how the religious discourse, as it appears in the sermonic sources, was mediated, the most important manuscripts containing sermonic material from Scandinavia are the *Norwegian Homily Book* (AM 619 4to) and the *Icelandic Homily Book* (Stock. Perg. 15 4to) both of which will receive special attention in this section.

As one of the best preserved manuscripts containing sermons and related material from medieval Scandinavia, it is necessary to take the *Norwegian Homily Book* into consideration for comparison and context although it does

---

161 Ibid., pp. 168–169.
162 Ibid., p. 170.
163 As noted elsewhere in this book, the lack of sermons in Latin is explained primarily because of the destruction of much material related to Roman Catholic Christianity after the 16th century reformation.
164 For a comprehensive list of manuscripts containing sermonic material, see Thomas N. Hall's contribution to *The Sermon*, "Old Norse-Icelandic Sermons,"pp. 661–709.

not feature in the analysis carried out later in this study. In view of the order of the manuscript's material and the content of its texts, the *Norwegian Homily Book* has been compared to collections of sermons like *St. Père de Chartres*, which is a collection of sermons in Latin composed around 820, and the *Blickling Homilies*.[165] Palaeographic analysis of the manuscript has revealed strong English influence.[166] It distinguishes itself, however, from these collections in several respects. It has relatively few sermons for Lent and Easter, which makes it impossible for the manuscript to have served as a liturgical homiliary on its own. Thus, Kirsten Berg has suggested that it might have served the purpose of storing sermons which were not accessible for the scribe in other collections available to him. Possibly supporting such a theory is the fact, which also separates the *Norwegian Homily Book* from the other two collections, is the space it gives to non-sermonic texts, most significantly Alcuin's *De virtutibus et vitiis*, the *vita* and *miracula* of King Ólafr Haraldsson, and a Debate of the body and soul (with the false heading *Visio sancti Pauli apostoli*). On such grounds, Berg proceeds to describe the manuscript first and foremost as a handbook and not a collection of sermons specifically intended for use at mass.[167] Although the possibility cannot be excluded, she is hesitant to place it in a context where the manuscript's content was mediated orally. She comes to the conclusion that the main role of the *Norwegian Homily Book* was for education purposes and belonged to an institution where clerics were being trained and suggests the John's Priory in Bergen or the cathedral of Bergen as a likely place of origin. The scribe might have been the school master of the cathedral school or, because of the musical notation which the manuscript contains, the cantor.[168]

The manuscript containing sermonic material by far the most important for the present research is the so-called *Icelandic Homily Book*.[169] The *Icelandic*

---

165   Kirsten Berg, "Homilieboka – for hvem og til hva?" in *Vår eldste bok: Skrift, miljø og biletbruk i den norske homilieboka*, eds. Odd Einar Haugen and Åslaug Ommundsen, Bibliotheca Nordica 3 (Oslo, 2010), p. 39.
166   Michael Gullick, "Skriveren og kunstneren bak homilieboken," in *Vår eldste bok: Skrift, miljø og biletbruk i den norske homilieboka*, eds. Odd Einar Haugen and Åslaug Ommundsen, Bibliotheca Nordica 3 (Oslo, 2010), pp. 94–97.
167   Berg, "Homilieboka – for hvem og til hva?" p. 43.
168   Ibid., pp. 74–76.
169   The *Icelandic Homily Book* has been edited several times both as a whole and in part since its first edition in 1872, made by Theodor Wisén. In 1993, there appeared two editions of the manuscript's content: A facsimile edition with a diplomatic transcription by Andrea de Leeuw van Weenen (*IHB*) and an edition for a broader audience edited by Gunnlaugur Ingólfsson, Guðrún Kvaran and Sigurbjörn Einarsson (*íH*). In this study, citations refer to

Homily Book was composed around 1200. Amounting to a total number of 102 sheets which contain 62 texts or fragments of texts, it remains by far the largest manuscript containing religious material dating to the formative years of the Church in Iceland. The largest part of the text it contains are homilies, hence its traditional title, *Icelandic Homily Book* (in contrast to the *Norwegian Homily Book*, composed around the same time). As the very first sentence of Andrea de Leuuw van Weenen's critical facsimile edition of the manuscript reflects, the manuscript does not offer any specific information as for its provenance: "We do not know where it was written, nor when, nor by whom, nor anything else about its history for certain until 1682," when the notorious manuscript collector Jón Eggertsson (1643–1689) bought it for the Swedish College of Antiquities.[170] On philological grounds, some scholars have attempted to classify the homily book with texts that exhibit influence from the *First Grammatical Treatise* and speculated for Skálholt episcopal seat as a possible place of composition. The manuscript itself, however, contains no evidence pointing in that direction. On the basis of the fact that the manuscript contains a part of the *Regula Benedicti*, others have argued for a Benedictine monastery as a place of origin. As de Leeuw van Weenen points out, this particular chapter of Benedict's Rule was a well known sermon in its own right and does not have to point to a Benedictine provenience, even though she herself seems to lean towards the Benedictine monastery of Þingeyrar as a likely place of composition.[171]

In addition to its sermons, the *Icelandic Homily Book* contains also other types of material. The arrangement of the material does not exhibit any systematic order throughout the manuscript although it follows the liturgical calendar in parts which are also interrupted with non-sermonic material. This has brought several scholars to describe the *Icelandic Homily Book* as a clerical handbook or a handbook for preaching, without necessarily specifying what that might have implied in praxis. Already in 1935, Fredrik Paasche described the Icelandic books of sermons as having "served their readers as books of devotion, and to many priests the written text probably also formed the basis of their sermons in church."[172] In view of their compilatory nature, Régis Boyer found the *Icelandic Homily Book* to bear the appearance of a manual and Svanhildur Óskarsdóttir describes both of the anthologies mentioned, the

---

the latter edition but for the few texts not published in the latter edition, de Leeuw van Weenen's edition has been consulted.

170 "Part 1: Introduction," in *IHB*, p. 3.
171 "Introduction," in *IHB*, p. 4.
172 Fredrik Paasche, *Homiliu-bók (Icelandic Sermons). Perg. 4to No. 15 in the Royal Library Stockholm*, Corpus Codicum Islandicorum Medii Aevi 8 (Copenhagen, 1935), p. 21.

Norwegian and the Icelandic one, as "handbooks in which priests could find sermons upon which they might model their own preaching."[173] Along similar lines, David McDougall is comfortable with categorizing the two manuscripts as "homiletic handbooks rather than homiliaries in the strict sense."[174] In an overview essay on Old Norse and Icelandic sermons, Thomas N. Hall expresses the same opinion, describing the *Icelandic Homily Book* as a "debased form of a liturgical homiliary" to which the term homiliary does actually not apply because of the lack of systematic order.[175] In view of the above, it seems prudent to follow Kirsten Berg in viewing the *Icelandic Homily Book* as belonging to the group of sermonic manuscripts which the French sermon scholar Louis-Jacques Bataillon compared to a 'commonplace book' or what in Italian is called a *zibaldone*.[176] The material in such manuscripts is not necessarily arranged in any particular order and contains "together with sermons, other texts not actually preached but useful as preaching material, such as *exempla, distinctiones*, or short moral or liturgical *opuscula*."[177] Thus, originally, it is likely that the *Icelandic Homily Book* was in the possession of an ecclesiastic – perhaps a monk of Þingeyrar-monastery but could also be a Northern cleric – who used it to collect and store material which he came across and considered of interest and potential use.[178]

Because of the fragmentary state of most other manuscripts belonging to the corpus under inspection, it is difficult to establish anything with certainty about their precise use. Hall has noted that a lack of order is somewhat of a special trait of the medieval sermon manuscripts preserved from Norway and Iceland.[179] It is thus well imaginable that some of the manuscript fragments containing mixed material originally belonged to anthologies similar to the *Icelandic Homily Book*. This might for example apply to AM 673 a I and II 4to which contain a version of the *Physiologus* in the vernacular and allegorical *exempla* on a ship and the rainbow. Another sizeable manuscript

---

173 Boyer, *La vie religieuse en Islande*, 273; Svanhildur Óskarsdóttir, "Prose of Christian Instruction," in *A Companion to Old Norse-Icelandic Literature and* Culture, ed. Rory McTurk (Oxford, 2005), p. 341.
174 McDougall, "Homilies (West Norse)," p. 290.
175 Thomas N. Hall, "Old Norse-Icelandic Sermons," in *The Sermon*, ed. Beverly Mayne Kienzle, Typologie des Sources du Moyen Âge Occidental (Turnhout, 2000), p. 670.
176 Berg, "Homilieboka – for hvem og til hva?" p. 38.
177 Bataillon, "Approaches to the Study of Medieval Sermons," p. 20.
178 For such an understanding of the use of the *Icelandic Homily Book*, it is necessary to accept the hypothesis that the manuscript only exhibits one scribal hand. See "Introduction" in *IHB*.
179 Thomas N. Hall, "Old Norse-Icelandic Sermons," p. 671.

containing mixed material, although it is predominated by material related to Pope Gregory the Great is AM 677 4to. 17 leaves contain 10 of Gregory's 40 *Homilliae in Evangelia*, other 12 contain parts of Gregory's *Dialogi*. The remaining seven leaves contain primarily *Prosper's epigrams* and a small fragment of *De XII abusivis saeculi*. Given Gregory's enormous popularity in the Middle Ages, his early literary presence in Iceland is of no surprise. How and whether this manuscript might have been used for preaching is uncertain although it is likely that the sermons could have served as model texts for preaching preparation. Among other manuscript fragments which might have belonged to such collections would be AM 655 XVII 4to containing texts which "are either homilies or could easily be adapted for preaching."[180] Several manuscript fragments contain only sermonic texts and could thus belong to larger sermonaries, as McDougall suggests about AM 237 4to, which would have been arranged according to the liturgical calendar but, as noted, it is impossible to state anything with certainty on the matter.

2.2.3 *Beyond the Manuscripts: The Materiality of Religious Discourse*

Although textual sources are central to the present study, it is necessary to take into account that their content was mediated in church spaces where the material surroundings and artifacts were bound to resonate with religious discourses in the texts. In praxis, this means including in the analysis visual and material manifestations of Christian religious discourse when possible. Well-known is Pope Gregory I's statement from his letter to Serenus, bishop of Marseilles, that "[w]hat writing does for the literate, a picture does for the illiterate looking at it."[181] Although Gregory's dictum has to be qualified by the historical and polemical context in which it emerged in such a way that visual imagery would never have replaced the written and spoken word entirely, it still served an important reinforcing or a supplementary function, making it easier for the people visiting the churches to imagine and visualize narratives which were being communicated by other means.[182]

Unfortunately, very few material objects and remains have survived from the period in question. Even so it is well-known that religious motifs figured

---

180   Pelle, "Twelfth-Century Sources," p. 52.
181   Translation from Lawrence G. Duggan, "Was Art Really the "Book of the Illiterate"?" in *Reading Images and Texts: Medieval Images and Texts as Forms of Communication*, eds. Mariëlle Hageman and Marco Mostert (Turnhout, 2005), p. 63.
182   Duggan, "Was Art Really the "Book of the Illiterate"?", pp. 63–107; Celia M. Chazelle, "Pictures, books, and the illiterate: Pope Gregory I's letters to Serenus of Marseilles," *Word & Image* 6 (1990), 138–153.

prominently in art and ornamentation found in churches in Free State Iceland. People attending churches were thus confronted with Christian religious discourse through visual representation all around the church space. Although Icelandic medieval churches and religious art has not been well preserved, the information that can be gained from church inventories and the little material evidence preserved gives no reason but to assume that like elsewhere in Western Europe, Icelandic churches would have offered their visitors a visual experience.[183] One should, nonetheless, assume for a considerable difference between churches. Smaller, low-income churches were perhaps only in possession of the most necessary equipment while wealthier churches were richly ornamented.[184] The episcopal seats were centers for craftsmanship and artistry in the Middle Ages and the great wooden cathedrals in Skálholt and Hólar – the largest wooden buildings in Scandinavia at the time – were the churches in the country which were ornamented with the most splendour.[185] The bishops hired artisans –carpenters, carvers, painters, textile makers – with the necessary skills to make the episcopal seats as impressive and magnificent as possible, reflecting at the same time the glory of God and the authority of the bishop. There are several descriptions in medieval sources of the cathedrals which were rebuilt several times during the Middle Ages either because of general disrepair or damages caused by storms or fires.

Most of the churches were made of wood and turf but after 1150 churches made exclusively of wood, often much larger than the turf-churches, became increasingly frequent. Some parts of the outside of the church – church-doors, door-frames and possibly other surfaces – were in some cases ornamented with carvings which were painted. These carvings were probably showing animal and plant patterns influenced by Viking age ornamentation, but they could also depict more specific scenes as can be seen on the renowned Door of Valþjófsstaður (see figure. 4). According to Guðbjörg Kristjánsdóttir, Icelanders were decorating their churches with traditional Christian motives as early as half a century after the official conversion in the year 999.[186] Wooden surfaces

---

183   Guðbjörg Kristjánsdóttir, "Messuföng og kirkjulist," pp. 246–259.
184   Guðbjörg Kristjánsdóttir, "Sóknarkirkjur og búnaður þeirra," in Kí II, p. 191.
185   Guðbjörg Kristjánsdóttir, "Dómkirkjur," in Kí II, p. 156.
186   As for the original location of the panel boards found at Flatatunga, Hörður Ágústsson has suggested Hólar cathedral as the most probable location where they might have been part of the cathedral's ciborium or covered the chancel-end of the church. See Hörður Ágústsson, Dómsdagur og helgir menn á Hólum: Endurskoðun fyrri hugmynda um fjalirnar frá Bjarnastaðahlíð og Flatatungu, Staðir og kirkjur II (Reykjavík, 1989), 123. Few have accepted Ágústsson's suggestion of Hólar as the original location of the panel boards and today most scholars lean towards Flatatunga, the finding place, without excluding some

FIGURE 4   Among the earliest and best preserved medieval ecclesiastical artefacts is the Door of Valþjófsstaður. The upper circle shows a knight fighting a lion. The lower circle shows four winged dragons. The door has been dated to the late 12th century. National Museum of Iceland

and artefacts inside the churches were also carved for example wooden columns as well as freestanding church artifacts like wooden baptismal fonts, lecterns, chests, chairs, and tabernacles. Among the few preserved material

other 11th century church in the region of Skagafjörður as the original location of the boards.

FIGURE 5   The image shows one fragment of the boards from Flatatunga. It depicts two figures with halos, possibly Christ and an apostle. National Museum of Iceland

remains from churches are wooden boards from the inside of a church with religious imagery. Surviving from a church at Möðrufell in Eyjafjörður are 16 parts of wooden boards. All of them show the same carved ornamentation, figures beginning in a spiral at the bottom reaching upwards ending in a stylized depiction of something which might be taken as both a cross and the crown of a tree, a frequent theme in medieval iconography. The panel was painted when it was first put up in the 11th century but no traces of coloring remain. A fragment of the same kind of wood panelling was also discovered at Hólar in Eyjafjörður (not to be confused with Hólar episcopal see in Skagafjörður) which might point to the frequency of this kind of ornamenation in the Eyjafjörður region during the 11th century. Stylistically, the ornamentation has been interpreted as showing characteristics of two viking age artistic styles, ringerike-style and mammen style.[187] More discussed by scholars are the wooden boards found in

---

187   Guðbjörg Kristjánsdóttir, "Fyrstu kirkjur landsins," in *KÍ* I, p. 184.

Flatatunga in Skagafjörður in 1952, depicting a series of saints with halos (see figure. 5). Above them is an elaborately carved ornamentation in ringerike-style. All of the boards are damaged but the original height of the panel decoration might have been around 2,2 m, covering the chancel-end of the church. Its style has been compared to decorations from the British Isles dating as far back as the 7th century.

Instead of carvings and wall paintings, inventories show that the walls of churches were also covered with curtains (*cortinae*). Such curtains would have been among the most conspicuous parts of the church embellishments and served both decorative and practical purposes as they could isolate from cold. Curtains were usually plain and unillustrated, although a few sources mention painted curtains which would then show patterns or religious motifs.[188] No curtains from the Free State period have been preserved but early charters show that they were part of how churches were decorated from very early on. More frequently, however, supplementing ribbons (*refill, borði*) made of better fabrics with embroidered images, would be fixed on or just above the curtains. Curtains of various types and sizes were used to cover and decorate different parts of the inside of churches, for example lecterns and baptismal fonts. It is known that hagiographic motives figured regularly on such ribbons.[189]

It can be assumed that the center of attention for the visitors of the church were the altar or altars of the church and other parts of the church which had direct religious significance as objects of veneration like crosses or statues of saints. Although in many cases they were at some distance from the people attending the churches, granted that only the ordained were allowed to step into the quire, they would have attracted considerable interest by the people attending the church. Altars in Icelandic churches were made of wood with an illustrated altarpiece. On top of the altarpiece might have been a cross with the Virgin Mary, the apostle John or a picture of a saint. The frontside of the altar could also have been illustrated or covered with altar cloths.[190] Figures of Christ – primarily as part of crucifixes – have been discovered from very early stages of the Church in Iceland. Statues of Mary and the saints do not

---

188   Guðbjörg Kristjánsdóttir, "Messuföng og kirkjulist," pp. 249–251.
189   Elsa E. Guðjónsson, *Reflar í íslenskum miðaldaheimildum fram til 1569* (Reykjavík, 1991), p. 23. See also, Elsa E. Guðjónsson, *Traditional Icelandic Embroidery* (Kópavogur, 2003); Agnes S. Arnórsdóttir, "Cultural Memory and Gender in Iceland from Mediveal to Early Modern Times," *Scandinavian Studies* 85 (2013), 378–399.
190   Other artwork, although less visible to the people attending churches, were various types of altar cloths. See Guðbjörg Kristjánsdóttir, "Sóknarkirkjur og búnaður þeirra," pp. 195–197.

appear frequently in church inventories until late in the Free State period but it is likely that they were found in larger churches before the 12th century.

Still another important field of visual impact was the clerical clothing and other accessories used when celebrating mass. The liturgical garments would vary according to the ordination of the ecclesiastic; the clothing of deacons would thus be different from the priests. Most important to take into account for the present purposes are the outer garments which could bear various kinds of religous images and symbols. Bishops and priests wore chasubles (*casula, planeta*) which often had a simple cross sign on their back but it is not impossible that wealthier churches, particularly cathedrals, might have been in the possession of illustrated chasubles. The oldest depictions of clerics wearing chasubles do not show illustrations and the earliest mentioning of such an item only specfies the color (a purple-white chasuble given by Bishop Gizurr Ísleifsson to the church he had built in Skálholt).[191] More likely to bear images was the cope (*pluviale*) which could be worn by clerics and came to be a distinctive trait of the episcopal ceremonial dress. The earliest mention of a liturgical cope (*pellz kantara kapa*) is found in a church inventory of the church at Skarð on Skarðsströnd of 1259. The only cope preserved from medieval Iceland dates to the Late Middle Ages, that of Bishop Jón Arason of Hólar (r. 1524–1550). That particular cope is richly decorated with images of saints and although it is a late item it may give some indication about how earlier copes were illustrated. The earliest items of liturgical vestments preserved from the medieval period are a stole (*stola, orarium*), a maniple and an amice from Hólar, dating to around 1200 (See Figure 6). Stoles were worn by all priests and several parts of stoles have been preserved from the medieval period. The stole shows the apostles Peter and Paul, each holding their attributive emblems, a key and a sword. The maniple depicts the bishops Þorlákr Þórhallsson and Jón Ögmundarson and the amice, worn on the head, depicts Christ and the apostles to his side. These liturgical vestments were imported from England and might just as well have been worn first by the legendary bishop Guðmundr Arason. Other items representing the material under inspection are various liturgical items which in many cases are showing images. These include chalices, patins, aquamaniles, baptismal fonts and other basins, and croziers.

2.2.4 *Conclusion: Texts in Motion*

It is evident from the above discussion that any study of the source material under analysis is bound to find itself *in medias res*. Such a description is

---

191 ÍF XVI, p. 16.

FIGURE 6 Part of an amice. Depicts Christ, sitting on a throne surrounded by the symbols of the evangelists and apostles to his side. It is believed to have been made around 1200 and used at the cathedral of Hólar in Hjaltadalur. National Museum of Iceland

particularly fitting for most of the manuscripts which are the products of a textual transmission which is both complex and somewhat unpredictable; in most cases, they represent only a single moment in a long line of copies and cannot be expected to represent exactly what was delivered, and if so it is not possible to say anything about where or when the delivery took place. It is, for example, not certain if and then how one of the most important manuscripts for this study, the *Icelandic Homily Book*, was used for delivery although it is quite certain that it was used for preparing sermons which were delivered aurally at some point. Similarly, while it cannot be stated with any amount of precision how the hagiographic manuscripts were used – although it is likely that they were used for aural delivery at one point or the other – it is sure that they were an important source for how central hagiographic themes were presented under diverse circumstances elsewhere. Thus, even though the source material does not provide a direct access to particular historical moments, it can still be seen to give indirect access to a broad array of diverse situations. Moreover, despite the fact of how problematic it is to pin-point individual manuscripts or material artefacts to a particular location or course of events, they should be seen as part of the same overarching sociopolitical process, namely that of the Christianization where they represent and, as is argued in this study, promote the position of the Roman Church. Such an open understanding of the medial context of the discourses under analysis makes it possible to disengage it from the location where the manuscripts were produced and view it as a significant part of the religious message being communicated by the Church to people around the country. Next section will attempt to reconstruct the main participants of such an event, most importantly the cleric and his audience.

2.3 Icelandic Ecclesiastics and Their Audiences

At the center of the discursive landscape of the early phases of the Church in Iceland are the historical agents producing, mediating and reproducing the ecclesiastical discourse. These are ecclesiastics of all ranks but most importantly, ordained clerics and their audiences. These were the primary users of the ecclesiastical texts under inspection and responsible for the constant reproduction and diffusion of their content. An important meeting point for these two groups was the ecclesiastical ceremony although such encounters were not restricted to such occasions. The identity of the priest in Free State Iceland is a much discussed topic in the field of Icelandic medieval church history and will be the subject of the first part of this section. Particular attention will be paid to how ecclesiastics represented the Roman Church, both as members of the church hierarchy but also through the education they received, shaping them and making them capable of mediating the content of the Christian religion as it was done elsewhere in the Christian West. In the second part of this section, the relatively unexplored topic of the composition of the cleric's audience will be taken into consideration and finally, in the third part, the attention will be directed to the medieval church building as a location of discourse.

2.3.1 *Representing Rome: Ecclesiastics in Iceland*
The year 1190 was an important one for Icelandic clergymen. In a letter sent to Icelandic chieftains, the archbishop of Niðarós, Eiríkr Ívarsson, prohibited them to be ordained as priests. Until then, Icelandic magnates had been able to serve the Church as clerics at the same time they were thoroughly involved in politics and other local affairs. For long, this had not been an incompatible task. In fact, the affiliation of the Icelandic elite with the Church was important for the swift and unproblematic introduction of the Christian religion in the country. As time passed, however, and claims for the independence and authority of the Church became louder, the conflict of interests became increasingly manifest. It became problematic, if not impossible, to reconcile the contending claims. In what follows, a closer look will be taken at the clerical caste with a special focus on how they can be understood to have been representing the Roman Church from the beginning.

2.3.1.1 Clerics in the Free State: Socially Diverse or Homogenous?

In the scholarly discussion of priests in the Icelandic Commonwealth, there has been a strong emphasis on their social and political status, primarily as chieftains, but also as servants and anything in between. In this respect, few stones have been left unturned by previous research.[192] The predominance of such concerns has to a certain degree eschewed the discussion, coming close to reducing an ordination of the clergy to being a matter of social and political interests. The following statement of a leading scholar in the field reflects such tendencies clearly: "It is difficult to see why the chieftains should have wanted to become priests if it did not in some way give them a firmer grip on their followers/subordinates and an edge over their rivals."[193] Without underestimating such factors, they should not be taken as the only motivation for seeking ordination. Important in that regard are also authentic religious convictions, a belief in the validity of the rituals they were performing and the truth of the religious message they were presenting. In view of how prominent questions pertaining to the social identity of Icelandic clerics have been in the scholarly discussion, it is inevitable to introduce its main findings.

Due to the limitations of the source material for the first centuries of Icelandic Christianity, most of the earliest priests remain unknown. At first, however, most scholars presume that there was a considerable number of foreign clergymen in the country.[194] According to the preserved accounts on the earliest missions in Iceland the first missionaries – such as Friðrekr and Þangbrandr – came from Saxony.[195] Others came from the British Isles such as Bjarnvarðr (Bjarnharðr) the learned and possibly Hróðólfr who according to one version of the *Book of Settlements* (that of Hauksbók) was said to have left three monks at Bær in Borgarfjörður interpreted by some as amounting to the founding of a monastery there.[196] From even further abroad, the Old Christian Law section in *Grágás* assumes for the possibility that non-Latin speaking bishops and priests might very well reach Icelandic shores

---

192 Jón Jóhannesson, *Íslendinga saga* I. *Þjóðveldisöld* (Reykjavík, 1956); Björn Þorsteinsson, *Ný Íslandssaga* (Reykjavík, 1966); Magnús Stefánsson, "Kirkjuvald eflist," in *Saga Íslands* II, ed. Sigurður Líndal (Reykjavík: Hið íslenska bókmenntafélag, Sögufélagið, 1975), 57–144; *KÍ* I; Orri Vésteinsson, *Christianization of Iceland*; Gunnar Karlsson, *Goðamenning*.

193 Orri Vésteinsson, *Christianization of Iceland*, p. 182.

194 *KÍ* I, p. 224.

195 *ÍF* I, p. 65; *ÍF* XV$_2$, pp. 4, 14, 60, and 114.

196 *ÍF* XVI, pp. 11–12. For a thorough discussion of the evidence for a monastery at Bær, see Steinunn Kristjánsdóttir, *Leitin að klaustrunum*, pp. 67–78.

and specifically singles out clergy of Greek (*girskir*) and Armenian (*ermskir*) origin.[197]

Very early on, however, there are reports of native Icelanders receiving ordination, the first one being Ísleifr Gizurarson (1006–1080), the first Icelandic bishop and a scion of the Haukdælir-family, highly influential in Icelandic society in the Free State period and in a dominating position in churchly matters well into the twelfth century. A certain Þórðr Sölvason was also ordained before 1055.[198] Ísleifr and Þórðr constitute the earliest examples of the sort of priests most notable in the sources for Icelandic Christianity's first two centuries, namely that of upper-class clerics. They were ordained chieftains and aristocratic householders who often owned their churches and had authority over men and territory. Some of the most powerful families of the Free State era seem to have been in close ties with the Church since the beginning, such as the Haukdælir family in Árnesþing, Oddaverjar family in Rangárþing, and well into the twelfth century the number of aristocratic families with an ordained commander in chief only increased.[199]

---

197   *Grágás: lagasafn íslenska þjóðveldisins*, eds. Gunnar Karlsson, Kristján Sveinsson and Mörður Árnason (Reykjavík, 2001), p. 19. After Magnús Már Lárusson, in a 1960 article, rejected A. D. Jørgensen's idea that the Old Christian Law section's paragraph on the non-Latin speaking bishops referred to the eastern religious movement of Paulicians, many accepted his suggestion, including the editors of the 1992 edition of *Grágás*, that the word 'ermskir' did not denote an Armenian origin but rather meant Eastern (Slavonic) rite clerics coming from Ermland, i.e. the region Warmia on the south eastern shore of the Baltic Sea. Magnús Már Lárusson, "On the so-called "Armenian" bishops," *Studia Islandica* xviii (1960), 23–38. Granted that Warmia was not Christianized until the 12th century the earliest, as several scholars have pointed out in recent years, it does not seem likely that there were many indigenous priests and bishops found in the region or, for that matter, travelling in the North. Also, there is no particular reason to doubt that Armenian clerics might – it is even well understandable considering Armenia's political situation being pestered by Turkish raids at the time – have been on the move. On that point, see Margaret Cormack's article, "Irish and Armenian ecclesiastics," in *West over Sea: Studies in Scandinavian Sea-Borne Expansion and Settlement before 1300*, ed. Barbara Crawford et al., Northern World 31 (Leiden, 2006), pp. 227–234, esp. pp. 232–233. The most recent contribution to this debate is that of Ólafur Haukur Árnason who has provided new philological evidence for reading the word 'ermskir' as denoting Armenian Christians. Árnason has also linked the presence of these Armenian clerics to King Haraldr Sigurðsson's (r. 1046–1066) close connections with the Byzantine Empire, arguing that they were Chalcedonian Christians of the Armenian rite. Ólafur Haukur Árnason, "Armenian and Byzantine Ecclesiastics in 11th-century Iceland," presented at the Oxford University Byzantine Society's 22nd International Graduate Conference, 2020 (unpublished).

198   Þórðr Sölvason is mentioned in genealogies in the *Book of Settlements* and *Sturlunga*. For further discussion, see Orri Vésteinsson, *Christianization of Iceland*, pp. 31–32.

199   Orri Vésteinsson, *Christianization of Iceland*, p. 187.

Despite the high presence of upper-class priests in the 12th century in narrative sources, there is evidence, albeit scant, for clerics stemming from other layers of society which has led some scholars to talk about different 'categories' of priests according to their differing social backgrounds and the general arrangement – legal and financial – of their studies and ministry.[200] The primary source for such members of the clergy is the Old Christian Law section (*Kristinna laga þáttr*) in which two other groups of priests appear not belonging to the upper layer of society. Interestingly, there is no mentioning of chieftain priests in the Old Christian Law section.[201] First there is what has been termed a church priest or a servile priest, a person of lower birth who had been adopted, as it were, by a church owner who paid for his allowance and education and obligated him thereby to serve at his church for the rest of his life.[202] According to the Old Christian Law section, the only ways for a priest to get out of such a contract was either by teaching a clerical candidate, who then would succeed him, or through a termination of the contract on the church owner's behalf in the case of the priest's longstanding illness. Even after his death, the church owner could claim a sizeable amount of the priest's assets for himself and the church.[203] In addition to ordained chieftains and servile priests, the third group of clergymen, growing in size in the 13th century, was that of district priests (*þingaprestar* or *leiguprestar*). Much of the Old Christian Law section seems to apply to priests working within this sort of an arrangement.[204] District priests were neither church owners nor householders. They probably lived on church-farms even though they were not required to do so. They only had to formally settle their abode every spring. They might have served more than one church but it is unclear whether they were employed by a single church owner or if the employers could be more than one. The Old Christian Law section describes their duties and demands in detail.[205]

---

200 *Kí* I, pp. 239–243.
201 The Old Christian Law section is the first part of the laws of the Icelandic Commonwealth, originally codified in 1122–1133 but its oldest surviving version was composed somewhat later, possibly as late as between 1199 and 1217, preserved in a manuscript (*Konungsbók*) older than from 1250 (and several other younger ones, the most important being *Staðarhólsbók* dating to around 1270). In addition to the necessary precaution when using normative legal material as historical sources, it is safest to apply the information it provides to the situation around 1200 even though sizable parts of it might date as far back as 1122–1133 but there is no knowing what is original and what later additions.
202 *Grágás*, pp. 14–15.
203 Ibid., p. 15.
204 Orri Vésteinsson, *Christianization of Iceland*, p. 195.
205 *Grágás*, pp. 17–18.

THE ROMAN CHURCH IN FREE STATE ICELAND 93

There is not a complete agreement among scholars about what kind of clergymen – upper class priests, servile priests and district priests – were most characteristic for the social composition of the clergy at given periods. The sources pose a certain discrepancy in this regard which has been interpreted differently by historians. To a significant degree, the difference in interpretations can be explained on the basis of the historiographical stance taken towards the source material. Thus, in his analysis of all the relevant sources for the Commonwealth period, Orri Vésteinsson seems to opt for narrative sources on the expense of legal sources, at least in his discussion of servile priests. Vésteinsson describes the development in the following way: During the 11th century, priests were few in number and those who are known were chieftains and some renowned for their learning and excellence such as Sæmundr in Oddi, Bishop Jón Ögmundarson, Teitr Ísleifsson of Haukadalur, Þórðr Sölvason in Reykholt and Illugi Bjarnarson in Hólar. After 1100 it seems to have become an established custom that chieftains had their sons ordained.[206] Around the mid-12th century a considerable number, possibly the majority, of chieftains and aristocratic householders was ordained.[207] Towards 1200 there are indicators that the top layer of the social and political elite is moving away from the priesthood. First heirs were not being ordained any more but younger sons and nephews instead. Families falling behind in the race for power began focusing on careers and influence within the Church. In increasing measure wealthy, non-elite individuals were ordained as they sought for social upwards mobility.[208]

From a sociopolitical perspective, therefore, active involvement in clerical ministry seems not to have been as predominantly elite in the latter half of the 12th and certainly the 13th century as it was before and it is at this point that the group of district priests really starts growing. This development must have taken a decisive step forward with the 1190 statute of Archbishop Eiríkr Ívarsson of Niðarós (r. 1188–1213) prohibiting the ordination of an owner of a chieftaincy (goðorðsmaðr) after which point chieftains were keeping to the lower orders of church ministry. But according to Vésteinsson's analysis, the general tendency of society's upper crust distancing itself from the priesthood seems to have been underway somewhat earlier.[209] With the necessary caveat that source material such as *Sturlunga* and Bishops' Sagas generally show limited interest in people of lower social standing, Vésteinsson interprets this in

---

206 Orri Vésteinsson, *Christianization of Iceland*, p. 183.
207 Ibid., p. 187.
208 Ibid., pp. 191–193.
209 Ibid., pp. 193–194.

such a way that during the 11th and 12th centuries the priesthood was primarily an upper-class concern. It is not until the 13th century that lower-class priests start appearing in the narrative sources.[210] And except for legal sources, servile priests are not mentioned at all.[211] This leads Vésteinsson to doubt that in the Commonwealth era "servile priests were in any way characteristic of the condition of Icelandic priests."[212]

Church historian Hjalti Hugason, describes the situation somewhat differently in his first volume of the history of Icelandic Christianity, as does Gunnar Karlsson in his 2004 book *Chieftain Culture*. Despite its normative value, both scholars hold *Grágás* in considerably high esteem as a historical source for the period. Accordingly, both scholars express the opinion that the silence about servile priests in narrative sources does not have to point to that they were few in numbers as Vésteinsson suggests. Karlsson even mentions a certain priest named Ljúfini who in his opinion is depicted as every other farm laborer (*vinnumaður*) and supposedly a lower-class priest emerging out of the subaltern for the sake of narrative.[213] In Hugason's opinion, the discrepancy between the legal sources and the narrative sources as to their mentioning or not of servile priests is sufficiently explained by the fact that they are different sources with different objectives. While the authors and editor of the *Sturlunga* collection had no problems with individuals belonging to the group of servile priests not surfacing in the accounts, the legislator of the Old Christian Law section saw a need to fix the arrangement of individuals of such standing into the law unlike ordained aristocrats whose legal arrangement posed no serious problems. They owned their own churches, served them themselves and went about their business as they wished; the less about it in legal codices, the better, Hugason contends.[214] And the fact that the group of ordained chieftains was large in number does not exclude the existence of priests coming from other layers of society. On the contrary, in Hugason's estimation a sizable number of elite clerics probably called for a corresponding number of servile priests so that behind each ordained chieftain must have been priests of a lower social rank carrying the weight of his pastoral duties.[215] Similarly, Karlsson asserts that

---

210 Ibid., pp. 188–189.
211 Jón Jóhannesson, *Íslendinga saga* I, 199; Gunnar Karlsson, "Frá þjóðveldi til konungsríkis" in *Saga Íslands* II, ed. Sigurður Líndal (Reykjavík, 1975), p. 22; Orri Vésteinsson, *Christianization of Iceland*, p. 179.
212 Orri Vésteinsson, *Christianization of Iceland*, p. 179.
213 Ibid., p. 426. The priest Ljúfini is mentioned in *Sturlunga* I, p. 64 (*Sturlu saga*).
214 *KÍ* I, p. 237.
215 Ibid., p. 238.

it can be established with certainty that the social status of priests was very diverse from the beginning.[216] Not all of them had to be 'servile priests' by the definition provided by the Old Christian Law section; there were other types of priests as Hugason points out and have already been mentioned, but they were certainly a part of the group of priests performing the pastoral duties chieftains were not bothering themselves with.[217]

2.3.1.2   Clerical Education: Practical but International

In light of the discussion above, it seems reasonable to assume that the Icelandic clergy was rather diverse, especially as more time had passed from the arrival of Christianity in the country. From the beginning, however, and until the archbishop of Niðarós prohibited magnates to receive ordination, it is likely that ordained chieftains stood out among them and added religious authority to the social and political authority they already possessed.[218] It is nonetheless important to emphasize that through their training and education, which in all likelihood was shaped by practices and traditions in other countries, all priests, irrespective of their social standing, had much in common.

The topic of the most important centers of clerical education has already been touched upon, although without addressing in any detail what men aspiring for the clergy might have been taught at episcopal seats, monasteries and large church farms like Oddi, Haukadalur, and later Reykholt (see Figure 1). It is most likely that the content of education was practical, directed at the most important tasks of clerics. There is a broad agreement among scholars that the content of education and proclamation was comparable to what was happening elsewhere in Europe, most importantly in the areas known to have influenced Christianity in Iceland such as Saxony and England via Norway.[219] The curriculum was grounded in the framework of the *septem artes liberales* although it should not be assumed that every student occupied himself with each branch of the *trivium* and the *quadrivium*. As in cathedral schools all around Europe, it is likely that the teaching concentrated on the written word, the *trivium*, and in most cases, clerical students must have been occupying themselves with the elementary principles of Christian theology and the praxis of the mass and other important rites. Given the state of literacy, many must have invested much time simply in practicing their reading skills and

---

216   Gunnar Karlsson, *Goðamenning*, p. 426.
217   KÍ I, p. 238.
218   Orri Vésteinsson, *Christianization of Iceland*, p. 189.
219   Sverrir Tómasson, *Formálar íslenskra sagnaritara*, pp. 19, 26, and 34; Orri Vésteinsson, *Christianization of Iceland*, p. 196; KÍ I, p. 232.

increasing their knowledge of Latin, granted that one of the most important requirements was being able to read through clerical handbooks when carrying out the most important Latin rites. An important elementary book for reading was the Latin Psalter which, of course, lay at the heart of the Office Liturgy. Such was the case in Europe since the Carolingian period and there is no reason to assume that much changed in the education and general requirements to the average priest until the late Middle Ages.[220]

A typical priest had to be able to know the 'Credo' and the 'Paternoster' by heart, be able to recite the liturgical prayers of mass, which psalms to chant and which biblical expositions to resort to. If no handbooks were available he had to be able to use his memory. In a handbook for episcopal visits composed by Regino of Prüm (d. 915), a bishop should ask clerics if they were in the possession of an adequately orthodox explanation of the Creeds and the Lord's Prayer, and if they could understand them completely and were able to teach their congregation accordingly. Moreover, they should be asked if they possessed a martyrology for announcing feast days to the congregation and the homilies of Gregory the Great and if they read them frequently with adequate understanding and also if they had the Roman Penitential in their possession. As it happens, such basic literature is among the oldest preserved manuscripts of the Icelandic manuscript tradition.[221] Two later manuscripts, one dating to 1350–1365 and the other more broadly dated to the 15th century, describe the duties and requirements of priests in a similar manner. There it says that a priest is to sing mass and consecrate salt and water on the Lord's day (Sunday).

---

220   Arnold Angenendt, *Geschichte der Religiosität im Mittelalter* (Darmstad, 2009 [1997]), p. 448. According to a certain Ulrich Engelberti (d. 1277), the minimal requirements seem to have become even more flexible seeing that a priest did not have to know more Latin grammar than being able to pronounce the words correctly and understand at least the literal meaning of what he was reading. The same applied to churchmen of lower orders. For the administering of the sacrament he had to know the necessary material and form of the sacrament and how to properly administer it. And only if pastoral care was part of his job description he had to know the principles of the Christian faith "as they manifest themselves in Love" and be able to distinguish between different sins as well as sins and not-sins. Citation in Friedrich Wilhelm Oediger, *Über die Bildung der Geistlichen im späten Mittelalter*, Studien und Texte zur Geistesgeschichte des Mittelalters (Leiden, 1953), p. 55. See also Angenendt, *Geschichte der Religiosität*, p. 447.

221   Translations of homilies of Gregory can be found in AM 677 4to as well as in the *Icelandic Homily Book* (Stock Perg 15. 4to). In the *Icelandic Homily Book* are also expositions of the Creed and the Lord's Prayer. Documents for computation are also among the oldest preserved Icelandic manuscripts, examples being AM 249b fol. dating to c. 1200. The oldest undamaged (practically) missal of Icelandic provenience (most likely) is AM 788 4to and dates to the 12th century.

He should consecrate crosses, incense and nourishment. A priest should know how to perform a wedding ceremony, hear confessions and grant absolution for sins. Moreover, he should know how to celebrate mass and as for his grammatical proficiency in Latin he should be aware whether he is using the masculine or feminine gender. He should be familiar with expositions of the gospels, homilies of Gregory and be versed in computation. He is to understand a penitential, be capable of overseeing baptism, extreme unction, burials and the *secreto* (*lágasöngur*) is particularly specified among those parts of the mass a priest should know.[222]

The topic of Latin skills of Icelandic ecclesiastics has been somewhat debated among scholars in the field. For long, the general scholarly tendency was to view the level of Latin learning in Iceland as limited, at least well below the standard elsewhere in Western Europe. The points of argument most frequently rehearsed supporting a weak position of Latin in Iceland have been the strong status of the vernacular and the meager preservation of original Icelandic manuscripts written in Latin dating to the Middle Ages.[223] Latin was, according to this view, only used when there was no other way possible and mostly restricted to the realm of liturgy and diplomatic exchange. Along those lines, Iceland (and often Norway as well) has often been mentioned as an exception in the overwhelmingly Latinized literary environment of the West.[224] As an example, such a view has been promoted by historian Gunnar Karlsson arguing that the power brokers of society did not need Latin for conducting their plots and business domestically and only used it when there was no other way possible. In a discussion of the cultural conditions behind the emergence of Icelandic medieval literature, Karlsson posits an early dismissal of Latin as a language of official proceedings and bureaucracy as a main reason.[225] For more than two centuries the Church in Iceland was governed by men – many of them priests themselves – who were conducting Icelandic society through their involvement in legislation, judicial proceedings, law

---

222   *Messuskýringar: Liturgisk symbolik frå den norsk-islandske kyrkja i millomalderen*, ed. Oluf Kolsrud (Oslo, 1952), p. 110.
223   According to a 2005 survey by Guðvarður Már Gunnlaugsson, the number of Latin fragments from Iceland is 218. Guðvarður Már Gunnlaugsson, "Iceland," in *The Beginnings of Nordic Scribal Culture, ca 1050–1300: Report from a Workshop on Parchment Fragments, Bergen 28–30 October 2005*, ed. Åslaug Ommundsen (Bergen, 2006). Gunnlaugsson defines 'fragment' as a manuscript which contains less than 50% of a book.
224   Jón Jóhannesson, *Íslendinga saga* I, 187–192. See also A. G. Rigg, "Latin literature," in *Dictionary of the Middle Ages*, vol. 7 (New York, 1986), p. 359 and Franz H. Bäuml, "Varieties and Consequences of Medieval Literacy and Illiteracy," *Speculum* 55 (1980), 238, n. 4.
225   Gunnar Karlsson, *Goðamenning*, p. 439.

enforcement, marriages, alliances and production. While doing so, they did not have time for busying themselves with Latin letters nor were they interested in doing so, Karlsson asserts. In his opinion, the Icelandic political elite did not have any interest in using such a 'secret language' (*leynimál*) for creating a special culture of their own and isolating themselves from society thereby.[226]

It seems reasonable to agree with Karlsson and others in assuming that people used their mother tongue whenever they could, even if they were ordained. Latin was a foreign language in Iceland just as it was elsewhere in Scandinavia, the British Isles and Germanic-speaking areas on the continent. Learning Latin demanded much time and effort and if one was to do so, it was with the specific aim in mind of becoming a member of the clergy. Given that education at the time concentrated on serving ecclesiastical office, it is reasonable to assume that in general literacy and Latinity went hand in hand; an elementary textbook for every clerical student was, for example, the Latin Psalter. In a society like 12th century Iceland, where the Roman Church had taken root, the Latin tongue as a central ecclesiastical language had become an inherent part of the linguistic environment and not something one could so easily dismiss.[227] While Karlsson is most certainly aware of the significance of Latin within ecclesiastical circles, his discussion indicates that it did not constitute a particularly notable component of Icelandic culture and society. There are however, several reasons for doubting such a view.

First of all, the boundaries between Latin and the vernacular were not clear-cut with each language existing relatively independent from the other.[228] Such an understanding is evident in Ernst Walter's research who assumes that all priests had knowledge of Latin at a considerably high level, that they were *lateinkundig* or skillful. Recent scholarship citing his findings has not seen reason to question his 'either-or' framework.[229] Not to mention that episodes from Icelandic medieval writings telling of priests with limited Latin knowledge speak against such a situation.[230] In general, it seems prudent to assume that

---

226 Ibid., p. 450.
227 For a further discussion of the term ecclesiastical language or church language, see Georg Kretschmar, "Kirchensprache", *Theologische Realenzyklopädie* 19, pp. 74–92.
228 Herbert Grundmann's essay, "Litteratus – illiteratus," *Archiv für Kulturgeschichte* 40 (1958), 1–65 stands as a classic example of such a dichotomizing view of medieval literacy and Latin proficiency.
229 Ernst Walter, "Die lateinische Sprache und Literatur auf Island und in Norwegen bis zum Beginn des 13. Jahrhunderts: Ein Orientierungsversuch." *Nordeuropa* 4 (1971), 201. Cf. Sverrir Tómasson, *Formálar íslenskra sagnaritara*, p. 34; Gottskálk Þór Jensson, "Lost Latin Literature of Medieval Iceland: The Fragments of the *Vita sancti Thorlaci* and Other Evidence," *Symbolae Osloenses* 79 (2004), 150–170.
230 *ÍF* XVI, p. 76; *ÍF* XVII, p. 273–274.

the historical reality was more complex than such a dichotomizing perspective between those who used Latin and those who did not. It is much more likely, as has been accentuated in scholarship on medieval Latinity and literacy in recent decades, that Latin proficiency varied on a scale ranging from complete illiteracy to the erudition of experts.[231] In between were individuals of differing capabilities of vernacular and Latin literacy; writing and reading laypeople, clerics partly literate in Latin or just even capable of reciting it by heart.[232] As ample evidence shows, such a broad view of literacy and Latinity seems particularly pertinent for the Icelandic context, granted that the unusually strong status of the vernacular on the one hand and the ecclesiastical use of Latin at a considerably high level on the other hand, produced a wide range of differing examples of literacy. In such a situation, it is understandable that religious texts such as homilies and hagiographical literature came to be translated at an early stage into the vernacular for those who did not have full control of the Latin. That does not mean, however, that the level of Latin-skills was as low as has been suggested. Icelandic priests were of differing capabilities when it came to the sacred language of the Church, on the one end of the scale there are priests so lacking in skills that Bishop Þorlákr only reluctantly ordained them, on the other there are learned men like brother Gunnlaugr Leifsson (d. 1219), monk at Þingeyrar-monastery and a prolific writer of Latin literature. In between were ecclesiastics of varying Latin proficiency whose vast majority must have been sufficiently well versed in order to carry out their office.

Second, Latin was a sacred language and, as such, was furnished with an aura of holiness, timelessness and universality.[233] Curiously for the perspective of the present study, an argument frequently employed by medieval exegetes for the sacredness of the Latin language was the intrinsic relationship between Latin and the divinely ordained Roman *imperium* and later the papacy.[234] As

---

231 Bäuml, "Varieties and Consequences of Medieval Literacy," p. 239.
232 Green, *Medieval Listening and Reading*, pp. 9–10.
233 In his article, "Lingua dei, lingua hominis: Sacred Language and Medieval Texts," *Viator* 21 (1990), 51–74, Irven M. Resnick thoroughly surveys patristic and medieval sources outlining the textual background for the idea that Hebrew, Greek and especially Latin were sacred languages. Along with Hebrew and Greek, Latin was one of the *tres linguae sacrae*, constituting the three languages on the *titulus* placed by Pilate over Christ's head.
234 Such reasoning goes back to Augustine's exegesis of the fourth gospel, *In Joannis Evangelium* 117.19.4, PL 35. An admittedly late but well-known instance of extending the sanctity of the *imperium* to the papacy is found in Johann Eck's attacks against Martin Luther, see the chapter "De missa latine dicenda" in Eck's *Enchiridion locorum communium adversus Lutherum et alios hostes ecclesiae* (1525–1543), Corpus catholicorum 34 (Münster, 1979), pp. 376–388.

the language of the Vulgate, it was through the Latin language that it was possible to gain access to God and his will as manifested in the biblical writings. Even though there existed partial translations of biblical texts into Icelandic very early, both in homilies and hagiography, and systematic translation efforts seem to have been underway already in the 13th century, evident from *Stjórn* II and III, Latin was, in Iceland as elsewhere in Christian Europe, the first language of the biblical revelation, making it theologically indispensable.[235] Furthermore, Latin liturgy constituted the setting in which most people were confronted with the use of Latin. Although there was room for the vernacular at particular points during ecclesiastical ceremonies it should be assumed that the readings, prayers and chants constituting the liturgical ceremony were recited in Latin. An early testimony to the centrality of Latin is found in the Old Christian Law section where it is prohibited to pay foreign priests or bishops for their services if they have had no knowledge of Latin.[236] Through the various liturgical ceremonies, people with no knowledge of Latin not only learned to recognize frequently occurring words and fixed phrases, but also patterns in the liturgical performance. The primary status of Latin in the liturgy also made it abundantly clear that Latin was the language of prayer and the optimal way of communicating with the divine, a fact which probably more than anything else might have led to the elevation of Latin in the ears of the audience. As a result, the status of Latin as the central language of theology and liturgy granted it a dominant place in the education of the cleric.

Even though Latin was a foreign language and for most people only heard during ecclesiastical ceremonies, as the church language at the time it existed in a symbiotic relationship with Icelanders and shaped their identity as members of the Christian Church.[237] In view of the above it should be clear that it held a special status as the first language of the Church, but for obvious reasons, for example that it was only known by a small percentage of the population, an exclusive use of Latin was impossible. While every cleric of a higher order had some minimal knowledge of Latin, needing to be able to get through each ceremony without much trouble, this is not to say that every cleric was fluent. There were plenty of occasions when ecclesiastics had to make use of the vernacular and many of them were probably more comfortable with using their mother tongue. This makes it possible to assume that a secondary

---

235 For the dating of the three parts of *Stjórn*, a partial medieval translation of the Old Testament into Icelandic, see *ÍB* I, 556–558. Cf. Reidar Astås' introduction to *Stjórn: tekst etter håndskriftene*, ed. Reidar Astås, Norrøne tekster 8 (Oslo, 2009), pp. xvii-xxxiii.
236 *Grágás*, p. 19.
237 Kretschmar, "Kirchensprache," pp. 74 and 80.

ecclesiastical language emerged, examples of which can be found in early homilies in the vernacular. By such a term "secondary ecclesiastical language," it is meant that a certain way of speaking in the vernacular distinguishes itself from the colloquial through its elevated character and frequent use of Latin loanwords, especially those well-known from ritual formulas.

A prime example for such a secondary church language is found in the *Icelandic Homily Book*. Not only do the homilies frequently resort to Latin, both in the use of standard loanwords (*fratres* being a common one) and ritual commonplaces (such as *per secula seculorum*), it also provides the user of the book with an explanation of the Apostles' Creed, containing an interlinear translation of the *textus receptus* of the creed, its earliest translation into a Scandinavian language.[238] At one point, the homilist even expresses his concern that the use of the vernacular might lead to something going amiss and apologizes for it.[239] Apologizing for one's inadequacy to express oneself is a common trope in medieval ecclesiastical writings – a literary *topos* stretching as far back as Exodus and the biblical prophets (e.g. Exod. 4:10 and Jer. 1:7) – but the mentioning of speaking in a language understandable to the audience shows that this was a concern of clerics at the time.

2.3.1.3   In Whose Authority?

It was the priest's role of wielding the divine words in the correct manner as he had been trained for; to use his competence to bring out – i.e. translate – what was necessary and customary out of the realm of the sacred and unintelligible, at least to most people. For such purposes, he need not be a Latin scholar, he simply had to be able to use the books that, among other things, legitimized his clerical status to make known the correct teaching to the people listening so as to facilitate their salvation.[240] Although it should

---

238   Lilli Gjerløw, *Liturgica Islandica* 1 *Text*, Bibliotheca Arnamagnæana XXXV (Copenhagen, 1980), p. 24.

239   *ÍH*, pp. 213–216.

"Nú þó að vér séim mjög vanbúnir til hvorrar, sem vér fremjum, guðsþjónustu, þeirra er nú hefi eg til tíndar, þá verður þó að hvoru yður það allra auðsýnst, hve mjög vér erum vanbúnir við því, er vér skulum Guði þjóna á þá tungu og á þá mállýsku, er ér kunnuð jamt skilja og um að mæla sem vér."[Now while we are very ill prepared to undertake the many kinds of service to God I have been enumerating, it should nonetheless be most clear to you how exceptionally ill prepared we are for serving God in the language and dialect which you are equally able to understand and speak as we]. *ÍH*, p. 3. Here and in what follows it applies that when no translation of an original is referenced, it is the work of the author of this book.

240   For examples of the correct teaching being singled out as the way to salvation (*heilsugata*, *himinríkis gata*) see e.g. *ÍH*, pp. 11, 20, 24–25, and 27.

be assumed that the learning of individual churchmen varied greatly, they were the holders of religious knowledge and had access to religious books the content of which they read or chanted and further adapted, retold, and paraphrased as needed. Due to this role, it can be assumed that all clerics received a considerable amount of authority and could well be described as religious specialists.[241] From such a point of view, the most important question is not necessarily how much learning Icelandic priests had in general, but rather how much Latin and literacy was sufficient to keep up appearances as a religious specialist.

The Old Christian Law section assumes that each priest had in his possession the most necessary books which he was to show to the presiding bishop regularly.[242] The appearance of the priest, especially in the setting of an ecclesiastical ceremony, was thus inextricably linked to the item of a book, and probably more often than not a book written in Latin. An informative episode is that of the brilliant priest Gísli Finnason in the *Saga of Bishop Jón of Hólar* who always kept a book in front of him when he spoke to the people, not because he needed it but because of his young age, "þótti þeim meira um vert er til hlýddu at þeir sæi þat at hann tók sínar kenningar af helgum bókum en eigi af einu saman brjóstviti" [the people listening considered it more worthy of note if they saw that he took his teachings of holy books and not of his own common sense.][243] Deeming from this text, it could happen that clerics, presumably more often in the case of more experienced preachers, might have preached to the people without resorting to written material, but also it clearly shows that the presence of a book would always add to the authority of the speaker. It was the priest's ability to wield such books which constituted his credibility and consequently his authority.

Thus, the authority of the cleric as cleric was thoroughly grounded in the corpus of writings, mythical narratives, religious traditions and rituals which – all local adaptions and idiosyncracies notwithstanding – were common to ecclesiastics all around the Christian West. Thereby, even if they were in possession of great social and political power, they were acknowledging the authority of an institution which, as time would tell, was bound to turn

---

241 Here, it might prove fruitful to make use of the theorizing of French sociologist Pierre Bourdieu who defined a religious specialist as "socially recognized" as the "exclusive holder of the specific competence necessary for the production or reproduction of a *deliberately organized corpus* of secret (and therefore rare) knowledge." Pierre Bourdieu, "Genesis and Structure of the Religious Field,"p. 9. Italics original.
242 *Grágás*, pp. 15 and 18.
243 *ÍF* XV₂, pp. 205–206.

against all local initiatives which disregarded the authority of the centralized Church, including the proprietary church system which had allowed for the growth of Christianity in the 11th and 12th centuries. In case they had some qualms, they would not stand a chance in negotiating their position as the Roman Church was in charge of the most important institutions and intellectual power.

2.3.2 Audiences of All Kinds

There is no dispute among scholars that hagiographic narratives and motifs were well known among the general Icelandic population. Such texts served both a liturgical and a pedagogical role, and are often said to have had a broader appeal than the often dark imagery and arguments found in sermonic sources such as the *Icelandic Homily Book*. In his thematic survey of Icelandic religious texts, Peter Hallberg maintains that works such as the *Icelandic Homily Book* and *Elucidarius* "were intended first and foremost for professionals, so to speak: theologians, future clerics, and for reading or lecturing in the monasteries."[244] On a similar note, Svanhildur Óskarsdóttir describes instructive literature such as Gregory's *Dialogi* and the *Vitae Patrum*, as well as the sermons of the *Icelandic Homily Book* and saints' lives as well, to have been "intended first and foremost for members of religious communities."[245] There is good reason to question such generalizations. Certainly, it can be assumed that theological writings such as the *Elucidarius* would not have reached far outside clerical circles but the same does not apply to hagiographic and sermonic material. On the contrary, it is a central premise for this study that both hagiographical and sermonic sources provide important examples of what was being communicated to people of differing social status all around the country. The evidence supporting such an inclusive view of the audience of the earliest religious discourse is threefold. First, the source material itself does not give a consistent picture of its audience which rather points to a diverse audience. Second, contemporary sources like Bishops' sagas and the *Sturlunga* collection show that Christian religious practices, including listening to hagiographic *lectiones* and sermons, constituted a prominent part of the lives of people of all standings. Third, the theoretical vantage point makes it possible not to restrict the discussion to the audience of specific manuscripts but to view the source material as examples of discourses which were being produced and reproduced in different contexts.

---

244   Hallberg, "Imagery in Religious Old Norse Prose Literature," p. 166.
245   Svanhildur Óskarsdóttir, "Prose of Christian Instruction," p. 341.

2.3.2.1 Audience according to Religious Source Material

The information gained from the religious source material itself is inconsistent, which is by no means surprising given the variety of its content. In the *Icelandic Homily Book* itself are prayers, exegetical homilies, moral sermons, hagiographical passages, and even a treatise on music. The information gained from manuscript sources is twofold: extratextual hints like manuscript rubrics and intratextual references to an audience.[246] There is not much extratextual evidence to be gained from the source material under inspection. The manuscripts are modest and unpretentious, predating large, illustrated manuscripts like the late 14th century *Codex Scardensis* (SÁM 1 fol.) or manuscripts of the Old Testament translation *Stjórn* such as AM 227 fol., dated to the mid-14th century. Unlike such manuscripts, the earlier source material was not supposed to impress through appearance and look rather like books that have been in much use over a longer period of time.[247] Along such lines, also keeping its varied content in mind, some scholars have suggested that the *Icelandic Homily Book* might have served the purpose of a clerical handbook or a 'commonplace book' as suggested above.[248]

Intratextual evidence for the actual situation of readings from the source material provide important information. An obvious piece of information is the language of the manuscripts. Some might take the sheer fact of the manuscripts being composed in the Old Icelandic vernacular as an indicator for them to have been intended for laypeople, assuming that Latin would be dominant in clerical circles. As already addressed, vernaculars were first used in ecclesiastical contexts where Latin had to be learned as a foreign language and Latin skills differed radically among the ordained. The Old Icelandic vernacular does not exclude a monastic setting, since other people than Latinate monks were living and working there, for example people from a nearby aristocratic family, lay brothers, or novices in training. Cloister churches could

---

246 Beverly Mayne Kienzle, "Introduction," in *The Sermon*, ed. Beverly Mayne Kienzle, Typologie des Sources du Moyen Âge Occidental 81–83 (Turnhout, 2000), p. 154.
247 Paleographic analysis of the *Icelandic Homily Book* has shown considerable changes in scribal hands, leading some scholars to conclude that it was written by as many as 14 different scribes. See for example Börje Westlund, *Skrivarproblemet i isländska Homilieboken*, Stockholm Studies in Scandinavian Philology 10 (Stockholm, 1974) and Eva Rode, "Palæografiske studier i Den islandske homiliebog med særligt henblik på skrivernes antal," Specialopgaver til magisterkonferens i Nordisk filologi (Copenhagen, 1974). Others find it more credible to see only one scribe at work over a longer period of time. See "Introduction" in *IHB*. Both theories support the view that it was a much-used book.
248 Svanhildur Óskarsdóttir, "Prose of Christian Instruction," p. 341. See also section 2.2.2.3 above.

also function as parish churches, serving others than the cloisterpeople living there.[249] In fact, if there is one particular setting in which the manuscripts in question can be located with considerable probability, it is a monastery. Given what is known about the book production of monasteries and the size of their libraries, monasteries remain the most probable locations of origin. It has, for example, been suggested that the *Icelandic Homily Book* was in the possession of Þingeyrar-monastery.[250]

A second piece of information is the occasion of the reading. Most of the speeches of the *Icelandic Homily Book* are written for a particular day of the calendar year including most of the central periods of the year: Christmas, Easter, Fast, Pentecost etc. This fact does not tell much about the audience of the speeches *per se* but begs the question as to who might have been present in churches at such occasions. The same applies for the hagiographic material. The earliest hagiographical writings, for example those found in AM 645 4to and AM 652/630 4to, frequently contain short introductions or prologues describing the occasion of the reading of text as the feast of the saint in question.[251] Such references seem to confirm what is usually assumed, that they were read on the feast day of the saint, either at a monastery, for example its refectory, or in a church.[252]

In later hagiographic works, such prologues become more informative. Even though they fall at the margins or outside the present study's chronological scope, there is no apparent reason not to see them as reflecting religious practices of earlier centuries and therefore worthy of a short consideration. One of the best-known hagiographical writers of the 14th century, the abbot Bergr Sokkason of Ver, explained in a prologue to the *Saga of Michael* that the writing should be read "á messuðagh Michaelis kirkiusoknar monnum til skemtanar, einkanlega í þeim stǫðum sem hann er kirkiudrottenn yfir"[253] [on the name day of Michael, for the entertainment of the men attending, especially in churches under his patronage]. The word 'kirkjusoknar menn,' literally 'the men attending church,' shows that hagiographic texts would be read in

---

249 Kirsten M. Berg, "Homilieboka – For hvem og til hva?" pp. 46–47.
250 *ÍH*, p. vii and Jón Þórarinsson, *Íslensk tónlistarsaga 1000–1800* (Reykjavík: Tónlistarsafn Íslands, 2012), p. 82.
251 "I dag holldum ver messudag Jacobo postola," *Post,* 513; "I dag hólldum ver dyrliga hatið postolum Philippo ok Jacobo ..." *Post,* p. 735; "Messudag holldum ver i dag Bartholomeo postola ...," *Post,* p. 743; "Mathias postoli guðs, er ver hólldum i dag hatið ...," *Post,* p. 767. For a source critical overview of such prologues, see Sverrir Tómasson, *Formálar íslenskra sagnaritara*, pp. 331–395.
252 Sverrir Tómasson, *ÍB* I, p. 422.
253 *HMS* I, p. 676.

churches as well as monasteries were people of differing standings might have attended and enjoyed the entertainment.[254] In another prologue, this time to his edition of the *Saga of Nicholas*, abbot Bergr gives instructions for how the reading of that particular text should be carried out. In that case, the author seems to have a monastic audience in mind, expressing the wish that "hverr maðr i herbergi nærri staddr i upphafi sogu þessarar lesi minni sal til fridar ok nada elskuligt vers Ave Maria"[255] [whoever in a room nearby when the beginning of the story is read, will read for the peace and grace of my soul the dear verse Ave Maria]. Here, the word 'herbergi' points rather to a monastic context than a church space.[256] It is also not likely that the author of a hagiographic narrative would give instructions for how to frame the reading of such a text in the relatively fixed context of a mass or the holy office. A bit earlier example is to be found in a letter from Grímr Hólmsteinsson (d. 1298), the author of the *Saga of John the Baptist,* to abbot Rúnólfr Sigmundarson of Ver (1264–1306) who had commissioned the composition of the work, Grímr seems to assume that his work was not restricted to clerical circles but also included unlearned men (*obóckfrodir menn*). In the letter he explains that he could not leave the "beautiful flowers and dark figures" ("hin fǫgru blom ok hinar myrku figurur") of the text uncommented on, since that would be as useless for unlearned men as gems are for pics ("sem gimsteinar ero svinum"), even though it had made the text longer.[257] The comments thus served a pedagogical purpose for those of lesser learning among the attending audience.

Further intratextual indicators consist of direct addresses to an audience in the source material. The most frequent address in the source material is some variation of 'brothers.'[258] The few addresses in the early hagiographic sources are also directed towards brothers.[259] It is true that the address 'brothers' hints

---

254 Sverrir Tómasson points out that the word 'skemtan' could have a twofold meaning, depending on whether it was taking place in an ecclesiastical context or secular. In the former case it refers to a pious, constructive entertainment pleasing to God, and in the latter, from a clerical point of view, the entertainment was false and frivolous. Sverrir Tómasson, *Formálar íslenskra sagnaritara*, p. 326.
255 HMS II, p. 49.
256 See for example Fritzner's entry, s.v. "herbergi," in which most of the examples refer to a room in a monastic context.
257 *Post*, p. 849.
258 In the *Icelandic Homily Book*, for example, one comes across the following variations: *brœður* [brothers], *góðir brœður* [good brothers], *innilegu brœður* [sincere brothers], *kærstu brœður* [dearest brothers], *fratres carissimi* [dearest brothers in Latin], *góðir fratres* [good fratres]. 55 instances in the *Icelandic Homily Book* alone.
259 For an example, see *Post*, p. 737; "Nu er enn skylldugt, goðir brøðr, at segia nǫkkut fra þeim enum dyrliga guðs postola óðrum."

at a monastic setting, but it is not a guarantee. It is not impossible that 'brothers' would have been used for addressing a mixed congregation including laypeople of both genders.[260] Of the 30 speeches in the *Icelandic Homily Book* with a direct address, a dozen of them contains an address to both brothers and siblings/ brothers and sisters.[261] In a Lenten sermon, two different addresses even follow immediately after one another: "Góð systkin, virðið ér, *fratres carissimi* hógværi Guðs." [Dear siblings, respect, *fratres carissimi*, God's humility.][262] It should also be noted that around half of the speeches and treatises found in the *Icelandic Homily Book* contain no direct address, which indicates the freedom of the preacher to add whatever addresses he found suitable each time, rather than he would not have addressed the congregation at all. In addition, it cannot be assumed that the text of the manuscript reflects precisely the delivered text itself. In many cases, the manuscript's speeches may have served as a blueprint to be adapted to the performative context each time.[263]

Before leaving the topic of direct addresses, a Christmas sermon deserves mentioning, bearing the heading "Alia sermonis," to be delivered on Christmas and provides an insight into how varied the audience might have been, at least at major festival like Christmas. The sermon begins by addressing "good siblings" and asking them to accept the speaker's admonition. After a moral reminder of the importance of repentance and purity of mind, the speaker proceeds to address different groups of the congregation. First, in celebration of the virgin birth, he addresses maidens (*til meyja*), which could simply mean an unmarried woman or have the more specific meaning of a nun. A little later, this address is expanded to include all men and women who lead a pure life ("karlar og konur, er hreinlífi haldið"), which probably means that there were both monks and nuns present. Next, the speaker addresses married men (*kvongaða men*) and reminds of them of maintaining an orderly marriage ("hafið þær stillilega"). In what follows, widows, poor people, and peasants are all addressed, indicating that people of all social standings could have been present during the sermon's delivery. Given that monastics were specifically addressed at the beginning of the sermon it is possible that the sermon was

---

260 In the hagiographic literature, when apostles and saints are shown to address a large number of people, described with words usually referring to both genders such as *mannfjoldi* [crowd] or *allur lýðr* [the entire population], they do not necessarily distinguish between men and women and only use "brothers." *Post*, pp. 176–177; *Post*, pp. 800.
261 On 25 occasions, the address is directed to "siblings" (*systkin* or *góð systkin* [good siblings]) and two times both brothers and sisters, *bræður og systur*.
262 *ÍH*, p. 128.
263 Svanhildur Óskarsdóttir, "Prose of Christian Instruction," p. 341.

intended for a mass at a monastery which also served as a parish church. In any case, it shows that even if sermons were prepared and delivered in a monastic setting, it does not mean that they were automatically reserved for members of such communities. Furthermore, the relative diversity in ways of addressing the congregation, shows how problematic it is to generalize about the audience of sources like the *Icelandic Homily Book*.

2.3.2.2 Audience According to Contemporary Narrative Sources

In a lecture presented at the Ninth International Saga Conference in 1994, Régis Boyer surveyed the evidence for Christian religious practices in the Contemporary Sagas and came to the conclusion that they show the Icelanders as observant Christians, participating in the ceremonies of the Church on a regular basis and in no way different from other Christians in Western Europe. In his lecture, Boyer was reacting to a longstanding research paradigm in Icelandic medieval history, according to which Christianity and the Church were viewed as a foreign to Icelandic culture and isolated from society.[264] Contrary to such a view, Boyer shows that Icelandic Christians of the 12th and 13th centuries were "actually 'good Christians' and that they would not seem quite foreign or strange if they would have happened to live in contintental Germany, or France, or other Christian countries, in that time."[265] Focusing exclusively on religious practices, Boyer provides plenty of examples from the relevant source material. He shows that attendance of offices seems to have been regular and important among them, the practice of the sacraments is "effective, regular and nothing allows us to take it for unsincere," fasting was widespread and usual, crosses were venerated (Boyer specifically mentions that the practice of praying with the arms crosswise was well-known and practiced).[266] Boyer takes issue with Sigurður Nordal's characterization of penance which he describes as foreign to the Nordic mindset.[267] On the contrary, Boyer contends, penance enjoyed a great importance among Icelanders, providing numerous examples for this case. Alms, charity and good works belonged to the "normal way of living" and vows in the form of gifts to churches or the poor, fasts or other devotive practices were frequent, all of this leading Boyer to the conclusion that there is nothing

---

264　See section 1.1.2 above.
265　Régis Boyer, "Were the Icelanders Good Christians according to Samtidarsogur?" in *Samtíðarsögur: The Contemporary Sagas* I, Preprint, The Ninth International Saga Conference (Akureyri, 1994), p. 113.
266　Boyer, "Were the Icelanders Good Christians?" p. 117.
267　Sigurður Nordal, *Íslensk menning* I, p. 198.

warranting such a view that Icelanders were adopting Christianity in a less authentic way and practicing it with less seriousness than other people in Western Europe.[268]

Whereas Boyer was successful in showing how prominent Christian religious practices were among medieval Icelandic Christians, he does not touch upon the related issue of the identity of those who were carrying out these religious practices. In what follows, Boyer's convincing account of what Icelandic medieval Christians actually were practicing, will be supplemented by approaching it from a slightly different angle, asking who these practicing Christians actually were. To a certain degree, Boyer's findings already indicate that if Christian practices were as inherent to the daily routine of the medieval Icelander as he shows, it is likely that they would have mobilized all sorts of people into participating which would also be in accordance with the situation elsewhere in Western Europe. And even though there is not much explicit evidence for audiences, it seems as if chieftains, warriors, women, and workers are all represented among the attending faithful.

The richest information about audiences of ecclesiastical discourse in medieval Iceland concerns the episcopal seats. The two episcopal seats, Skálholt in the South and Hólar in the North, were the most populous farmsteads of medieval Iceland. According to the saga of Bishop Páll Jónsson (r. 1195–1211), around 120 people resided at Skálholt during his episcopacy, including 70–80 workers.[269] This number multiplied during major Christian feast days. One of the best known episodes on the practice of preaching and the attending audience is found in the saga of Bishop Jón Ögmundarson of Hólar. Gísli Finnason, the cleric from Gothland in Sweden hired by Bishop Jón to oversee the clerical education taking place at Hólar episcopal seat. According to the saga, Gísli was a gifted preacher and not infrequently would those who listened to him be touched by his speeches. Compared to other sources, Gísli's audience is described in considerable detail:

> Kenningar hans váru linar ok léttbærar ǫllum góðum mǫnnum, en vitrum mǫnnum þóttu vera skapligar ok skemmtiligar, en vándum mǫnnum varð ótti at mikill ok sǫnn hirting. Um allar stórhátíðar þá var þar fjǫlmenni mikit, því at þannug var þá mikit erendi margra manna, fyrst at hlýða tíðum, svá fagrliga sem þær váru fram fœrðar, þar með boðorðum byskups ok kenningum þeim inum dýrligum er þar var þá kostr at heyra,

---

268 Boyer, "Were the Icelanders Good Christians?" p. 122.
269 ÍF XVI, p. 305.

hvárt sem heldr váru fram fluttar af sjálfum byskupi eða þessum manni er nú var frá sagt.²⁷⁰

[His teachings were lenient and light to all good men, while wise men found them reasonable and entertaining, but evil men experienced a great fear and true reprimand. A large crowd of people came there for every major feast, for many men wished to hear mass there, as beautifully as they were carried out, with message of the bishop and the glorious teachings one could hear there, either delivered by the bishop himself or this man we now tell of.]

The first part of this citation, dividing the audience into good men, wise men and evil men, could be taken to reflect the diversity of people among the attending congregation but the description is in all probability theologically inspired, reflecting the Augustinian understanding of the Church as a *corpus permixtum*.²⁷¹ What is more important for the present discussion is the attraction of crowds to Hólar episcopal seat in order to participate in the celebration taking place there with a special emphasis on listening to what was being said there (*hlýða, heyra*). This point is further expanded on a little later in the saga:

[Á] hverri hátíð sóttu menn á fund byskups, hundrað manna eða stundum tvau hundruð eða nǫkkuru fleiri, því at inn heilagi Jón byskup hafði þat í formælum sínum at honum þótti því at einu til fullls ef hverr maðr í hans sýslu ok allra helzt innan heraðs, sá er fǫng hefði á, kæmi um sinn it sjaldnasta at vitja staðarins á Hólum á tólf mánuðum. Ok fyrir þá sǫk varð þar svá fjǫlmennt at skírdegi eða páskum skorti þá eigi fjǫgur hundruð manna, allt saman karlar ok konur.²⁷²

[For feast, men came to meet the bishop, one hundred and sometimes two hundreds or more, for the holy bishop Jón instructed that it was only sufficient for every person capable from his county and preferably from his district, would visit the episcopal seat once every twelve months. For

---

270 *ÍF* XV₂, p. 206.
271 In a Christmas sermon from the *Icelandic Homily Book*, it is also explained that evil men are necessary for good men to prove their integrity: "Eigi megu góðir menn án of vera vonda mennina. [...] Til þess þarf illa mennina með góðum, að þeir reyna þá, hvort þeir sé góðir. Þeir reyna í meingerðum og í mótstöðu, svo sem fjándinn reynir mennina innan í hugskotinu og teygir þá til rangs." [Good men cannot be without evil men. [...] Therefore are evil men needed among good men, that they test them, if they are good. They test them with evil doings and adversity, just like the Devil tests the men in their minds and leads them to wrongdoings.] *ÍH*, p. 237–238.
272 *ÍF* XV₂, pp. 215–216.

this reason, the number of people present there on Maundy Thursday or Easter amounted to no less than four hundreds, counting both men and women.]

Thus, large crowds of men and women are said to have come to Hólar episcopal seat during the major feasts. The people travelling to Hólar were those who were capable of leaving their farmsteads in the care of their workers and servants, that is farmers of higher standing. This does not mean, however, that clerical preaching did not reach the lower layers of society. It is well known that people from diverse social layers were residing at the episcopal seats for longer or shorter periods. According to canon law, bishops were obligated to care for the poor and, as pointed out by Vilborg Auður Ísleifsdóttir, who has extensively studied poverty in medieval and post-reformation Iceland, both episcopal seats in Iceland must have been crowded with impoverished people throughout the period.[273] There can be no doubt that both episcopal seats – and monasteries as well – were locations where people of all standings would have encountered ecclesiastical discourses such as those under analysis in this study.

Even though Skálholt and Hólar episcopal seats remained the centers of Christianity in Iceland, the Christian message reached around the country through the constant activities taking place in the parish churches. Preaching and reading hagiography was not among the interests of the authors of the contemporary sagas and thus descriptions of such activities are scarce. Churches rose all around the country at an early stage in the Christianization process. However, even though religious practices are not central to the narratives of the *Sturlunga* collection, for example, it stands to reason that the Roman Church is one of the most important background elements, already integral to the society in which the events are taking place. The society described in the *Sturlunga* sagas is a thoroughly Christian society, a tumultuous one, but thoroughly Christian nonetheless. Frequently when events come to pass, people are on their way to church or returning home; people are attending *tíðir* which could refer to mass or participating in the holy office.[274] And these can be people of all social standings: chieftains,[275]

---

273 Vilborg Auður Ísleifsdóttir, "Öreigar og umrenningar: Um fátækraframfærslu á síðmiðöldum og hrun hennar," *Saga* XLI/2 (2003), 105. In her article, Ísleifsdóttir provides numerous examples of how medieval bishops cared for the poor, see pp. 105–112.

274 The *Icelandic Homily Book* for example uses the word *tíðir* both in a treatise on the mass and on the holy office. *ÍH*, p. 165 (office) and p. 190 (mass).

275 "Og um vorið eftir fór Hafliði Másson suður yfir heiði í Haukadal til kirkjudags tveggja postula messu, Filippuss og Jakobs ..." [In the following spring Hafliði Másson went south

farmers,[276] workers,[277] young people,[278] women,[279] and children.[280] There are a few more expansive accounts in the source material, but none of them detail the attending audience. In *Prestssaga Guðmundar Arasonar* for example, the following is said to have happened when a woman named Hallfríður Ófeigsdóttir attended the mass of Guðmundr Arason in Miklibær in Skagafjörður:

> Hún stóð hjá messu Guðmundar prests og hugði að sér vel sem jafnan var hún vön og horfði jafnan á hann um messuna. En er lesið var guðspjall og hann snerist utar og sagði dominus vobiscum þá sá hún eld fara af munni honum í loft upp, bjartara miklu en hún hefði fyrr slíkan séð.[281]
>
> [She was present when Guðmund said Mass and, as was her custom, she followed the Mass closely and attentively, observing Guðmund throughout. When the gospel had been read and he turned towards the congregation and said: "Dominus vobiscum," then she saw fire issuing from his mouth into the air, much brighter than any she had ever seen before.]

Other instances show people entering churches late, interrupting the mass, even when a bishop was celebrating. Over Christmas in the year 1252, the chieftain Þorgils skarði Böðvarsson was dwelling at Hólar episcopal seat under the auspices of Bishop Heinrekr Kársson. In *Þorgils saga skarða*, there is an

---

across the heath to Haukadal on the day of the Feast of the Two Apostles] *Þorgils saga og Hafliða*. Sturlunga I, p. 34. Trans. McGrew, *Sturlunga* II, p. 56.

276 "En um morguninn eftir hlýðir bóndi tíðum" [The following morning the bóndis (sic) went to divine services] *Þorgils saga Skarða*. Sturlunga II, p. 575. Trans. McGrew, *Sturlunga* II, p. 352.

277 "Kjartan, hann var húskarl Óspaks í Holti, en Guðbjörg kona [...] Svo bar eitt sinn er þau fóru frá tíðum."[[Kjartan] was a housecarl of Óspak in Holt. There was a woman named Guðbjörg [...] It happened that one time when they were coming from Mass]. *Sturlu saga*. Sturlunga I, p. 68. Trans. McGrew, *Sturlunga* I, p. 78.

278 "Brandur [...] var ungur maður og frálegur [...] Og einn helgan dag fór Brandur til tíða þangað." [Brand [...] was a fine, young man of promise. [...] One saint's day Brand went across to divine service] *Guðmundar saga dýra*. Sturlunga I, p. 136. Trans. R. George Thomas, *Sturlunga* II, p. 163.

279 Þórdís the daughter of Þorgils Skeggjason is accompanied from *tíðir* by a certain Guðmundr Steinsson. Ibid., p. 184.

280 When Snorri Sturluson is only a few years old he accompanies his father to Oddi in Rangárþing, where he was fostered by the chieftain Jón Loptsson. *Sturlu saga. Sturlunga* I, pp. 98–99.

281 *Prestssaga Guðmundar Arasonar*. Sturlunga I, p. 122. Trans. R. George Thomas, *Sturlunga* II, p. 118–119.

interesting description of how an evensong sung by Bishop Heinrekr on the 12th day of Christmas (January 5, 1253) was interrupted:

> En hinn tólfta dag er biskup var að aftansöng gekk maður í kirkju. Var hann snjóugur allur. Hann var lágur og kollóttur að sjá en þó gekk hann heldur en valt. En er hann kom í kirkjuna mælti Þorgils við Þórð: „Þessi maður er Loðinn Sigurðarson frændi minn." Gekk Þorgils að honum og minntist við hann. Var þá sunginn aftansöngur til lykta.[282]
>
> [On Twelfth Night while the bishop was at Evensong a man came into the church. He was entirely covered with snow; he was a short, bald man, rather unsteady in his walk. When he entered the church, Þorgils said to Þórð, "That is my kinsman Loðin Sigurðarson." Þorgils went over to him and embraced him while Evensong was being completed.]

Later in the same saga, there appears one of the most explicit example about a reading from a hagiographic narrative in the entire corpus of the contemporary sagas and it so happens that it takes place outside a church. Shortly before his final and, for Þorgils skarði, fatal encounter with his one remaining enemy, Þorvarðr Þórarinsson, Þorgils had ridden over to Eyjafjörður and was staying at the farmstead Hrafnagil. In the evening, he is offered entertainment, either the reading of sagas or dancing.

> Hann [Þorgils] spurði hverjar sögur í vali væru. Honum var sagt að til væri saga Tómass erkibiskups og kaus hann hana því að hann elskaði hann framar en aðra helga menn. Var þá lesin sagan og allt þar til er unnið var á erkibiskupi í kirkjunni og höggin af honum krónan. Segja menn að Þorgils hætti þá og mælti: „Það mundi vera allfagur dauði."[283]
>
> He [Þorgils] asked what sagas there were to chose among and was told there was the saga of Archbishop Thomas, and he chose this for he loved him above all other saints. The saga was then read aloud right up to the part when the Archbishop was assaulted in the church and the crown of his head struck off. Men said that Þorgils paused at this, and then remarked, "that would be a fine death."

A similar episode, showing hagiographic material being told in people's homes for enjoyment and spiritual reflection, is found in *Hrafns saga*

---

282   *Þorgils saga skarða*. *Sturlunga* II, p. 608. Trans. McGrew, *Sturlunga* II, p. 389.
283   *Þorgils saga skarða*. *Sturlunga* II, p. 734. Trans. McGrew, *Sturlunga* II, p. 476.

Sveinbjarnarsonar. When experiencing difficulties falling a sleep, the chieftain Hrafn Sveinbjarnarson asks for a poem on the apostle Andrew (*Andrésdrápa*) to be recounted to him.[284] As in the case of Þorgils skarði, this reading takes place shortly before the death of the protagonist, Hrafn, who was killed that very night. It could well be the case that these two episodes are literary constructs but still they reflect that people would resort to the reading of hagiographic material in their homes in times of fear and worry, either read from a manuscript or recounted by memory. The readings of hagiographic material could thus take place in various settings and the audiences do not necessarily have to be restricted to the people who might have attended church.

2.3.3 Pastor and Flock: Points of Encounter

Medieval Icelanders could come across the religious discourses under inspection in various forms under diverse circumstances all around society. The pastoral obligations of priests required them to be mobile around their ministries and in close contact with their parishioners as they engaged in private communication, for example through the sacrament of penance or other instances of pastoral care. Apart from such duties, ecclesiastics of all levels of ordination were actively participating in society as magnates, heads of households, and farmers. In a sporadic and fragmented manner, the ordained servants of the Church thus had plenty of opportunities to reproduce and apply religious discourses in their daily routines. The same applies to devout laypeople, who in all likelihood went about in a similar way.[285] As the last section showed, hagiographic material was accessible on the farmsteads of well-to-do farmers where they were read as spiritual nourishment and late-night entertainment. The most important location for the dissemination of the early religious discourse, however, was the church building which was the center of religious activities in each parish.

2.3.3.1 Translatio Ecclesiae: A Medieval Icelandic Textual Community

In addition to the few passages referred to above, relatively little is known about how the communication between a cleric and his audience took place exactly. Recent theorizing in the field of medieval literacy and critical theory may, however, provide useful conceptual tools to reconstruct important elements of the nature of such a communication. As can be seen from the

---

284 *Hrafns saga Sveinbjarnarsonar. Sturlunga* I, p. 242.
285 Such sporadic applications of ecclesiastical discourses will be explored in the last part of this study.

above discussion on clerical authority, holy books increased the credibility of individuals who might have lacked it for some other reason, such as young age or low social ranking.[286] And even if they were not lacking in credibility at all, each book would always increase it insofar that it represented and in a sense contained the body of sacred literature acknowledged and accepted by the gathered congregation, which would be inaccessible were it not for the cleric. In a semi-literate society such as the Icelandic one during the Commonwealth era, the group was dependent upon individuals who mediated the content to those who could not acquire it, either because they did not know the language in which it was composed, in this case Latin, or they were illiterate. As the Church was establishing itself in Iceland, it is possible to describe its operation in terms of a textual community, particularly in the event of its communicating its messages to a wider public.[287] While this concept does perhaps not need to be applied to all aspects of medieval life in Iceland, it is instructive for understanding the dynamics of the relationship between the learned clergy and their audience, particularly in the event of an ecclesiastical ceremony.

A textual community consists of a small group of literate individuals accompanied by a larger group of semi-literates and non-literates; although not everybody in the group is literate, all of the members acknowledge the fact that behind the communication taking place is a text or a corpus of texts. The communicative discourses and practices depend on the basic tenets of the text being familiar to and at least recognized by those present. As a result, central texts or 'organizing texts' were not necessarily read and not even at hand each time the members of a textual community convened. What mattered was that the textual basis was accepted as a common frame of reference, within which different varations of particular themes could be presented and rehearsed each time. As a religious specialist, the cleric was expected to have mastered the content of the sacred books through his training and was supposed to mediate orally to those who could not receive it otherwise, presumably a sizable portion of Icelandic Christians at the time.

In this view, it is not so far-fetched to describe the role of the clerics as that of a translator, not only between oral and written modes of reception but also between the ecclesiastical language of Latin and the Icelandic vernacular.

---

286 See section 2.3.1.3 above.
287 The concept of a 'textual community' is set forth and explained by Brian Stock in his research of the relationship between the oral and the written medium in the 11th and 12th centuries. See Brian Stock, *Implications of Literacy: Written Language and Models of Interpretation in the Eleventh and Twelfth Centuries* (Princeton, 1983), pp. 88–92.

Even though Latin was a foreign language and for most people only heard during ecclesiastical ceremonies, as the church language at the time it existed in a symbiotic relationship with the Icelanders and shaped their identity as members of the Christian Church.[288] It held a special status as the first language of the Church, but for obvious reasons, for example that it was only known by a small percentage of the population, an exclusive use of Latin was impossible. As already discussed at some length, every cleric of a higher order had some minimal knowledge of Latin. But while he had to be able to get through each ceremony without much trouble, this is not to say that every cleric was fluent. They were, nonetheless, in the position of having to relate with people with limited or no knowledge of Latin while still keeping their ground in the inherently Latinized reference frame of medieval Christian religiosity.

What the cleric said to his audience was always a version of something that had been said in Latin before. Contrary to the tendency of modern scholars to reduce ecclesiastical texts to secondary importance as translations, the exact opposite was the case in the Middle Ages. To Icelandic medievals with limited understanding of Latin, ecclesiastical texts and paraphrased on-the-spot explanations in the vernacular were important because they were translations. It was because they were not originally Icelandic which significantly increased their value.[289] For if one wanted to say something of note during the Middle Ages, not to mention if one wanted to say something new, one had to do it through words uttered before by an authority vouching for what was being said.[290] It is essential to keep this backdrop in mind for the interpretation of ecclesiastical texts in the vernacular. In the communication between a priest and his congregation, the vernacular was an exegetical medium, and at no point was it intended to replace Latin as a holy language. Instead, "it gave access to the holy without representing it directly."[291] What the cleric said to his congregation in the vernacular was always boosted by the framework in which it took place, the Latin liturgy that is, which, in turn, was common to all members of the holy and universal Roman Church.

---

[288] For a further discussion of the term 'ecclesiastical language' or 'church language,' see Georg Kretschmar, "Kirchensprache", *Theologische Realenzyklopädie* 19, pp. 74–92, see esp. pp. 74 and 80.
[289] Svanhildur Óskarsdóttir, "Prose of Christian Instruction," p. 340.
[290] Umberto Eco, "Auf dem Wege zu einem Neuen Mittelalter," in *Über Gott und die Welt: Essays und Glossen*, trans. Burkhart Kroeber (München, 2013 [1987]), pp. 25–27.
[291] Mortensen, "Den formative dialog," p. 263.

2.3.3.2 Social Significance of the Church Building: Panopticon or a Heterotopia?

Although Icelandic clerics came into contact with their parishioners in diverse ways around their parish, it is the church building which offers itself as the most significant meeting point between the clergy and the flock. During the communication, the church building itself should, of course, not be seen as a neutral social space as scholars of medieval Iceland have pointed out. Much rather, it should be viewed as actively supplementing – as a framework and an extention of – the interaction taking place between the clergy and the attending faithful. After the cultural and later the material turn in the humanities, medieval scholarship has in increasing measure directed its focus towards the church building as the context or the venue for a "medieval experience of religion."[292] Some scholars have even spoken of the church building as constituting an 'experience' in itself, defined as a shift in focus towards the audience or the visitors of the church, i.e. how they were affected by and within the space. Such a view entails taking a look at how different aspects of the church experience – architecture, ornamentation, and liturgy – worked together to produce a particular experience.[293]

This process has also been explained from the theoretical and methodological standpoint of memory studies. In her discussion of the importance of space and particularly architectonic structures for the preservation of cultural memory, Pernille Hermann points out that in medieval Scandinavia, the church building was a "central site for the preservation and transmission of rituals and narratives that secure the cultural memory of the Christian congregation."[294] Without expanding further on the processes through which the congregation sustained its cultural memory – a point to be addressed later in this section – Hermann proceeds to explain how the importance of the church building is reflected through its serving "as a metaphor for a mnemonic construction in the mind."[295] Using the example of the so-called stave church

---

292 Beth Williamson, "Material Culture and Medieval Christianity" in *The Oxford Handbook for Medieval Christianity*, ed. John H. Arnold (Oxford, 2014), p. 68.

293 Paul Crossley, "Ductus *and* memoria: Chartres Cathedral and the Workings of Rhetoric," in *Rhetoric Beyond Words: Delight and Persuasion in the Arts of the Middle Ages,* ed. Mary Carruthers (Cambridge, Eng., 2010), p. 214. In his analysis, Crossley makes use of the analogy between rhetorics and ecclesiastical art which was employed throughout the Middle Ages.

294 Pernille Hermann, "The Mind's Eye: The Triad of Memory, Space and the Senses in Old Norse Literature," *European Journal of Scandinavian Studies* 47 (2017), 205. See also the discussion in Henning Laugerud, "To See with the Eyes of the Soul: Memory and Visual Culture in Medieval Europe," *Arv: Nordic Yearbook of Folklore* 66 (2010), 43–68.

295 Hermann, "The Mind's Eye," p. 206.

homily (sometimes called the dedication homily) which is preserved in both the Icelandic and the Norwegian homily books, she notes how that particular sermon, building upon a rhetorical tradition involving the making of mental images, evokes a picture of a church in the audience's mind which should then serve as a mnemonic device.[296] An important term from the religious vocabulary of medieval Scandinavia reflecting how the mental faculties of thought and memory were based on inner visualization is the 'mind's eyes' (*hugskots augu*). Seen with the mind's eyes, the church building itself and the church inventory, furniture and ornaments, could acquire a spiritual layer of meaning which went far beyond the surface of the material things.[297] Thus, through such an allegorical reading, the church building itself became a medium for religious messages and a storage place for religious truths.

For describing this role of the church, archaeologist Steinunn Kristjánsdóttir has made use of Michel Foucault's theories, comparing the church building in medieval Icelandic society to a panopticon fraught with social power, providing people with instructions for their behavior and controlling it.[298] In her article, Kristjánsdóttir maintains that the role of representing the 'Christian agenda' superceded other purposes the church might have been intended to serve, for example the economic interests of the church owner. Thus, it had to be made clear that the church fulfilled all the basic structural elements and be built according to a certain architectural style in order that it might function in such a way.

Another scholar making use of Foucault's work for a more detailed analysis of the social significance of the church building in medieval Icelandic society is Sverrir Jakobsson. Combining Foucault's theory on the spatial situation of power with Henri Lefebvre's definitions of social space, Jakobsson addresses the question as for "how the Church used spatial discourse to redefine power relations in a society where the state was not present as an agent of support to the agenda of the Church."[299] On grounds on Lefebvre's tripartite scheme of the social production of space (Lefebvre's Spatial Triad), Jakobsson emphasizes the significance of the church as a 'space of representation' or, to use a

---

296 Ibid., 206–207. Mental image-making and other aspects of the medieval *ars memoria* or mnemothechnics have been thoroughly studied by Mary Carruthers, *The Craft of Thought: Meditation, Rhetoric, and the Making of Images* (Cambridge, Eng., 1998).

297 Such interpretations appear very early. An 8th century example from St. Gallen in which different parts of the church are allegorized is cited in Arnold Angenendt's *Geschichte der Religiosität im Mittelalter*, p. 438.

298 Steinunn Kristjánsdóttir, "Becoming Christian," pp. 34–35.

299 Sverrir Jakobsson, "Heaven is a Place on Earth: Church and Sacred Space in Thirteenth-Century Iceland," *Scandinavian Studies* 82 (2010), 7.

more transparent term, as a 'lived space' reffering to the ways in which a space is experienced – physically, mentally, emotionally. The churches in Iceland served as centers "of wealth and social control within the community," but no less important was their religious significance as sacred spaces linking heaven and earth, frequently noted by earlier generations of historians of religions; it was an *axis mundi*, the meeting point of heaven, earth and hell.[300] Furthermore, it served as a typological point of contact between the present time and the sacred past of the Church and, with a particular bearing for the present study, the papacy and Peter the apostle's successor in Rome.

In his attempt to reconstruct how such conceptualizations of the church space played out in the social reality of medieval Iceland, Jakobsson resorts to the example of medieval churches serving as sanctuaries in social unrest and warfare, a function he defines as "a product of their symbolic and ideological significance as sacred places, as the places on Earth where Heaven was represented, but also the hallowed sites of sacred events and the past that belonged to the Bible and the saints." Such an understanding of the church space had gained enough momentum in the 12th and 13th century for warring forces not to proceed with violence towards those who had sought refuge in churches. Through this particular conception of the church space, it had become or at least was in the process of becoming a 'heterotopia' of sorts, where the social rules and conventions were not fully operating.[301]

2.3.4 Conclusion: Conflicts of Interests

It has been established that it was the cleric who was the most important distributor of the religious discourses in Free State Iceland. In churches and around his parish, the cleric would come into contact with people from all social strata and in one way or the other, mediate the Christian message. That could be through various practices of pastoral care but also in sermons, readings and other less formal addresses. In the first two centuries of Christianity in the country, it is likely that the most prominent clerics were also in possession of much social and political capital as chieftains. This has led scholars to

---

300   Mircea Eliade, *Cosmos and History: The Myth of the Eternal Return*, Trans. Williard R. Trask (New York: Harper and Brothers, 1959), p. 12. On grounds of different biblical locations, the church has been described as both the meeting place of God and man, in the words of the patriarch Jacob, "This is none other than the house of God, and this is the gate of heaven" (Gen. 28:17) and also the meeting place of Christians who came together as one (1Cor. 11:20) as living stones (1Pet. 2:15) of God's temple (1Cor. 3:17).
301   Although in a different way, Richard Cole has applied the notion of 'heterotopia' to the medieval Icelandic context in his article, "Homotopia, or Reading Sagas on an Industrial Estate," *Exemplaria* (2018), 105–128, see esp. 105–108.

assume that the interests of the Church might have fallen in the shadow of their own political interests or those of their family. It must, however, be kept in mind that their education, their behavior, their role, the very words they spoke, were strongly shaped according to the traditions of the Roman Church. It is likely that individual clerics, especially if they were in power over people and property, negotiated their interests and allegiances in different ways – within themselves and to other people. However, even if they were outspoken opponents of ecclesiastical authorities or policies at a given time, they were bound to reproduce and reinforce the supreme position of the Church through the religious discourses they were diffusing, in the liturgy, through prayers and sermons, through the entire world view and perception of reality, which will be the subject of next section.

2.4 Ecclesiastical Imagination

The Church did not only import books and woods for church building. It also brought with it an entire metaphysical and ontological framework which was in formation during its early stages. With the aid of this framework, which was introduced very early in the history of Christianity in Iceland, medieval Icelanders were not only provided with an entire worldview, but also ways to think about the progress of time and history and their own place in that process. For the purposes of the present study, it is important to explore its main features and the evidence for its use in the Icelandic Free State, for without it the significance of the discourses under inspection would be unintelligible, granted the great extent in which it determined the ways in which the discursive themes under inspection were understood and applied.

2.4.1 *Icelanders in the Sixth Age*

Very possibly the oldest Icelandic manuscript preserved is AM 732 a VII 4to. It contains an Easter Table (*tabula computistica*) with a suggested dating between 1121 and 1139.[302] As elsewhere in Western Europe, the Church in Iceland based its calcuation of Easter on the *computus* of the sixth century monk Dionysius Exiguus (470–544) which spread around Western and Northern Europe

---

302 For the most detailed analysis and discussion of the manuscript to date, see Ólafía Einarsdóttir's *Studier i kronologisk metode i tidlig islandsk historieskrivning*. See also Halldór Laxness' laudatory assessment of Ólafía Einarsdóttir's work in his article "Tímatalsrabb: Dr. Ólafía Einarsdóttir brýtur í blað," *Tímarit Máls og menningar* 27/1 (1966), 31–42.

through Bede's writings on computation. It has been suggested that for the writing of his *Book of Icelanders,* Ari *the Wise* made use of an Easter Table similar to the one in AM 732 a VII 4to.[303] There, Ari uses the phrase *at alþýðu tali* which is an Icelandic translation of the Latin phrase *secundum æram vulgarem* for referring to the Dionysiac calendar while at the same time acknowledging the existence of alternative computational methods.[304] It is likely that the Dionysiac calendar was taught at the learning center of the Haukdælir family, including Skálholt episcopal seat, during the first two centuries.[305] Less is known about which version was used in the diocese of Hólar. A modified version of Dionysius' calendar, the *computus* of Garland (d. 1103) according to which Christ's date of birth took place seven years later than Exiguus and Bede had assumed, gained considerable popularity in Iceland during the 12th and 13th, decades after it had become outdated on the European mainland.[306] It has been argued that the Garlandian computational methods were adopted by Bishop Jón Ögmundarson of Hólar in the 12th century but fallen out of use all around the country in the 13th century, possibly due to the influence of the Fourth Lateran council.[307] Many of the most important sources for the development of the Christian religion during the Free State Era, such as *Hungrvaka* and the *vitae* of bishops Þorlákr, Jón, and Páll, make use of the Garlandian *computus* for their dating of events.

Despite the differences between competing computational methods, they were all grounded in the same underlying metaphysical framework of how to think about time and the progress of history. According to this view, the history of the world and its order was intrinsically connected to the biblical *Heilsgeschichte* and the history of the Church. History is divided into six stages or ages (*aetates*) until it reaches the end of the world, the heavenly Jerusalem. Some versions count eight ages, adding a seventh age of rest and an age beyond time after the Last judgment.[308] Such an understanding is reflected in a sermon in the *Icelandic Homily Book* to be delivered on the feast of Christ's circumcision:

---

303   Jakob Benediktsson, "Formáli," in *ÍF* I, p. xxxi.
304   Ibid., pp. xxix-xxx.
305   Gunnar Karlsson, *Inngangur að miðöldum,* p. 395.
306   Another alternative, which did not catch on in Iceland, was set forth by Marianus Scotus of Mainz (1028–1082 or 1083), according to which Christ was born 22 years after the point in time championed by Dionysius and Bede. For a further discussion on the popularity of Garland' computus in 12th and 13th century Iceland, see Jón Jóhannesson, "Tímatal Gerlands," *Skírnir* 126 (1952), pp. 76–93.
307   Jón Jóhannesson, "Tímatal Gerlands,"pp. 76–93.
308   Jakob Benediktsson, "Verdensaldre" in *KLNM* XIX, cols. 651–653.

Sex eru aldrar heims þessa. Nú er það nauðsyn, að menn nýti sér veittar stundir og vinni sér til eilífrar hvíldar í heiminum. Inn sjöundi aldur er paradísarvist til dómsdags. Inn átti aldur er sjálfur upprisudagur með eilífri sælu, þá er góðri önd er eigi mein að líkama sínum, því að þau eru þá samþykk og eru ávallt hjá skapera sínum.[309]

[This world has six ages. It is necessary now that men use the time given to them and earn their eternal rest in the world. The seventh age is a paradisal stay till the Day of Judgment. The eighth age is the resurrection day itself, with eternal bliss, when a good soul suffers no harm from the body, for they are in accordance with each other and eternally with their creator.]

The version of this scheme most widespread in the Middle Ages had its origins with Augustine but gained influence in medieval Western and Northern Europe through popular authors such as Isidore of Seville, Bede the venerable, and Honorius Augustodunensis.[310] Beginning with the moment of creation, the first age ranged from Adam to Moses, the second period extended from Noah to Abraham, the third spanned the period between Abraham and David, the fourth between David and the Babylonian Exile, and the fifth lasted from the Exile until the birth of Christ. From a medieval point of view, the period before Christ (*ante Christum natum*), generally conceptulized with respect to the Mosaic law (in Latin *ante legem* or *sub lege*; in Icelandic *fyrir lög* or *undir lögum*), served the sole purpose of being fulfilled with the birth of Christ. The Christ-event marked the beginning of a new era, the sixth age of history, a period of grace (in Latin *sub gratia*; in Icelandic, *undir miskunn*) in which medieval Icelanders, as elsewhere, found themselves.[311]

At the center of this historical framework stood the human being. The Christian *Heilsgeschichte* revolved, after all, around the salvation of humanity. The human lot, caused by the sin of the first man was to remain in the fleating mortal and temporal existence as a result of divine justice, wrath, and revenge.[312]

---

309   *ÍH*, p. 79. See also a reference to this scheme in *ÍH*, p. 37. The world chronicle *Veraldar saga* is also organized according to the framework of six *aetates*.
310   Sverrir Jakobsson, *Við og veröldin,* pp. 112–113; Svanhildur Óskarsdóttir, "Universal history in fourteenth-century Iceland: Studies in AM 764 4to" (Doctoral thesis, University of London, 2000), 63–68.
311   See *ÍH*, p. 57.
312   On the tension between divine justice and divine mercy, see *ÍH*, pp. 40–41.

> Frá honum [Adam] er komið allt mannkyn í þenna heim og var ávallt bundið stríðlega af sekt ins fyrsta manns, og mátti engi maður komast undan því oki, heldur féllu allir undir ríki eilífs dauða og djöfullegs máttar.[313]
>
> [From him [Adam] is the entire human race descended in this world and is always harshly bound by the guilt of the first man, and for no man was it possible to escape this plight, but everybody was bound to fall under the sway of eternal death and devilish power.]

This affects every human being and nobody is able to escape it, not even the holiest of men, with the exception of the Lord himself. "No men in this world have been so holy that they have not done something wrong, although the faults of some are both few and small."[314] The world is covered in the darkness of sins:

> Svo kalla helgar bækur sem nótt myrk synda og villu og þar með reiði Guðs lægi yfir allri veröld frá synd ins fyrsta manns allt til upprisu *Domini*, sú er allt mannkyn leiddi til dauða og til helvítis myrkra héðan úr heimi.[315]
>
> [The period between the sin of the first man – which led the human race into death and the darkness of hell out of this world – until the resurrection of the Lord [*Domini*], holy books name as the dark night of sins and error as the wrath of God lay over the entire world.]

And the dark night is evidently seen in the material existence of all people. Each individual is striving to endure "í vesöld veraldar þessar, í sóttum og sárleik, hríðum og frostum og óárum, sulti og manndauð og margháttuðum meinlætum, þeim er hér verða að hafa þeir menn, er heiminn byggva" [in the misery of this world, in diseases and pains, snowstorms, colds, and bad years, hunger and losses and all kinds of hardships, the lot of those men who inhabit the world.][316] Other indicators are the existence, persistence, and success of all kinds of enemies: pagans, heretics, Jews and of course devils and other monsters.[317] Each prayer of the Lord's Prayer, at least according to one of its interpretations found in the *Icelandic Homily Book*, is meant to counter such

---

313 *ÍH*, p. 65.
314 "Hafa engir menn svo helgir verið í heiminum, að eigi hafi nekkvað misgjört, þótt sumir hafi bæði fátt og smátt ..." *ÍH*, p. 223.
315 *ÍH*, p. 103.
316 *ÍH*, p. 242.
317 See section 3.2. below.

evils, which are ultimately related to the "evil of the Devil, sins and betrayal, diseases and sorrow and all kind of this-worldly ailments."[318] And in spite of everything, the battle for survival is bound to end with the inescapable destinity of death, for "nobody became so potent in the world that he might avoid death, everybody should accept it, the powerful as the powerless, noble and humble, old as young, and then receive their recompence in accordance with their performance."[319]

The religious truth of Christ's resurrection constituted the dawn of "the day of the bright and correct faith and mercy of the Lord [Domini]" – in several senses.[320] The eschatological hope of the imminent day of reckoning provided faithful Christians with some consolation – and certainly a considerable amount of dread as well. And in addition to the ultimate judgment day of the second coming of Christ and his heavenly hosts, there was the judgment day of every individual Christian taking place at the end of her or his life.[321]

2.4.2 Typological Thought

With the fall of man, human beings' access to God and divine truth was obstructed and their understanding of the divine distorted. As explained by Hugh of St. Victor, the only eyes unclouded after the fall were the eyes of flesh, while the eyes of reason (*ratio*) and the eyes of contemplation (*contemplatio*) were darkened.[322] These correspond roughly to the distinction made by Honorius Augustodunensis between bodily vision (*corporalis*), spiritual vision (*spiritualis*), and intellectual vision (*intellectualis*) which might lie behind the Old Icelandic phrase *hugskots augu*.[323] The only way to reach an understanding

---

318 "[D]jöfuls illsku, [...] syndum og svikum, sóttum og sorgum og allri þessa heims meinsemi." *ÍH*, p. 43.
319 *ÍH*, pp. 69–70.
320 *ÍH*, p. 103.
321 For the judgment of the individual at the end of life see: "En svo er hverjum komi dómadagur, þegar er hann andast, fyr því að veit hver þá þegar sinn hluta, hvort hann skal helvítis kvalar hafa, þær er aldregi skal þrjóta, eða skal hann hafa hreinsunareld nekkverja stund og þau meinlæti, er af honum brenni inar smærri syndir, þær er hann hefir óbættar, áður hann andist" [And upon the death of each arrives his judgment day, as each comes to know his share, if he will receive eternal tortures in hell, or if he shall have to endure purgatory for some while and the hardship meant to burn of him the smaller, unsettled sins, before he passes.] *ÍH*, p. 223. To the ultimate day of judgment there are numerous references, for examples see *ÍH*, pp. 19, 25, 27, 26, 33, 41, 44, 60, 62, 69, 72, 85, 92, 94, 107, 124 125, 160, 175, 177, 274, 292, 296–297, 301.
322 Hugh of St. Victor, *The Didascalicon of Hugh of St. Victor: A Medieval Guide to the Arts*, trans. and ed. Jerome Taylor (New York, 1961), pp. 6.
323 Honorius Augustodunensis, *Liber duodecim quaestionum* 10. PL 172. Col. 1183A.

of God and his will was through symbols which could only give indirect access; still it was the only bridge to the eternal reality of God. The symbol, which in the Middle Ages was more frequently referred to as a resemblance (*similitudo*), image (*imago*), type (*typus*) or figure (*figura*), belonged to the earthly and visible reality but was also 'real' through its participation in the divine reality it represented. To take a well-known example, such an understanding of the symbol was central to the medieval doctrine of the sacraments. The bread and the wine, or the *species* as the physical properties of the sacrament were called, were conceived as symbols, referring as sacred symbols to the thing itself (*res*), that is the body and blood of Christ. Central to such thinking is the notion – ultimately grounded in Platonic dualism – that beyond the visible reality – fleeting, fallible, and unreliable as it is – is another world, more real and more true than the physical world visible to human eyes.

The divine reality remains beyond temporal progress as known to human perception, as reflected in the following translation of Prosper of Aquitaine's 57th epigram, found in AM 677 4to:

> "Fyr vtan tid er skipan tiþana i eilifri gvds specd enda ero ongver lvter nyradliger fyr þeim sem von er at er skapþa hever þa hluti þegar er en eru ocomnir fram oc coma muno"[324]
>
> [Outside time is the order of times in the eternal wisdom of God for no things are new for the one who has created those things which already exist as well as those which have not emerged and will come to pass.]

Historical events are only a faint image of the heavenly eternity which allowed for an interpretation of historical events and a historical consciousness which has been termed symbolic, figural, or typological. This means that two historical events or persons, distant in time and space according to human conception, can be taken to reflect symbolically the same eternal, constant, and divine truth. Other well-known metaphors for the relationship between type and antitype are those of shadow and the figure projecting the shadow, childhood and maturity, or a sketch and a painting that is already finished. From the point of view of biblical exegesis, typological thought is grounded in the notion that the Old and New Testament form an entire whole constituting the revelation of God.

A short definition of typological interpretation, often also termed figural interpretation, is, according to Erich Auerbach, the establishing of "a

---

[324] *Leifar*, p. 13.

connection between two events or persons, the first of which signifies not only itself but also the second, while the second encompasses or fulfills the first."[325] Another specialist on the subject, Friedrich Ohly, defined typology along similar lines:

> Sie besteht in der Zusammenschau zweier Geschehnisse, Einrichtungen, Personen oder Dinge, deren je eines aus dem Alten und dem Neuen Testament gegriffen und zu einem Ereignispaar derart verbunden wird, daß durch die Zuordnung zu einem spiegelnden Sichbeleuchten ein Sinnzusammenhang zwischen den beiden an den Tag gebracht wird.[326]

As Ohly's citation indicates, such a hermeneutical stance can be traced back to how biblical exegesis was practiced already in late antiquity, throughout the Middle Ages, and beyond.[327] As the revealed word of God, the biblical text was understood to give acess to divine truth which, according to medieval exegetes, manifested itself in the four (sometimes three) different senses of scripture. The plain, literal meaning of the text was referred to as *sensus historicus* which concerned itself exclusively with facts (*res gestae*). Beyond the historical sense of scripture, which did not always lend itself to much theological speculation in itself, medieval exegetes could find different layers of spiritual meaning (*sensus spiritualis*). *Allegoria*, the allegorical, mystical or spiritual sense of scripture, gave access to another, transcendent meaning; as noted by Honorius Augustodunensis, it refers to those parts of scripture by which something else is meant than the facts (*res*) recounted.[328] Another spiritual sense of scripture was the tropological or moral sense (*sensus tropologicus* or *sensus moralis*) on the grounds of which exegetes would construct guidance for human action. The fourth sense of scripture, which in fact is a type of allegory, was the so-called anagogical sense which deals with allegorical similitudes referring specifically to the eschatological future. By aid of this hermeneutical framework, which was grounded in the same symbolic thought mentioned above, medieval exegetes had access to the eternal and divine reality.

---

325 Erich Auerbach, "'Figura,'" in *Scenes from the Drama of European Literature*, foreword by Paolo Valesio, Theory and History of Literature 9 (Minneapolis, 1984), p. 53.
326 Friedrich Ohly, "Typologie als Denkform der Geschichtsbetrachtung," in *Natur, Religion, Sprache, Universität: Universitätsvorträge 1982/1983*, Schriftenreihe der Westfälischen Wilhelms-Universität Münster 7 (Münster, 1983), p. 68.
327 For a clear and informative overview of medieval hermeneutics, see Hans-Werner Goetz, *Geschichtschreibung und Geschichtsbewußtsein im hohen Mittelalter*, 2nd ed., Orbis mediaevalis. Vorstellungswelten des Mittelalters 1 (Berlin, 2008 [1999]), pp. 78–91.
328 Honorius Augustodunensis, *De animae exsilio et patria* 12. PL 172. Col. 1245C.

The typological or figural understanding was constituted on grounds of the same ontological principles as the notion of the fourfold meaning of scripture. Historical persons, events or courses of events could be interpreted in view of the past in order to make a statement of general validity. From such a point of view, a preceding type would be taken to refer to its later antitype; a historical figure was understood to 'prefigure' a corresponding later figure. When applied to the progress of history, however, the interpretation was obviously not restricted to the biblical history although the biblical history enjoyed a central position for typological interpretation. As can be seen in various works of medieval historiography, the entire history of the Church and also historical developments of a more secular nature, for example in politics, reflect this view of the world and history. Thus, to take two frequently rehearsed examples, medieval authors would view emperor Constantine as a new Moses and Charlemagne as a new David.[329] History was thus not only understood to tell of past things but could also be symbolically understood to reflect the fact – inevitable to medieval Christians – that every course of events had a place in God's divine order of things.

2.4.3 Typological Thought in Medieval Icelandic Culture

The outlines described above should only be taken as an ideal type of the *Weltanschauung* constituted by the theological worldview and hermeneutic framework promoted by the Christian Church, internalized and adapted by unlike individuals in different ways and measure. Written sources from medieval Iceland testify about the diverse ways in which such a typological historical consciousness could manifest itself, ranging from the practice of name giving to the composition of large works of literature.[330] In the late 20th century scholars were beginning to pay attention to such issues. Lars Lönnroth, Gerd Wolfgang Weber, and Hermann Pálsson, emphasized how medieval Scandinavian historiographers viewed the pagan past of the North in terms of the Christian understanding of history described above.[331] In recent years, the discussion on such topics has become increasingly lively and the number of

---

329 Ohly, "Typologie als Denkform der Geschichtsbetrachtung," p. 75, see also p. 96, footnote 19.
330 Sverrir Jakobsson maintains that the extent to which such thinking, shaped by a vertical sense of space and a typological sense of history, was brought to Iceland by the Church is unclear. It might for example be reflected in texts of Norse mythology but whether such texts can be understood to reflect pre-Christian though is subject to debate. There is however, no doubt that the Church made use of it for presenting its message. Sverrir Jakobsson, *Við og veröldin*, pp. 83 and 97.
331 See discussion in section 1.1.2 of the present work.

examples of how Icelandic sagas portray the influence of Christian symbolic thought (what some scholars would call the inculturation of the Christian *Heilsgeschichte* into medieval works of literature) has increase significantly.[332] In very recent years, for example, two extensive monographs on hagiography and medieval Icelandic literature have been published, both dealing with it from a literary historical point of view with the primary goal of bringing out how hagiographic themes appear in saga writing and to some extent poetry as well.[333] It would exceed the scope of this study to provide an exhaustive summary of the debate but a few examples will suffice for explaining how the 'ecclesiastical imagination' manifested itself in the literary production of the time.

In his work on *Heiðarvíga saga*, among the oldest sagas of the Icelanders, Bjarni Guðnason argues that the text should not be taken as a narrative of actual events but as an "epic novel laden with spiritual meaning."[334] The family dispute occupying the largest share of the saga, climaxing in a battle between the rivaling parties taking place on the heath Tvídægra, should rather be understood spiritually as a symbolic representation of the constant tension between Christianity and paganism, forgiveness and revenge, peace and unrest. According to such a reading, Guðnason suggests that medieval Icelanders would have aligned Víga-Styr, the villain of the saga who mistreats the farmers in his district, with antagonists from the Hebrew Bible, for example the Egyptian pharaoh or the Philistean warrior Goliath. Similarly, the protagonist of the story who eventually kills Víga-Styr would have been paralleled with King David. Although one should be careful when applying such detailed typological interpretations to texts which do not explicitly mention them, Guðnason's general point on the constant and recurring battle between

---

332   For a discussion of the term inculturation, see Bruno Quast's introduction, "Literarische Inkulturation. Zur Einleitung" in *Inkulturation. Strategien bibelepischen Schreibens in Mittelalter und Früher Neuzeit*, eds. Bruno Quast und Susanne Spreckelmeier, Literatur - Theorie - Geschichte 12 (Berlin, 2017), pp. 1–13.

333   Siân E. Grønlie, *The Saint and the Saga Hero: Hagiography and Early Icelandic Literature*, Studies in Old Norse Literature (Woodbridge, 2017) and Haki Antonsson, *Damnation and Salvation in Old Norse Literature*, Studies in Old Norse Literature (Woodbridge, 2018). See also Antonsson's article, "The Construction of Auðunar þáttr vestfirzka: A Case of Typological Thinking in Early Old Norse Prose," *Scandinavian Studies* 90 (2018), 485–508.

334   Bjarni Guðnason, *Túlkun Heiðarvígasögu*, Studia Islandica 50 (Reykjavík, 1993), p. 265. Guðnason's interpretation has been criticized by both Alison Finlay, "Interpretation or Over-Interpretation? The dating of two *Íslendingasögur*," *Gripla* XIV (2003), 61–91 and Uwe Ebel, "Ex oriente lux: Zum Problem theologischer Sinngebung in der Heiðarvíga saga" in *International Scandinavian and Medieval Studies in Memory of Gerd Wolfgang Weber*, ed. Michael Dallapiazza et al. (Trieste, 2000).

Christianity and heathendom seems reasonable, testifying to the vividness of typological thinking in medieval Iceland.[335]

Another early family saga which has been shown to be fraught with Christian symbolism is *Egils saga*. In books and articles, Torfi H. Tulinius has striven to show how the author of the saga about the eventful life of the warrior-poet Egil Skallagrimsson has incorporated manifold layers of biblical typology into the work. Most significant to Tulinius' reading of the text, are the typological parallels between the protagonist Egil and two characters from the Hebrew Bible, Cain (and Judas Iscarioth, Cain's antetype from the New Testament, by extention) and King David. Not only did Egil share several characteristics of outward appearance with Cain and Judas as they were depicted in medieval ecclesiastical iconography – baldness, vivid eyebrows, and, according to some interpretations, a shivering head – but he also had a very ambiguous relationship towards his brother Þórólfr and his actions would eventually lead to his death.[336] Furthermore, Egil's killing of the Christ-figure Rögnvaldr, son of King Erik and queen Gunnhild, fits such a reading quite well.[337] A more convincing analogy can be drawn between Egil and King David. Like David, Egil is a poet; he desires the wife of another man and his actions lead to the death of the competing husband, who in Egil's case is his brother. The death of both Egil's brother Þórólfr and Uriah, David's competitor, happen in battle under similar circumstances. Furthermore, both David and Egil loose a beloved friend and later a son conceived with the woman desired and originally betrothed to another.[338] Through these parallels and other, Tulinius uncovers a spiritual layer of meaning according to which Egil emerges as a highly ambigous character with a hybrid religious identity. In that sense, Egil's life can be understood as a conversion event, as he moves from paganism and sin to Christianity, repentance, and forgiveness.[339] In her more recent treatment of the topic, Siân E. Grønlie emphasizes the way in which the saga author is resisting and inverting standard hagiographic *topoi* and suggests that Egil might be conceived of as an "'anti-saint', who challenges and subverts supposedly saintly norms."[340]

The clearest cases of typological thought are found in hagiographical literature. In many cases, the type or the prefiguration does not necessarily stem from a biblical apocryphal past. To mention an obvious example from *Ólafs*

---

335 Bjarni Guðnason, *Túlkun Heiðarvígasögu*, p. 266.
336 Torfi H. Tulinius, *Enigma of Egill*, pp. 90–93.
337 Ibid., pp. 82–86.
338 Ibid., pp. 97–100 et passim.
339 Ibid., pp. 119–131.
340 Grønlie, *Saint and the Saga Hero*, p. 108.

saga Tryggvasonar by the monk Oddr Snorrason, the relationship between the two kings, Ólafr Tryggvason and Ólafr Haraldsson, is paralelled with the relationship between John the Baptist and Christ.[341] Ólafr Tryggvason holds Ólafr Haraldsson during his baptism and thus becomes, as John did for the Lord.

> Ok svá sem hann var hans fyrirrennari ens helga Óláfs konungs, svá var ok Óláfr konungr Tryggvason fyrirrenari hins helga Óláfs konungs, ok heldu þeir sínar sifjar sem allir skyldu í sínum helgum krapti ok dýrligum verkum, ok þat kom þar fram sem Jóan mælti við Dróttin: „Þér hœfir at vaxa, en mér at þverra."[342]
>
> [And as John was His precursor, so was King Olaf Tryggvason the precursor of the sainted King Olaf. They maintained their kinship as everyone should, with holy strength and glorious deeds. It then came to pass as John said to the Lord: "You are destined to grow and I to diminish."]

Such typological parallelism between two saints is even more evident in another group of Icelandic hagiography. The Icelandic bishops' sagas clearly exhibit the same sort of typological patterns as other hagiographic texts composed in the Latin West.[343] Model bishops like Þorlákr and Jón, are depicted in a saintly manner, imitating Christ's paradigmatic actions each in their own way.[344] Some of them, like Þorlákr, are even explicitly presented as apostles for Iceland.[345] Their earthly enemies similarly represent the enemies of the Church and Christianity and the fight being fought should be understood in the elevated sense of the constant battle between the cosmic forces of good and evil.

2.4.4 Conclusion: Beyond the Written Word

The above examples show that typological thought was a vivid part of how medieval Icelanders thought about the world and their place in it. It was the self-evident framework within which the authors of medieval writings, whether hagiographical or of a less explicitly religious nature, formulated their

---

341 For a more thorough discussion on hagiographic elements in this text see Grønlie, *Saint and the Saga Hero*, pp. 39–77.

342 *ÍF* XXV, p. 125. Trans. Theodore M. Andersson in Oddr Snorrason, *The Saga of Olaf Tryggvason*, Islandica LII (Ithaca, 2003), p. 35.

343 Ásdís Egilsdóttir, "The Beginnings of Local Hagiography in Iceland: The Lives of Bishops Þorlákr and Jón," in *Fræðinæmi: Greinar gefnar út í tilefni 70 ára afmælis Ásdísar Egilsdóttur* (Reykjavík, 2016), pp. 39–41.

344 *ÍF* XVI, pp. lxxi–lxxvi.

345 *ÍF* XV, p. 43.

versions of past events and their significance for the present. While it is safe to assume that the authors of hagiographical works were by and large ecclesiastics, the identity of those who composed the family sagas is less certain and subject to a long-standing debate. In some cases they could have been ecclesiastics but not necessarily. They could very well have been literate laymen like Snorri Sturluson who has been suggested as the author of *Egils saga* but better known for his composition of *Heimskringla* – a collection of sagas of Norwegian kings – and the *Prose Edda*. The ontological framework and the historical consciousness described above were not only restricted to ecclesiastics, but inherent to Icelandic culture and society at the time and shared by laypeople and the ordained, although people would have made use of it in different ways and measure. It should be emphasized, for the present purposes, that it was also not restricted to the production of written texts, although they provide the clearest evidence for it. The same ontological structures – symbolism, figuralism, typology – provided the framework in which people made sense of the events taking place around them even though they were not always put into writing. The written evidence for typological thought in medieval Iceland does not provide the only versions of how it was carried out but first and foremost testifies to the vividness of the phenomenon and its significance in medieval Icelandic culture.

CHAPTER 3

Force of Words: Constructing a Christian Society

As other religious texts, the source material under inspection contains discourses on things transcendent and eternal. It also contains a set of ideas, often inscribed in the same discourses, promoting a particular social framework and particular power relations. The dispersion of such discourses around society serves to stabilize and consolidate the suggested social order as well as it legitimates the authority of certain groups while confirming and naturalizing the subordination of others.[1] Since its arrival in Iceland, messages of such sociopolitical import were part of the proclamation of the Church. The Church introduced notions and categories supporting and reinforcing its position through the mythical corpus represented most prominently through the religious texts constituting the backbone of the analysis in this third chapter. In other words, the institutional growth of the Church, so thoroughly treated by scholars of medieval Iceland, was grounded in and reinforced by a corpus of religious myth that has not been as thoroughly studied in that context. Surveying the religious discourses of the source material, the following three sections will explore and analyse the ways in which it can be seen to prescribe to its audiences a vision of a particular societal order. To that end, three major themes from the source material are explored, all of which played a crucial role for the social formation taking place through the religious discourse.[2] These themes remain stable, that is the way in which they are constructed stays similar or the same throughout the 13th century and, as will be further argued in the fourth chapter of this book, all of these themes carried considerable social weight in the Icelandic Free State.

Guided by the imperial hermeneutic perspective, the discursive themes explored here are intended to throw light on a particular configuration of power, namely how the Church constructed for itself a position of 'powering over' other people and especially any opposition that stood in its way.[3] In

---

[1] Such an understanding of the nature of religious texts is based on the theorizing of Bruce Lincoln who has defined mythical texts as containing "ideology in narrative form." Bruce Lincoln, *Theorizing Myth: Narrative, Ideology, and Scholarship* (Chicago, 1999), p. 147.

[2] For a methodological discussion on the identifying and organizing of such a thematic, see Lincoln, *Theorizing Myth*, pp. 150–151. See also, Lincoln, "How to Read a Religious Text," pp. 9–10.

[3] The phrase 'power over,' is frequently used by scholars adhering to an atemporal understanding of the postcolonial as an 'imperial experience.' Such a point of view calls for an

that regard, the present study shares the premises of those scholars who have analysed Christian religious texts from the perspective of postcolonial and imperial studies.[4] The thematic set forth in the three sections of this chapter thus reflects what has been termed the 'imperial ethos' inscribed in the texts and, consequently, the religious discourse to which they attest.[5] That is, how they aimed at social control, through enforcing the power and authority of the Roman Church and reinforcing the submission and obedience of other social groups. Along these lines, the first two themes concern the most important socioreligious groups and the boundaries between them, of course from the point of view of the Roman Church. Thus, the first section discusses the discursive representation of the Church itself and its representatives. It explores how the position of the Church was explained and defended and why those who belonged to it—and particularly those who had been chosen to represent it—enjoy a privileged position of powering over other people. The second part of the chapter deals with how those who set themselves apart from the Church by disregarding its instructions or opposing it in other ways are represented in the discourse. The third part looks into the retributive structures inscribed in the discourse, preserving the social order by insisting on the benefits of the social order promoted by the Church and the negative consequences of undermining it.

3.1 Authority

This section, headlined by the relatively broad term 'authority,' seeks to show how the early religious discourse of the Roman Church in Iceland contributed to elevate the Church as an institution and its representatives to a position of powering over other people in society. The notion of authority is

---

explanation of which power is powering over each time, but as already noted it is the Roman Church which assumes that role in the present analysis. For a more detailed discussion of this issue, see sections 1.2.2.1 and 1.2.2.2 above.

4   For examples of the employment of such an approach, see Elisabeth Schüssler Fiorenza's *Power of the Word*, Warren Carter's, *Matthew and Empire: Initial Explorations* (Harrisburg, 2001), and Stephen D. Moore's *Empire and Apocalypse: Postcolonialism and the New Testament*, The Bible in the Modern World 12 (Sheffield, 2006). For further examples and an overview of the diversity of approaches within this field of scholarship, see Fernardo F. Segovia, "Introduction: Configurations, Approaches, Findings, Stances," in *Postcolonial Commentary on the New Testament Writings*, eds. Fernando F. Segovia and R. S. Sugirtharajah, The Bible and Postcolonialism 13 (London, 2009), pp. 1–68.

5   Schüssler Fiorenza, *Power of the Word*, p. 149.

here understood as an aspect of discourse, following scholars such as Pierre Bourdieu, Michel Foucault, James C. Scott, and in particular Bruce Lincoln whose work on religious discourse has already been cited on several occasions. In his book on authority, Lincoln explains how he views discursive authority as "(1) an effect; (2) the capacity for producing that effect; and (3) the commonly shared opinion that a given actor has the capacity for producing that effect."[6] As for what sort of effect exactly, Lincoln states on a very general note that authority is best conceived in relational terms "as the effect of a posited, perceived, or institutionally ascribed asymmetry between speaker and audience" and as such can manifest itself in various ways in different cultural and historical surroundings.[7] As a form of communication, authority stands close to persuasion and may lead to or even legitimize the use of force, but if it is necessary to resort to either one of those measures to have an influence, it usually means that authority is lacking.[8] In this part of the study, it will be asked how the ecclesiastical discourse could have contributed to producing such an effect of "asymmetry between speaker and audience."[9] In this section, three core components of the authority of the Church and its representatives will be explored: first, the notion of the Church's teaching will be discussed which will, in turn, call for a further discussion of the topic of apostolic authority and domination. Finally, the attention will be directed to the institutional organization of the Church, the ecclesiastical hierarchy that is to say, and how it was grounded in the religious discourse.

3.1.1   *Teaching*

A central term from the religious discourse contributing to the Church's authority is that of a 'teaching' or 'doctrine,' rendered in Icelandic as *kenning*. It was mediated by *kennimenn* which literally means a teacher.[10] In medieval Iceland it was exclusively used about priests who were, as already discussed, in control of the new technology of literacy which distinguished them from most other people and, of no less importance, gave access to the sacred doctrines of the Church. The term *kenning* referred, broadly, to the knowledge which

---

6   Lincoln, *Authority: Construction and Corrosion*, pp. 10–11.
7   Ibid., p. 4.
8   Ibid., p. 4.
9   To such ends, the source material is read in the sense provided by religion scholar Elisabeth Schüssler Fiorenza that "all discourses about the Divine are articulated in specific socio-political situations, by particular people, with certain interests in mind, and for a certain audience with whom they share cultural codes and religious traditions." Schüssler Fiorenza, *Power of the Word*, p. 196.
10   *Cleasby-Vigfusson*, p. 336.

the Church preserved in its books and learning and the ways in which it was promoted and mediated. It should be noted that an important way for imperial formations like the medieval Roman Church to stay in power over their subjects is to maintain control over the production and mediation of knowledge. Teaching was a highly significant part of of medieval Christian religiosity; accepting it was a *sine qua non* for any Christian, and opposing it meant exclusion. In what follows, the term will be explored with a particular emphasis on how clerical authority was bolstered through the Church's religious discourse in which the teaching exclusively accessible to the clergy, was being constructed as superior to any other knowledge.

3.1.1.1 The Original Teaching

Anybody listening to what was being said in Icelandic churches during Christianity's first centuries would sooner or later come across the word *kenning*. In the sagas of the apostles, a central theme is the apostles' teaching which they deliver to all sorts of audiences they encounter on their travels. The preaching of the apostles could be directly traced to their own teacher, Christ himself, one of whose many attributes was that of a teacher (*kennimaðr*)[11] and a mentor to the apostles (*lærifaðir*).[12] The apostles were speaking the teaching of Jesus through their own mouths as it is described by the apostle Matthew in his saga.[13] An example of how prominent the notion could be in the Church's discourse is found in the following passage from the *Saga of the Apostle Andrew*:

> Þa for Mattheus postoli a braut þaðan ok ut a Blaland, ok leiddi þar margan lyð til guðs fyrir sina *kenning*, ok let þar lif sitt fyrir guðs nafni, þa er hann hafði aðr snuit þeim hinum ofagrliga lyð ok gervan fagran i guðligri tru af sinum *kenningum*. Þegar er Mattheus var a braut farinn, tok Andreas postoli at kenna *kenningar* i borginni berliga. Ok þegar er borgarmenn heyrðu hans *kenningar* þeir er eggiaðir voru af diofuls krapti at svivirða *guðs kenningar* þa toku þeir þegar hondum Andream postola ok drogu hann um borgina innan a hari sva harðliga, at a hverium steini

---

11 *Post*, p. 185.
12 *Post*, p. 185 (Christ as *kennimaðr*). *Post*, p. 342 (Christ as *lærifaðir*).
13 "Þu hefir enn eigi heyrða kenning drottins mins Jesus Kristz af munni minum," [You have not yet heard the teaching of my Lord Jesus Christ from my mouth] *Post*, p. 801. Trans. Roughton II, p. 820. See also the apostle Paul's response to emperor Nero: "En su kenning er mer eigi af monnum gefin, helldr af guði Jesu Kristo ok dyrðar foður," [This doctrine was not given to me by men but rather by God, Jesus Christ, the father of glory] *Post*, 191. Trans. Roughton II, p. 542.

ok stræti var hans blóð set. Postolinn let eigi at helldr af *kenning* sinni, sa er fullr var af miskunn heilags and, ok bað fyrir þeim overðum.[14]

[The apostle Matthew departed and went to Africa, and he brought a large number of people there to God through his *teaching*, and he lost his life there for the name of God after he had converted those inelegant people and made them beautiful in godly faith by his *teachings*. As soon as Matthew was gone, the apostle Andrew began to *teach and to preach* [kenna kenningar] openly in the city. When the people of the city, who were urged on by the power of the Devil to dishonour the *teachings of God*, heard his *teachings*, they immediately seized the apostle Andrew and dragged him by the hair so violently through the city that his blood spilled out onto every stone and street. The apostle, however, who was filled with the grace of the Holy Spirit, desisted in no way from his *teachings*, and he prayed for those unworthy ones.]

Despite the prevalence of the topic of the teaching in the hagiographical sources, one should be careful not to read any complex dogmatic instruction into the religious shaping taking place at the time. In the hagiographic texts, the apostles' teaching can be described in various ways and most often it did not reach a high level of complexity. Surely, most apostolic *vitae* contain at least one speech from an apostle where the audience gets direct access to their teaching. The speeches can vary greatly in length and content, ranging from short recapitulations of the life of Jesus to short theological treatises on topics such as original sin.[15] Some texts contain more speeches than others, like the lengthy sagas of apostles Peter, Paul, Andrew and John. In others there is only one speech like in the *Saga of the Apostles Philip and James* or even none at all as in the *Saga of the Apostle Matthias*. More often than not, however, the teaching itself is left unsaid and key words or phrases kept instead. Thus, the apostles are said to be preaching the teaching of Jesus (or simply preaching Jesus), the teaching of life, words of God, or other equally open description of the teaching.[16] In other instances, they are said to be teaching the correct faith (*tru*

---

[14] *Post*, pp. 320–321. Trans. Roughton II, pp. 613–614. Italics added. As Roughton points out, the passage quoted is an addition by the Icelandic translator to the Latin source text so the word must have been closely linked to the apostles as imagined by a 12th century Icelandic cleric. Roughton I, pp. 201–202.

[15] See the apostle Bartholomew's two speeches for King Polimius in the *Saga of the Apostle Bartholomew*, *Post*, pp. 746–748.

[16] *Post*, p. 165 (faith of Jesus Christ); *Post*, p. 167 (word of life); *Post*, p. 178 (teaching of life); *Post*, p. 328 (preaching Jesus Christ); *Post*, p. 515 (teaching of the Lord Jesus Christ).

retta) and the true faith (*sanna trú*).[17] On other instances the content description is completely left out and the immediate result described. If the teaching is successful, it leads to repentance and conversion and if not, it can lead to anger and violence, as described by the apostle Peter in one of his speeches:

> Þvi mun hverr batna eða versna við helgar kenningar, at sumir leggia a hug, en sumir abbaz við, þa er þeir verða vitaðir fyrir gløpi sina, sva sem þa er drottinn taldi tru fyrir Gyðingum, at sumir hlyddu honum, en sumir stygðuz við hann ok reðu um hann fiörraðum.[18]
>
> [Everyone will either improve or worsen upon hearing the holy teachings, for some wil take it to heart when they are rebuked for their crimes, and some will be vexed, just as when the Lord preached the faith to the Jews: some heeded him, but some were offended and plotted against his life.]

An important feature of the teaching is its universal scope as it was seen to unite the Christian world, from its center to the fringes. Such an idea is rooted in the great commission of Matt. 28:19 where the resurrected Jesus instructs his disciples to spread his teachings around the entire world.[19] The faith which the Church emerging in Iceland preached was, after all, catholic, in Icelandic *almennilig trúa* which literally means that which applies to all men: "ein er almennileg trúa boðuð í öllum áttum heims" [one is the catholic faith preached in all of the world's quarters].[20] Through these and similar remarks it was made clear to the Icelandic audience that the preaching delivered to them was the same elsewhere in the Christian world. Inherent to their identity as Christians was that they belonged to a much larger whole extending around the entire world.[21]

For the universal dispersion of the teaching, the missionary activities of the apostles were imperative. They had received from Jesus "þat hit agæta umboð almattigs guðs at boða hans erindi um allan heim" [the excellent mandate of almighty God to proclaim his message around the entire world].[22] This same

---

17 *Post*, pp. 131, 723, 739 (correct faith); *Post*, p, 372 (true faith).
18 *Post*, p. 178. Trans. Roughton II, p. 521.
19 This particular verse is not preserved in an Icelandic manuscript, neither in Latin nor Icelandic, but it can be assumed with certainty that it was well-known to Icelandic clergy.
20 *ÍH*, p. 22.
21 Sverrir Jakobsson, *Við og veröldin*, pp. 128–129.
22 *Post*, p. 767. An interesting variation of this theme is the turn of the phrase "naliga um allan heim" [almost the entire world] which appears both in an original prologue to the *Saga of the Apostle James* and in what appears to be an original addition to the *Saga of the Apostles Philip and James*. *Post*, p. 736.

understanding is reflected in a sermon to be delivered on the Feast of All Saints where the apostles are described as "þeir, er sjálfur Drottinn valdi af alþýðu og sendi of heim innan að setja grundvöll kristni sinnar, svo að kenningar þeirra efldist of allan heim" [those chosen from the common people by the Lord himself and sent into the world to lay the foundation of his Christianity in order that their teachings might gain in force around the entire world].[23] Another particularly interesting example deserving to be quoted in full is from a sermon intended for delivery on Christmas day.[24] The passage juxtaposes the taxation of Emperor Augustus to the allegiance to Christ's commands, carried around the world by the apostles:

> Cesar, það er höfðingjanafn. Það merkir Krist þann, er heldur höfðingsskap liðinna hluta, nýlegra og óorðinna. Sjá keiseri Augustus sendi boð of allan heim, að hver maður, jafnt auðugur sem fátækur, ungur og gamall, karlar og konur, að hver maður skyldi gjalda honum einn penning heilan, þann er denarius heitir. Sá er við aðra tíu. Svo sendi Dominus vor, Jesús Kristur, postula sína of allan heim, að hver sem einn gyldi honum penning boðorða hans. [...] En þá er þetta var að gjört, þá var allur heimurinn saman samnaður svo vandvirklega, að engi mátti komast undan skattgildinu. Svo er nú engi sá í þessum heimi, er komast megi undan skattgildi konungs vors og Domini Iesu Christi, sá er borinn var í dag til hjálpar heiminum.[25]
>
> [Caesar, it's a chieftain's name. It refers to that Christ which keeps the overlordship of things past, recent and those that have not taken place. This emperor, Augustus, announced to the entire world, that each man, rich and poor, young and old, men and women, that each man should pay tribute to him, an entire coin, which is called a denar. Those responsible for others, ten. In the same way, our Lord Jesus Christ sent his apostles around the entire world, so that each and everyone would pay what is due to his commands. [...] And when this had been done [the counting and taxation of the population of the three thirds of the world: Asia, Africa and Euope], the entire world had been gathered so carefully together that nobody could escape paying tribute. Similarly now, there is nobody in

---

23 *ÍH*, p. 58.
24 A direct source for the passage has not been identified but as de Leeuw van Weenen points out it echoes ideas set forth by Pseudo-Alcuin's *De Divinis Officiis Liber*. "Introduction" in *IHB*, p. 9.
25 *ÍH*, pp. 67–68.

this world who can escape paying tribute to our king and Dominus Jesus Christ, who today was born to save the world.]

In addition to the unmistakable imperial metaphor, which was by no means a rare occurrence in medieval ecclesiastical literature, the passage shows that the teaching of the Church, here equated with heeding the Lord's commands, is considered just as actual and relevant at the moment of the preaching, as it was when it was originally set forth by the apostles.[26] To quickly summarize, the hagiographical literature does not provide a clear outline of what the teaching entailed. What was made clear, however, was that the *kenning* proclaimed in 11th, 12th, and 13th century Iceland was the same around the entire world and, furthermore, reached back to the Church's sacred past; it was the same apostolic teaching they heard of in sagas of the apostles and other saints.

3.1.1.2   Teaching in the Icelandic Free State

For the medieval Icelander, it is likely that the vague outlines of the apostles' teaching were filled with more concrete material through the religious shaping and education they received either from a priest or, more often, at home with their parents or godparents.[27] In its most concise form, the teaching was found in the Apostolic creed and the *Pater noster* which were the only texts that every layperson was obligated to know.[28] The Old Christian Law section states clearly that every man and woman should know the *Credo* and the *Pater noster* and those failing to do so would be subject to punishment of three years of outlawry (*fjörbaugsgarðr*).[29] And even though most people would learn the basic tenets of their Christian religion at home, it can be assumed that they also knew that the demands for a minimum knowedge was made by the Church and that it was the priest's responsibility to make sure that his parishioners knew the most important texts, their significance and the meaning of particular key words.[30] It should also be kept in mind that these texts were

---

26   For another example of an imperial metaphor from an ecclesiastical writing, admittedly not so wide-spread, see for example Walahfrid Strabo's ninth century exposition of the liturgy where he for example states: "Just as Roman emperors are said to have held the absolute rule of the entire world, so the head bishop in the Roman see who holds blessed Peter's office is elevated to the highest position of the entire Church [...]" Alice L. Harting-Correa, *Walahfrid Strabo's* Libellus de exordiis et incrementis quarundam in observationibus ecclesiasticis rerum: *A Translation and Liturgical Commentary*, Mittellateinische Studien und Texte XIX (Leiden, 1996), p. 191.
27   Kí II, p. 203; see also Kí I, p. 368.
28   Angenendt, *Geschichte der Religiosität im Mittelalter*, p. 470.
29   *Grágás*, p. 5.
30   Kí II, p. 203.

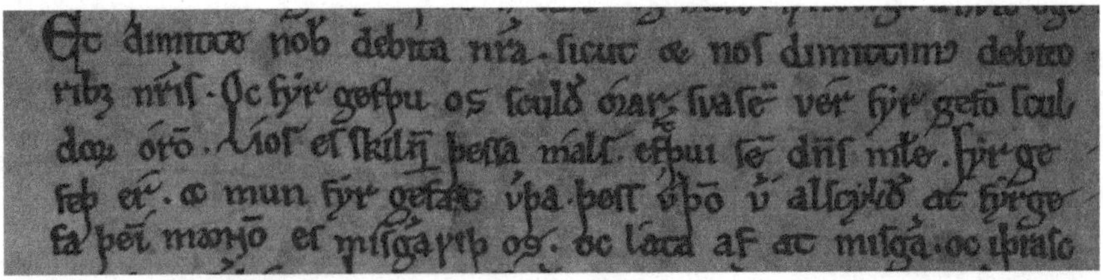

FIGURE 7   Icelandic Homily Book, Stock. Perg. 15 4to, 93r. The Árni Magnússon Institute for Icelandic Studies

presented and most often recited in Latin which was the official language of the teaching so people with no or limited understanding of Latin were thus dependent upon the clergy for access to it.[31]

The *Icelandic Homily Book* contains explanations and commentary of both texts; three on the *Pater noster* and two on the apostolic creed.[32] It can be assumed that these texts reflect how a member of the clergy might have explained the content of these two central texts to Icelandic Christians at the time. The texts provide a version of the confession and the Lord's Prayer in the Icelandic vernacular but the Latin is usually kept very central as well (see figure. 7). In all three versions of the *Pater noster* and one of the *Credo*, each section of interpretation begins by providing the Latin text, then an Icelandic version, ending with a short theological commentary. The other version of the apostolic creed is an extended version in the Icelandic vernacular containing a summary of Christ's life. It is the type of a confession which in German speaking scholarship is called a *Gemeinde-Symbol* and Lilli Gjerløw has pointed out certain similarities with two creeds preserved in the Old High

---

31   Stefán Karlsson has argued that the degree of difference between the versions of the *Pater noster* preserved in the Icelandic vernacular from the High Middle Ages suggests that it had not acquired a status of a fixed formula intended for people to know by heart. Stefán Karlsson, "Drottinleg bæn á móðurmáli," *Studia theologica islandica* 4 (1990), 163. As Arnold Angenendt points out there was a growing tendency in non-Roman Europe throughout the Middle Ages that the *Pater noster*, and the *Credo* as well, were translated into the various vernaculars and that the sacred status of the three *linguae sacrae* – Hebrew, Greek, and Latin (the only applicable one in the West) – gradually receded. Angenendt, *Geschichte der Religiosität im Mittelalter*, pp. 470–471. Keeping in mind that both the Icelandic vernacular and the 'sacred' Latin were, each in its own way, living languages in much use, it does not seem helpful to limit the question of the language of the liturgy to either Latin or vernacular. It is more likely that there was a vivid interaction between the two languages, even in some parts of the liturgy. See also section 2.3.1.2.

32   *Pater noster* in *ÍH*, pp. 39–44, 45–48, and 280–286; *Credo* in *ÍH*, pp. 209–210 and 213–216.

German vernacular which were used for catechetical instruction.³³ There is no reason to give a detailed account of the content of the exegesis found in the commentaries on these texts. Few texts have been commented upon as much as the *Credo* and the *Pater noster* and the *Icelandic Homily Book* mostly reproduces what could be found in similar commentaries around Western Europe.³⁴ What should be pointed out, however, is that these two texts were presented as belonging to the sacred past of the Church. The author of the *Pater noster* was of course Jesus himself who is said to have 'composed' the prayer – as a poet might compose a poem – and 'taught' it to his disciples.³⁵ Similarly, in the Latin version of the creed, which is the apostolic creed's *textus receptus* with an interlinear translation and a commentary, the apostles are described as the authors of the creed. Each article of the creed is assigned to one of the twelve apostles as can be seen on the image below. Peter says *Credo in deum*, Andrew says *et in iesum christum*, and so on (see Figure. 8). This is a tradition which can be traced back to Rufinus of Aquileia and the earliest manuscripts of the *textus receptus* as well as those of the Old Roman Creed.³⁶

Still another way of referring to how the teaching would be mediated was through the gospels (*guðspjöll*), as can be seen for example in the Stave Church Homily's allegorizing of the corner pillars of the church building: "Fjórir hornstafar kirkju merkja fjögur guðspjöll, því að þeirra kenningar eru inar sterkstu stöður allrar kristninnar."³⁷ [The four corner pillars of the church signify the four gospels, because their teachings constitute the strongest foundations of entire Christianity.] The evangelists, frequently referred to in Icelandic as gospel poets (*guðspjallaskáld*), belonged either to the group of disciples like Matthew and John or received their trusty information through other disciples like Luke through Paul or Mark through Peter and thus provided the only

---

33   These are on the one hand the 11th century Wessobrun confession and, on the other, the 12th century Bamberg confession. Gjerløw points out that, like the Icelandic confession, these two texts contain a rare article specifically stating a belief in that Jesus' body on the cross was stuck by a spear and that both blood and water poured out of the side of his chest. Gjerløw, *Liturgica Islandica* 1, p. 24. In her source list, de Leeuw van Weenen does not provide a direct source for the text. "Introduction" in *IHB*, p. 13.
34   Among sources are Alcuin and Caesarius of Arles, but for significant parts direct sources have not been identified. See "Introduction" in *IHB*, pp., 8, 13, and 15.
35   "Postular báðu Drottin vorn kenna sér bæn" [The apostles asked the Lord to teach them a prayer], *ÍH*, p. 39; "En Jesús Kristr, er þessa bæn orti" [But Jesus Christ who composed this prayer], *ÍH*, p. 43. "Orti" is the past tense of the verb "yrkja" which often refers to the activities of poets (*skáld*). Fritzner, s.v. "yrkja."
36   Gjerløw, *Liturgica Islandica* 1, p. 23; "Introduction" in *IHB* p. 13.
37   *ÍH*, p. 150.

FIGURE 8   Icelandic Homily Book, Stock. Perg. 15 4to, 68r. The Árni Magnússon Institute for Icelandic Studies

reliable account for the Christ event.[38] But the significance of the gospels was naturally not restricted to their mere historical value. The reading of the text of the gospel was a religious event in and of itself and marked the high point of the first part of the mass, the service of the word. It was always read by a cleric of a higher order, traditionally a deacon (*djákn*) or the priest himself in the absence of a deacon. As the following passage from a treatise on the mass found in the *Icelandic Homily Book* based on the *Gemma animæ* by Honorius Augustodunensis makes clear, the gospel was the word of God:

> En þá er djákn les guðspjall, þá jarteinir hann Iesum Christum, því að hann boðar þá orð Guðs. Sá er guðspjall les, snýst í norður, því að hann sýnir það, að Guðs orð er til skjóls mönnum á mót djöfli, er norðurátt táknar.[39]
>
> [And when the deacon reads the gospel, he signifies Jesus Christ, for at that point he is proclaiming the word of God. The reader of the gospel faces North thereby showing that the word of God shields men from the Devil, signified by the direction North.]

In medieval theological treatises, hearing the word of God amounted to the presence of Christ in the same way as hearing somebody's voice guaranteed

38   *Post*, p. 181.
39   *ÍH*, p. 185. For a more detailed discussion on the representation of the apostles in early ecclesiastical discourse, see section 3.1.2.1 below.

the presence of the person's body (*Vox Christi*).⁴⁰ Such a religious reality demanded the utmost level of reverence as described in the mass explanation just cited: the congregation should stand, make the sign of the cross, take off their hats and put away their walking rods. The book from which the gospel was read was itself an object of reverence, introduced by a symbolic kiss followed by a formal procession with lights and burning incense.⁴¹ All these ritual practices, as the treatise makes clear through theological allegory, were there for a good reason. Standing up signifies the attention of the mind, the mark of the cross similarly cleans the mind and keeps evil away, removing one's hat signified the importance of keeping the ears open, especially the ears of the mind (*hugskots hlust*). The kiss of the book signified the peace brought around the world by the apostles manifesting itself in the acceptance and confession of the teaching by the people.⁴²

As for the practical outcome of listening to the gospels, they are said to preserve the trinitarian faith (*brenningar trúa*).⁴³ They also contain moral and practical instructions for how to lead one's life. In that sense they are called commandments (*boðorð*) and even laws ("nýjum lögum er í guðspjöllunum standa").⁴⁴ It can be assumed that in the service of the word the gospels were read in Latin so if its content was to reach an audience which did not know Latin it had to be mediated by the cleric. The teaching of the gospels thus provided the ground for the instruction priests gave to their parishioners and extended itself into their homilies and even pastoral care, legitimized with phrases like "as it says in the gospel" ("svo er sagt í guðspjalli").

---

40   Thomas Lentes, "Textus Evangelii: Materialität und Inszenierung des *textus* in der Liturgie," in *'Textus' im Mittelalter: Komponenten und Situationen des Wortgebrauchs im schriftsemantischen Feld*, eds. Ludolf Kuchenbuch and Uta Kleine, Veröffentlichungen des Max-Planck-Instituts für Geschichte 216 (Göttingen, 2016), pp. 138–139.

41   The books from which the gospel was read were of different types in the Medieval Church. There were ordinary gospel books containing the canonical gospels, rarely entire Bibles. They might have contained a list of pericopes, either at the beginning but more often at the end of the manuscript, telling which readings were supposed to be read each liturgical day (*capitularia evangeliorum*). If not, the readings might have been marked out with marginal notations but that was not a particularly frequent practice. Then there existed also books containing the material of the gospel already arranged according to the capitularies, the so-called *evangeliarium* or the evangeliary. Eventually, there was the emergence of the missal which contained all the texts needed for the celebration of the mass. Palazzo, *A History of Liturgical Books*, pp. 86–110.

42   *ÍH*, p. 185.

43   *ÍH*, p. 24.

44   *ÍH*, p. 234 (laws); *ÍH*, p. 261 (commandments).

3.1.2 *Apostolic Authority*

As pointed out by Jan Assmann, authority is grounded in its point of origin, be it a place or a person.[45] In the early Christian discourse in Iceland, one such point of origin was Christ himself as discussed above.[46] Another, even more prevalent in the discourse, is constituted by the apostles and their special relationship to the divine. The tendency to align oneself, one's group, writings, and tradition with an apostle is apparent already in the 1st century with the figures of the apostles and later the emerging notion of apostolicity playing a central role for the development of the early Christian religion.[47] What matters for the present discussion is the privileged position of enjoying a special relationship to the divine. The term 'apostle' (*postoli*) means 'messenger' or 'envoy,' literally 'one who is sent' and in the Christian context the act of sending is generally attributed to God or Christ. Such a mandate is bound to empower and bestow the one who carries it with increased authority. On the level of discourse, it could be said that in the event of competing discourses, a speech act with a stronger claim to apostolicity is immediately aligned more closely with truth and consequently with power. It is much more likely to be heard and is in a stronger position to silence, suppress and even eliminate disagreeing voices. A main concern of the following discussion is to show how the ecclesiastical discourse consistently bolsters the apostle's exalted position as a figure fraught with power. It suggests that a fitting way to describe the position of the apostle as it is constructed is with the concept *dominus* which is inspired by feminist biblical scholar Elisabeth Schüssler Fiorenza's critical theorizing and analysis of early Christian texts.[48] By applying it to the ecclesiastical discourse it is

---

45 Jan Assmann, *Das kulturelle Gedächtnis: Schrift, Erinnerung und politische Identität in frühen Hochkulturen*, Beck'sche Reihe 1307 (München, 2007), p. 71.

46 See section 3.1.1.2.

47 The earliest mention of an apostle is to be found in Paul's letter to the Galatians (1:1): "Paul an apostle—sent neither by human commission nor from human authorities, but through Jesus Christ and God the Father, who raised him from the dead." The Pauline corpus of authentic letters constitutes the group of earliest extant sources for the Christian religion and the letter to the Galatians is usually dated to the period between 50 and 60.

48 Schüssler Fiorenza defines 'kyriocentrism' and 'kyriarchy' in the following way: "Kyriarchy means the domination of the emperor, lord, slave master, husband, the elite freeborn educated and propertied male colonizer who has power over all wo/men and subaltern men. It is to be distinguished from kyriocentrism, which has the ideological function of naturalizing and legitimating not just gender but all forms of domination. Kyriarchal relations of domination are built on elite male property rights over wo/men who are marked by the intersection of gender, race, class imperial domination, as well as dependency, subordination and obedience or second class citizenship." Schüssler Fiorenza, *Power of the Word*, 158. To better fit the linguistic and historical context of this research, it seems apt to replace the Greek word κύριος (master, ruler, lord), from which the words *kyriocentrism*

stressed how the apostles are shown to enter every situation with the intention of demanding submission and obedience and turning the people they come across into subjects of the Lord; in short, dominating.

3.1.2.1 Apostolic Mandate

Although the special relationship between the apostles and the Christian God remains as one of the best known facts about the Christian religion, the topic nonetheless deserves special highlighting, if only to gather some basic information about the representations of the apostles in medieval Icelandic culture. The apostles were highly visible in the spectacle of the Church in Iceland. Like elsewhere in medieval Christian Europe, their position came to be regarded as a theological axiom and as such elevated far beyond doubt. In the cult of the saints, they were located at the very top, second only to Jesus' mother Mary and along with Christ and Mary the most depicted figures of Christian medieval iconography. Countless churches were devoted to them, including some of the most frequented pilgrimage sites in the medieval West and their feast days were among the most highly celebrated in the liturgical calendar. Even though the preservation of Icelandic ecclesiastical source material from the period is limited when compared to many other areas of Western Europe it clearly portrays the considerable extent to which the apostles put its mark on Icelandic culture and religion in various ways.[49]

The basis for the apostles' special relationship and their unique position consists of three encounters of the apostle with the divine; exceptions are apostles Paul and Matthias whose apostolic career differs in significant ways since they were not part of the original twelve.[50] These three encounters consist of: 1) a personal relationship of the apostle with Jesus of Nazareth during his earthly career as a member of the group of disciples who came to witness

---

and *kyriarchy* are derived, with its Latin equivalent *dominus* but in effect it assumes the same position within the hermeneutical framework.

49 For an overview, see Cormack, *Saints in Iceland*.
50 The traditional number of the apostles is twelve but such a number can be problematized on several grounds. Thus, early Christian sources make mention of people outside the group of twelve being called apostles, the apostle Paul being an obvious case in point. Later, Acts 14:4 and 14:14 refers to Paul's companion Barnabas as an apostle whereas Paul himself does not. Paul, on the other hand, might or might not have referred to James the brother of the Lord as an apostle (Gal 1:19) and also a woman named Junia (Rom. 16:7), whom tradition turned into the male Junias, see Eldon Jay Epp, *Junia: The First Woman Apostle* (Fortress, 2005). It should also be mentioned that the canonical lists of the apostles differ among themselves in so far that Matt. 10:2–4 and Mark 3:16–19 include Thaddeus while Luke 6:14–16 (and consequently Acts 1:13) brings in Jude the son of Jacob.

Jesus' life, death and resurrection, 2) being present at the Great Commission as described in Matt. 28:16–20, 3) receiving of the holy spirit from Jesus himself as recounted in John 20:22 but also, appearing more frequently in medieval discourse, through the descension of the holy spirit, who came over the disciples at Pentecost as described in Acts 2:1–13.

All of these encounters figure prominently in 12th and 13th century Icelandic ecclesiastical discourse. The personal relationship of individual apostles with Jesus is depicted in various ways; about some apostles is much to be said, such as Peter and John, primarily because of the substantial amount of information to be found in the gospels, but about others, such as Simon and Jude, close to nothing. Thus, many of the translated *vitae* begin with an account of Jesus' calling of individual apostles. The famous accounts of the calling of Peter and Andrew to become fishers of men stands at the beginning of the *Saga of the Apostle Peter* and the *Saga of the Apostle Andrew* (Matt. 4:19). Similarly, the sagas of apostles John and James sons of Zebedee both open with an account of their calling which, according to the Gospel of Matthew (Matt. 4:21–22), took place only later during the same day that Jesus had called Peter and Andrew.[51] Accounts of events involving Jesus and different apostles serve a similar purpose of portraying the nature of their relationship. The *Saga of the Apostle Peter* duly records events such as Jesus' appointment of Peter as rock of the Church endowed with the power of loosing and binding (Matt. 16:13–19), Peter's three denials of Jesus (Matt. 26:69–75; Mark 14:66–72; Luke 22:56–62; John 18:25–27) and later the threefold acknowledgement of Peter, "You know, Lord, that I love you," ("Þu veist, drottinn, at ek elska þik") as told in the Gospel of John (21:15–19).[52] The *Saga of the Apostle John* mentions that along with Peter both James and John were present at the transfiguration (Matt. 17:1–8)[53] and at the end of the *Saga of the Apostle Thomas* it refers to Thomas' experience of the resurrected Jesus as described in John 20 although Thomas' doubts are practically eliminated and only those parts of the episode cited which affirm his firm belief after he had "touched his hands to the side of the Lord and said: 'You are my Lord and my God'" (John 20:28).[54] That John, James, and James the less were related to Jesus through family ties was probably not unimportant to

---

51 "Drottinn kallaði þá Johannem ok Jacobum bræður á enum sama degi til sinnar fylgðar sem þá Petrum og Andream,"[The Lord called the brothers John and James on the same day as Peter and Andrew into his company] *Post*, p. 513. Trans. Roughton II, p. 710.
52 *Post*, pp. 159–163.
53 *Post*, pp. 412–413.
54 *Post*, p. 727. Trans. Roughton II, p. 742.

the medieval audience and is carefully noted in the source material.[55] Because of the close relationship the apostle John had with his Lord, the *Saga of the Apostle John* is particularly illuminating for showing what kind of an effect a contact with Jesus had on those who stood closest to him, as the following example shows:

> [Þ]a var enum sæla Joani postola logð su virðing til handa, at hann var sofnaðr yfir briosti sialfs guðs sonar, ok hlaut hann þa sva mikla speki af sialfum spektarbrunninum drottni varum Jesu Kristo. Ok sva sem vattaz i heilagri ritningu hans, at hann hefir umfram komiz aðra mennina i sinum skilningi ok nærr flogit guðdominum hinum hæsta i sinu guðspialli, en naliga se vit til annarra manna skilningu at at koma.[56]
>
> [[T]he blessed John was granted the honor of sleeping at the breast of the son of God himself, and it was then that he received such great wisdom from the well of wisdom of our Lord Jesus Christ himself. And just as it is affirmed in his holy writings, that he surpassed other men in his understanding and has flown to nearly the highest divinity in his gospel so that other men lack the wisdom to fully comprehend it.]

Surely, not all apostles could have had as close a relationship with Jesus as the beloved disciple John but all of them, each in his own way, was considered to have an extraordinary connection with the divine even though there was not much information available about them.[57] Knowledge on apostles Philip, Jude,

---

55 *Post*, p. 412 (John), *Post*, p. 513 (James), *Post*, p. 737 (James the Less). The *Saga of the Apostle John* calls James the Less "the brother of the Lord" as some traditions hold. *Post*, p. 417. In the manuscript AM 655 XII-XIII 4to (dated to the late 13th century), it suggests that Simon and Jude were brothers of James the Less and thus also related to Jesus: "Sva segir enn helgi Jeronimus prestr, at þeir havi verit systrungar drottins og brœþr Jacobi, er um varit a dag með Philippo, oc havi Maria verit moþir þeirra, dottir Cleophe og systir Marie drotningar. En eigi hofum ver set a bocum ritað, með hverium atburð þeir comu til fylgþar og foruneytis með drotne varum, en með honum varo þeir allar stundir til hans piningar" [Thus says the holy priest Jerome, that they were the cousins of the Lord and brothers of Jacob, who in springtime has a day with Philip, and that Mary, the daughter of Cleophas and Queen Mary's sister, was their mother. But we have not seen written on books how they came to follow and accompany our Lord, but they were with him every hour until his passion.] *Post*, pp. 791–792.
56 *Post*, p. 413. Trans. Roughton II, pp. 655–656.
57 The title 'beloved disciple' stems from the gospel itself which on several occasions refers to "the disciple whom Jesus loved" whom tradition has since the 1st century equated with John the son of Zebedee. "Pétur postuli vissi [...] að Jesús unni honum mest [The apostle Peter knew [...] that Jesus loved him the most], *Post*, p. 413. The supernatural insights of

Simon, James the Less, and even Matthew, was limited but they enjoyed their position as apostles as members of the original group of twelve.[58] Even though the Christian tradition is rich in details about individual apostles, there was an important sense in which they had received their mandate as a group. Such a collective view of the apostles is much in agreement with the idea that the group of apostles were strongly united, so that the veneration of an individual apostle amounted to a veneration of the entire group and vice versa.[59] Some medieval churches were even devoted to the apostles as a group (*Apostoli*), an Icelandic example being that of the church at Mikligarður in Eyjafjörður.[60]

This is also important to keep in mind when considering apostles such as Paul and Matthias who were well known, especially Paul, but were not members of the original group of the twelve and their apostleship had to be accounted for differently. As told in Acts 9, the risen Jesus appeared to Paul on his way to Damascus and the *Saga of the Apostle Paul*, for the most part a translation of the canonical Acts of the Apostles, opens with that account.[61] Similarly, the passage from Acts 1:12–23 telling of how Matthias was chosen to replace Judas Iscariot appears early on in the *Saga of the Apostle Matthias* but the topic of Matthias' unusual rise to apostleship had already been brought up in the prologue so as to clear out all doubts about his apostolic merits:

> hann var gøddr hinu haleitasta tignarnafni, ok tok þar með gipt heilags anda ok þat hit agæta umboð almattigs guðs at boða hans erendi um allan heim sem aðrir postolar, hann var ok oss gefinn til hofðingia ok forstiora i stað Judas Skarioths, er drottin varn selldi við verði.[62]
>
> [he was endowed with the most sublime rank, and received along with that the gift of the Holy Spirit and the outstanding mandate of Almighty

---

John are again rehearsed in *Post*, p. 420, then in the context of the so-called prologue of John (John 1:1–18).

58 It should be noted that there exist accounts on the calling of both Philip and Matthew in the canonical gospels. As is briefly mentioned in the Gospel of John (1:43), Philip was called by Jesus the next day after the two pairs of brothers were called. *The Saga of the Apostles Philip and James* adds that he was of low origin which according to Kirby is also to be found in the *Legenda Aurea*, Kirby II, 33. *Post*, 735. As for the apostle Matthew, Matt. 9:9 tells of his calling but the earliest Icelandic account of that is AM 655 XII-XIII 4to (1275–1300) which mentioning his strictness as a publican and further merges him with the tax collector Levi which appears in the other synoptics (Mark 2:14; Luke 5:27).

59 See e.g. *ÍH*, pp. 20 and 25 and the epilogue of the *Saga of the Apostle Matthew* in *Post*, pp. 774–775.

60 Cormack, *Saints in Iceland*, pp. 81–82.

61 *Post*, p. 216.

62 *Post*, p. 767. Trans. Roughton II, p. 775.

God to preach his message throughout the world, just like the other apostles. He was also granted to us as a chieftain and leader in place of Judas Iscariot, who sold our Lord for a price.]

Particulars about the calling of individual apostles provided a scriptural basis which surely was important for clerics and others ready to dwell on such matters, but for most listeners it was likely just background information. More likely to have gained a broader audience is the simple fact of the apostles' possession of power and authority which they had received directly from God through their contact with Jesus and the holy spirit allowing them to preach in God's name and perform wondrous deeds. All of the apostles had been accepted by Jesus himself to his group of followers and later sent into the world to proclaim his name. The standard account of that event is the Great Commission (Matt. 28:16–20), only partly extant in Icelandic medieval translations but indirectly referred to on numerous occasions in the religious source material.[63] On numerous occasions, for example when they come across new people or need to prove themselves in one way or the other, the apostles state that they have been sent by God or Jesus and received their power from the same source, clearly referring to the Great Commission. In the *Saga of the Apostle Matthew*, partly preserved in AM 655 IX 4to, one of the oldest manuscripts of the Icelandic manuscript tradition, the apostle Matthew, just after he had slain a terrible dragon, addresses the people present in the following way:

> Høriþ brøþr oc synir, oc aller þeir, es leysa vilia ander sinar fra enom forna dreca, þat er djofle, fyrir heilso yþra sendi goþ mic hingat, at ér firerletet villo scurþgoþa en tryþet skapara yþrom.[64]
>
> [Listen, brothers and sons, and all those who wish to release your souls from the ancient dragon, which is the Devil! God sent me hither for your health, that you forsake the heresy of idol-worship and believe in your creator.]

---

63 In translation it is extant in one of the very oldest Icelandic manuscripts from the 1st quarter of the 13th century, AM 677 4to, where it appears at the end of the translated treatise *De duodecim abusivis saeculi* (*On the Twelve Abuses of the World*), very popular throughout medieval Europe. There, in a final section, it explains the importance of the apostles as legitimate witnesses through whom Christ is made accessible among all nations. *Leifar*, p. 2.

64 *Post*, p. 815. Trans. Roughton II, p. 815.

Also running through the religious discourse of the Church is the apostles' special endowment of the Holy Spirit. On two occasions they had come to receive the holy spirit through what in *The Saga of the Apostle John* is called "tvenn heilags anda ástgjöf" ("twofold gift of love of the holy spirit"), referring on the one hand to Jesus' gift of the holy spirit as narrated in John 20:22 and translated in John's saga as follows: "Siðan bles hann a þa, ok gaf þeim helgan anda og þar með valld at fyrirgefa syndir ollom monnum, þeim er þess væri makligir, en þeim skylldi eigi fyrirgefaz, er þeir villdu at sva væri [Then he blew on them, and gave them the Holy Spirit and with that the power to forgive the sins of all men who were worthy of forgiveness, but those should not be forgiven whom they wished not to forgive].[65] On the other hand, the holy spirit was granted to the apostles on the day of Pentecost: "[Þ]a kom hinn helgi andi yfir þa alla postolana, og toku þeir allir iafna gipt og iafnan styrk og iafna gøzku og atgervi af hans tikomu á hvitasunnudegi; kendu þeir þa ok allir kenningar eptir þat" [[T]he Holy Spirit came over all of them, and they all received equal fortune and equal strength and equal grace and endowments from its coming on Whitsunday. Afterward they all went out and preached the faith.][66]

3.1.2.2   Apostolic Domination

On grounds of their special mandate, the apostles were God's representatives of the highest rank and the most important champions for the advancement of God's reign all around the world. An apostle could be described as a man of God (*Guðs maðr*), holy man of God (*heilagr maðr Guðs*), friend of God (*vinr Guðs*), and God's beloved friend (*ástvinr Guðs*), to give but a few examples of epithets used to demonstrate the proximity between the apostle and God.[67] Of still more significance for the purposes of the present study, however, is the frequent practice of comparing the apostle's connection with God to the relationship between a king or some other worldly lord and his subordinate. The apostles are presented as faithful emissaries promoting the ruler's absolute claim to rule and dominion, by whatever means and despite the consequences. Within such a framework, the apostles are described as the servants of God (*þjónn, þjónustumaðr*), courtiers of God (*hirðmaðr*), and

---

65   *Post*, p. 414. Trans. Roughton II, p. 657 (corrected: "he blew on them" instead of Roughton's "he blessed them").

66   *Post*, p. 770. Trans. Roughton II, p. 781.

67   *Post*, pp. 185, 323, 340, 347, and 716 (friend of God); 325 (holy man of God); *Post*, p. 414 (Christ's beloved friend); *Post*, p. 319 (God's beloved friend). About the term "friend" and its association to sainthood in medieval Iceland, see Jón Viðar Sigurðsson, *Viking Friendship: The Social Bond in Iceland and Norway*, c. 900–1300 (Ithaca, 2017), pp. 72–103.

even God's slaves, underlining the apostle's complete submission to his master.[68] This sort of description is very characteristic for how the figures of the apostles are construed in the ecclesiastical discourse but rarely does it manifest itself more clearly than in the *Saga of the Apostle Bartholomew* in the apostle's second speech before King Polimius of Farthest India (*Hið ysta Indíaland*):

> Ok sva sem þu ser, at konungr stigr yfir ovin sinn ok sendir riddara sina ok liðsmenn i alla staði, þa er ovinr hans hafði velldi yfir ok leggr sitt mark ok eigu a allt, sva gerði og Jesus Kristr, þa er hann ste yfir fiandann, at hann sendi oss i oll lond, at ver rekim a braut alla þiona djöfuls, þá er byggja í hofum og í skurðgoðum, en vér leysum menn úr ánauð þeirra og frá veldi þess er yfir var stiginn.[69]
>
> [And just as you have seen, when a king overcomes his enemy and sends his knights and troops to all the places over which his enemy had power, and places his sign of victory and ownership of everything, Jesus Christ did the same, when he overcame the fiend, for he sent us into all lands, that we should drive away all the servants of the devils that dwell in temples and in idols, and we free men from their misery and from the power of the one who was overcome.]

The apostles are in this sense emissaries who have been entrusted with the assignment of overcoming and expelling whomever stands in the way of their Lord's reign which, as a matter of fact, constitutes the *cantus firmus* of the apostles' sagas: The apostles are sent to subdue.

For further illustrating the position of the apostles, attention should be directed to a term from the Old Icelandic vernacular, frequently appearing in the religious discourse of the Church referring to the different ways in which the apostles are exalted and endowed with power, namely *veldi* (also *velldi* and *vellde*). The word has a considerably broad range of meaning but depending on the context, the term can roughly be said to either refer to power or authority (in Norwegian: *magt, myndighed*) or what belongs to or falls under someone's power or authority (in Norwegian: "hvad der er ens magt og myndighed underlagt"), in many cases a political geographical entity like *Noregs veldi* meaning Norway's dominion or *biskups veldi* which would be the dominion

---

68 In the *Saga of the Apostle Peter*, the apostle Paul proclaims to be a "courtier of the eternal King" [hirðmaðr hins eilífa konungs], *Post*, p. 200.
69 *Post*, p. 748. Trans. Roughton II, p. 763.

of a particular bishop.[70] Both of these senses, primarily political, can certainly prove helpful for explaining the apostle's power but in the ecclesiastical discourse its meaning is expanded so as to include the religious and theological dimensions in at least three interrelated ways, all of which are of great importance for this study. Firstly, it can refer to the rather intangible notion of God's *power over* people as opposed to the Devil's power over people. Secondly, in a political sense, to the dominion of God as a polity or a body of ruled people much related to the political notion of the dominion of a king or a bishop. Finally, to the *power to* perform divine wonders granted to the apostles and by extension other apostolic agents.

Firstly, as can be seen the last citation to the *Saga of the Apostle Bartholomew*, the apostles are presented as agents in an intense power play between God and the Devil contesting for power over people. Both God and the Devil possess their own *veldi* and in that sense the word veldi is often a translation of Latin words such as *dominatio, regnum*, or *potestas*.[71] Although the battle was unfolding on a cosmological level it extended itself throughout all planes of reality and was understood to manifest itself on the temporal level in the fight over the souls of human individuals. From such a perspective, it is important to note that people are never free in the sense of not being under the sway of some superior power; either they were under the control of God or the Devil, *tertium non datur*.

The second of the above mentioned senses of the word *veldi* is closely related to the first one, they could even be described as two sides of the same coin. It does not take a lot of imagination to see how the power of God or his representatives over individuals or sporadic groups of people came to correspond to the notion of a more coherent body of subjects in the sense of a dominion of God or a rule of God and even an empire of God.[72] The apostles' pioneering work of mission constituted the foundation for the earthly manifestation of God's rule which in their time was still in an immature state but would gradually assume the form of the Church. It is highly important to keep in mind for a complete understanding of the Church's politics in the discussion that follows, particularly in the concluding synthetical part of this study, that the understanding of the Church as an expanding religio-political entity bound to reach its zenith

---

70 See the entry on "veldi" in Fritzner, pp. 737–738. A third possibility offered by Fritzner is "3) Betydning; stafr hefir þrenn tilfelli, nafn, figúru, veldi, eða mátt."

71 See *Post*, p. 747, cf. Mombritius I (dominatio), p. 142; *Post*, p. 748, cf. Mombritius I, p. 142 (potestas); *Post*, p. 751, cf. Mombritius I, p. 144 (regnum).

72 *Post*, p. 748, cf. Mombritius I, p. 144 (imperium).

in an eschatological *imperium* of Christ was constantly being rehearsed on the level of discourse.[73]

Thirdly, in order to be able to fulfill their assigned role in the supernatural warfare between God and the Devil, the apostles had been granted power, *veldi*, to perform all kinds of extraordinary things. The discursive manifestations of this sort of power appear frequently in the sagas of the apostles and what remains of this section will be devoted to it, beginning with the following excerpt from the *Saga of the Apostle Thomas*:

> Heilagur, ósýnilegur, óskiptilegur guð, er sendir oss hið himneska ljós drottin vorn Jesúm Krist son þinn, en hann gaf oss postulum sínum það veldi, að vér græddum allar sóttir og gætum það allt, er vér bæðum guð föður í nafni hans sonar.[74]
>
> [Holy, invisible, indivisible God, who sends us the heavenly light our Lord Jesus Christ your son, who gave to us his apostles the power to cure all ills and accomplish all that we ask God the Father in the name of his son]

In such instances, *veldi* is usually a translation of the Latin word *potestas* in its general sense of being capable of doing something.[75] The capabilities granted

---

73 In the *Saga of the Apostle Bartholomew* Christ's eternal "veldi" as described in *Post*, p. 748 is a translation of the Latin "imperium", see "ubi solum eius regnat imperium" from *Passio Sancti Bartolomaei Apostoli*, Mombritius I, p. 142. For source critical observations, see Roughton I, pp. 301–302.

74 *Post*, p. 718 / *Frá Sýrlandi til Íslands*, p. 302. Trans. Roughton II, p. 726. Also later in the same saga, it says that God gave them the "veldi" for the sake of the son: "Þú Guð, skapari allra hluta sýnilegra og ósýnilegra, er oss gafst það veldi fyrir son þinn ..." [You, God, creator of all things seen and unseen, who through your son gave us the power ...] *Post*, p. 723. Trans. Roughton II, p. 734. See also *The Saga of the Apostles Philip and James* where the apostles are also said to have received might: "Hann [Jesus] reis upp af dauða a þriðia degi, ok gaf oss til þess veldi og matt lærisveinum sínum, at gefa syn blindum monnum ok grøða allar sottir ok reisa dauða menn til lifs." [He [Jesus] rose from death on the third day, and gave to us his disciples power and might to give sight to blind men and cure all illnesses and raise dead men to life.] *Post*, p. 739. Trans. Roughton II, p. 752.

75 Cf. a likely Latin source text for the above citation from the *Saga of the Apostle Thomas*: "invisibilis et incomprehensibilis et immutabilis perseverans, qui misisti nobis illuminatorem filium tuum, deum et dominum nostrum Iesum Christum, qui veniens dedit nobis apostolis suis potestatem," Klaus Zelzer's edition, printed in *Frá Sýrlandi til Íslands*, p. 337. See also the *Saga of the Apostle Bartholomew*: "Drottinn vor gaf oss það velldi í nafni sínu," *Post*, p. 750 which is a translation of the following text from a *Passio* of the apostle Bartholomew: "Qui in suo nomine dedit hanc potestatem," Mombritius I, p. 143.

to the apostles are described almost invariably in a formulaic statement like the one just cited where they are said to have received the power to perform miracles (*jartegnir*) like granting sight to the blind, hearing to the deaf, enabling the limp and lame to walk, and raising dead to life. This standard description of the apostolic program, originally found in the Book of Isaiah (32:3–4), is in its medieval versions, based on Jesus' command to the apostles as found in Matt. 10:8 and Jesus' own activities as described in the gospels (Matt. 11:5; Luke 7:21; translated into Icelandic in the *Saga of the Apostle James* (*Post* 518)). Not infrequently is it complemented by mentioning their teaching and preaching activities leading people away from error and idol worshiping. The obvious power needed to perform such deeds was in and of itself a sign of the apostle's extraordinary relationship with Christ. In theological principle it was not even the apostle himself who was working the miracles in his own might but Christ working through the apostle. This is evident from the many occasions in which the apostle performs a miracle after having said a prayer addressed directly to Christ or stated explicitly that the particular deed is being done in the name of Jesus.[76] It is likely, however, that such a distinction was not always clear or highly significant to a popular audience since obviously the apostles possessed power and enjoyed a level of sanctity of their own.

Through the practice of wondrous deeds, the apostles were able to carry out their duty and calling to serve their Lord at the same time they were expanding God's sphere of dominion. The sagas of the apostles consist mainly of episodes which each in its own way presents the audience with a variation of the major theme of the frequently rehearsed apostolic formula.[77] The episodes describe the apostles' encounter with people, demons, dragons and other figures whose receptiveness to their proclamation differs immensely. Collectively, these encounters amount to the narrative of the early spread of the Christian religion as it was known to people in the Middle Ages. On the grounds of their role in such texts, the apostles became stereotypes for missionaries and their work similarly paradigmatic for how missionary work was perceived, reproduced, and practiced in the medieval West. Such narrative episodes were also the

---

76 See e.g. *Post*, pp. 329, 718, 750. Such an appeal was sometimes left untranslated, see for instance the following command from the *Saga of the Apostle Paul*: "In nomine Jesu Cristi byþ ec þer, ohreinn andi, at þu farer braut fra kono þessi," [In nomine Jesu Cristi I command you, unclean spirit, to leave this woman] *Post*, p. 220.

77 See discussion in Benedicta Ward, *Miracles and the Medieval Mind: Theory, Record and Event 1000–1215* (London, 1982), pp. 170–171. For such formulaic description of the apostolic program see *Post*, p. 185 (Peter), p. 320 (Andrew), p. 417 (John), p. 719 (Thomas), p. 737 (Philip), p. 739 (James the Less), p. 750 (Bartholomew), p. 786 (Simon and Jude), p. 818 (Matthew).

most important means by which the power and authority of the apostle was presented, not only through his success in performing his deeds but also their dominating position from which they demanded obedience and submission. Although the apostles are frequently described as humble in appearance and attitude and amicable in demeanor, their structural position is always that of a conqueror or, to come back to Schüssler Fiorenza's hermeneutic framework, a *dominus*.[78] In any event of resistance, the apostles invariably come out on top and any audience familiar with the genre would expect it to play out in the following way:

1) Apostle encounters resistance
2) Apostle overcomes resistance
3) Witnesses to the encounter accept the Christian faith

There are both minor and major variances of this scheme among the great number of episodes existing in the source material, but as a general description for the apostles' encounters with the external world the above structure holds true. Only in the case of their ultimate defeat as martyrs, which was not even the fate of all apostles since the apostle John died in old age, does it not apply, but even then, their martyrdom was often presented as a victory (*píningarsigur*) and would only boost their elevated status (see Figure 9).

Through the many episodes of the apostles' encounters, it becomes clear that an apostle is capable of affecting his surroundings in various ways. One way, as already noted, consists of his capabilities of performing miracles. Another would be through persuasion as they present their audience with

---

78   For examples of the apostle's humble attire, see the following citation from the *Saga of Apostles Simon and Jude*: "Af því styggiz þer eigi við herfiligan fatabuning okkarn, þviat þeir hlutir leynaz fyrir innan, er þer megit af þeim finna eilifa dyrð ok lif," [Therefore do not abhor our ragged apparel, for those things by which you may find eternal glory and life are concealed on the inside], *Post*, p. 783. Trans. Roughton II, p. 799. See also the reasoning behind Matthias having been chosen to apostledom in the *Saga of the Apostle Matthias*: "En sva sem Mathias var pryddr morgum öðrum mannkostum, þa er þo þat fra sagt, at litillætit hafi mest upphafit hann til ennar mestu tignar" [But although Matthias was adorned with many other virtues, it is related that it was humility that raised him to the highest rank], *Post*, p. 770. Trans Roughton II, p. 781. See also *ÍH:* "Dúfur kallast þeir við glugga sína, því að þeir litu einföldum augum til allra hluta, þeirra er þeir sáu á jörðu, og girntust þeir engra hluta líkamlegra" [Doves they are called at their windows, for they looked with simple eyes to all things they saw on earth and not did they yearn for any bodily thing], *ÍH*, p. 21. For examples of their gentle manner, see the description of John as "bliðligr ok glaðligr ok þekkiligr i ollu yfirbragði" [pleased and happy and handsome in his whole demeanor] *Post*, p. 432. Trans. Roughton II, p. 690. See also the following description of the apostle Bartholomew: "Ávallt er hann með hinum sama hug, blíður er hann jafnan og glaður" [He is singleminded in disposition, so that he is always cheerful and never unhappy]. *Post*, p. 745. Trans. Roughton II, p. 757.

FIGURE 9   An image showing the crucifixion of the apostle Andrew dating to the 13th century. Andrew's X shaped cross is missing. The statue belonged to the church at Teigur in Fljótshllíð. National Museum of Iceland

the teaching they had been entrusted with.[79] In addition, at least three ways in which the apostles affected their surroundings should be mentioned since they were bound to increase the awe and reverence related to the figure of the apostle. First, the simple fact of their presence is often shown to have wondrous effect on both material things and living beings, secondly, their prayers are described as extremely powerful, and thirdly, they are also frequently portrayed to successfully get their way through rebuke and demand for obedience.

A number of episodes from the apostles' sagas describe how it is simply enough for the apostles to show up in a particular place for their influence to become manifest. Frequently it is often demons who sense the apostles' presence first, reminiscent of gospel episodes like Jesus' healing of the Gerasene

---

79   See section 3.1.1 above.

demoniac (Mark 5:1–13). This is for example the case in the *Saga of the Apostles Simon and Jude* describing the apostles entering a pagan temple: "Þá voru postularnir höndlaðir og leiddir til sólarhofs. En er þeir gengu í hofið, þá kölluðu djöflar fyrir óða menn: 'Hvat søkit þit at oss, postolar guðs lifanda? Ver brennum i tilkvamu ykkarri'" [The apostles were seized and led to the temple of the sun. When they entered the temple, devils cried out from demoniacs: "What do you want from us, apostles of the living God? We burn at your arrival!].[80] As the apostle Matthew is dealing with the sorcerers Zaroes and Arfaxath, who are accompanied by fierce flying dragons, the dragons are said to have reached the apostle's knees and immediately fallen asleep.[81] The apostles' presence could also affect inanimate objects as can be seen when the apostle Andrew wanted to save his fellow apostle Matthew from a dungeon where he was being held prisoner, that "er Andreas postuli kom at myrkvastofunni, þa spruttu þegar fra lasarnir, og skein lios solu biartara fyrir honum i myrkvastofuna" [[w]hen the apostle Andrew went up to the prison door, however, the locks immediately burst open, and a light brighter than the sun lit his way into the prison].[82] On top of such wondrous events, it should not be overlooked that the people immediately start gathering around the apostles for no apparent reason except their powerful presence when they arrive in a new territory.

In contrast to the apostles' simple presence, there is ample evidence in the source material showing them being more active in manipulating their surroundings, for example through prayers or other verbal exchange. On numerous occasions the power of the apostles' words are shown to strongly influence people and other beings of less terrestrial nature. As for the power of the apostles' prayers, *The Saga of the Apostle Andrew* is particularly rich in examples. On one occasion Andrew prays "[o]k i þvi bili varð landskialfti mikill ok þar með reiðarþrumur storar og fell iarlinn or hasæti sinu, ok allir fellu til iarðar, þeir er aðr satu. Moðir sveinsins fell allt til jarðar ok do þvi næst" [[a]t that moment there was a huge earthquake accompanied by great and terrible thunder, and the earl fell from his throne and all those who had been sitting there fell to the ground].[83] A little later it tells of how Andrew's prayer made him able to calm a storm and still further into the saga it is shown how the power of his prayer was capable of granting life to the dead.[84] Not infrequently does the line between the apostle's prayer and his command for obedience become

---

80   *Post,* p. 788. Trans. Roughton II, p. 807.
81   *Post,* p. 814.
82   *Post,* p. 320. Trans. Roughton II, p. 612.
83   *Post,* p. 322. Trans. Roughton II, p. 617.
84   *Post,* p. 324 (storm) and p. 333 (raises body cast upon the shore from the dead).

vague like the following episode involving the apostles Jude and Simon and a pair of tigers shows:

> Þat gerðiz enn, at dyr .ii. akafliga grimm, þau er tigris heita, urðu laus or bondum ok slitu allt og rifu, þat er fyrir þeim varð ok þau mattu taka. Þa flyði allr lyðr til postola guðs. En þeir hetu a Jesum Krist og buðu dyrunum, að þau sefaðiz ok fylgði þeim heim til huss með ser. En þau hlyddu boðorði postolanna ok voru i husi þeirra þria daga.[85]
>
> [It also happened that two vehemently ferocious wild animals called tigers got loose from their chains and tore into and ripped apart everything in their way, or whatever they could get hold of. Everyone fled to the apostles of God, and they called on Jesus Christ and commanded the animals to be calm and to follow them home. The tigers heeded the apostles' command and remained in their house for three days.]

Such events are related both through the usual form of 3rd person narrative but also through the more vivid exchange in the 1st person which was bound to have a stronger influence on the audience present. It is helpful to keep in mind when considering the many occurrences of direct speech in textual sources such as the apostolic *vitae* that they are performative texts. When reading a particular saga about an apostle, in the refectory of a monastery, during holy orders and perhaps less frequently in mass, examples of intense prayers, heated verbal exchange between an apostle and his antagonist or a booming apostolic command would have provided the reader with a good opportunity to carry out a performance as effective and memorable as possible. Consider, for example, the following excerpt from *The Saga of the Apostle John*:

> Ok er allir menn höfðu sva gort, sem postolinn bauð, þa mælir postolinn biartri röddu, sva at allir menn heyrðu: „Drottinn minn Jesu Kriste, ek bið þik, at þu briotir niðr hofit þetta með ollum þeim skurðgoðum, sem i þvi eru, sva at engum manni verði mein at, en menn megi at sönnu þvi trua ok vita, at þetta hof Gefionar og skurðgoð hefir djofull bygt en eigi Guð." Og iafnskiott sem postolinn hafði þetta mællt, þa brotnaði allt senn hofit ok þau öll skurðgoð, er i þvi voru, og siðan varð þat allt at dupti einu.[86]
>
> [After everyone did as the apostle ordered, the apostle spoke in a clear voice, so that everyone could hear: "My Lord Jesus Christ, I pray you to

---

85   *Post*, p. 786. Trans. Roughton II, p. 807.
86   *Post*, p. 430. Trans. Roughton II, pp. 687–688.

demolish this temple and all of the pagan idols in it, so that no one is injured, and so that people may truly believe in you and know that the Devil, and not God, has built his temple of Gefion and the idols" As soon as the apostle said this the temple and all the idols that were in it were demolished at once, and it all turned to dust.]

Even more likely to give a strong impression of the apostle's power through a dramatic performance are the second person direct commands and rebukes which are close to indispensable to any account of an apostle's conflict with an adversary. In such moments, in contrast to the depiction of the apostles as kind and peaceful, it becomes manifest that when there is something endangering their mission, all kindness is set aside and whatever power and authority the apostle had access to was used.[87]

3.1.3 *Hierarchy*

Even though the term hierarchy is not to be found in the source material, the notion of a particular organization of power through an arrangement of offices is of high significance in the ecclesisatical discourse. This ecclesiastical hierarchy has its origins in the Church's sacred past and it was divinely instituted. Priests and bishops received a good deal of reverence through their position in this system in addition to their role and appearance as celebrants in the liturgy. Their role segregated them from others, a segregation accentuated with

---

[87] For such examples: Paul to a certain wise woman: "In nomine Jesu Cristi, byþ ec þer, ohreinn andi, at þu farer braut fra kono þessi" [In nomine Jesu Cristi, I command you, unclean spirit, to leave this woman], *Post,* p. 220; Andrew to an unclean spirit possessing a boy: "Fly þu, ovinr mannkyns, fra þioni guðs. Ok þegar flyði hann fra honum øpandi" [Flee, you enemy of mankind, away from the servant of God. And immediately he ran away from him screaming], *Post,* p. 323; Andrew to demons in the city of Nicaea: "Fari þer braut i þurra staði ok avaxtalausa, ok gerit engum manni mein, þar er nafn drottins verðr kallat, uns þer takit skyllda kvol helvitis loga." Er hann hafði þetta mællt, þa yldu fjandarnir og hurfu fra syn lyðsins" [Go from here into a dry and barren place, and do harm to no man who calls upon the name of the Lord, until you suffer the torments of hellfire."] When he had said this, the fiends howled and disappeared from the sight of the people.] *Post,* p. 324. Trans. Roughton II, p. 620; Andrew to the earl Egeas: "Heyrðu, dauða sonr og elldibrandr eilifs loga! Hlyð þu mer þræli og postola drottins mins Jesu Kristz! [Hear me, son of death and firebrand of eternal flame! Listen to me, the servant and apostle of my Lord Jesus Christ], *Post,* p. 340. Trans. Roughton II, p. 647; Bartholomew to a demoniac: "Þegi þu, ohreinn andi, og far fra honum" [Be silent, unclean spirit, and leave him], *Post,* p. 745. Trans. Roughton II, p. 758; Bartholomew to a demon living in an idol: "Ef þu villt eigi, at ek senda þik i undirdiup, þa gakk þu brott," [If you do not wish me to send you to the deepest abyss, then leave], *Post,* p. 749. Trans. Roughton II, p. 766.

differences in looks and attire, but it was their position in a divinely instituted hierarchy which ultimately decided the nature of the power they possessed.

3.1.3.1 Primatus Petri

There is nothing unexpected about the representation of the apostle Peter in early Icelandic ecclesiastical discourse. All his traditional attributes are found, both in sermons and sagas. In what follows, the most significant Petrine themes will be explored, particularly those relating to how the authority of Rome and the pope was being constructed. In the beginning of the *Saga of the Apostle Peter*, Peter is introduced as the *princeps apostolorum*, 'chieftain among other apostles' (*hofðingi annarra postola*)[88] and 'the gatekeeper of the kingdom of heaven' (*durvǫrðr himinrikis*)[89]

Peter's status as the leader of the apostles is underpinned by biblical passages, a central one being that of Matt. 16:16–19 where Jesus describes Peter as the rock upon which he will build his Church. He receives the keys to the kingdom of heaven and the power of binding and loosing. It appears as a part of a string of Petrine New Testament passages placed at the beginning of his saga and deserves to be quoted in full:

> Þa svaraði Simon Petrus: Þu ert Kristus sonr guðs lifanda." Jesus mællti við hann: "Sæll ertu Simon dufu sonr, þviat eigi vitraði þer þetta holld ok bloð, helldr faðir minn er a himnum er. En ek segi þer, at þu skallt heita Petrus - en þat er steinn a vara tungu - ok mun ek yfir þann stein smiða kristni mina ok gera sva styrka, at eigi munu helvitis hlið mega i mot henni; ek gef þer lykla himinrikis, ok allt þat er þu bindr a iorðu, skal a himnum bundit.[90]
>
> [Simon Peter answered: "You are Christ, the son of the living God." Jesus said to him: "Blessed are you Simon, son of a dove, for flesh and blood did not reveal this to you, but rather my father who is in heaven. But I say unto you, that you shall be called Peter - that is stone in our language - and upon this stone I will build my church and make it so strong that the gates of Hell will not be able to oppose it; I give to you the keys to the kingdom of heaven, and everything that you bind on earth shall be bound in heaven.]

---

88 Roughton translates it as "the leader of the other apostles" which does not quite capture the connotation that the word "hofdingi" might have had among 12th and 13th century audiences. *Post*, p. 159. Trans. Roughton II, p. 487.
89 *Post*, p. 159. Trans. Roughton II, p. 488. *ÍH*, p. 123.
90 *Post*, p. 161. Trans. Roughton II, p. 489.

Together with Luke 22:32 and John 21:15–17, this passage was cited most frequently as the religious foundation for the authority of the pope and the Roman See. Studies on the history of the interpretation of Matt. 16:16–19, however, have shown that during the Middle Ages such an understanding was only one of several possible interpretations and until the reign of Innocent III (r. 1198–1216) not even a prevailing one.[91] Although the text was used in support of the primacy of the bishop of Rome as early as the works of popes Leo I (r. 440–461) and Gelasius I (r. 492–496), exegetical and theological works show that it did not belong to the mainstream of interpretations until much later.[92] Throughout Late Antiquity and much of the Middle Ages, two other interpretations remained more popular, both of which do not understand Peter as the 'rock' on which the Church is built. First, according to the 'eastern' interpretation, so-called because of how prevalent it was in Greek exegesis since it was originally set forth by Origen in the 3rd century, Peter stands as a type for all Christians and it is not him personally that is the 'rock' that Jesus speaks of but his confession of faith. This interpretation was advocated in the West by late antique authors such as Ambrose, Hilary of Poitiers, and Ambrosiaster. Second, there was the christological interpretation, frequently named after Augustine who repeatedly promoted it in his writings. According to that interpretation, Peter could be seen as a 'second' foundation for the Church, at best. With recourse to the 'rock' of 1Cor. 10:4, it is Christ who is the only rock and fundament on which the Church stands.[93] The third option espoused by medieval exegetes was the one which sees Peter and later the pope as the rock in the text. The sermons of Pope Leo I to the pontificate are often cited among the earliest examples where he directly links his authority to the confession of Peter.[94]

---

91 For a detailed overview of the pericope's history of interpretation during the Middle Ages, see Karlfried Froehlich, "Saint Peter, Papal Primacy, and the Exegetical Tradition, 1150–1300," in *The Religious Roles of the Papacy: Ideals and Realities*, 1150–1300, ed. Christopher Ryan, Papers in Mediaeval Studies 8 (Toronto, 1989), pp. 3–43. With a broader time span and more condense is Ulrich Luz's discussion in his *Matthew 8–20*, Hermeneia (Minneapolis, 2001), pp. 370–375.

92 Donald J. Grimes provides interesting early medieval examples from the British Isles by showing that neither Pseudo Jerome nor Bede the learned were thoroughly papal in their interpretation, even though they are aware of the significance of Peter's role. Donald J. Grimes, "Petrine Primacy: Perspectives of two Insular Commentators (A.D. 600–800)," *Proceedings of the PMR Conference* 12/13 (1987–1988), 149–158.

93 1Cor. 10:4 (Vg.): "et omnes eundem potum spiritalem biberunt bibebant autem de spiritali consequenti eos petra petra autem erat Christus." Elsewhere in the same epistle, it says that there can be no other *fundamentum* than Christ, see 1Cor. 3:11 (Vg.): "fundamentum enim aliud nemo potest ponere praeter id quod positum est qui est Christus Iesus."

94 Madigan, *Medieval Christianity*, pp. 124–126.

Whatever is properly done by the bishop of Rome should be ascribed to Peter, the rock who provides his successors with his strength.[95] Such an interpretation runs through papal documents, letters and decrees throughout the Middle Ages, for example *Decretum Gelasianum* in which Matt. 16:18 is cited as proof for the divine and not human origin of the primacy of the pope and the 12th century law collection *Decretum Gratiani*.[96]

The Icelandic translation quoted above, the earliest one preserved, clearly reflects the Roman interpretation by adding a well-known etymological explanation of the meaning of Peter's name to the text of the Vulgate.[97] It can be assumed that this etymology was well known among Icelanders at the time.[98] By doing so, the translator directed the audience towards a Roman interpretation of the passage in a decisive way. It is difficult to identify the rock on which the Church is built as anything else—be it the faith of the Christian or Christ himself—than Peter, and his successors in Rome by extension, when the text already states that Petrus "means stone in our language" ("en þat er steinn a vara tungu").[99] The translation further eliminates the ambivalence produced by the difference between 'Petrus' and 'petra,' which authorities such as Augustine used for their exegesis.

This is further commented upon in the following passage of the *Saga of the Apostle Peter*, a translation of Matt. 18:15–17 and Matt. 18:21–22, introduced by the translator as how "the Lord revealed to Peter how he was to use this power (*velldi*)."[100] In the case of a sinning brother, he should be first reproached in private and if that does not work out, then in a group of two or three others. If that turns out to be unsuccessful then he should be reproached before a crowd in church. In the original context of the Gospel of Matthew, Jesus is speaking

---

95   Frequently cited are sermons 3 and 4 given on the anniversary of Leo's elevation to the pontificate. Available in English translation in St Leo the Great, *Sermons*, trans. Jane Patricia Freeland C.S.B.J. and Agnes Josephine Conway, S.S.J. *Fathers of the Church* 93 (Washington, D.C., 1996), pp. 17–32 and sermon 82 given at the feast of Peter and Paul, *PL* 54: 422C-428A.

96   The canons in which Matt. 16:18 is used in such a way are provided by Franz Gillmann, "Zur scholastischen Auslegung von Mt 16, 18." *Archiv für katholisches Kirchenrecht* 104 (1924), 41–53, esp. pp. 42–43.

97   Matt. 16:18 (Vg.): "Et ego dico tibi, quia tu es Petrus, et super hanc petram aedificabo Ecclesiam meam, et portae inferi non praevalebunt adversus eam." The meaning of Peter's name is also clearly stated in John 1:42 which does not, however, survive in translation until the 14th century manuscript *Codex Scardensis*, where it is included both in the *vita* of Peter, *Post*, 2, and Andrew, *Post*, 354.

98   *ÍH*, p. 22.

99   *Post*, p. 161.

100 *Post*, p. 161. Trans. Roughton II, p. 489.

to the disciples as a group and not only Peter as it is presented in this version of the *Saga of the Apostle Peter*. In the gospel itself, Peter is not directly addressed until the question on the limits of forgiveness and how often he should forgive the one who sins against him (Matt. 18:21–22). By presenting the entire passage as an instruction for how Peter should exercise his authority, the *Saga of the Apostle Peter* throws a different light on words such as 'reproach' (*hirta* in Icelandic, *corripere* in Latin) and 'heed' (*hlyðnaz* in Icelandic, *audire* in Latin) which in its original context has to do with conflict solving among equals in the Church. What in the original context of the gospel has to do with conflict solving within the Church, the *Saga of the Apostle Peter* turns into a discussion on Petrine authority and church discipline. There is an interesting ambivalence to this passage. On the one hand, Peter is in the position of demanding obedience, reproaching and in the case of a sinning brother unwilling to heed his words, even punishment: "En ef hann hlyðnaz þa eigi þer, þa se hann sem bersyndugr eða heiðinn."[101] [If he still does not obey you, he should be treated as a shameless sinner or a heathen.] On the other hand, he receives the command to show practically boundless mercy to the sinner.

However, from what can be gathered about the representation of Peter in medieval Iceland, it rather accentuated the dominating aspects of the apostle. Certainly, following the Petrine passages of the gospels, Peter is shown as a frail human who fears, doubts, commits violent acts and ultimately denies his Lord three times.[102] But in the early ecclesiastical discourse, this would only become

---

101   *Post*, p. 161.
102   Fearing: "Hræðumst vér, bræður, er sæll Petrus apostolus hræddist" [We fear, brothers, as the apostle Peter feared] *fH*, p. 93; Doubting: "En er hann [Petrus] sa sio storan ok vind mikinn, þa hræddiz hann. [...] Þa retti drottinn hond sina til hans ok mællti við hann: "Litil er trua þin, fyrir hveria sok efaðir þu nu?" [But when he [Peter] saw such huge waves and such a strong wind, he was afraid [...] The Lord reached out to him and said: "Your faith is weak; why did you doubt?] *Post*, p. 160. Trans. Roughton II, p. 488. Violence: "Dominus lét eigi hefna sín né verja sig, þá er hann var höndlaður og bundinn af Gyðingum, heldur græddi hann eyra þræls eins, er Petrus hafði af höggvið" [The Lord did not want to be revenged nor defended when he was captured and bound by Jews, but rather healed the ear of a slave whose ear Petei had chopped off], *fH*, p. 96; "En er sendimenn Gyðinga höndluðu Jesúm, þá brá Símon Pettar sverði og hjó af eyra ið hægra af þræli einum, en sá hét Malkus" [But when the envoys of the Jews had captured Jesus, Simon Peter took up a sword and chopped the right ear of a slave named Malkus], *fH*, p. 245; "þa bra Petrus sverði ok hio eyra af einum þræli Gyðinga, ok syndi sva öruggleik sinn" [Peter drew a sword and hewed off the ear of one of the Jews' servants, thereby showing his fearlessness], *Post*, p. 161. Trans. Roughton II, p. 490; Denial: "Petrus neitti Kristi og leiðréttist" [Peter denied Christ and was redeemed], *fH*, p. 98; "Hví væri eigi Pétar postuli í munni hans, þá er hann neitti Drottni?" [Why would the apostle Peter not be in his [Leviathan's] mouth, as he rejected the Lord], *fH*, p. 109; "Þá neitti Pétur með svardaga,

the background out of which Peter would emerge as a strong leader, a champion of faith and an a prime example of a repenting sinner. Unlike Judas who committed his misdeeds of evil and repented in despair (*örvilnun*), Peter's sins were caused by weakness and he repented with hope (*vilnun*), as is explained in the sermon *Passio Domini* from the *Icelandic Homily Book*.[103] Another sermon from the Homily Book, entitled *Resurrectio Domini*, encourages its audience to look to Peter for hope, especially in case of weakness or loss of faith.[104]

It should also be noted that in 11th and 12th century Icelandic culture, Peter's willingness to grab arms in defence of his Lord would not necessarily have been interpreted as a negative trait, even though two sermons from the *Icelandic Homily Book* take a critical stance towards the apostle's behavior.[105] Such a tolerant attitude is best seen in the *Saga of the Apostle Peter* where the translator adds that by cutting the ear of the servant, Peter is said to have been "showing his fortitude" ("syndi sva öruggleik sinn").[106]

After his threefold confession of love, Peter emerges as the true leader of the apostles. This confession, a translation of John 21:15–19, is explicitly explained by the translator as a recompense for his denial of Christ.[107] After this, the source of the saga has shifted from the gospels to the Acts of the Apostles. Peter gives his Pentecost-speech, successfully calling the audience to repentance. Along with the Holy Spirit, Peter is introduced as the one who managed the mission of the apostles.[108] He gives inspired speeches, converting people by the thousands, performs miracles and fights any opposition vigorously.[109] It

---

að hann hafði aldregi með Jesú verið" [Then Peter swore that he had never accompanied Jesus] *ÍH*, p. 246; "En hann neitti i hvert sinn, er þau spurðu, ok kvaðz eigi vita, hver Jesus var," [Peter denied everything they asked and said that he did not know who Jesus was] *Post*, p. 161. Trans. Roughton II, p. 491.

103   *ÍH*, p. 98.
104   *ÍH*, p. 110.
105   Esp. *ÍH*, p. 96. See also *ÍH*, p. 245.
106   *Post*, p. 161.
107   "En til þess beiddi hann Petrum þrysvar iata elsku sinni, at hann bøtti þat i þrefalldri iatningu, er hann hafði guði þrysvar neitat." [He asked Peter to acknowledge his love three times in order to repair in a threefold acknowledgement the fact that Peter had denied God thrice.] *Post*, p. 163. Roughton II, p. 493.
108   "Postolar skylldu fara a yms lond, sem siðan for fram at vitran heilags anda ok fyrirsogn Petrs postola." [the apostles should go to various countries, which occurred after the vision of the Holy Spirit and under the leadership of the apostle Peter] *Post*, p. 164. Cf. Roughton II, p. 496.
109   For speeches, see for example Peter's pentecostal speech on *Post*, pp. 163–165. "En er Petrus hafði þetta mællt, þat toku tru ok skirn þriar þusundir manna, ok voru staðfastir a bønum ok hlyðnir kenningum postulanna." [After Peter said this, three thousand men accepted the faith and were baptized, and they were steadfast in their prayers and heeded

is the image of the strong Peter that dominates the largest part of Peter's vita. And whatever ambivalence might mark Peter's persona in the New Testament source material, it was uniformly interpreted with the outcome of Peter as an example of hope and repentance. Later in the story, in his conflict against Simon Magus, Peter's fear is also completely disappeared: "Eigi mun ek hræðaz engla þina, en þeir munu mik hræðaz i krapti drottins Jesu Kristz" [I will not fear your angels, but they will fear me by the power of my Lord Jesus Christ].[110] And furthermore, while sitting in a dungeon: "Petrus hræddiz eigi pislir, helldr let hann at bøn lyðsins ok gerðiz braut at fara."[111] [Peter did not fear suffering, but he listened to the prayers and made his departure.]

Not to be overlooked are Peter's capabilities of producing fear and awe. These elements of Peter's character are especially prominent in Petrine material based on other source texts than the New Testament although they can also be found there, beginning with the canonical Acts of the Apostles. A particularly effective account, translation of Acts 5:1–11, tells of the couple Annanias and Saphira who did not heed the commands of the apostles to share everything with the Christian community but hid some of the profit from a field they sold. When Peter found out about this he severely rebuked Annanias, explaining that he had thereby not lied to men but God. Upon hearing Peter's scolding, Annanias fell down dead as did his wife Saphira after she persisted in lying about hiding the profit. The passage ends by stating that: "Nu varð hræzla mikil yfir ollum lyð"[112] [All the people were stricken with great fear.] Linking directly to this is a version of Acts 5:12–42 where it is highlighted that even Peter's shadow could heal and make miracles. What follows is a recapitulation of Acts 5–12 including Peter's vision, the conversion of Cornelius, the important account of the angel rescuing Peter as he awaited his execution chained in prison (*vincula Petri*).

All of this leads up to the encounter with Simon Magus which is biblically based in Acts 8 but came to be greatly expanded in the patristic and medieval traditions. After Peter had been serving as bishop at Antiochia for seven years, he hears that Simon Magus is preaching his heresy in Rome:

---

the apostle's teachings.] *Post*, p. 164, Roughton II, p. 496; "En er Petrus hafði lokit tölu sinni, þa toku tru fimm þusundir manna, er heyrt hofðu þessi orð." [When Peter finished his speeech five thousand men who heard his words accepted tha faith.] *Post*, p. 165. Roughton II, p. 498.

110 *Post*, pp. 187–188. Trans. Roughton II, p. 536.
111 *Post*, p. 196.
112 *Post*, p. 166. Trans. Roughton II, p. 500.

> Því var þat ráð allra manna kristinna, at Petr postoli føri til Romaborgar ok gengi a mot villu Simonar ok eyddi, ok þotti þat makligast, at hinn øzti hofðingi kristninnar gengi a moti hofðingia villumanna.[113]
>
> [Then all Christians agreed that Peter would go to Rome to oppose Simon's heresy and eliminate it, and they thought it most fitting that the highest leader of Christianity should oppose the leader of the heretics.]

The skirmish of Peter, and Paul as well to a certain degree, with Simon Magus, was a paradigmatic strife between an apostle/saint and an opponent. This will be discussed in more detail in the next section of this chapter (3.2), but it should be noted how the authority of the Christian representative in such skirmishes is boosted through the confrontation with his enemy.

3.1.3.2 Church Hierarchy

The sagas of the apostles contain accounts of how central offices of the Church, the papacy, episcopacy, and the priestly office, were already existing and functioning during the apostolic age.[114] According to these texts, the apostles ordained bishops and priests and Peter is shown to have ordained his successors as popes. As is made clear in the *Saga of Clement* and the *Saga of the Apostle Peter*, before he became bishop of Rome, he had been a bishop of Antioch. In the saga of Clement, Peter is said to have ordained three popes:

> Enn fyrste pave af Petro vigþr oc til kǫrenn var Linus, oc var hann litla stund. En annarr pave var Cletus efter Linum at forraþe Petrs postola, oc lifþe scamma stund. Enn þriþi pave fra Petro var sia inn gøfge Clemens.[115]
>
> [The first pope ordained and chosen by Peter was Linus, and he was pope for a short time. The next pope after Linus, as prescribed by Peter, was Cletus who lived for a short while. The third pope after Peter was the noble Clement]

---

113 *Post*, p. 180.
114 The word 'byskup' has sometimes the broad meaning of a religious leader and is thus not always restricted to the hierarchy of the Roman Church. Thus, the high priest Abiathar can be called 'byskup,' (see e.g. *Post*, p. 518) and pagan religious leaders are frequently referred to by the term 'blotbyskup' (see e.g. *Post*, p. 748 and throughout the *Saga of the Apostle Bartholomew*, see also *Saga of Simon and Jude*).
115 *Post*, p. 180.

FORCE OF WORDS: CONSTRUCTING A CHRISTIAN SOCIETY   167

In the *Saga of the Apostle Peter*, however, Clement is introduced as the first pope and Linus and Cletus have been relegated to bishops.[116] The text explains that as bishops in Rome, they were responsible for administrative matters relating to clerics while Peter himself "var a bønum iafnan ok kendi monnum tru" [was always at his prayers and preaching the faith],[117] giving the impression that there already existed a functioning hierarchy at the time. Despite the discrepancy between the two texts, they have in common that Clement enjoys a special status, singled out by Peter and ordained in a special ceremony as the rightful successor of Peter's cathedral.[118] In the *Saga of Clement*, it is explained in elaborate terms that Clement was expected to keep up the holy teachings and commandments of God. He is said to be invested with the power to govern (*styra*) and rule (*raþa*) over as the ordained "bishop and pope" over Christianity in its entirety.[119] In addition to describing how Peter ordained Clement, with the laying over of hands, the text also says that Peter provided Clement with detailed instructions about "hversu hann scy(l)de halda byscopdom eþa hvé hann scilde styra cristne þeire, es hann var þá iver setr."[120] [as to how he should hold the bishopric and how he should steer the Christians over whom he was placed.][121] This ceremony is described in the following way in the *Saga of the Apostle Peter*:

> Hlyði þer mer, goðir brøðr! [...] ek hefi mann valdan til þess velldis, er drottinn minn gaf mer, Clement lærisvein minn, þann er mer hefir lengi fylgt, ok eru honum oll guðs lôg einna mest i kunnleika [...] Fyrir þvi sel

---

116 There is no apparent reason for this discrepancy between the two texts. Roughton suggests that it might have been to "avoid confusion of Peter's consecration of Clement as his immediate successor to the papal seat." Roughton I, p. 150. It is right, the *Saga of the Apostle Peter* could reflect the opinion that it would have been problematic to think of many popes to have been in office at the same time with Linus and Cletus being the contemporaries of Peter. Such difficulties do not seem to have bothered the composer of the *Saga of Clement* who names all of them as popes, although Clement is specifically named by Peter as his successor. This position towards the papal succession could have been adopted from any late antique or medieval source, resolving the contradiction in differing ways. See Roughton I, p. 105–106.
117 *Post*, p. 181. Trans. Roughton II, p. 181.
118 "Nu set ec þenna mann Clementem i stol minn," [Now I place this man, Clement, in my seat] *Post*, p. 142. Trans. Roughton II, p. 469.
119 "hann vigþe hann til byscops oc til pava iver alre cristne" [ordained him as bishop and pope over entire Christianity] *Post*, p. 142. Cf. translation in Rouhgton II, p. 470.
120 *Post*, p. 142. Trans. Roughton II, p. 470.
121 In this sentence, the word 'cristne' as 'the Christians' would more accurately be replaced with the world 'Christendom.'

ek honum þat velldi, er guð gaf mer at leysa ok binda, ok hans atkvæði skal standa um alla kristni." Siðan lagði hann hendr yfir hofuð honum ok setti hann i stol sinn ok vigði hann til pava.¹²²

[Hear me, good brothers! [...] I have chosen a man to take the power that my Lord granted to me, Clement my disciple, who has followed me for a long time, and who is most well-versed in all the laws of God. [...] Therefore I give to him the power that God gave me to release and to bind, and his decisions shall stand throughout all of Christendom." Then he laid hands over his head and seated him in his throne and consecrated him as pope.]

This passage provides an interesting example of how the divine power Peter received from Jesus as described in Matt. 16:19 is transferred to the ecclesiastical hierarchy, reflected in the use of the word *veldi* already discussed earlier in this chapter. In the text, the word *veldi* merges with the power or authority given to Peter by God being exclusively restricted to the one who holds the office.

As for the involvement of other apostles in the emerging ecclesiastical hierarchy, there is a number of examples. If not bishops themselves, the apostles are frequently represented as founding episcopal sees in the regions where they were proclaiming the faith and ordaining other men they found fitting for service. Those coming across the *Saga of the Apostle John* would, for example, hear how the apostle James was installed as the bishop of Jerusalem by his fellow disciples and how that very event served as a model for a bishop's ordination still a thousand years later:

En eptir þat er postolar hofðu skipat guðs kristni a Gyðingalandi, eptir þvi sem fong voru a, þa skipuðu þeir Jacobo postola broður drottins yfir kristnina ok settu hann byskup yfir Jorsalaborg, ok logðu þeir hendr yfir hofuð honum, Petrus postoli fyrst at upphafi, ok þar siðan með honum Jacobus ok Johannes brøðr. Ok þaðan af er skynsemi til þess tekin, at engan byskup skal sva vigia, at færi byskupar se við en þrir, erkibyskup, sa er vigir, ok aðrir tveir byskupar með honum, þeir er styði þat hit haleita embætti.¹²³

[After the apostles organized God's Christians in Judea as best they could, they then appointed the apostle James, the brother of the Lord, as the leader of the Christians and bishop over Jerusalem, and they laid

---

122 *Post*, p. 181.
123 *Post*, p. 417. Trans. Roughton II, p. 662.

their hands over his head, first Peter, and the brothers James and John along with him. And this is the reason why no bishop shall be consecrated unless there are no less than three bishops present, the archbishop, who consecrates, and two other bishops with him, who uphold that sublime office.]

Andrew is said to have ordained a certain Celestine as bishop over Nicaea. He is described as a wise man who took good care of his flock as Andrew had commanded him ("sem Andreas postoli hafði honum boðit").[124] In their travels around Babylon, Simon and Jude then ordained a bishop for the region, a certain Abdias (the same one as the so-called Pseudo-Abdian collection took its name from) who had followed them from Judea: "postolarnir vigðu byskup i Babylon, þann er Abdias het"[125] [[t]he apostles ordained a bishop in Babylon, Abdias by name].

Furthermore, with the increasing success of the Christian mission and the growing number of Christians around the world, the source material regularly describes how the apostolic emissaries built up the administrative structure around the nascent Christian religion. Having succeeded in converting a sufficient number of people, a first step is to eradicate the last traces of the previous pagan religions and replace it with Christian churches. The *Saga of Clement*, for instance, describes how

> vel efldesc þar cristenn domr, at at þeim misserom var halfr atti tǫgr kirkna þar gorr oc vigþar af kennimonnom, oc sva øll scurþgoþ broten i þeim heroþom oc øll hof eyd oc aller blótstallar brennder. Oc þa hlógo cristner menn at otru heiþinna manna oc blotom þeira.[126]
>
> [Christendom was so well strenghtened there that during the same season forty churches were raised and consecrated by clerics there, and all the heathen ideols in that district were torn down and all the temples destroyed and all the places of sacrifice burned. The Christians scorned the heresy of the heathens and their sacrifices.]

The apostle Philip is described to have travelled around many regions and cities where he "vigði byskupa, presta ok diakna, ok marga aðra klerka, ok let þar margar kirkiur reisa ok efla þar miok kristinn dom. Ok var hann þar.xx. ar kenningar at kenna"[127] [ordained bishops, priests, and deacons, and many other

---

124 *Post*, p. 324.
125 *Post*, p. 787. Trans. Roughton II, p. 806.
126 *Post*, p. 149. Trans. Roughton II, p. 483.
127 *Post*, p. 737. Trans. Roughton II, p. 747.

clerics and had many churches erected, and greatly strengthened the Christian faith there. He preached there for twenty years]. Another particularly rich example is found in the *Saga of the Apostle John*, describing the activities of the apostle after he returns from exile on the island Pathmos. Having returned, he continues to travel around, preaching the word of God but he also proceeds to

> vigia kirkiur eða lata reisa i þeim stöðum, sem eigi voru aðr. Hann setti ok kennimenn til varðveizlu kirkiunnar eða kristninnar, bæði byskupa ok presta ok aðra lærða menn, a þann pall hvern, at vigslunum fylgði, eða stað, sem honum var aðr af helgum anda til visat. En er hann var kominn til einhverrar borgar ok hafði þar tiðir veittar ok alla þa luti, er til guðligrar þionostu komu.[128]
>
> [consecrate churches and to build them in places where none been built before. He also appointed clerics to supervise the churches and Christians, both bishops and priests and other learned men, at the steps of the altar where each consecration took place or in each place where he had been directed by the Holy Spirit. When he came to a certain city and had celebrated mass and done all of the things appertaining to the worship of God ...]

According to this passage, the apostle John himself arranged his congregations within a hierarchical order, inspired by the Holy Spirit, ordering all learned men, both bishops, priests and others to a position (*a þann pall*) fitting to the ordination of each and every one.

3.1.4 Conclusion: Powering Over

The above discussion has highlighted the layer of the early Christian discourse in Iceland concerned with enhancing the authority of the Church and elevating the position of its ordained servants. To that end, inspired by the critical approaches towards religious text material discussed earlier in this study, it has paid particular attention to how the position of the Church was carved out in the religious discourse. Central to such practices was the Church's emphasis on its special relationship with the divine which was made possible through an exclusive access to the divine teaching and by association with religious figures like the apostles. What is also emphasized is the organizational context in which the discourse is carried out, namely the ecclesiastical hierarchy which can be traced back to the apostles themselves. Such discursive practices served

---

128   *Post*, p. 427. Trans. Roughton II, p. 682.

the purpose of setting ecclesiastics apart from other people, elevating them to a position from which they could tell others what to do, teach them.

Furthermore, in particular in the discussion of the teaching, the discourse has been placed in the context of the liturgical performance taking place within the church building. Although the term 'teaching,' as it is constructed in the earliest Icelandic religious discourse, does not offer itself to any clear-cut content description, the examples above show that in an important sense it was regarded as the same teaching preached by Christ and carried on by the apostles and later by their successors. Contentwise, the teaching remained relatively open but at the same time it entailed a fixed structural relationship between a cleric and laypeople, learned and unlearned, those in the knowing and those in the unknowing. This is of course not to say that the content was not there or unclear, only that it was diverse and shaped by the circumstances each time. The teaching was thus an umbrella term for the message the Church wanted to get through in different circumstances and was not defined by the specifics of its content but the power relationship lying at its core.

3.2   The 'Other'

Ecclesiastical discourse during the Free State era was filled with descriptions and images of various kinds of opponents. Demons, pagans, heretics and inimical Jews frequently turn up in sermons and in hagiographical texts, the enemy-figure amounts to a structural necessity. From the point of view of critical theory, these figures constituted an 'other' over against which those who belonged to the Church could measure themselves.[129] As it gradually paved its way to a position as the most powerful institution in the country, the Church in Iceland was taking measures in order to mark out the boundary-lines between

---

129   The concept of the 'other' has been traced back to Georg Wilhelm Friedrich Hegel's (1770–1831) 'Master-Slave Dialectic,' an influential chapter of his *Phenomenology of the Spirit* in which he explains that the consciousness of self, of identity, is shaped through the dialectical master-slave relationship or better, that of lord (*Herr*) and bondsman (*Knecht*). It is in this text where the notion of self as constructed by an 'other' is put forth which has since then resurfaced "fundamentally in any critical discourse that wrestles with some idea of the "other" as that against which you define yourself." Andrew Cole, "What Hegel's Master/Slave Dialectic Really Means," *Journal of Medieval and Early Modern Studies* 34/3 (2004), 578. Variations of this theme are numerous, two influential those of philosophers Alexandre Kojève (1902–1968) and Simone de Beauvoir (1908–1986). In the following, the discussion will be limited to the political and social aspects of the concept and how it can become of use for analyzing and explaining historical and social processes.

'us' and 'them,' between those who were 'like us' and those who were 'not like us.' As Jonathan Z. Smith points out, such a comparison is essentially hierarchical and political:

> Difference is seldom a comparison between entities judged to be equivalent. Difference most frequently entails a hierarchy of prestige and the concomitant political ranking of *superordinate* and *subordinate*.[130]

This was of course by no means a specifically Icelandic concern. Such discursive practices came naturally to the Roman Church wherever it was settling itself. As this section will show, much of the discourse analysed, particularly the one grounded in hagiographical narratives, is structured around the binary opposition between an apostolic protagonist and a hostile 'other.' The main reason for bringing up the notion of the 'other' in the context of the early Icelandic ecclesiastical discourse is to highlight the inherently political nature of such discursive structures and the kind of power relationships it was able to produce and sustain in the social realm.

3.2.1 Enemies of the Church

It should be stressed right at the outset that the image of the 'other' in the ecclesiastical discourse was also an image of an enemy (*Feindbild*). The notion of an enemy-image has increasingly come into use in recent decades, especially in the German speaking world, both in popular discussion as well as scholarship across the various fields of the humanities and social sciences.[131] It is important to keep in mind a distinction between enemy-images and other boundary formations between 'us' and 'them.' Not every criticism, not every negative representation, not every prejudice or image of an 'other,' should be

---

130 Jonathan Z. Smith, "What a Difference a Difference Makes," in *Relating Religion: Essays in the Study of Religion* (Chicago, 2004), p. 253. Italics added.

131 A transdisciplinary collection of essays on enemy-images, grounded in the work of a research group within the Cluster of Excellence: Religion and Politics in Münster is Alfons Fürst, Harutyun Harutyunyan, Eva-Maria Schrage et al., eds., *Von Ketzern und Terroristen: Interdisziplinäre Studien zur Konstruktion und Rezeption von Feindbildern* (Münster, 2012). Other examples include Anne Katrin Flohr, *Feindbilder in der internationalen Politik: Ihre Entstehung und ihre Funktion*, Bonner Beiträge zur Politikwissenschaft 2 (Münster, 1991); Anton Pelinka, ed., *Feindbilder in Europa: Analysen und Perspektiven*, Studienreihe Konfliktforschung 23 (Vienna, 2008); Ingrid Hartl, *Das Feindbild der Kreuzzugslyrik: Das Aufeinandertreffen von Christen und Muslimen*, Wiener Arbeiten zur germanischen Altertumskunde und Philologie 40 (Bern, 2009); Dennis Weiter, *Feindbildkonstruktionen im Nahostkonflikt: Ursache für das Scheitern der Roadmap 2003?* (Hamburg, 2012).

perceived as an enemy-image. Prejudices and images of the 'other' contribute to the construction of an identity, just as enemy-images do. But unlike enemy-images, they are not directly linked to the origin of evil and it is not a matter of ultimate importance to overcome them as is usually the case with an enemy.[132]

In a passage in the *Icelandic Homily Book* with the heading *Oratio. Passio Domini* one can find a succinct summary of the enemies of the Church:

> Nú skulum vér biðja fyr villumönnum og þrætumönnum, að Guð og vor *Dominus* leiði af öllum villum og leiði þá til heilagrar og postullegrar kristni. Biðjum vér fyr ótrúum Gyðingum, að Guð og vor Drottinn taki ótrúumyrkur af hjörtum þeirra, svo að þeir kenni sinn *Dominum* vera Jesúm Krist vorn Drottin. Nú skulum vér biðja fyr heiðnum mönnum, að Guð almáttugur færi illsku frá hjörtum þeirra og þeir fyrláti skurðgoð, en þeir snúist til Guðs lifanda og sanns og einkasonar hans Jesú Krists, Guðs og Drottins vors.[133]
>
> [Let us pray for heretics and quarrelers, that God, our *Dominus* may lead them away from all error and lead them to holy and apostolic Christianity. We pray for incredulous Jews, that God and our Lord remove the darkness of unbelief from their hearts, so they will recognize their Dominum as Jesus Christ our Lord. Now let us pray for heathen men, that almighty God remove evil from their hearts and that they forsake idols, but turn to the living and true God and his only son Jesus Christ, God and our Lord.]

Following Jesus' instruction (Matt. 5:44; Luke 6:28) to pray for one's persecutors, the passage distinguishes relatively clearly between three groups of enemies: quarreling heretics opposed to apostolic Christianity,[134] incredulous Jews whose hearts are filled with unbelief (*ótrú*), and idolatrous heathens with hearts filled with evil. Another summary can be found at the end of the *Saga of the Apostle Thomas* but there the differentiation between enemies is not as

---

132 Eva-Maria Schrage, "Von Ketzern und Terroristen? Zum analytischen Nutzen eines interdisziplinären Feindbildbegriffs," in *Von Ketzern und Terroristen: Interdisziplinäre Studien zur Konstruktion und Rezeption von Feindbildern* (Münster, 2012), pp. 220–221.
133 *ÍH*, p. 102.
134 According to the strict definition of a heretic, it is somebody who has already been baptized and accepted the Christian faith but departed from its correct interpretation provided by the Catholic Church. Here the word *villa* in *villumenn* is used in the narrow sense of the word, referring to heresy and heretics. This is clear from the context, which associates them with quarrelers, separated from holy and apostolic Christianity and later makes a distinction from heathens.

clear. After the apostle's martyrdom in India, his body was taken to the city of Edessa and placed in a silver casket. Because of the apostle's sanctity, enemies of Christianity are not allowed in the city, described as follows: "I þeiri borg ma eigi vera villumaðr ne blotmaðr ne Gyðingr, ok eigi megu heiðnir menn þangat heria" [Heretics, heathen worshippers, or Jews are not to be found in that city, and heathens cannot harry there].[135] The enemies enumerated here are heretics, men participating in worship including sacrifical ceremonies (*blót*), heathens, and Jews. This distinction seems to derive from the Latin source text, which differentiates between *haereticus, Iudaeus, idolorum cultor*, and *barbarus*.[136] While each of the Latin terms has its specific reference distinguishing them from the others, the same distinction does not carry over to the Icelandic. *Blótmenn* and *heiðnir menn* can, for example, simply refer to the same group of people, and in a certain sense *villumenn* also.[137] The following discussion is intended to further explore the three groups of enemies referred to above: heretics, heathens, and Jews.

3.2.1.1 Heretics

In Sverrir Jakobsson's estimation, medieval Icelanders only had superficial knowledge about conflicts and debates between disagreeing Christians. Icelandic sources do not, for example, show much awareness of the great schism between East and West which seems to have been understood as a temporary disagreement.[138] Jakobsson even goes as far to describe the situation in Iceland as "free of heresy and other original thoughts on religious matters" and Icelanders by and large indifferent to religious matters.[139] Although Jakobsson is most likely right in assuming that Icelanders were not fully up-to-date in

---

135 *Post*, p. 726. Cf. *Frá Sýrlandi til Íslands*, p. 316. Here, a narrow understanding of the word "villumaðr" seems reasonable. Roughton's translation of *blótmaðr*, however, with the word pagan does not suffice as it stands in contrast with the word *heiðinn maðr* later in the same sentence.

136 Lucy Grace Collings has identified as the closest source text the version of *Passio Sancti Thomae Apostoli* (BHL 8136), edited by Max Bonnet in *Acta Thomae* (Leipzig, 1883), p. 159. See discussion in Collings, *Codex Scardensis*, pp. 14–17 and Roughton I, p. 270–271.

137 The 14th century manuscript SÁM 1 (Codex Scardensis) replaces "blotmaðr ne Gyðingr" with the word "gudnidingr" [one who denigrates (commits *nið*) against God]. For a further discussion of the terms "nid" and "gudnidingr," see Richard Cole, "*Kyn / Fólk / Þjóð / Ætt*: Proto-Racial Thinking and its Application to Jews in Old Norse Literature," in *Fear and Loathing in the North: Jews and Muslims in Medieval Scandinavia and the Baltic Region*, eds. Cordelia Heß and Jonathan Adams (Berlin, 2015), pp. 248–249.

138 As an example thereof, he points out the rather imprecise account of the Second Council of Lyon in 1274 found in *Árna saga biskups*. Sverrir Jakobsson, *Við og veröldin*, pp. 127–128.

139 Ibid., p. 128.

religious conflicts carried out in distant lands, the notions of 'heresy' and 'heretics' were by no means foreign to them given how prominent a spot they enjoy in early ecclesiastical discourse.

The religious texts under inspection in the present study contain numerous examples of heretics and mention well-known heretical movements from the Church's past. In the *Saga of the Apostles Philip and James*, the apostle Philip is said to have encountered "villa þeira manna, er Hebioniti voru kallaðir" [heresy of the men called Hebionites], which he is then said to have destroyed and "førði kristnina i lag sem þa er bezt hafði verit" [brought Christianity in its place, as it had been best there before].[140] At the beginning of the *Saga of Bishop Martin*, the Arian heresy (*Arrius villa*) is said to be spreading around the entire world and Martin had to endure beatings for being the only one who objected to the faithlessness of the teachers (*otru kennemanna*). The saga further tells that the bishop Hilarius, "var rekenn fra byscopsstole sinom fyrer ofriþe villomanna" [had been driven from his bishop's seat by the hostility of the heretics]. Although the texts do not go into the details of the nature of these different heresies, it is made clear that they constitute a corruption of true Christianity, lack of faith and unrest which was to result in physical violence.

In addition to such sporadic mentionings of well-known heretical movements, heretical behavior receives its clearest manifestation in the figure of Simon Magus, a prototypical heretic from the early Christian and medieval tradition, figuring prominently in writings related to the apostle Peter and Bishop Clement of Rome. In the Icelandic medieval tradition, he plays a significant role in the *Saga of the Apostle Peter* and the *Saga of Clement*. In the biblical canon, Simon Magus is first named in the canonical Acts of the Apostles (8:9–24) but traditions around him grew rapidly during the first three centuries CE as can be seen from Apocryphal Acts of the Apostles, the Pseudo Clementine Corpus and later in patristic writings by authors such as Justin Martyr, Irenaeus, and Tertullian. In such writings and others, Simon has been charged with the founding of simony - the sin of purchasing the gifts of God (*giafir guðs*) which in the Middle Ages came to be applied to the purchasing of ecclesiastical office.[141] He is presented as the archenemy of Peter and the climax of the *Saga of Peter the Apostle* is reached in the conflict between him and the apostles Peter and Paul in front of the Roman emperor Nero.

---

140   *Post*, p. 737. Trans. Roughton II, p. 747.
141   See the description of the origin of simony in *Post*, p. 171.

In the religious discourse of the Church, a characteristic frequently attributed to Simon is his exuberant arrogance, the capital sin of *superbia*, the "queen of all evil things," as its Icelandic equivalent *dramb* or *dramblæti* is called in a Lenten service in the *Icelandic Homily Book*.[142] In fact, the saga depicts Simon as guilty of other capital sins as well, such as envy (*ǫfund*) and anger (*reiði*), but it is safe to say that his arrogance stands out.[143] At various points during his clashes with the apostles, he claims to be Christ, the son of God descended from heaven, the supreme power of God and the sun itself.[144] As the conflict between him and the apostles Peter and Paul escalates in Rome, the emperor asks who the true one is, which immediately prompt's the following answer from Simon: "Ek em hann enn sanni" [I am the true one]. Again, when the emperor later asks who is "konungr ok drottinn" [king and Lord], Simon responds in the same way as before: "Ek em hann sa, ek em hann sa" [I am him, I am him].[145] In his vaingloriousness, Simon thus repeatedly claims power and prestige for himself, which is due only to God alone.

Such actions, however, bring him nothing but shame from the apostles, as the following passage from the *Saga of the Apostle Peter* clearly illustrates:

> En hann [Petrus] mællti, at menn skylldu sia við svikum Simonar ok við allri villu hans, ok lata eigi at velum diofuls, þviat hann kvað Simon vera lygimann ok fiolkunnigan galldramann ok vándan þiof, ovin guðs ok allz hins retta, ok kvað bratt augliosa mundu verða hans illzku fyrir ollum lyð.[146]
>
> [He [Peter] said that men should see through Simon's treachery and all his heresy, and not be fooled by the Devil's wiles, for he said that Simon was a liar and a sorcerous conjurer and an evil thief, an enemy of God and all righteousness, and he said that soon his evil would be publicized before all the people.]

---

142   *ÍH*, p. 87. At one point, the *Saga of the Apostle Peter* specifically uses the term 'dramb,' when stating that Simon "drambaði mikit." *Post*, p. 171.

143   Envy: "En Simon magnus fylldiz ófundar ok mællti mart illt um Petrum," [Simon Magnus was filled with envy and spoke great ill of Peter] *Post*, 185. Trans. Roughton II, p. 532. Anger: "Þa reiddiz Simon," [Simon became angry] *Post*, p. 188. Trans. Roughton II, p. 538.

144   *Post*, p. 186 (son of God); *Post*, p. 172 (Christ); *Post*, p. 132 (the sun); *Post*, pp. 133 and 174 (supreme power).

145   *Post*, p. 192–193. Trans. Roughton II, p. 544, 547.

146   *Post*, p. 185. Trans. Roughton II, p. 533.

Throughout the apostles' dealings with Simon, they do not miss a chance to scold him harshly, exposing him as a heretic associated with sourcery, treachery, falsity and the Devil himself.[147]

Another feature regularly associated with Simon Magus that should be mentioned is his tendency to engage in what in Icelandic is conveyed with the word *þræta*. The noun 'þræta' can mean a quarreling, altercation or an objection, and the verb *þræta* simply means engaging in such activities.[148] Inherent to such altercations, as suggested by a translation option in Fritzner's dictionary, is the practice of objecting or countering the standpoint of another[149] which is precisely what Simon does in his exchange with the apostles: "Þvi þurfum ver ekki at mæla til friðar helldr til þrætu" [Therefore we do not need to speak in the name of peace but rather to debate].[150] Time and again, Simon calls the apostles' teachings into question and corrupts them, offering his own alternative teachings sometimes with great success. At the same time, it remains clear that his teachings are harmful (*skaðsamlig*)[151] and, more importantly, untrue, a fact most clearly articulated in one of Peter's retorts to Simon in front of emperor Nero: "Engi er sannleikr i þer, helldr gerir þu ok mælir allt með lygi" [There is no truth in you; everything that you do and say is a lie].[152] Thus, in the ecclesiastical discourse, the true teaching of the apostles is opposed to the false and demonic teaching of the archheretic Simon Magus. By the same token, the very practice of questioning the apostles' teaching, not to mention taking a stance against it, is counted among heretical practices.

3.2.1.2 Heathens

The opponents most frequently encountered in the hagiographic source material are heathens, referred to by a variation of the adjective *heiðinn*, cognate with the English word 'heathen.'[153] Heathens are those who worship other gods than the Christian one, either because they have not been introduced to the Christian religion or they have not accepted it. A standard way to describe the situation of heathens is that of darkness, they have not seen the light. In a

---

147 *Post,* p. 189.
148 According to Cleasby-Vigfusson, *þræta* is defined as a "quarrel, wrangling, litigation."
149 In Norwegian: "Modsigelse hvormed nogen imødegaar ens Paastand," Fritzner, s.v. "þræta."
150 *Post,* p. 174. Trans. Roughton II, p. 513. For other references to quarrels between Simon and the apostles, see *Post,* pp. 132–134 and pp. 172–173.
151 *Post,* p. 180.
152 *Post,* p. 192. Trans. Roughton II, p. 544.
153 Fritzner's dictionary translates 'heiðinn' as a heathen (In Norwegian: *hedensk*), that is somebody who is excluded from or stands outside (Christian) human society, and does not share their peace nor their laws. Fritzner, s.v. "heiðinn".

sermon to be held on feast of the Presentation (*Purificatio s. Marie*), heathen peoples are said to be in darkness of mind: "Heiðnar þjóðir vóru í hugarmyrkri, því að þeir sáu eigi ið sanna ljós, þá er þeir kunnu eigi skapera sinn" [Heathen peoples remained in darkness of mind, for they did not see the true light, when they did not know their creator].[154] Since as early as the Apostle Paul, Christian authors have shown a certain ambivalence towards the figure of the pagan, especially when it comes to the question what to make of 'noble heathens,' that is people who excelled in wisdom or moral virtue without having access to the truth of the Christian gospel.[155] For such reasons, as well as the fact that they always have the opportunity to convert to Christiantiy and are as such the main object of the apostolic mission, the figure of the pagan should not be regarded as automatically negative. As pointed out by Sverrir Jakobsson in his discussion of the identity of medieval Icelanders, the contours of heathendom are malleable and not an ultimate dividing line between 'us' and 'them.'[156] Despite such ambiguities regarding the identity of medieval Icelanders in general, it cannot be overlooked that the figure of the heathen is represented as overwhelmingly negative in early Christian religious discourse.

Following their Latin source texts, the Old Icelandic texts base their representation of the pagan religion on the polytheistic religious landscape of the Roman empire. The only difference between the Icelandic texts and their source texts is the occasional replacing of the names of Greco-Roman deities with names from Old Norse mythology, a practice sometimes refferred to as *interpretatio Norræna* (comparable to Tacitus' *interpretatio Romana*).[157] Just as often, however, deities keep their foreign names. The substituting of the deities' names is carried out with relative ease, minimizing any differences between the Old Norse gods and the Greco Roman ones. As shown by Simonetta Battista, there is not an inner coherence to be detected in the Old

---

154 *ÍH*, p. 122.
155 For a classic article on the topic of the 'noble heathen' for the medieval Scandinavian context, see Lars Lönnroth, "The Noble Heathen: A Theme in the Sagas," *Scandinavian Studies* 41 (1969): 1–29. For a more recent contribution, see Grønlie, *Saint and the Saga Hero*, pp. 111–162.
156 Sverrir Jakobsson, *Við og veröldin*, p. 139.
157 The topic has been the subject of two fairly recent contributions, by philologist Simonetta Battista "Interpretations of the Roman Pantheon in the Old Norse Hagiographic Sagas," in *Old Norse Myths, Literature and Society*, The Viking Collection 14, ed. Margaret Clunies Ross (Odense, 2003), pp. 175–197 and literary scholar Ármann Jakobsson, "'Er Saturnús er kallaðr en vér köllum Frey': The Roman Spring of the Old Norse Gods," in *Between Paganism and Christianity in the North*, eds. Leszek P. Słupecki and Jakub Morawiec (Rzeszów, 2009), pp. 158–164, esp. p. 161–164.

Icelandic translations as for which Old Norse god corresponds to which Greco Roman god.[158] Sometimes, Óðinn and Þórr are made into collective representatives of the entire pantheon.[159] In Ármann Jakobsson's opinion, the reason for such inconsistencies is that for the medieval cleric and his audience "this diversity does not matter: one heathen god is just as wicked as another, and it serves no purpose to distinguish between them."[160]

A distinctive feature of heathens as they are represented in the source material is their adherence to their own local deities. Each city or region had its own deity, worshipped through idols (*skurðgoð*). In the *Saga of the Apostle Bartholomew*, the popularity of idols is explained in the following way:

> En hinn lygni guð tælir sva þa, er eigi truðu eða kunnu sannan guð, at hann kastar a þa sottum ok meinum ok skôðum, ok gefr svôr or skurðgoðum, at þeir bloti honum; en þa syniz heimskum monnum sem hann grøði, þa er hann lætr af at meiða. En hann bergr engum, helldr grandar hann, ok syniz þa biarga, er hann lætr af at granda.[161]
>
> [The lying god swindles those who do not believe in or know the true God by casting upon them sickness and wounds and injuries, and by giving answers from out of idols in order to get them to worship him, and then it seems to stupid people as if he cures them, when he only ceases to injure them. But he saves no one, and indeed only does injury, and he seems to save when he stops doing harm.]

According to such explanations, idols are only vehicles for forces of evil to trick people into following them. In the *Saga of the Apostle Andrew*, the apostle quotes Jesus Christ himself on having said that "skurðgoð þessi eigi guð vera helldr hina verstu diofla ok ovini allz mannkyns, þa er þess eggia menn at gera þat, er guð reiðiz þeim ok hverfi fra þeim ok heyri eigi bøner þeira" [these idols not to be gods but rather the worst devils and the enemies of all mankind, who urge men to do things that anger God, and then he turns from them and will not hear their prayers].[162] In a speech, given by the apostle Bartholomew in the *Saga of the Apostle Bartholomew*, he explains how the apostolic mission was in part directly aimed at the devils living in pagan idols and temples. Just as Jesus has conquered the Devil, his emissaries were intended to finish the task

---

158   Battista "Interpretations of the Roman Pantheon," pp. 26–30.
159   Ibid., p. 26.
160   Ármann Jakobsson, "Roman Spring of the Old Norse Gods," p. 163.
161   *Post*, p. 744. Trans. Roughton II, p. 756.
162   *Post*, p. 337. Trans. Roughton II, p. 640.

he had begun, following his command: "at ver rekim a braut alla þiona diöfuls, þa er byggja i hofum ok i skurðgoðum, en ver leysim menn or anuð þeira ok fra velldi þess, er yfir var stiginn" [that we should drive away all the servants of the Devil that dwell in temples and in idols, and we free men from their misery and from the power of the one who was overcome].[163] Thus, following their master's commandments, the apostolic protagonists programmatically seek out the idols and expose them as the abodes of devils.

Inevitably, the fight against idols includes encounters with their worshippers. As noted, however, the heathens who the apostle or saint meet when entering new territories, either in groups or as individuals, are by no means an automatically negative force in the hagiographic narratives. They are also potential converts and an object of mission. An illustrative example is found in the *Saga of Martin*:

> En for Martinus hia bø nøcqeriom fiolmennom of dag, oc com lið mikit heiþinna manna a mot honum, þviat engi maþr cunne Crist a þeim bø. En þa var morgom forvitni at (sia) Martinum, þviat þeir heyrþo mart ogorligt sagt fra honom. Þa toc Martinus at boþa heiþnom mønnom guþs orþ, oc comsc hann viþ af øllom hug, es sva micell mannfiolþe scylde eigi cunna scapara sinn.[164]
>
> [One day Martin was passing by a farm with some followers, and a great crowd of heathens came against him, for no man on that farm knew Christ. There were many who were curious to see Martin, because they had heard many terrible things said about him. Martin began to preach the word of God to the heathens, and he rued with all his heart the fact that such a great number of people should not know their creator.]

The hagiographic material also contains numerous passages, modelled after the healing miracles of the New Testament gospels, where heathen individuals approach the apostles and saints, most often in desperate need for help because of a sick or a demon-possessed relative, and ask for their assistance.[165] These encounters are usually shown to lead to the conversion of a great number of people.

There is, of course, a more antagonistic side to the heathens very prominent in the source material and contributes to the image of the heathens as

---

163 *Post*, p. 748. Trans. Roughton II, p. 763.
164 *HMS* I, p. 566. Trans. Roughton II, p. 856.
165 A prime example is the *Saga of the Apostle Andrew* which contains a large number of such passages. *Post*, pp. 318–343.

enemies. This side comes out when the Christian message does not fall into fertile soil and is received with hostility and violence. As described in the *Saga of the Apostle Andrew* the apostle Matthew was apprehended by heathens ("tekinn af heiðnum monnum") in the city of Mirmidon, blinded in both eyes, and thrown into a prison where he was kept in shackles.[166] When the apostle Andrew comes to the city – having healed his fellow apostle Matthew and sent him on to Ethiopia (*Blaland*) – he continues where Matthew left off and is not received with any more leniency. Only after a while and many fervent prayers to his Lord to "open the hearts' eyes of these men," do the people of the city desist in torturing the apostle. These confrontations with heathens can also lead to the saint's martyrdom. The martyrdom of the apostle Philip, for example, is described in the following way:

> Segia sva helgar bøkr, at þa kømi þar heiðnir menn með ofriði miklum ok hǫndluðu postolann ok dømdu hann þegar til liflatz, ok var hann siðan krossfestr, ok gryttu þeir hann siðan a krossinum, ok for hann með þeim piningarsigri a þessum degi til almattigs guðs.[167]
>
> [It says in the holy books that heathen men came there with great hostility, and they arrested the apostle and commanded that he be put to death, and he was then crucified, and they stoned him while he was on the cross, and he went with those victorious sufferings upon that day to Almighty God.]

Such encounters constitute a recurring theme in the religious discourse of the Church. In the *Saga of Sebastian,* the Christian convert Tranquillinus, having defended the Christian faith against a Roman count, is "gripinn af heidnum monnum ok grioti bardr ok kastad liki hans ut a ana Tibr" [caught by heathen men, hit with rocks and his body thrown into the river Tiber].[168] These reactions reflect one of the main characteristic of the heathen mindset which is, as construed in early ecclesiastical discourse, stubbornness produced by a hardenened heart.

Important representatives of heathens are the spokesmen or leaders of the people of a particular region. These can be, on the one hand, religious leaders, and, on the other hand, political officials. The opposition of religious leaders consists of heathen temple officials – referred to most frequently in Icelandic with words such as *blotbyskupar* and *blotmenn* – but also popular

---

166   *Post*, p. 319.
167   *Post*, p. 737. Trans. Roughton II, p. 748.
168   *HMS* II, p. 231.

sourcerers – denoted with the phrase *fiolkunnigir menn*.[169] Such religious opponents are more harmful than the political officials insofar that they are more persistent in their opposition to the Christian religion and its proponents, which they carry out with lies and deceit. Oftentimes, they are also the ones bringing the activities of the apostles and saints to the attention of the political leaders. The hostility of the religious leaders is usually spurred by envy towards the success of the Christian religion as can be seen widely in hagiographic sources. The sourcerers Zaroes and Arfaxath, opponents of the apostles Simon and Jude and the apostle Matthew, are said to be filled with envy ("fyllduz ófundar") when they hear about how Simon and Jude have overcome the *blotmenn* in the region.[170] The same is said of the sourcerer Ermoginis when his disciple Filetus tells him about the success of James' apostolic project: "Þa fylldiz Ermogenis ófundar, er hann heyrði þetta" [Hermogenes became filled with envy when he heard this].[171] In the *Saga of the Apostle John*, the apostle John is at one point said to have twelve thousand heathens which produced the following reaction in a certain Aristodimus:

> Ok er þessi tiðendi ser byskup sa er Aristodimus er nefndr, sa hafði yfirmaðr verit allra blota, þa verðr hann fullr af hinum versta anda ok hinum illgiarnasta ok vekr ofrið i moti Joani postola.[172]
>
> [And when the bishop named Aristodimus, who had been in charge of all the sacrifices, beholds all of these things, he is filled with the worst and most ill-natured spirit and raises enmity against the apostle.]

What follows in the saga, and in the general run of things in other hagiographic narratives, is an altercation between the apostle and his enemies during which the heathen religious leaders are exposed as the followers of false idols and demons.

Also posing great danger to the champions of the Christian religion are the political authorities – emperors, kings, governors, earls and counts – in the area where the apostle or the saint is carrying out his missionary work. Hearing about the apostle's or the saint's mission, they confront him and try to force him to stop his missionary practices and worship the traditional idols of the area, and when they realize that it is in vain, they have the saint

---

169 The word *blotbyskup* literally means a bishop of *blot*, the worship of a heathen deity. The adjective *fiolkunnigr* refers to individuals skilled in sourcery.
170 *Post*, p. 782.
171 *Post*, p. 514. Trans. Roughton II, p. 700.
172 *Post*, p. 430. Trans. Roughton II, p. 688.

tortured and sometimes executed. These figures merge the political and religious aspects of the enemy-figure as they are not only opposed to the Christian religion on religious grounds but because of their disobedience and the potential social unrest it might cause. Thus, the Greek earl Egeas, at the beginning of the *passio* section of the *Saga of the Apostle Andrew* calls the apostle to his court because he was told that after the apostle had entered the region, the people of the land had stopped following the law of the kings ("hallda eigi lǫg konunga").[173]

While the religious leaders are depicted as driven by envy in their hostility, the actions of the political leaders are usually motivated by anger, when they realize that their authority is being disregarded or undermined through the deviant behavior of the Christians or the direct disobedience of the apostles and saints. A prime example can be found in the *Saga of Blaise* or *Blasius* which existed in translation at a very early stage of the Icelandic manuscript tradition. In the text, Bishop Blasius encounters the governor of Cappadocia, Agricolaus, who at one point utters the following words: "I qvolom mon ec heimta at yþr þat er ec mæ eigi i ordum" [What I cannot get from with you with words, I will acquire through your agony].[174] Agricolaus not only tries to keep Blasius from preaching the Christian message and gathering converts by throwing him in a prison cell but also viciously tortures a group of women who were Blasius' most faithful followers. Blasius himself also suffers horrible torments which only seemed to increase the saint's strength and love for God, even when tortured with wool combs (which remain one of his symbols in Christian iconography). These episodes highlight the cruelty and anger of the governor as the following excerpt reflects:

> Þa fylldisc iarll mikillar rę(i)þi oc let omn mikinn kynda i avgsyn þeim, oc syndi þeim iarnkamba, þa er til þess voru gørvir at slita holld heilagra manna; oc enn let hann þangat bera gloandi eirkyrtla, þeim scylldi steypa yfir þęr.[175]
>
> [Then the governor was filled with great anger and had a great oven heated before their eyes, and showed them combs made of steel, such that were meant for ripping apart the flesh of holy men; and had glowing copper gowns brought to that place, which were intended to be thrown over them.]

---

173   *Post*, p. 336.
174   *HMS* I, p. 264.
175   Ibid.

Oftentimes, however, these authorities do not immediately emerge as antagonistic. It is, for example, not clear until it draws close to the end of the *Saga of the Apostle Peter* after Simon Magus has fallen to his death at the Sacra Via in Rome that Nero announces that the apostles Peter and Paul have distressed his mind greatly ("þið gerðut hug minn ahyggiufullan") and that he will therefore bring a cruel death upon them.[176] In still other instances, the authorities ultimately react very positively to the Christian message, for example the King Polimius in India who was converted by the apostle Bartholomew and later baptized along with his entire court, after which he became bishop.[177]

Most significant for the construction of the heathen opponent, however, is the multitude of occasions in which there is no doubt whatsoever about the evil of the political authorities. A notorious example is that of the Roman emperor Domitian, who is shown as a hostile secular power *par excellence*, in possession of "riki [...] yfir heiminum" [dominion [...] over the world] and exhibiting all of the worst character traits most frequently attributed to heathen rulers.[178] He is described as a "grimmr maðr, otrur ok fegiarn ok vanstilltr miok um flesta luti" [a wicked man, an unbeliever and avaricious and terribly excessive in most things].[179] In the Christian tradition, he is infamous for his persecutions, thoroughly recorded in the Icelandic sources. In a sermon for the Feast of All Saints in the *Icelandic Homily Book*, he is said to have been "verstur við kristna menn, þeirra er keisera nöfn höfðu haft" [worst towards Christian men of those who had borne the title of an emperor].[180] His violence towards Christians is described in the sermon just cited but in more detail in the *Saga of the Apostle John*.[181] Having heard about John's preaching of Christ and is opposition to the worship of heathen idols which by implication entails transgressing the commandments of the emperor, Domitian becomes furious (*akafliga oðr*) thus adding anger to his list of unfeasible character traits. He further has John moved to Rome where he seeks to execute him by placing him in a burning kettle filled with boiling oil which does not do any harm to the apostle, leading the emperor to exile John to the island Pathmos wherefrom he

---

176   *Post*, p. 195. In the *Saga of the Apostle John*, however, Nero is introduced as "Nero hinn vandi keisari" [Nero the evil emperor] which points to a less ambiguous repetition. *Post*, p. 417.
177   *Post*, p. 752.
178   *Post*, p. 417. Roughton translates *riki* as "control," but the word "dominion" captures better the political implications. See Roughton II, p. 663.
179   *Post*, p. 417. Trans. Roughton II, p. 663.
180   *ÍH*, p. 217.
181   *Post*, pp. 418–419.

returns after Domitian's death. The description of Domitian's fate shows him receiving the death of the tyrant he was:

> En a hinu sama ari, sem Joan var i Pathmos, toku Romveriar Domicianum af lifi með mikilli ovinsælld ok odømum, at þeir attu þing i borginni eptir liflat hans ok dømdu þat a þingi, at þat skylldi allt vera leyft, er hann hefði bannat, en þat bannat allt, er hann hafði leyft.[182]
>
> [In the same year that John was on Pathmos the Romans killed Domicianus with great enmity and violence, and they held a meeting in the city after his death and decided at the meeting that everything that he had forbidden should be allowed, and everything banned that he had allowed].

3.2.1.3   Jews

The image of the Jews in the source material corresponds by and large to the stereotype of the Jew in medieval Christian thought. In the words of Umberto Eco, "[t]he Jew has been described as monstrous and smelly since at least the birth of Christianity, given that he is modeled on the Antichrist, the archenemy, the foe not only of man but of God[.]"[183] This reputation is to a significant extent based on the depiction of the Jewish opponents of Jesus and his followers as they are described in the New Testament, particularly that of the gospels' passion narratives and the canonical Acts of the Apostles, and patristic writings.[184] Such anti-judaistic attitudes manifested themselves in diverse ways around the Christian West, irrespective of whether there were actual Jews present. Since there were no Jews in Iceland during the Middle Ages, representations of Jews in Iceland's ecclesiastical discouse can be categorized as examples of the Jew's paradoxical position as a figure which is physically absent from a particular society but still contributes to the construction of Christian identity among its members. This status of Jews in some parts of medieval Western art and culture has been a much-discussed topic since the 1990s and

---

182   *Post*, p. 419. Trans. Roughton II, p. 666.

183   Umberto Eco, "Inventing the Enemy," in *Inventing the Enemy and Other Occasional Writings*, Trans. Richard Dixon, (Boston, 2012), p. 7. See also David Nirenberg, *Anti-Judaism: The History of a Way of Thinking* (London, 2013), pp. 183–216.

184   The *Icelandic Homily Book* contains one sermon on the passion of the Lord recapitulating the passion narrative (mostly according to the Gospel of John) and both the *Saga of the Apostle Peter* and the *Saga of the Apostle John* contain shorter passages from it. The *Saga of the Apostle Peter* is also to a large part a translation of the New Testament Acts of the Apostles.

has been referred to in various ways, for example as the "hermeneutical Jew" or the "virtual Jew."[185]

As has been pointed out by Richard Cole, written sources from Norway and Iceland usually do not describe Jews by commenting on their physical appearance.[186] Much rather, Cole asserts, Jews are described with regard to their behavior and, it should be added, their malevolent intentions.[187] The greatest offense of the Jews lies in the accusation repeatedly rehearsed that it was they who crucified Jesus or at least apprehended him and called for his crucifixion as the following concise summary from the *Saga of the Apostle Andrew* of the Jews' role in the passion story has it: "hann var [...] hondlaðr af Gyðingum ok leiddr fyrir Pilatum iarl ok krossfestr af riddorum iarlsins at raði Gyðinga" [he was [...] arrested by the Jews and brought before the earl Pilate and crucified by the earl's soldiers at the insistence of the Jews].[188] In the course of his passion, Christ had to suffer "bönd og bardaga, brigsli og hlátur, háðung og lygi" [bonds and distress, shame and laughter, mockery and lies] as a Palm Sunday Sermon from the *Icelandic Homily Book* so lyrically expresses it. This is the source for attributing to the Jews malevolence (*illska*) and cruelty (*grimmd*), which they are then shown to show repeatedly to the apostolic proponents of the Christian faith, beginning with Stephen the protomartyr and soon also several of the apostles.[189]

This image is supplemented by theological reflections, which do not reach any serious degree of complexity, on the position of the Jews in the historical scheme of salvation where they hold a special position. Before the arrival of

---

185   Jeremy Cohen introduced the phrase "hermeneutical Jew" or the "hermeneutically crafted Jew" in his *Living Letters of the Law: Ideas of the Jew in Medieval Christianity* (Berkeley, 1999), pp. 1–17. In an article from the year 2000, Sylvia Thomasch explains the phrase 'virtual Jew' as not referring directly to "any actual Jew, nor present[ing] an accurate depiction of one, nor even a faulty fiction of one; instead it 'surrounds' Jews with a 'reality' that displaces and supplants their actuality." Sylvia Tomasch, "Postcolonial Chaucer and the Virtual Jew," in *The Postcolonial Middle Ages*, ed. Jeffrey Jerome Cohen (New York, 2000), p. 253.
186   Cole, "*Kyn / Fólk / Þjóð / Ætt*," p. 245.
187   On the basis of a number of late medieval *miracula* as well as several visual representations of what were probably Jews, the earliest one dating to the early 14th century, Cole argues that there existed in the Old Norse speaking world what he terms proto-racial thinking. At least since then, although Cole does not address the question as to when such thinking might have begun, 'Jewishness' was being understood in racial terms, as something "irremovable" and "inheritable." Cole, "*Kyn / Fólk / Þjóð / Ætt*," pp. 251 and 264–265.
188   *Post*, p. 337. Trans. Roughton II, pp. 641–642. For other examples of this point, see *Post*, pp. 164, 184, 725, 739, and 748.
189   *ÍH*, p. 96. For a detailed description of *grimmleikr Gyðinga* [cruelty of the Jews] based on Acts see a sermon for the Second Christmas Day in *ÍH*, pp. 254–256.

Christ, they were the sole possessors of the correct faith among the nations of the world: "þeir höfðu ið æðsta sæti að samkundu Guðs, meðan þeir héldu trúu réttri" [they held the supreme seat at the assembly of God, while they kept the correct faith].[190] In the *Saga of Clement*, Pope Clement describes the ancestors (*langfedur*) of his Jewish sympathizers as holy men and great friends of God ("helga menn oc goþs vine micla") and that nobody would be admitted to the kingdom of heaven without believing what their holy prophets (*helger spamenn*) had foretold.[191] It is the birthplace of the Christian faith which is even reflected in the celebration of the mass, as the following passage from a treatise on the mass makes evident:

> Því er ljós og bók færð á ið nyrðra horn altera eða ið vinstra að guðspjalli, að ljós guðspjallskenningar færðu postular heiðnum lýð, er vóru af kyni Gyðinga, er vóru í fyrnd lýður innar hægri handar Drottins. Því er inn fyrsti hlutur og inn efsti messu sunginn á inu hægra horni altera, að trúa hófst í Gyðingafólki.[192]
>
> [That is why the light and the book is moved to the northern corner of the altar when the gospel is read, for the light of the gospel was brought to the heathen people of the Jews, who in ancient times were the people of the right hand of the Lord. For that reason, the first part and the first of the mass is sung on the right corner of the alter, for the faith began with the Jews.]

Through the course of the biblical salvation history, the position of the Jews shifted from that of God's chosen people to becoming serious opponents of the true faith. As described in one sermon in the *Icelandic Homily Book*, they became outcasts (*rekningar*) on grounds of their faithlessness (*ótrúa*).[193] They lost the light given to them and fell into error, *villa Gydinga* [error of the Jews] as it is regularly referred to.[194]

While keeping some special traits, the Jews assume very similar characteristics as other inimical forces – heretics and heathens – who have fallen prey to error, depicted as evil,[195] scornful,[196] lying,[197] and even quarreling.[198] In a

---

190 *ÍH*, p. 271.
191 *Post*, p. 143.
192 *ÍH*, p. 186.
193 *Post*, p. 184.
194 *Post*, pp. 516, 738, and 739.
195 *ÍH*, p. 31.
196 *ÍH*, pp. 243, 248, and 250.
197 *ÍH*, pp. 96 and 246. *Post*, p. 187.
198 *Post*, p. 185.

sermon for the feast of the Purification of Mary, they are described as blind because they "kenndust eigi við Guð þá er hann var hjá þeim, þó að þeir vissi tilkomu hans" [did not know God while he was with them, even though they were expecting his arrival].[199] This is framed slightly differently in another sermon from the *Icelandic Homily Book*, where the position of the gentiles or heathens (*heiðnar þjóðir*) is contrasted to that of the Jews:

> Heiðnar þjóðir vóru í hugarmyrkri, því að þeir sáu eigi ið sanna ljós, þá er þeir kunnu eigi skapera sinn. En Gyðingar höfðu ljós, því að þeir trúðu rétt á Guð. En af því kallast Kristur heldur ljós heiðinna þjóða en Gyðinga, að heiðnar þjóðir lýstust í hingaðkvomu hans, en Gyðingar margir týndu þá því ljósi, er áður höfðu þeir, því að þeir vildu eigi trúa á hann.[200]
>
> [Heathen nations remained in the darkness of mind, for they did not see the true light, as they did not recognize their creator. But Jews had their light, for they had a correct faith in God. But therefore Christ is rather called the light of the heathen nations, for the heathen nations were enlightened through his arrival, but the Jews lost the light they had had before, for they did not want to believe in him.]

Like heathens and heretics, the Jews are depicted as envious, with one of the main motivating factors behind Jesus' crucifixion being the Jews' envy.[201] Similarly, the Jewish leaders envied the apostles when the crowds started gathering around them which led them to acts of violence to the Christians.[202] At the same time, envy is described as the force which brought condemnation over them: "Gyðingar fyrirdømdu sik ok kynsmenn sina af ófund sinni" [the Jews condemned themselves and their kinsmen with their envy].[203]

3.2.2 Encountering the 'Other'

As can be seen from the above discussion, there exist illustrious examples of different groups of opponents in the hagiographical literature of the 12th and 13th century, ranging from arch-heretics such as Simon Magus to pagan kings in foreign lands. However, it is likely that Icelandic clerics were not very preoccupied with the difference between such opponents. Surely, it was not the case that Icelandic clerics had problems understanding the rudimentary differences

---

199 *ÍH*, p. 83.
200 *ÍH*, p. 122.
201 *Post*, p. 184. See also *ÍH*, p. 243.
202 *Post*, pp. 165 and 167.
203 *Post*, p. 187.

between a pagan and a heretic like some scholars have suggested.[204] When pushed, most learned clerics would probably have been able to explain it, but what is more likely is that the difference did not make such a big difference to them.[205] There were probably few pagans and even fewer heretics to be found in 12th and 13th century Iceland, at least according the definition above. More important for the purposes of this study, however, is what they had in common, that is to say their opposition, resistance and disobedience to the representatives of the Church, which, unlike actual pagans and actual heretics was not lacking in the Icelandic Free State.

3.2.2.1   Expansion of Error

As noted, medieval Icelanders did not expect to encounter the enemies discussed above as they were described exactly in homiletic and hagiographic texts. That, however, did not mean that they would not encounter enemies of the Church who could be expected to behave in similar ways. All enemies of the Church were, namely, sprung of the same root and were manifestations of the same cardinal error of turning away from God. In fact, there even existed a term which could include this general opposition, namely, *villa*. The term can be translated as 'heresy' in the strict sense of a dissenting Christian but it can also carry a considerably broader meaning so as to include a much larger group of people, pagans, Jews, and others who have turned their back on God and the Church.[206]

An account of the origin of error is found in the *Saga of the Apostles Simon and Jude* in a speech given by the apostle Simon to the wise men of Persia on how the angel of envy (*ófundarengill*) lured the first human beings into disobedience. He tells them that humankind was born into the world from one man and one woman, created and placed in the region of life (*lífsherad*) by God. Soon, however the angel of envy enters the stage:

---

204   Sverrir Jakobsson, *Við og veröldin*, p. 150.
205   "Difference is rarely something to be noted; it is, most often, something in which one has a stake. Above all, it is a political matter." Smith, "What a Difference a Difference makes," p. 252.
206   In the *Saga of the Apostle Andrew*, the apostle Matthew is captured by "pagans" ("tekinn af heiðnum monnum"), but a little later their position is described as *villa*. *Post*, pp. 319–320. As for Jews, in the *Saga of the Apostle James* it says that many converted to the Christian faith and abandoned the error of the Jews (*villu Gyðinga*). *Post*, pp. 516, 522 (AM 652/630 4to), 526 (AM 645 4to). Interestingly, in this case, the phrase *villa Gyðinga* [Jewish Heresy] is not to be found in the Latin original and therefore a likely addition by the Icelandic translator.

> [Þ]a teygði ófundarengill þau til þess at briota guðs boðorð skapara sins, ok voru þau þa anauðguð af diofli, þviat þau hlyddu teygingum hans, ok voru ger utlæg hingat i heim or lifs heraði.²⁰⁷
>
> [the Angel of Envy allured them into breaking the commandment of God their Creator, and they were enslaved by the Devil, for they paid heed to his temptations, and were made outcasts here in the world from out of the district of life].

In his mercy, however, God granted that men would not become subject to death if they would love their creator which called for the following response of the inimical angel:

> En sa hinn versti engill gerði sva, at maðrinn hvarf fra skapara sinum guði atmatkum (sic) ok truði a skurðgoð, ok kallaði þat guð sinn, er hann gerði sialfr. En er maðrinn hvarf fra guði grøðara sinum, þa varð hann i velldi ovinar sins, en ófundarengill føddi af þvi þessa villu með monnum, at hann mætti hafa velldi yfir þeim, at gera við þa, sem hann villdi.²⁰⁸
>
> [But the Worst Angel made it so that the man turned from his Creator Almighty God and professed faith in heathen idols, and proclaimed things that he made himself to be gods. And when man turned from God his Savior, he gave himself over to the power of his enemy, and the Angel of Envy feeds this [error] in men so that he can have power over them and do with them as he wishes].²⁰⁹

According to this version of the fall, error is taken to mean a turning from the "Creator Almighty God" into a state of being lost. This turning away from God is denoted with the Icelandic verb *hverfa fra* which in this case is a rendering of the Latin verb *recedere*.²¹⁰ Such a version of the fall understands error as a

---

207   *Post*, p. 783. Trans. Roughton II, p. 800.
208   *Post*, pp. 783–784. Trans. Roughton II, pp. 799–800.
209   Here, Roughton's translation has been modified by replacing the word 'heresy' with the word 'error.' Such a translation does not have as restricted a meaning to theological or religious content and is also closer to the Latin source text, which Roughton has identified as a version of the *Virtutes* of Simon and Jude, going as follows: "Hunc autem errorem in omnibus hic angelus princeps inuidiæ ideo nutriit: ut ipse eis dominetur: et faciat de eis: quod ipse uoluerit." Mombritius II, pp. 536–537. Other improvements of this translation would be to replace "Savior" with "healer," which is a more precise rendering of the word "grøðari."
210   "Egit autem hic ipse pessimus homo ut a creatore suo recedens idola coleret et elementa adoraret." Mombritius II, p. 536.

movement away from God, keeping it relatively open where to the movement is directed. In such a state of disorientation, it does not really matter what one stumbles upon as one's object of worship – be it of gold, silver, wood, stone or other human beings – it is going to be an error.

Those who did not obey the Church were in danger of being counted as 'heretics,' immediately aligned with notorious heretics and violent pagan kings. They have turned away from God and become subject to the power, or better, the dominion of the enemy (*veldi*). Therefore, although this understanding of 'error' or 'heresy' was in effect relatively broad, one point remains clear. Error amounts to being lead into enslavement and dominion of the Devil. As an example, in the *Saga of the Apostles Simon and Jude,* the apostles are shown following two Babylonian sorcerers, described as men of error (*villumenn*) performing erroneous deeds (*villuverk*), with the eventual result of exposing their teaching as being of the Devil.[211] In a dualistic religious framework like the one encountered in this text, there is no neutral zone; disobedience to God and his commandments equals submitting to the rule of God's enemy, the Devil.[212]

A similarly open understanding of the term *villa* is found in the sermons preserved from the Free State period. In many sermons found in the *Icelandic Homily Book*, the state of error is described as a state of darkness, blindness, or being covered by clouds. It is the "dark night of sins and error" as an Easter Day sermon puts it.[213] In a sermon entitled *Postulamál* the apostles are compared to a light, "því að kenningar þeirra lýstu of allan heim þá, er áður vóru í villumyrkri" [for their teachings lighted up those people around the world who before remained in darkness of error].[214] In a Christmas day sermon, Christ is described as "sá er lýsir allan heim af villu eilífs blindleiks" [the one who lights up the entire world from the error of eternal blindness].[215] In a sermon on the meaning of the Sunday, the darkness of error (*villumyrkur*) is said to recede to the light of faith just as the primordial darkness gave way to the light at the

---

211 "[P]ostolarnir [...] syndu kenning þeira vera af diöfli," *Post*, p. 787.
212 This conception of the notion of error is related to what the German historian Herbert Grundmann termed in a 1927 article as the figure or the type of the heretic, broadly applied to any sort of religious deviance or departure from other prevailing norms. Inspecting and placing the heretic over against the most significant theological frameworks of the day, Grundmann located him in the *civitas diaboli* from an Augustinian point of view, and eschatologically the heretic belongs to the hosts of the antichrist. Herbert Grundmann, "Der Typus des Ketzers in Mittelalterlicher Anschauung," in *Kultur- und Universalgeschichte: Walter Goetz zu seinem 60. Geburtstage* (Leipzig/Berlin, 1927), p. 93.
213 *ÍH*, p. 103.
214 *ÍH*, p. 21.
215 *ÍH*, p. 67.

moment of God's creation.[216] The apostle John is taken as an example of an individual whose eyes of the mind were never covered with the clouds of error (*villuský*).[217]

Such an inclusive use of 'error' has been the subject of much discussion as it links into the notion of heresy as it came to be used in High Medieval Europe. In his York Quodlibet lecture from 2000, Alexander Patschovsky stated that although the concept was lacking a clear definition and dogmatic grounding, "[h]eresy is to be found at the basis, not at the margin of medieval society."[218] It should be emphasized that Patschovsky is concerned with the fact that medieval society was, at this point in time, marked by incessant conflicts; it was a 'persecuting society' as R. I. Moore described this social reality.[219] In his lecture, Patschovsky describes how political hostilities increasingly came to be expressed in religious terms and took the shape of religion. He further asserts that the concept of heresy inflated and increasingly became a weapon in political conflicts. In that light, he states "that in the course of time, *the* heresy par excellence had become disobedience instead of disbelief."[220] In that sense, *villa* and its adherents, *villumenn*, can be broadly applied to all who do not conform with the Church's prescriptions, whether in the field of religion and morality or regarding issues of more political nature such as taxation and property rights. And when so used, the term did not lose its meaning of 'heresy' in the religious sense, with all its repercussions, but much rather inflated.

3.2.2.2 Becoming Other

Although the 'other' was primarily found in the books of clergymen or painted on church walls, such figures should not be regarded as insignificant but as actual part of the world where they could influence and even participate in the events taking place. As for where and how is another question which will be

---

216 *ÍH*, p. 36.
217 *ÍH*, p. 260.
218 Alexander Patschovsky, "Heresy and Society: On the Political Function of Heresy in the Medieval World," in *Texts and the Repression of Medieval Heresy*, eds. Caterina Bruschi and Peter Biller, York Studies in Medieval Theology IV (Suffolk, 2003), p. 41.
219 R. I. Moore, *The Formation of a Persecuting Society: Authority and Deviance in Western Europe 950–1250*, 2nd ed. (Oxford, 2007).
220 Patschovsky, "Heresy and Society," p. 26. For a more recent discussion of the heresy of disobedience, see Gerd Althoff's discussion of the "the heresy of the disobedient" (*Die Häresie des Ungehorsams*) which he traces back to the polemical rhetoric of the reforming pope Gregory VII who did not hesitate to dub those who did not obey his instructions as heretics (neither did he have any problems backing it up with biblical prooftexts). Gerd Althoff, *"Selig sind, die Verfolgung Ausüben": Päpste und Gewalt im Hochmittelalter* (Darmstadt, 2013), pp. 47–53 and 189–213.

addressed in the following paragraphs. As noted, the construction of an 'other' and creating an enemy is, namely, not simply another way of denoting difference. It is, as stressed at the beginning of this section, sociopolitical, insofar that it is concerned with sub- and superordination within a social hierarchy of prestige. Different things may exist without their paths ever crossing while the 'other' always entails reciprocity; it is a relational concept which does not exist in and of itself. Despite its connotations of something far-off and exotic, the 'other' should not be taken as referring to what is remote but rather what is close, at least what is in sight and reach. Construing otherness is a way of grappling with something one has come across and experienced as different. Thus, an 'other' is most often a 'proximate other,' a relational category, a term of interaction.

That said, it might seem peculiar to discuss the 'other,' not to speak of a 'proximate other' in the context of the Church's enemies discussed above, who were absent in the Icelandic Free State. As it happens, however, the source material contains explanations of how these enemies could break out of the realm of the purely mythical into history and become real. To that end, it is necessary to keep in mind the backdrop of the cosmic battle ongoing every day and no one questioned.[221] As described in a translation of Gregory the Great's *Dialogi*, it is "difficult to fight off the Devil's guile, as it was in a constant battle" [erfiðlegt [...] að sjá við vélum óvinarins og sem í orrustu sé ávallt].[222] The Devil and his forces ambush the thoughts, words, and deeds of the people, leading them off the right way. As can be seen in the hagiographic sources, however, it was not necessarily the demons themselves which could prove the most harmful to the apostolic protagonists, although there are certainly examples thereof, but the actual, human agents which had been successfully led astray by the demonic forces. All of them share the same capital fault of having turned away from God and joined the group of the outsiders, those who have been driven away "frá Guði og í sveit rekninga hans" [from God to the team of his outcasts], as it says in a homily from the *Icelandic Homily Book* entitled *In Passione Domini*.[223]

It should be stressed at this point that according to the elaborate body of thought existing on the topic in the High Middle Ages, the change which people underwent in the spiritual struggle was not only a mental or a metaphorical change, but an actual physical change. The following excerpt from the longest sermon of the *Icelandic Homily Book* describes what is happening in the body

---

221 For further discussion, see section 3.3.2.1 below.
222 *Leifar*, pp. 99–100.
223 *ÍH*, p. 130.

when people fight evil forces with the means offered by the Medieval Western Church:

> Skulum vér og það líkja eftir honum að þröngva líkamanum til þess, að eitrið fari úr hugnum, þröngva með meinlætum, föstum og vökum, að vaka um tíðir vel, í erfiðlífi að vinna trúlega, þeir er verkmenn eru, eða þótt eigi heiti verkmenn, og er þó hverjum hjálpvænlegt að erfiða sér í nökkvi, ef hann er heill, svo sem hver er helst til fær, sumir í bænahaldi og knébeðjarföllum, í smíðum, þeir er hagir eru, fylgja ófærum mönnum yfir vötn, eða slíkt er Guð skýtur hverjum í hug að gera til hjálpar sér og strýkva svo eitrið úr hugnum, reiði og ranglæti, bölvun og bakmæli, öfund og ofmetnuð. Eitur er slíkt kallað.[224]
>
> [Let us imitate him to force the body so that the poison can leave the mind, force it with ascetic practices, fasts and through waking, to pay close attention to the offices, to work faithfully in difficult times, those who are workers, or if they are not workers, since it is beneficient for all to work hard at some project, if he is healthy, and to the extent one can manage, some in prayers or kneefall, in carpentry for those who are skillful, help those who can't cross waters over them, or whatever God may invoke with anybody to do for one's sake and thus push the poison out of the mind, anger and wrongdoing, cursing and gossiping, envy and ambition. Such things we call poision.]

As this passage makes clear, the physical and the spiritual sides of the human being were closely connected in medieval Christian thought. There are physical practices which force the poision out of the mind of the person bringing about changes in the entire being of the individual – from the outmost layers of the skin to the innermost spiritual capacities. The individual in question becomes clean, light, and healed.

The process was understood to affect the entire being of the individual – body and soul, and spirit, understood as a psychosomatic unity, much in line with what was happening elsewhere in the Christian West in the 12th and 13th centuries.[225] Another example of that is when those attending mass are asked to take off their hats so the words of the gospel will reach their minds more easily: "Því tökum vér höttu af höfði oss, að ekki sé þess, er byrgi hlust vora og

---

224 *ÍH*, p. 226.
225 See Caroline Walker Bynum, *The Resurrection of the Body in Western Christianity, 200–1336* (New York, 1995), pp. 156–199; Caroline Walker Bynum, "Soul and Body," in *Dictionary of the Middle Ages, Supplement 1* (New York, 2004), pp. 590–592.

allra helst hugskots vors hlust frá orði Drottins" [therefore do we remove our hats so they do not cover our ears and most importantly the ears of our minds from hearing the word of the Lord].²²⁶

In an Old Icelandic translation of *Elucidarius*, the soul and spirit are said to be so thoroughly combined that the body appears to be doing everything which the soul does ("líkamur sýnist allt gera það er önd gerir").²²⁷ It should be stressed, however, that the attitude towards the body was not necessarily negative, although it was highly ambiguous.²²⁸ It was only negative if the person failed to pay heed to the Church's instructions and turn over to the side of the enemy. Or better, to become an enemy oneself. In that sense, in a society such as the Icelandic Free State were the Roman Church was establishing itself, everyone could become an enemy and join the group of heretics, Jews, and heathens.

For exploring this point further, it can prove illustrative to consider notions of presence and absence prevalent in medieval Scandinavian culture. In a 2016 article, Richard Cole sets out a typology of absence in Old Norse literature in which he divides absence into seven types that he places on a scale ranging from perfect absence to perfect presence.²²⁹ It seems helpful to think of the opponents of the Church as being in a state of 'becoming,' a term Cole adopts from Gilles Deleuze, either that of 'becoming-present' or 'becoming-absent.' As an example of a phenomenon reflecting the state of becoming absent, Cole discusses a phenomenon recurring in Old Norse literary works, that of a ghost (*draugr*) which he describes as the "agressively present bodies of the deceased,"

---

226   *ÍH*, p. 185. The connection between outer looks and religious piety have been studied recently in studies on disability in medieval societies. Irina Metzler, *Disability in Medieval Europe: Thinking about Physical Impairment During the High Middle Ages, c. 1100–1400*, Routledge Studies in Medieval Religion and Culture 5 (London, 2006). For an overview article about disability in Icelandic medieval literature, see Ármann Jakobsson, "Fötlun á Íslandi á miðöldum: svipmyndir," in *Fötlun og menning* (Reykjavík, 2013), pp. 51–69. Jakobsson does, however, only shortly touch upon religious interpretations of physical impairment and disabilities in Icelandic medieval society.

227   *Þrjár þýðingar lærðar*, p. 103.

228   See especially Caroline Walker Bynum, *Holy Feast and Holy Fast: The Religious Significance of Food to Medieval Women*, New Historicism (Berkeley, 1987).

229   The types of absence Cole suggests are i) never-here-never there (perfect absence), ii) never-here-now-there, iii) once-here-now-gone, iv) once-here-now-there, v) becoming-absent, vi) becoming-present, vii) here (perfect presence). Richard Cole, "Towards a Typology of Absence in Old Norse Literature," *Exemplaria* 28 (2016): 137–160. Cole's typology is grounded in Patric Fuery's theorizing on absence, see his *The Theory of Absence: Subjectivity, Signification, and Desire*, Contributions in Philosophy 55 (London, 1995).

disappearing in daylight and reappearing when they are least wanted. Ármann Jakobsson places ghosts in a group with a number of phenomena which he collectively terms "anti-social others."[230] When ghosts appear, they are physically there, but they are also able to suddenly vanish. Cole suggests that the best way to describe the absence of a ghost is not in terms of a static entity but rather as moving on a trajectory between presence and absence. To be clear, the enemies of the Church were no ghosts. As regards their presence, however, they are similar to ghosts insofar that they were in a constant state of becoming either absent or present, which was primarily determined by the degree of piety and obedience they showed or failed to show.

3.2.3 Conclusion: Making Enemies

The information preserved in medieval hagiographic and homiletic writings about the adversities and persecutions suffered by the early Church was a rich source about the Church's enemies. At first glance at least, these enemies seem foreign – not to say irrelevant – to the homogenous society of the Icelandic Free State. There were no Jews in medieval Iceland, religious deviance was rare if existent, and the presence of heathendom or the Old Norse religion seems to have waned consistently after the arrival of Christianity. As has been emphasized in this section, however, the rich collection of opponents one encounters in the early Christian source material was by no means unimportant in the sociopolitical conflicts in which the Church found itself during this time. On the contrary, it provided Christians in Iceland with figures, ideas, and imagery to interpret and understand any opposition they might face. It is likely that these images produced feelings of fear and horror among the audience which could be mobilized in the Church's favor in moments of conflict. Out of the diverse groups of enemies there emerges a fluid and flexible notion of an 'other.' The religious discourse of the Church provided churchmen with a template or a type of an enemy which could be adapted to different situations and different opponents with relative ease. The enemies of the Church were real although the exact nature of their deviance would continue to change. For the Roman Church in Iceland, in the social and political conflicts of the day, what mattered the most was to realize whether or not somebody was an opponent. After somebody had been singled out as an enemy, it was among the most powerful discursive strategies of the Church to juxtapose that enemy with the hosts of enemies from the Church's past. There existed even elaborate

---

230   Ármann Jakobsson, "The Fearless Vampire Killers: A Note about the Icelandic Draugr and Demonic Contamination in Grettis Saga," *Folklore* 120 (2008), 310.

ideas explaining how people, through the sinful defilement of their body and soul (and sometimes spirit) could turn into enemies. In such a way, the groups and individuals 'othered' in the texts provided historical agents in medieval Iceland with tools to grapple with what they had experienced as an 'other' in their own historical reality.

3.3 Perish or Prosper

In the first two sections of this chapter, it has been shown how clearly the lines between the opposite sides of 'us' and 'them,' the known and the 'other,' good and evil, God and the Devil, the Church and its enemies are constructed in the earliest Christian discourse of the Icelandic Free State. These dividing lines were paramount for the construction of the Christian world-view. The world, the stage on which history unfolded itself, was represented as a field of constant tension and conflict between these two sides. This inherently dualistic framework does not allow for much impartiality or undecidedness. In accordance with this world-view, the early Christian discourse presented its audience with clear alternatives and demanded reaction from its audiences with great urgency. Much in line with Jesus' saying in Matt. 12:30, "Whoever is not with me is against me," they were urged to take a stance with the Church, accept its message and follow its commands, or they would oppose it and face the consequences. Coming back to the imperial hermeneutical framework, subjects of empires are programmatically provided with these kinds of alternatives: either to submit, enjoy, and prosper or resist, suffer and perish.[231] In this final part of the source analysis, the question will be addressed as to how such alternatives were presented to Icelandic Christians in the Free State era. In the first part of this section, attention will be directed to the benefits of accepting the social order promoted in ecclesiastical discourse and, although to a lesser degree, the perils of rejecting it. In the second part, the discussion will move beyond questions of merely social nature and explore how the early ecclesiastical discourse raised the stakes to ultimate proportions. As they were constructed, the alternatives posed to the Icelandic audience were of no mundane significance. Siding for or against the message of the Church amounted to taking sides in a battle between the cosmic forces of good and evil and was, in the end, a matter of one's own eternal salvation.

---

231 Münkler, *Empires*, pp. 81–84 and pp. 101–107.

3.3.1 Peace or Unrest?

Peace is a contested concept and can acquire diverse meanings in different historical and cultural contexts. Understood either negatively as an absence of war and conflict or positively as a state of harmony and well-being, most, if not all of the world's traditional religions view peace as a desirable goal for any society to reach.[232] The Icelandic term *friðr* appears frequently in the earliest discourse of the Church in Iceland which is hardly a surprise given how prominent a place it has enjoyed in the Christian religion from the beginning.[233] In the texts under inspection, the concept of peace covers a range of meanings.[234] More often than not, *friðr* is generally a translation of the word *pax*, which is highly charged both religiously and politically.[235] In contrast, its opposite *ófriðr* refers to violence and aggression and in the earliest religious discourse of the Church almost without exception towards the proponents of the Christian religion. Considering the frequent association of peace with tranquility, care and harmony, it may come as a surprise that peace and peacemaking have often been used in order to justify overlordship and domination. According to a narrative which seems to emerge again and again around imperial formations, true and lasting peace can only be reached through imperial rule while everything outside the imperial boundaries is portrayed as disruptive

---

232 For different representations of peace in several world religions, s.v. "Frieden," in *Religion in Geschichte und Gegenwart*, 4th ed. The distinction between positive and negative peace is usually attributed to the Norwegian peace researcher Johan Galtung but similar formulations had been set forth by American activists Jane Addams in her *Newer Ideals of Peace: The Moral Substitutes for War* (Chester, 2005) and Martin Luther King Jr, see esp. his "Letter from Birmingham Jail" in *Letter From Birmingham Jail*, Penguin Modern (New York, 2018).

233 To bring up a few important examples from the New Testament writings, Jesus greets his disciples by wishing them peace and as he sends them out to preach his message, similarly instructs them to address those they meet with greetings of peace (Luke 10:5). In the sermon on the Mount, Jesus blesses the bringers of peace and elsewhere he tells them to "have salt in yourselves, and be at peace with one another" (Mark 9:50). Furthermore, peace is a standard part of the greetings in the New Testament epistles attributed to the apostles Paul, Peter and John.

234 Fritzner defines *friðr* as either "love" or "peace between persons and countries, as well as the safety from whatever harmful situation." Fritzner, s.v. "friðr", 489. Etymologically, *friðr* is derived from the Proto-Germanic word *friþuz* which means either tranquility or the absence of conflict or sanctuary or refuge.

235 As for the religio-political significance of the term *pax*, it has been concisely described by Croatian-Austrian philosopher Ivan Illich: "[T]he term [*pax*] was exploited by Constantine to turn the cross into ideology. Charlemagne utilized it to justify the genocide of the Saxons. Pax was the term employed by Innocent III to subject the sword to the cross." Ivan Illich, "Peace vs Development," *Democracy* 2 (January, 1981), 45.

FORCE OF WORDS: CONSTRUCTING A CHRISTIAN SOCIETY 199

and in turmoil, in opposition to the peace. As formulated by political scientist Herfried Münkler: "Imperial ideology counters the supposed naturalness of small-scale political orders by pointing to their notorious lack of peace."[236] As the narrative goes, which has appeared in diverse shapes and forms throughout history as Münkler has shown, it is only by succumbing to a grand-scale political order through a rule of an imperial center that disorder and hostility can be put to rest.[237] Running through the source material of this research, is a narrative thread conceptualizing peace in those terms. As has been emphasized earlier, however, multilayered religious concepts like peace should not be reduced to their sociopolitical conflict potentials. Even though this section will focus on how peace was constructed in the Church's earliest discourse in order to counter and suppress opposition, it does not mean that it loses its religious and existential dimensions. On the contrary, the sociopolitical significance of the concept of peace lies to a considerable degree in its multiple layers of meaning.

3.3.1.1   Performing Peace

The liturgy of the mass provides an illuminating point of departure for a discussion of the topic of peace and unrest as constructed in ecclesiastical discourse. Anybody regularly attending a mass would inevitably have to come to grips with the notion of peace as *pax* through the liturgical performance of the celebrant. In addition to the references to peace an audience came across in scriptural readings over the course of the church year, it was also a fixed part of the medieval mass through the liturgical salutation *pax vobis* (or equivalent greetings of peace such as *pax vobiscum* or *pax tecum*). As a rule, greetings of peace would occur at two occasions in medieval masses following the Roman rite. Assuming that the explanation of the mass found in the *Icelandic Homily Book* reflects actual liturgical practices, the same applies for masses held in Iceland in the 12th and 13th centuries. This explanation is based on the *Gemma animæ* by Honorius Augustodunensis and is also found in later manuscripts.[238] First, while an ordinary cleric would greet his congregation before the collect with the salutation *Dominus vobiscum*, a greeting of peace, *pax vobiscum*, was used by a bishop at the same point in the course of the mass. This is explained in the following way in the *Homily Book*: "Biskup kveður: Pax vobiscum, friður með yður, því að Drottinn boðaði mönnum frið í hingaðkomu sinni" [Bishop

---

236   Münkler, *Empires*, p. 81.
237   Ibid., pp. 81–84.
238   "Introduction" in *IHB*, p. 12.

says: Pax vobiscum, peace be with you, for in his arrival the Lord proclaimed peace to men].[239] Another point in the mass where the congregation would be greeted with peace by the celebrant – bishops and priests alike – was between the consecration of the Eucharistic elements and communion. This greeting was accentuated with a kiss of peace (*osculum sanctum, osculum pacis*) carried around the congregation from the altar.[240]

What a person could learn about peace in terms of detailed content as it was being presented in the liturgy of the mass was probably not much. It is not at all certain that everybody would have known the meaning of *pax* and unlikely that everybody would have taken it the same way. It is not even likely that people were interested in learning anything concrete about it at all. The Latin liturgy probably left people with vague outlines of a mysterious idea, repeatedly uttered by the celebrant. Nonetheless, peace was being represented as a phenomenon in the possession of the Church and in the power of its ordained servants to bestow. Although the liturgy of the mass itself did not offer much room for expounding upon the notion of peace, a priest might have provided his congregation with an explanation of the symbolic meaning of the ritual kissing of peace along the lines found in the *Icelandic Homily Book*. "Því gefur hver frið öðrum í friðarkossi, að sá má frið öðlast af Guði, er friðsamur er við náunga sína."[241] [Therefore does one give peace to each other through the kiss of peace, that he receives peace from God, who is peaceful towards his neighbours.]. In this sense, peace has a meaning similar to love (*ást*), care (*alúð*) and agreement (*sátt*). Such was also the mentality required of those who attended mass in general: "Þá er vér komum til kirkju og sækjum tíðir, þá höfum vér ást og frið hver við annan, því að ósæmt er, að vér hafim hatur í hjörtum órum, þá er vér stöndum að sáttarfundi Guðs og manna."[242] [When we come to Church and attend holy office, we should show love and peace to one another, for it is not fitting that we harvest hate in our hearts, as we attend the meeting of reconciliation of God and men.]. Thus, the references to peace in the liturgy refers to a trouble-free and harmonious relationship between individuals but also between men and divine beings, such as God and his saints.

---

239 *ÍH*, pp. 183–184.
240 Magnús Már Lárusson, "Fredskys" in *KLNM* IV, cols. 608–610. A kiss of peace is also described before the execution of the apostle James where it symbolized the faith of the Jewish official Josias who decided to convert to Christianity. *Post*, pp. 519 and 529.
241 *ÍH*, p. 189.
242 *ÍH*, p. 153.

3.3.1.2 Peace of the Church

The outlines of the notion of peace encountered in the liturgy were being filled in, modified and expanded elsewhere. Certainly, the positive conception of peace as active love and care as seen in the mass explanation is also present in the hagiographic and sermonic texts from the same period. In the *Saga of the Apostle Peter*, the apostle Paul describes his preaching for example as "þat er til friðar er ok astar" [the things that engender peace and love] and further that he went "með friðarboði allt i Jerusalem" [with a message of peace around all Jerusalem].[243] Such a peace, however, was not available for everybody but a privilege for Christians and the Church reserved the right to establish the conditions under which people were entitled to enjoy the Church's peace and the requirements that had to be fulfillled.

On several occasions, both in sermons and hagiographic translations, the conditions of peace are defined considerably clearly. In a sermon from the *Icelandic Homily Book* to be delivered on the Feast of the Annunciation it is stated that peace is available for all men of good will. As for who men of good will are, the sermon clearly states: "Þeir eru með góðum vilja, er á Guð almáttkan trúa og hans boðorð halda og þykjast und honum allt traust eiga, en ekki und sjálfum sér." [They are of good will who believe in almighty God and keep his commandments and know that all their trust should be on him and not themselves.][244] This explanation of men of good will and consequently those who are entitled to peace contains two of the most frequently expressed requirements for the peace offered by the Church: adhering to the correct doctrine and behaving accordingly, which in the Middle Ages were the main constituents of the Christian faith. Before the growth of scholastic theology, there would not be a great distinction between matters of doctrine and moral practice. The confession of faith would always entail adhering to moral instructions and religious ceremonies.[245] Another example of how doctrine was portrayed as constituting the grounds for peace can be found in the *Saga of the Apostle Andrew*. In a prologue to the *passio* section of the saga the following connection is made between peace and faith:

> Friðr se yðr ollum kristnum monnum, er settir eruð i Kristz nafni i austri ok vestri, i norðri ok suðri, ok ollum þeim, er trua a einn guð i algørri þrenningu, sannan föður ogetinn, sannan son eingetinn af feðr, sannan

---

243 *Post*, p. 190. Trans. Roughton II, p. 541.
244 *ÍH*, p. 194.
245 Jaroslav Pelikan, *The Growth of Medieval Theology 600–1300*, The Christian Tradition 3 (Chicago, 1978), pp. 11–23.

helgan anda framfaranda af feðr ok syni, ok þann foður almatkan truum ver allan einn vera, er gat son, ok son eingetinn, þann er getinn er af almatkum feðr.²⁴⁶

[Peace be with you, all Christian men who are established in Christ's name in the east and west, north and south, and all who believe in one God in the perfect Trinity, the true father unbegotten, the one true Son begotten of the Father, the true Holy Spirit proceeding from the Father and Son, and that Almighty Father we believe to be entirely one, who begot the Son, and the Son only begotten, who was begotten by the Almighty Father.]

While the phrase "Peace be with you," is clearly modelled after the salutation formula, "Grace and peace be with you" from the New Testament epistles, and should by no means be taken as original, the passage still shows how the correct faith – summed up in a formula with an unmistakable Nicene flavor – is a prerequisite for enjoying the peace offered by the medieval Church, in this case the author of the text ("sa er sǫguna hefir setta").²⁴⁷ Thus, peace had its boundaries and as it was constructed by the medieval Church in Iceland, the area of peace corresponded to the area where the Church had secured its ground, between Christians in Christian territories.

The premises for peace are established on a more practical level in a passage from a Christmas sermon from the *Icelandic Homily Book*. Interestingly for the purposes of this study, it does so by means of an imperial metaphor, comparing Christ's bringing of peace to emperor Augustus' *Pax Romana*.

Þá er Augustus kom í Rúmsborg og gaf alla skuld, þá er fólkið átti að gjalda honum á því ári, svo að vísu gefur oss Dominus noster syndir órar og skuldir fyr helga skírn og fyr sanna játning og algjörva iðrun glæpa vorra, þeirra er vér gerðum í gegn vilja hans. Í hans ríki gerðist svo mikill friður of allan heim, svo að engi maður bar hervopn, því að horvetna var friður og samþykki og eitt ríki. Fyr það boðast friðsamt ríki sonar Guðs lifanda, sá er frið gerði á meðal himins og jarðar, og hann gerði eitt ríki.²⁴⁸

[As Augustus came to the City of Rome and exempted the people from the debts they had due that year, in the same way does Dominus noster forgive us our sins and debts through holy baptism for a true confession, and a complete repentance of the crimes we committed against his will.

---

246 *Post*, p. 336. Trans. Roughton II, p. 639.
247 *Post*, p. 336.
248 *ÍH*, p. 67.

There was such a great peace around the entire world in his domain that no one carried arms, for everywhere was peace and agreement and one domain. For this we proclaim the peaceful domain of the Son of God, who made peace between heaven and earth, and he made one domain.]

There is an interesting discrepancy between the peace brought around by Augustus and that of Christ. Emperor Augustus is said to have simply exempted the people from their debts while it is assumed that Christ's forgiveness and thereby his peace is given for a specific price—namely the religious practices of baptism, confession, and penance. The peace promised by the Church is thus dependent on the religious beliefs and practices constituting a Christian society and corresponds in an important sense to the social order which the Church strove to maintain.

The Western Church had at its disposal a long-standing interpretative tradition equating peace with the natural order of things. At the heart of that tradition lie Augustine's formulations of the concept of peace from the nineteenth book of the *City of God*. A large part of the book is devoted to explaining how peace manifests itself on the different levels of human existence, ranging from the level of body and soul to different relationships such as the household, the relationship between God and man and ending with the entire universe. On all these levels, Augustine contends, the state of peace is maintained by heeding the proper order of things established by God:

> [P]eace between mortal man and God is an ordered obedience, in faith, in subjection to an everlasting law; peace between men is an ordered agreement of mind with mind; the peace of a home is the ordered agreement among those who live together about giving and obeying orders[.][249]

Coming to the manifestation of peace at the level of the entire universe, Augustine describes it along the same lines, but now with the highly influential notion of peace as a 'tranquility of order,' (*tranquillitas ordinis*) which he further defines as "the arrangement of things equal and unequal in a pattern which assigns to each its proper position."[250] Such a state of peace could, according to Augustine, not materialize fully in the temporal, earthly reality. It is only with the eternal peace of the heavenly city that a perfect tranquility of order can be reached. Nonetheless, there is always the possibility of achieving

---

249 Augustine, *Concerning the City of God against the Pagans*, ed. David Knowles, trans. Henry Bettenson (Harmondsworth, 1972), pp. XIX, 13, 870.
250 Ibid.

'some tranquility of order' and 'some peace' and during the Middle Ages the Church had developed various ways to define itself as the channel of peace in the world and its laws and articles of faith as its main constituents.

Clearly discernible in the sources is the representation of the Church and its proponents as the bringers of peace as the correct order of things. A particularly illustrative case is found in the *Saga of the Apostle Peter*, when the apostle Peter ends his speech against Simon Magus in Caesarea by saying: "Þvi hof ek þetta mal friðsamliga, at ek vil frið ollum bioða."[251] [I delivered this speech peacefully because I wish peace for all.] As the apostle is forced by his remonstrant Simon to expand on the advantages of peace, he provides an answer harmonizing with Augustinian understanding of peace as the tranquility of order. He explains that all of God's laws are given in peace, that they maintain peace and that all of God's commandments stand with peace.[252] Wherever the peace is broken, Peter says, there will be disunity among men, robberies, many battles and all sorts of disgrace committed. The only way to mend such a sinful state of affairs is returning to the state of peace, leading Peter to end his speech in the following way: "Ok verðr af því friðrinn upphaf ok niðrlag guðs laga.[253] [therefore peace is the beginning and end of God's laws]. Coming from the mouth of the apostle Peter such a claim would have been highly charged and must have resounded in the Church political landscape of the time.

3.3.1.3 Fighting for Peace

In the sense of a lasting state of love and harmony, peace can be described as an important goal in the Church's program for a fallen world. The eschatological hope for eternal and universal peace does not, however, reflect how the Church's representatives carried out their errands on a day-to-day basis. There is no lack of medieval examples showing how the Church's fondness of peace did not keep it from entering skirmishes and political conflicts where its representatives did all but refrain from using intimidation, coercion and violence.[254] Paradoxically, peace could be used as a legitimation for such measures. The Church's peace does not refer to whatever love, care and agreement can be attained but that of accepting the new state of affairs presented by the

---

251 *Post*, p. 173. Trans. Roughton II, p. 512.
252 *Post*, p. 174. "oll guðs lög eru i friði ok til friðar sett" and "með friði standa oll guðs boðorð".
253 *Post*, p. 174. Roughton II, p. 514.
254 See Althoff, *"Selig sind, die Verfolgung ausüben"*; Philippe Buc, *Holy War, Martyrdom, and Terror: Christianity, Violence, and the West, ca. 70-C.E. to the Iraq War* (Philadelphia, 2015); Craig M. Nakashian, *Warrior Churchmen of Medieval England 1000–1250: Theory and Reality* (Suffolk, 2016.)

Christian religion. Such a situation was something that had to be defended and fought for and could, with recourse to authorities no smaller than Augustine, serve to legitimize its opposite, conflicts and violence.[255] As it is often constructed in the source material, peace is not a means but an end which can be reached in various ways. It is the type of peace which by later thinkers has been called 'peace at any price' or even 'peace of the cemetery.'[256]

Illustrating this is a part from a homily in the *Icelandic Homily Book* to be delivered on All Saints Day. In accordance with the feast day's dedication, a major part of the sermon is devoted to enumerating the large number of saints honored including kings who fought for the kingdom of heaven "by using physical and spiritual weapons" ("með líkamlegum vopnum og andlegum") bringing peace through conquest in war against "God's enemies and their own" ("Guðs andskota og sína").[257] Corroborating further what has been said about the understanding of peace as order, the kings are said to have used them in order to uphold the peace once it had been established through conquest of the opponents. The saintly kings are said to have fought each day against the sins and crimes,

> og ráku svo fyrir ósýnilega fjándur með andlegum vopnum, það er siðum góðum og stjórn, að þeir stýrðu bæði sér og sínu fólki til lagahalds og Guðs boðorða varðveislu sem þeir ráku sýnilega andskota af höndum með sýnilegum vopnum.[258]
>
> [and so they drove out invisible fiends, with spiritual weapons, which are good mores and governance, that they instructed both themselves and their people to keep the laws and the commandments of God just as they drove away visible enemies with visible weaponry.]

The list includes the biblical King David, Roman Emperor Constantine, legendary missionary kings such as King Oswald of Northumbria and Edmund of East Anglia. It ends with King Ólafr "who fought for order and peace in Norway and

---

255   Such a conception of peace harmonizes well with Augustine's much discussed lines from the nineteenth book of the *City of God*: "For every man is in quest of peace, even in waging war, whereas no one is in quest of war when making peace. In fact, even when men wish a present state of peace to be disturbed they do so not because they hate peace, but because they desire the present peace to be exchanged for one that suits their wishes. *Thus their desire is not that there should not be peace but the peace they wish for.*" Augustine, *City of God* XIX, 13, p. 866. Emphasis added.
256   Münkler, *Empires*, p. 82.
257   *ÍH*, p. 227.
258   *ÍH*, p. 228.

righteous laws of the land" ("er til siðar og friðar barðist í Norvegi og landslaga réttra").²⁵⁹

The introduction of Christianity by force into non-Christian territories is a repeated theme in the corpus of preserved hagiographical literature dating to the 12th and 13th century Iceland. The missionary kings stood in a long tradition of apostles and saints who were presented as the bringers of peace at the same time they cause nothing but havoc in the areas where they carry out their mission. The peace brought by the Church is not an acceptance of the *status quo* but an introduction of a new order, the Christian order, which in non-Christian territories would inevitably subvert local customs. The hagiographic literature of course abounds with examples of apostles and saints converting people in great numbers, thereby causing disorder and provoking hostile reactions from local authorities. And until their eventual martyrdom, they might well take all sorts of violent measures.

3.3.1.4 The Danger of Unrest

The construction of peace as the privilege of the Christian society also produced a clear image of an 'other,' constituted by any threat made to the ideal state of peace. These were the disturbers of the peace, referred to with words such as 'prætumenn' [*quarrellers*] or 'ófriðarmenn' [*men of unrest*].²⁶⁰ As noted, according to Augustine and other authors after him, perfect peace was an eschatological state and not attainable in a fallen world.²⁶¹ A very prominent thread in the religious discourse of the Church consists in the Church and its promoters always having to endure opposition and violence which is not infrequently described with the word unrest (*ófriðr*): "En þeir sendimenn Guðs, er hann sendi að boða og reka sín erindi, fyrst spámenn, en síðan postular, þoldu ófrið mikinn af vondum mönnum."²⁶² [But those emissaries of God, who he sent to preach and carry out his errands, first prophets, and later apostles, suffered a great unrest by evil men.] Of this there exist numerous

---

259 *íH*, pp. 227–228. Interestingly, by mentioning King Ólafr, the passage contextualizes the sermon's message in Scandinavian culture which is rare for the sermons found in the Homily Book and never is it done so explicitly.
260 See more detailed discussion on quarreling as a characteristic of the enemies of the Church in section 3.2.1 above.
261 "Jerúsalem þýðist: „friðar sýn" og merkir himneskan frið, þann er Guð gefur vinum sínum með sér á himnum." [Jerusalem means "vision of peace" and means the heavenly peace which God grants to his friends in heaven.] *íH*, p. 22.
262 *íH*, p. 234.

examples in the sagas of the apostles where *ófriðr* refers to any sort of opposition towards Christians ranging from minor acts of violence to wide ranging persecution.[263]

Illustrative of how the ecclesiastical discourse produced an 'other' through the notion of peace is an episode, already discussed in the last section of this study, from the *Saga of the Apostle Peter* where Peter meets and enters into a debate with the arch-heretic Simon magus. The theme of peace, unrest, and quarreling figures prominently in the debate from the beginning on.[264] Simon ferociously attacks Peter on account of a seemingly harmless greeting of peace at the end of his speech and is thus revealed as a quarreler of the worst sort:

> Ver þurfum ekki friðar þins, en ef frið ok samþykki skal til þess hafa at vita, hvat hit sanna er, þa höfum ver miok at þarfleysu hingat farit.[265]
> [We do not need your peace, and if peace and concord are necessary to know the truth then we have come here unncessarily.]

Simon continues by asserting that peace is not the most productive phenomenon for achieving truth. The people who had come to witness the debate were not interested in hearing Simon and Peter to agreeing on all things. Rather, Simon explains, they want to hear about their differences so they can assess the truthfulness of their teachings respectively. He concludes his response saying:

> Þvi þurfum ver ekki at mæla til friðar helldr til þrætu, at þu megir sigr vega a oss, ef þu treystir þer, ok stiga yfir villu vara með rettri skynsemi, ef þu ert við þvi buinn.[266]
> [Therefore we do not need to speak in the name of peace but rather to quarrel so that you might defeat us if you trust yourself, and overcome our heresy with right reason if you are prepared to use it.]

---

263 In the *Icelandic Homily Book* and the hagiographic works subject to the present research, the word *ófriðr* exclusively refers to violence towards Christians.
264 "Menn eru komnir margir ok biða þin, Petrus, ok er Simon oddviti þess liðs, sa er nu er buinn at eiga þrætu við þik." [Many people are here awaiting you, Peter, and Simon is their leader, the one you have had quarrels with already]. *Post*, pp. 172–173.
265 *Post*, p. 173. Trans. Roughton II, p. 512.
266 *Post*, p. 174. For translation, cf. Roughton II, p. 513. His translation of *þræta* as debate and *rett skynsemi* as righteous wisdom is not accurate.

It is of no trivial importance that Simon is introduced as a quarreler. Given Simon's status as a prototypical enemy of the Church, it shows how significantly quarreling and disturbing the established Church order impacted the identity of an enemy of the Christian religion. Those who could be shown to undermine the peace and order established by the Church were dangerously close to the groups of 'others' which have been discussed earlier. It could even be asserted that disturbing the peace and producing unrest is a common attribute for the enemies of the Church. On one occasion in the *Icelandic Homily Book*, for example, those who are said to bring about unrest are simply called "evil men" (*vondir menn*).[267] There are more concrete examples to be found in the source material. In a prayer from the *Icelandic Homily Book*, quarrelers are grouped together with heretics: "Nú skulum vér biðja fyr villumönnum og þrætumönnum, að Guð og vor Dominus leiði af öllum villum og leiði þá til heilagrar og postullegrar kristni."[268] [Let us now pray for heretics and quarrelers, that God and our Dominus will lead them from all error and lead them to holy and apostolic Christianity.] The hagiographic translations show how the instigators of the unrest can be secular authorities like King Herod who is said to have had the apostle James executed or Roman emperors Nero and Domitian. Other less historical figures, earls, governors and pagan religious leaders (*blótbyskupar*) in the areas visited by the apostles are also said to produce unrest as well as unspecified mobs of pagans or Jews.[269]

Whatever harmony and order attainable in this world would be brought about by the Church. Those who threatened to disrupt that order became guilty of a grave offense. They were enemies of the peace, violators of the peace (*perturbator pacis, pacis violator*) and would be treated with anything but mercy. Consider the following excerpt from a speech made by the apostle Matthew in which the apostle expounds on the importance of keeping up "laws of God" and "right customs" from several perspectives.

> Manndrap er ilt, þar er saclaus maþr verþr veginn, oc vitom ver þo stundom lovaþ manndrapet vera oc rétt, þar er ovinr friþarens es drepinn eþa þiofr eþa vikingr.[270]

---

267 *ÍH*, p. 263.
268 *ÍH*, p. 102.
269 For examples see *Post*, p. 170 (Herod) and p. 417 (Nero and Domitian), pp. 737 and 771 (pagans), p. 738 (Jews). See also *Icelandic Homily Book*: "Drottinn flæði til Egiptalands og firrtist Herodem, því að Guðs kenningar hurfu til heiðinna þjóða, þá er Gyðingar gjörðu ófrið Guðs vinum." *ÍH*, p. 264.
270 *Post*, p. 819; Ólafur Halldórsson, *Mattheus saga postula*, p. 49. Trans. Roughton II, p. 824.

[Murder is evil when an innocent man is killed, and yet we know that sometimes murder is permitted and is right, when an enemy of the peace or a thief or a viking is killed.]

Traditionally, the Church renounced the shedding of blood which of course was in violation of the Fifth Commandment. *Ecclesia abhorret a sanguine* is a formula often rehearsed in patristic literature and conciliar proceedings. But there were instances, coming up in increasing measure after the 10th century, in which the killing of another person could be defended.[271]

3.3.2 Heaven or Hell?

In return for their obedience, the Church not only offered order and peace to the Icelanders and their society. Individuals were also offered promises of a more lasting value pertaining to their fate in the hereafter. While faithful and obedient Christians could expect eternal salvation with God in Heaven, those who failed to comply with the Church's instructions and regulations were destined for torturous punishment in Hell. As elsewhere in medieval Christian Europe, matters pertaining to the afterlife figure prominently in Iceland.[272] They also constitute an important part of the imperial logic of domination embedded into the religious discourse of the Church in the Icelandic Free State, whereas the religious specialists of the Church monopolized the knowledge and practical means by which the ordinary Christians could avoid Hell and obtain salvation. On such grounds, they possessed authority to demand people's obedience and influence their behavior.

3.3.2.1 War

On a cosmological plane, there was an ongoing battle between the powers of God and the Devil, often constructed with royal, imperial, and military vocabulary well known from both the Hebrew Bible and Early Christian Writings. God is described as "allsvaldandi himinríkis konungur" [almighty king of the kingdom of heaven], reigning over his dominion (*ríki, veldi*), governing his hosts of angels (*englafylki, englalið, engla sveitir*) in the battle against the enemy of God and humanity (see Figure 10).[273] Similarly, the Devil reigns as the lord of

---

271 Tomaž Mastnak, *Crusading Peace: Christendom, the Muslim World, and Western Political Order* (Berkeley, 2002), p. 16.
272 For an extensive study on how this theme appears in 'original' medieval Icelandic literature, see Haki Antonsson's monograph *Damnation and Salvation in Old Norse Literature*.
273 *ÍH*, p. 56. Devil as the enemy of humanity (*gagnstaðligr ovinr mannkynsins*), Post, p. 332.

darkness (*myrkra höfðingi*) or the lord of the underworld (*Heliar höfðingi*).[274] In the *Saga of the Apostle Bartholomew*, the underworld is represented by its queen Hel upon which Christ made war ("heriadi a Hel drottning vara").[275] The Devil governs his hosts of demons (*djöflar, árar*), urging them to hurt faithful believers,[276] in his own power (*veldi*), promoting "ríki eilífs dauða og djöfullegs máttar"[277] [the dominion of eternal death and demonic power].

In his comprehensive work on medieval Christian religiosity in Western Europe, Arnold Angenendt describes the battle between the opposing sides as being carried out all around and at all times: "In drastischer Allgegenwärtigkeit ist der Teufel am Werk."[278] In realms beyond the human eye, hosts of demons and unclean and maleficient spirits plan their schemes and carry out their attacks on the agents of the Church and faithful Christians (see Figure 11).[279] In early Icelandic Christian discourse, the activities of the Devil, demons and spirits are constructed much in the same way. The hagiographic sources show the inimical forces at work at every corner. They are rarely visible to the ordinary layperson but to the protagonists of the Old Icelandic *vitae*, they appear frequently as shown in the *Saga of Bishop Martin* as found in AM 645 4to:

> Petar og Pol postola letzc hann oft sia. Dioflar como oc stundom at freista hans i ymsom lic(i)om, oc allra oftast i like Þors eþa Oþens eþa Freyio. En Martinus hafði crossmarc at scildi við allre freistne þeira. En hann kende þa, i hverionge likio(m) sem þeir varo, oc nemndi hvern þeira a namn oc fec hveriom þeira þa qveðio, er (þeir) varo verþer: Þor callaþi hann heimscan, en Oþen deigan, en Freyio portcono. Engla guþs sa hann oc oft, oc melto þeir við hann oc sogðo honom fyrer oorþna hluti.[280]

---

274   For the phrase "Myrkra höfðingi" see *Post*, pp. 434 and 718. For "heliar hofdingi" see *Post*, p. 748.

275   *Post*, p. 748. Even though the name Hel is also found in Old Norse mythology, where it refers to the goddess of the underworld, it is clear, as L. Michael Bell points out, that the figure in the *Saga of the Apostle Bartholomew* is the queen of the Christian underworld and not the heathen one. Bell further suggests that it is related to the ambiguous figure of Infer(n)us from the *Gospel of Nicodemus* which in an Old English translation of the gospel took on the guise of the female demoness *seo hell*. L. Michael Bell, "'Hel our Queen': An Old Norse Analogue to an old English Female Hell," *Harvard Theological Review* 76/2 (1983), 263–268, esp. 264–265.

276   "Djöfull fær sinni sveit fjötra til meina oss." [The demon provides his hosts with shackles to inflict pain on us] *ÍH*, p. 28.

277   *ÍH*, p. 65.

278   Angenendt, *Geschichte der Religiosität in Mittelalter*, p. 155.

279   Ibid., pp. 154–156.

280   *HMS* I, p. 569. Trans. Roughton II, pp. 861–862.

FIGURE 10   God as King. Illustration from a mid 14th century manuscript AM 227 fol. containing a Norse translation of the Old Testament. Árni Magnússon Institute for Icelandic Studies

[The apostles Peter and Paul often appeared to him. Devils also came sometimes to tempt him with various temptations, most often in the likeness of Þórr or Óðinn or Freyja, but Martin had the sign of the cross as a shield against all of their temptations. And he recognized them in whatever form they assumed, and named each of them by name and addressed each of them according to their "worth: he called Þórr an idiot, Óðinn timid, and Freyja a whore. He often saw angels of God, and they spoke to him and told him of future events.]

An important part of the activities of the apostles, and consequently a significant message of the hagiographic source material, is simply proving the existence of the inimical forces by exposing them and illustrating that the misfortunes people are suffering from are caused by demons and evil spirits. The theme of exposing Satan's wiles can ultimately be traced back to the temptation narrative of the synoptic gospels (Matt. 4:1–11, Luke 4:1–13). Arriving in the city of Nicaea, the apostle Andrew came across seven devils who practiced throwing rocks at people at a certain street corner, causing people injury and

FIGURE 11   Demon. Illustration from a mid 14th century manuscript AM 227 fol. containing a Norse translation of the Old Testament. Árni Magnússon Institute for Icelandic Studies

death. Andrew explains to the people that in order to be released from their troubles, they have to believe in Jesus Christ, the Almighty God and the Holy Spirit, "einn guð i þrenningu"[281] [one God in Trinity]. When they had accepted his suggestions, the apostle Andrew: "bauð [...] dioflunum at standa i augliti allz lyðs. Þa synduz fiandr i hunda likium. Þa sneriz Andreas postoli til folksins ok mællti: Siai þer nu her diofla, þa er yðr eru gagnstaðligir" [commanded the devils to show themselves to all the people. The fiends appeared in the bodies of dogs. The apostle Andrew turned to the people and said: 'See here now the devils who oppose you'].[282] Even though it is more frequent that demons and unclean spirits only become visible to ordinary people by possessing objects and living beings already existing in the material world, there is an interesting description of an actual appearance of a demon in the *Saga of the Apostle Bartholomew*:

---

281   *Post*, p. 323.
282   *Post*, p. 324. Trans. Roughton II, p. 620.

Þa syndi hann þeim mikinn skugga hræðiligan hrafni svartara; nef hans var hvast ok skegg hans var sitt, har hans tok allt a føtr niðr; elldr brann or augum hans, en gneistar flugu or munni hans sem af gloanda iarni, en brennusteins log rauk or nôsum hans; fiaðrar hans voru sva sem þyrnar, en hendr hans voru bundnar a bak aptr með elldligum bôndum.[283]

[Then he showed them a great and terrible shadow blacker than a raven; its nose was sharp and its beard long, its hair hung all the way down to its feet, fire burned from its eyes and sparks flew from its mouth as if from glowing iron, and sulphuric flames shot out ofts nose. Its feathers were like thorns, and its hands were bound behind its back with fiery bonds.]

Exploring this particular episode, Philip Roughton points out that it parallels typologically the description of the apostle Bartholomew at the beginning of the narrative where the apostle is depicted in a complete contrast to the demon. While the apostle is depicted as having sublime physical features, wearing impeccable clothes, capable of almost anything with the help of angels, the demon, with his iron, flames, and thorns, is bound behind the back, incapable of doing anything in the presence of the apostle. A further parallel is found in the mutual exposure of the opposing forces. Just as it was the demon Berith who gave the description of Bartholomew at the beginning of the saga, it is Bartholomew who exposes the idol as a demonic shadow in, as Roughton puts it "a literal enactment of the theme of the exposure of Satan's wiles."[284]

As for how the demons are shown to carry out their deeds, they most often proceed by taking hold of either people or idols (*skurðgoð, likneski*). Demonic possession is shown to have severe consequences, as the demon causes physical torments, illnesses and even death to the possessed person, as well as it can force it to do harm to other people. Driving demons out of mad people is a standard part of the apostolic routine during their travels, formulaically described with the phrase "rak diofla fra oðum monnum" [drove demons from mad men].[285] Another frequent practice of the demons is their possession of idols through which they demand veneration and obedience, misleading people from the true God. In the *Saga of the Apostle Bartholomew* it is explained how the demons trick their adherents into believing that they have healing

---

283 *Post*, p. 750. Trans. Roughton II, pp. 767–768.
284 Philip Roughton, "'Þa syndi hann þeim mikinn skugga': Unmasking the Fantastic in the *Postola Sögur*," in *The Fantastic in Old Norse/Icelandic Litearture. Sagas and the British Isles*, eds. John McKinnel, David Ashurst, and Donata Kick (Durham, 2006), p. 850.
285 For examples see, *Post*, pp. 185, 336, 336, 424, 427, 440, 514, 717, 719, 726, 728, and 750.

powers as they inflict harm to the people and only let go of them when he or she begin to worship the possessed idol.

> I skurðgoðinu var diófull, sa er sagðiz grøða siuka menn, en þa eina grøddi hann, er hann meiddi; þviat Indialandz men kunnu eigi sannan guð, ok urðu þeir af þvi tældir af osónnum guðum. En hinn lygni guð tælir sva þa, er eigi truðu eða kunnu sannan guð, at hann kastar a þa sottum ok meinum ok skóðum, ok gefr svór or skurðgoðum, at þeir bloti honum; en þa syniz heimskum monnum sem hann grøði, þa er hann lætr af at meiða. En hann bergr engum, helldr grandar hann, ok syniz þa biarga, er hann lætr af at granda.[286]
> [In the idol was a devil who claimed to cure sick people, but he actually only cured those whom he himself injured, for the people of India did not know the true God, and they were therefore swindled by false gods. The lying god swindles those who do not believe in or know the true God by casting upon them sickness and wounds and injuries, and by giving answers from out of idols in order to get them to worship him, and then it seems to stupid people as if he cures them, when he only ceases to injure them. But he saves no one, and indeed only does injury, and he seems to save when he stops doing harm.]

This way, the demons first get hold of the person's body and then, when the person starts worshiping the idol, are in control of the person's soul, as the demon explains himself a little later in the same saga: "Hófðingi varr sendir oss at granda monnum, fyrst likomum þeira meðan ver hofum eigi velldi yfir ondunum; en þa er þeir blota oss til heilsu likama sinna, þa latum ver af at meiða þeira likami, þviat þa hofum ver velldi yfir ondum þeirra"[287] [Our chieftain sent us to harm people, first their bodies while we have no power over their souls; and then when they sacrifice to us in order that their bodies might be healed, we cease injuring their bodies, for we then have power over their souls]. Sustaining the injury for as long as possible, they eventually force the possessed to believe that they are gods and worship them.[288]

3.3.2.2 Anger of God
God's wrath is an inherent part of certain biblical traditions, particularly visible in the conceptualization of history as it appears in the writings of the

---

286 *Post*, p. 744; Trans. Roughton II, p. 756.
287 *Post*, p. 749. Trans. Roughton II, pp. 764–765.
288 *Post*, p. 749.

Deuteronomic body of writings characterized by the notion of divine retribution or punishment because of human sin. Such a characteristic marked the medieval Christian image of God quite decisively.[289] All sort of catastrophes - be it natural disasters, plagues, or human evil - could ultimately be explained with reference to the wrath of God culminating on the Day of Judgment. In this respect, Icelandic ecclesiastical discourse was no different than elsewhere in the Medieval West as wrath remained a notable attribute of God.

From the perspective of salvation history, God's anger (*reiði, styggð*) was understood to have been lying over the earth like a dark night, like it is described in an Easter homily, "ever since the sin of the first man until the resurrection of the Lord, leading humanity to death and to the darkness of hell out of this world."[290] Adam did not want to obey divine commandments and therefore he was outlawed to the misery of the earthly life.[291] The dark night of sins was only lifted with the resurrection of Christ "from which arose the day of correct faith and the mercy of the Lord."[292] Even so, God's wrath had still to be reckoned with, for human sinfulness was still quite capable of arousing the wrath of God as can be seen on the leaves of the *Icelandic Homily Book* and should be avoided at all costs: "Oft skulum vér órum hug til þess renna [...] hve þungt er að verða fyr reiði hans."[293] [We should often direct our minds to [...] how severe it will prove to meet his anger.] It could not be forgotten, had to be kept in mind at all times and reckoned with. It was even scribed unto the creation itself. In a short allegorical sermon fragment on the rainbow, found in the so-called *Physiologus*-manuscript (AM 673 a II 4to), the three colors of the rainbow are said to symbolize water, sulphur-flame, and fire which collectively are supposed to remind of the threefold wrath: "[Á] regnboga eru þrír litir: vatns ok brennusteinsloga ok elds. Þat minnir oss á at óttask þrefalda reiði Guðs, þá er kømr yfir heiminn". [In the rainbow there are three colours: of water and of sulphur-flame and of fire. This reminds us of fearing the threefold wrath of God, which comes over the world.][294]

The anger of God is also a frequent topic in the hagiographic source material. God's emissaries frequently bring up the threats of God's anger and even more frequently does one encounter it in the words of repenting sinners after they have been convinced of their error by the apostles and their miracles.

---

289   Angenendt, *Geschichte der Religiosität im Mittelalter*, pp. 101–104.
290   *ÍH*, p. 103.
291   *ÍH*, p. 65.
292   *ÍH*, p. 103.
293   *ÍH*, p. 130.
294   Cucina, "The Rainbow Allegory," pp. 73–74.

Having been tortured by the authorities of the city Mirmidon in Achaea, the apostle Andrew persisted in praying for his persecutors and teaching those who listened, which eventually lead to the inhabitants of the city being convinced of their error, approaching the apostle with the following words:

> Misgert hofum ver við þik, af því at ver vissum eigi hvat ver gerðum. Biðium ver þik, at þu fyrirgefir oss þat, er ver hofum misgert við þik, ok synir oss heilsugotu, at eigi stigi guðs reiði yfir borg þessa.[295]
>
> [We have done evil to you, for we knew not what we were doing. We beseech you, forgive us our transgressions against you, and show us the path of salvation, so that the wrath of God does not descend upon this city.]

This is a fairly standard reaction of a repenting opponent approaching an apostle or a saint in fear and awe which the readers and audiences of the religious discourses of the Church would have come across quite frequently.[296] A rather elaborate account of the anger of God is found in a speech given by the apostle Matthew at the end of a version of *Passio sancti Mathei apostoli* found in the manuscript AM 645 4to. In the speech the apostle compares the power of an earthly king to that of the heavenly king. The power of the earthly lasts only for a short time but the power of the heavenly king is eternal, and so also his rewards and punishments. And regarding God's anger, the apostle continues:

> Ef konongs reiþe er ogorlig, hyggit at ér, hvor ogorligre er goþs reiþe eþa mannz. Mannz reiþi endesc á eino augabragþi stundar meþ elde eþa iarne, en goþs reiþe cinder eil(i)fan loga misgerøndom. Dominus goþ, kennande ens sanna, visse firer oorþna hluti oc melte: „Ér scoloþ eigi hręþasc þá, es licomom granda einom saman, en þeir mego eigi øndena vega, heldr scoloþ ér þann hreþasc, es beþi hefir veldi at firerfara bøþi ǫnd oc licama i helvites eldi. Sva segi ec yþr, at þann scolot ér hręþasc.[297]
>
> [If the anger of the king is horrible, consider which is more horrible, the wrath of God or of man. The wrath of a man ends in the blink of an eye with fire or iron, but the wrath of God kindles eternal fires for evildoers. The Lord God, the teacher of the truth, knew the future and said: 'Do not fear those things which hurt the body and yet which can not scathe the soul; rather should you fear that which has power both to destroy

---

295 *Post*, p. 321. Trans. Roughton II, p. 614.
296 For more examples see *Post*, p. 721 and p. 784.
297 *Post*, p. 821. Trans. Roughton II, p. 826.

the soul and the body in hellfire.' So I say unto you, it is this which you should fear."

What exactly those could expect who had called God's anger upon themselves will be addressed in the upcoming section but on that topic, as will be shown, the sources under inspection were by no means silent.

3.3.2.3   Justice

As noted, the notion of last judgment was central to medieval Christian religiosity as the following words from the *Icelandic Homily Book* reflect: "Hræðstu dómsdag ávallt og óast helvítiseld."[298] [Fear at all times the Day of Judgment and dread the fire of hell.] And the judgment is not far ahead, as a sermon on the Purification of Mary reminds the audience with considerable urgency: "minnumst á það, að Guð mun koma skjótt að dæma af allar þjóðir og munum þá taka slíkan dóm af Guði sem vér dæmum órum misbjóðöndum nú í þessi veröld."[299] [Let us remember that God will come soon to judge all people and we will then receive such judgment of God like we offer to our mistreaters in this world.] In another sermon to be delivered on the feast of Epiphany, a translation of Gregory's 10th homilia in Evangelia, the audience is encouraged to envision the stringency of the divine judge: "Setjum vér fyrir hugskotsaugu oss annmarka óra og þar með ógn dómadags. Virðum vér, hve stríður dómandinn kemur, sá er ógnar dóminum og leynist hann, sýnir hann ógnir syndgum mönnum og bíður."[300] [Let us place before our mind's eyes our shortcomings and the threat of judgment therewith. Let us look at how strict the judge is who comes, the one who threats with judgment and hides, he shows threats to sinful men and waits.]

The Icelandic Christians did not always have to rely on their mind's eyes because they had the material illustrations of the topic already there in front of them. Carved onto a set of thirteen wooden panels, brought to the Icelandic National Museum from the farm Bjarnastaðahlíð in Skagafjörður in the year 1924, are depictions of various human figures and other creatures. Although much is missing from the work as a whole, scholars agree that the panels originally belonged to a grandiose illustration of the last judgment and hell. It showed the "frightful day of judgment" (*dagur ógurlegur dóms*) when the Lord will come as a "strict judge" (*stríður dómandi*), a prominent theme in the early religious discourse of the Church.[301] The panels give an important insight in

---

298   *ÍH*, p. 274.
299   *ÍH*, p. 125.
300   *ÍH*, p. 85.
301   *ÍH*, pp. 69–70 and 85.

how early religious discourses concerning divine punishment in Hell manifested itself in visual, material form. As shown by art historian Selma Jónsdóttir, the illustration is carved out in a characteristically Byzantine style.[302] Not many church illustrations of this type have been preserved in the Latin West but an important example is a mosaic found in the cathedral of Torcello in North East Italy.[303] How this style of ornamentation reached Iceland is unclear but Guðbjörg Kristjánsdóttir has pointed out that an Italian-Byzantine style was wide-spread in Benedictine monasteries and on such grounds she has connected the making of the decoration to the first Benedictine monastery in Iceland at Þingeyrar in Húnaþing. It is very likely that this illustration was originally located in the cathedral of Hólar, built after the foundation of the episcopal see in 1106. If the making of the picture was somehow related to Þingeyrar-monastery, its point of composition has to be moved a bit forward in time, possibly to the episcopacy of Ketill Þorsteinsson (r. 1122–1145), as Guðbjörg Kristjánsdóttir suggests.[304] Hypothetical reconstructions of the picture suggest that it must have been over 7.3 meters long and 2.8 meters high, most likely painted in colors.[305]

In line with other preserved Byzantine judgment illustrations, the decoration in Hólar cathedral was divided horizontally into two halves with each half showing many different sections and scenes. Its upper part probably showed the Godhead surrounded by angels, apostles, and saints. One panel from the upper half (marked *k* on figure. 12) thus shows Mary, mother of Jesus and a figure venerating her. Most of the preserved panels, however, seem to stem from the decoration's lower part, depicting judgment scenes and the fate of people sentenced either for salvation in Heaven and damnation in Hell. Figuring prominently on the panels preserved from Bjarnastaðahlíð, are images of snakes or monsters surrounding Satan's throne and damned individuals. Panel *e* shows an angel pushing a human being in the direction of such a creature and panel *i* shows another one devouring or regurgitating a person.

It is likely that such a decoration, aweing as it was in its size and bright colors, made a great deal of impact on those who came across it. Placed on the eastern wall of the cathedral, this impressive work of art was the last image

---

302 Selma Jónsdóttir, *An 11th Century Byzantine Last Judgment in Iceland* (Reykjavík, 1959).
303 An important difference between Byzantine judgment scenes and those done in a Western style, is that the former tradition does not restrict itself to Biblical imagery. Especially prevalent, for example, are motives from the Homilies of the Syrian deacon Ephrem. Guðbjörg Kristjánsdóttir, "Dómsdagsmynd frá Bjarnastaðahlíð," in *KÍ* I, p. 274.
304 Guðbjörg Kristjánsdóttir, "Dómsdagsmynd frá Bjarnastaðahlíð," in *KÍ* I, p. 277.
305 Ibid., p. 276.

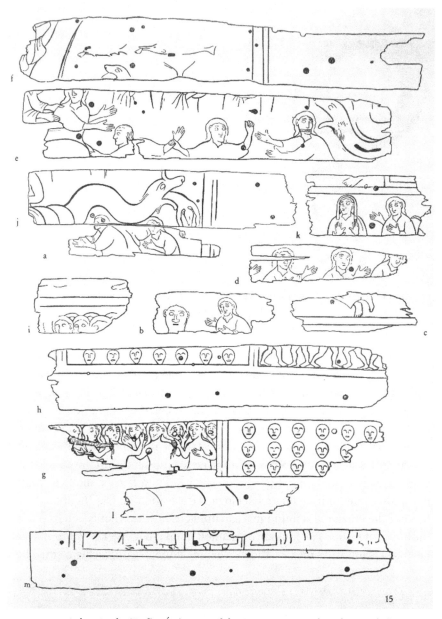

FIGURE 12   A drawing by Hörður Ágústsson of the images preserved on the panels from Bjarnastaðahlíð. Image: Hörður Ágústsson, *Dómsdagur og helgir menn á Hólum*, 15

FIGURE 13   The Crozier's head shows a gaping creature. It was discovered in Bishop Páll's grave in 1954. National Museum of Iceland

seen before the attending faithful left the sacred space of the church on their way into the world. It reminded people of the urgency of the Christian message and the severe consequences they could expect if they failed to recognize it. Similar reminders of the impending judgment could be identified in various contexts, intended and unintended, even on clerical clothing and liturgical accessories. There are, for example, unmistakable resemblances between how the creatures surrounding Satan's throne were represented on the panels from Bjarnastaðahlíð and animal images on the head of a crozier, made of walrus ivory, discovered during an archaeological excavation in 1954 (figure. 13). The head of the crozier was found in a sarcophagus next to what is believed to be the bones of Bishop Páll Jónsson of Skálholt (r. 1195–1211).[306] The volute-formed head of Bishop Páll's crozier, shows a gaping animal head, facing a small lion

---

[306] Archaeologist Kristján Eldjárn suggested the crozier head to have been carved out in Iceland around the year 1200. Kristján Eldjárn, "Stav II, Ísland" in *KLNM* XVII, col. 78. Sveinbjörn Rafnsson has questioned Eldjárn's conclusion, deeming the quality of the craftwork too high to have been carried out in Iceland or Norway. A more likely place of origin, in Rafnsson's opinion, would be a city on the British Isles with a rich tradition craftsmanship, even though the walrus ivory could not have been found elsewhere than in the North. Sveinbjörn Rafnsson, *Páll Jónsson Skálholtsbiskup: Nokkrar athuganir á sögu hans og kirkjustjórn*, Ritsafn sagnfræðistofnunar 33 (Reykjavík, 1993), p. 126.

engraved on the crozier. Kristján Eldjárn has suggested the animal on the crozier to be a lion and a reference to the lion of Judah.[307] Contextualizing it more thoroughly, Sveinbjörn Rafnsson points out the resemblances of the creature with Norwegian decorative art under Anglo-Norman influence, for example that which can be seen on the Olaf's chapel (Olavskapellet) in the cathedral of Niðarós and, more importantly, on the famous Urnes Stave church in Sogn and Fjordane county in Norway.[308] In the church in Urnes, one can even see a carved-out figure of a bishop or an abbot holding a crozier very similar to the crozier of Bishop Páll.[309]

Animal figures were prominent in medieval Scandinavian decorative art and Icelandic Christians were probably used to seeing various types of animal ornamention in their surroundings. There is, however, no agreement among scholars on what kind of a figure is being depicted at the end of the crozier's volute. Is it a lion, like Eldjárn suggested, or is it perhaps more reasonable to take it as a dragon or a serpent, a widespread motif on medieval crozier-heads?[310] In a short picture commentary on the crozier's iconography, art historian Guðbjörg Kristjánsdóttir decidedly states that the animal is a dragon, symbolizing the Devil.[311] At the end of a long bishop's staff, it appears more likely to have looked like a serpent's head, with the entire crozier representing the rest of the snake's body (see figure. 14). It should also be noted that a gaping animal was a frequent way of symbolically referring to hell in the Middle Ages. In a speech to be delivered on Annunciation Day, the apostles are for example to have led God's people "úr úlfs munni, það er djöfuls veldi"[312] [out of the wolf's mouth, that is the Devil's dominion] and in the *Saga of the Apostle Matthew*, the apostle calls on the audience to redeem their souls "fra hinum forna dreka, þat er fra diofli!"[313] [from the ancient dragon, that is the Devil]. At any rate, to people of differing knowledge of Christian iconography, not to mention if it was from afar, it is not far-fetched to assume that it might have seemed reminiscent of the serpents surrounding Satan's throne in hell, similar to those depicted on the panels from Bjarnastaðahlíð discussed above. From such a point of view, it should not be excluded that figures of doom and dread

---

307 Gen. 49: "Judah is a lion's whelp; from the prey, my son, you have gone up. He crouches down, he stretches out like a lion, like a lioness—who dares rouse him up?"
308 Sveinbjörn Rafnsson, *Páll Jónsson Skálholtsbiskup*, pp. 124–125.
309 See image in Roar Hauglid, *Norse stavkirker: Dekor og utstyr* (Oslo: Dreyer, 1973), p. 333.
310 As hinted at by Ellen Marie Magerøy, "Carving: Bone, Horn, and Walrus Tusk," in *Medieval Scandinavia: An Encyclopedia*, ed. Phillip Pulsiano (New York, 1993), p. 70.
311 Guðbjörg Kristjánsdóttir, *KÍ* II, marginal picture commentary, p. 142.
312 *ÍH*, p. 192.
313 *Post*, p. 800.

FIGURE 14   A creature from a panel from Bjarnastaðahlíð, believed to repesent a serpent surrounding Satan's throne. National Museum of Iceland

merged into how episcopal authority came to be visually represented on episcopal insignia such as Páll Jónsson's crozier.

3.3.2.4   Punishment

The illustration on the panels from Bjarnastaðahlíð, and other comparable decorative objects, represent an important part of the religious discourse of judgment people would come across during mass and other ecclesiastical ceremonies. The topic of judgment was of course inseparable from what it would eventually lead to, that is the tortures of hell or the glories of paradise, topics which will be taken into consideration in what follows.

In the sermonic and hagiographic source material, there is no lack of forceful depictions of the punishments of Hell. As with other themes already explored in this study, there is no striking difference between the Icelandic religious discourse and the ways in which Hell was conceptualized elsewhere in the Christian West.[314] Hell is a place of darkness (*myrkur*), misery (*nauðir*), suffering (*kvalar*) and torture (*píningar*) carried out in eternal fire.[315] Hell is the dominon of the Devil and is often referred to with the word 'veldi' which has already cropped up several times in this analysis ("djöfuls veldi," [dominion of the Devil], "veldi fjandans" [dominion of the fiend], "veldi myrkra," [dominion of darkness]).[316] The accounts of Hell in such sources, the sermonic ones in particular, have been said to have a more popular appeal and be of a more simple or folksy nature (*folkeleg*) than more elaborate descriptions in for example *Elucidarius* and religious poetry such as *Harmsól* and *Sólarljóð*.[317] It is correct, that in medieval Icelandic sermons, Hell is often used as a simple key word for what Christ conquered through his atonement much like the

---

314   Olav Bø, "Helvete," in *KLNM* VI, col. 428.
315   For examples see, *ÍH*, "myrkur," p. 241; "kvalar," pp, 223, 241, and 297; "nauðir," pp. 104 and 106; "píningar,"pp. 64 and 210 "eternal fire," pp. 72, 207, and 302.
316   For examples see *ÍH*, "djöfuls veldi," p. 20, "veldi myrkra," p. 245; "veldi fjandans," p. 209.
317   Olav Bø, "Helvete," in *KLNM* VI, col. 428.

following sentence from a sermon with the heading *Resurrectio Domini* conveys: "Christus [...] leysti oss úr syndaböndum og frá kvölum helvítis og frá vélum og hlátri djöfulsins." [Christus [...] redeemed us from the shackles of sin and from the suffering of hell and the tricks and laughter of the Devil].[318] Such simple references, however, would of course always have hinted towards more elaborate descriptions of Hell which were not only found in vision literature but also in the sources for the earliest religious Christian discourse as it has previously been defined in this study. Consider for example the following description from a treatise consisting of parts of Pseudo-Ambrose's *Acta S. Sebastiani martyris*. Originally it was part of a speech given by the martyr Sebastian but in the *Icelandic Homily Book* it stands as an independent speech. It is also partly preserved in the late 13th century manuscript fragment AM 238 XXVIII fol. but it is unclear if that manuscript fragment was originally part of Sebastian's *vita* or part of an independent homily like the one in the *Icelandic Homily Book*:[319]

> En sá er eigi vill elska þetta ið bjarta líf, þá má sá eigi til þess komast, heldur verður hann tekinn af eilífum dauða og haldinn í eilífum loga. Þar eru hræðilegir fjándur. Þeirra augu skjóta af sér eldlegum örum, þeirra rödd er svo sem grenjun hinna óörgu dýra, þeirra viðurlit gera hræðslu og sárleik og dauða. Og væri svo vel, að dauðinn mætti bjarga við þessum meinum. Heldur er hitt þyngra, að þar er til þess lifað, að ávallt sé þeir í kvölum, er þar eru. Og til þess endurnýjast liðir þeirra, að þeir sé ávallt slitnir af höggormum, fyr því að þeir vildu ekki geyma Guðs boðorða.[320]
>
> [But the one who does not want to love this bright life, he will not arrive there, but will be seized by eternal death and kept in an eternal flame. There are horrible demons. Their eyes shoot fiery arrows, their voice is like the cry of wild animals, their look produce fear, harm, and death. And it would be well if death would save from these pains, but on the contrary are those living there subject to the severity of eternal pain. Their joints are constantly renewed after having been torn by snakes, for they did not want to heed the commandments of God.]

Another description is to be found in the *Saga of the Apostle John*, based on a Latin version of the apostle's life as found in the *Passio Iohannis* by

---

318 *ÍH*, p. 107.
319 See Stefán Karlsson, "Om himmel og helvede på gammelnorsk AM 238 XXVIII fol.," in *Festskrift til Ludvig Holm-Olsen* (Øvre Ervik, 1984), pp. 185–195.
320 *ÍH*, p. 207.

Pseudo-Melito and the *Virtutes Iohannis*.[321] In the account a man named Stactaeus, brought to life by the apostle John, explains to the audience present what he had experienced in the hereafter. Those who resist the message of the apostle, like the people present have rejected the reward of paradise and will instead be receiving the suffering of Hell:

> Slika luti hafi þit fyrirlatna, en fengit ykkr þa staði i moti, er fullir eru af myrkrum, fullir af drekum ok gnistondum logum, fullir af kvǫlum ok ollum oumrøðiligum piningum, fullir af otta, fullir af óskurligri ogn. En þit hafit fyrirlatið þa staði, er fullir eru af öllum blomum, þeim er alldri kunnu at fyrnaz, af allzkonar fǫgrum röddum, ok tekit þar a moti þa staði, sem eilifr gratr er ok ylun bæði nætr ok daga[322]
>
> [You have forsaken these things and have received in their place places full of darkness, full of dragons and biting flames, full of torments and all unspeakable tortures, full of dread, full of hideous terrors. You have forsaken the places that are full of all sorts of flowers that can never decay, of all sorts of beautiful voices, and you have taken in their place the place where there is eternal wailing and howling both night and day.]

Also noteworthy about this particular account is the reaction of the crowds who immediately repent after having heard their prospects.

In light of the previous discussion on the Church's enemies, it is important to note that Hell is reserved for God's enemies: "ógurlegt er að gera í gegn Guði, því að hann má sínum óvinum steypa í helvíti"[323] [it is frightening to act against God, for he will throw his enemies into Hell], as it says in a sermon on the Holy Spirit. Through his resurrection and descent into Hell, Christ further saved his friends in Hell (*vinir Guðs í helvíti*), i.e. noble and upright men who had passed before Christ, and brought all his men (*alla sína menn*) away from the misery of hell into eternal joy.[324] In a Christmas speech, it is made clear that being an enemy of God is no abstract notion but referred to those who disturb the peace and oppose his agents:

---

321 Roughton I, p. 245.
322 *Post*, p. 426. Trans. Roughton II, p. 680.
323 *ÍH*, p. 33.
324 *ÍH*, p. 106. See also the following description of Judgment Day in a speech to be delivered on All Saints Day, *ÍH*, p. 63: "en úr þeim eldi lesa englar Guðs og hefja í loft upp Guðs vini alla. En Guðs óvinir verða í eldinum eftir og eigu þaðan til Drottins að sjá og að líta." [out of the fire the angels of God will elevate all of God's friends. But God's enemies will remain in the fire and from there they have to see and observe the Lord.]

Svo gerir Guð jafnan við þá, er ófrið veita og mótstöðu erindrekum hans, að hann tekur þá fyrst af lífi, en síðan brennir hann og borgir þeirra, það eru líkamir þeirra, er byggðu andir þeirra í svo sem í borgum, meðan þeir lifðu, en kvelur hann hvort tveggja og brennir í helvíti, önd þeirra og líkama.[325]

[So God does to those who produce unrest and oppose his agents, that he first executes them, then he burns also their cities, that is their bodies, in which their souls lived as it were cities, while they lived, but tortures both and burns in hell, their soul and body.]

3.3.2.5 Rewards

As set forth in the Church's religious discourse, the goal of all medieval Christians was to attain salvation and enter the kingdom of heaven which was systematically associated with key words such as glory (*himinríkis dýrð*),[326] joy (*himinríkis fagnaður*),[327] and bliss (*himinríkis sæla* or *fullsæla*).[328] Just as they were encouraged to imitate the saints during their lives they would also follow them in death, but they are repeatedly said to go after their death to the eternal bliss of the glory of heaven ("til himinrikis dyrðar ok eilifrar sælu an enda").[329] According to Hörður Ágústsson's reconstruction of the judgement picture from Bjarnastaðahlíð (see Figure 15), its depiction of heaven consisted first and foremost of images of those who were already saved. At the bottom, it shows Abraham surrounded by children, signifying passed souls, the virgin Mary surrounded by her worshippers, and the thief crucified next to Jesus (Luke 23:33–43). Above these motifs is a group of saved people following Peter into Paradise and hosts of angels.[330]

As has already been touched upon earlier, the prerequisites for entering the kingdom of heaven are made plain in early ecclesiastical discourse. Baptism and holding on to the correct trinitarian faith are both central premises for entering the kingdom of heaven.[331] This is clearly summarized in a sermon to be held on the Feast of All Saints:

---

325   *ÍH*, p. 236.
326   For examples, see *Post*, pp. 421 and 743; *ÍH*, pp. 12, 22, 33, 35, 63, 64, 86, 92, 94, 107, 113, 148, 210, and 242.
327   For examples, see *Post*, p. 735; *ÍH*, pp. 78, 202, 228, 229, 242.
328   For examples, see, *ÍH*, pp. 141, 201, and 241 (sæla) and *ÍH*, p. 27 (fullsæla).
329   *Post*, pp. 513 and 521.
330   Hörður Ágústsson, *Dómsdagur og helgir menn á Hólum*, pp. 56–65.
331   *Post*, pp. 739 (baptism), 789, and 799 (correct trinitarian faith).

FIGURE 15   Hörður Ágústsson's reconstruction of the Judgment picture. Unpaginated picture sheets between pages 62 and 63 in Hörður Ágústsson, *Dómsdagur og helgir menn á Hólum*

Það vil eg láta fylgja máli mínu, er mér þykir oss hjálpvænlegast vera og mestur leiðarvísir til paradísarvistar, að það er upphaf hjálpar vorrar allrar, að vér haldim trúu rétta, þá sem töld er í credo, skiljim það allt undir þá trúu, er helgir menn hafa oss til kennt.[332]

[I wish to attach to my sermon what I find most helpful and the best guidance for attaining a stay in heaven, that it is the beginning of our entire salvation that we keep the correct faith, as it is recounted in credo, and understand that as the faith which holy men have taught us].

As has also been noted, but necessary to stress at this point, the ultimate authority of admittance had been committed to the apostle Peter, although

---

332   *ÍH*, p. 61.

some texts allow the possibility of other apostles having such authority as well.³³³ At the end of a version of the *Saga of the Apostle Peter*, preserved in AM 655 XII–XIII 4to, dating to the period 1250–1275 is a prayer composed for the Feast of Peter and Paul.³³⁴ The prayer's text asks for the guidance of the teachings of the apostle Paul in order to get to the doors of heaven which in turn are opened by the apostle Peter "meþ sinu valldi oc vilia" [by his power and will].³³⁵ The prayer ends with the following request:

> [O]c leiþi þessir hinir œzstu hofþingiar oss til samvistu viþ almatkan guþ, oc ver niotim þar i sifello eilifrar fullsælu i samneyti allra heilagra um allar veralldir verallda. Amen.³³⁶
>
> [And may these supreme magnates lead us to a cohabitation with God almighty, and that we will incessantly enjoy there an eternal bliss together with all saints for ever and ever. Amen.]

Heaven is not frequently the subject of detailed description and mostly referred to with key words such as glory, bliss, and joy. There exist, however, descriptions indicating how it might have been imagined in more detail. The *Saga of the Apostle John*, contains a description of heaven given by a man named Stactaeus after he had been resurrected from the dead by the apostle. He describes the things that he saw before he was resurrected by John and is asked by the apostle to direct his words specifically to two brothers in order to bring them from sinning. Stacteus tells the brothers about the things they would forego if they would continue on their path of sins. He describes the kingdom of heaven, a place with eternally blossoming flowers and all kinds of beautiful voices. There were a multitude of rooms made of shining gems, "þau voru full af eilifu liosi, full af eilifum krasum ok eilifri skemtan" [they were full of eternal light, full of eternal dainties and eternal delight].³³⁷ Instead they would get rooms filled with darkness, dragons, and sparkling fires, pain, tortures, fear and screaming threats. Naturally, after this speech, the two brothers fell on their knees in front of the apostle asking him for mercy.

---

333   See, for example the *Saga of the Apostle Thomas* where it says that "hann [Thomas] mun luka upp himinrikis durum fyrir ykkr" [but he will open the doors of heaven for you]. *Post*, p. 715. Trans. Roughton II, p. 721.
334   Wolf, *Legends of the Saints*, pp. 310–311.
335   *Post*, p. 216.
336   *Post*, p. 216.
337   *Post*, p. 426. Trans. Roughton II, pp. 679–680.

Another description is found among the very oldest preserved manuscripts in the Icelandic manuscript tradition, AM 655 4to IX, probably written by a Norwegian in Iceland in the second part of the 12th century.[338] This manuscript contains a fragment of the *Saga of the Apostle Matthew* which is also preserved in several later manuscripts, including AM 645 4to and AM 652/630 4to.[339] The saga contains a lengthy description of the bliss of Paradise which Jesus Christ opened in his resurrection for "alra sanctorum ǫndum, þa er þeir fara or licømom sinom, svat aller mego nu þangat comasc ón iva, þeir er þiona Cristo" [for all holy souls, when they go from their bodies, so that all those who serve Christ may now come thither without doubt].[340]

> [Þ]ar ero aller hluter bliþer oc aller cyrrer oc hogvęrer; þar er aldregi himens fegrþ siokom hulit; þar fliuga aldregi eldingar, þar verþa eigi reiþarþrumor, heldr er þar gleþi avalt on enda, oc hotiþ su er eigi hefir endemarc.[341]
>
> [[A]ll things there are pleasant and all things quiet and gentle; the beauty of the sky is never covered by clouds in that place; lightning never flies there, there are no claps of thunder, but rather there is always joy without end, and a feast-day which never has a stopping point.]

It is described as a "staþr góþr ollom fiǫllom øþre oc nalęgr himne" [good place, higher than all mountains and near to heaven], containing whatever one could wish for.[342] It is a place of beauty and perfection, where there is never bad weather, always a good smell in the air, plants and flowers do not wither, and animals and insects cause no harm. Nobody has to fear lack of food or other ailments, whether caused by old age or illnesses.

3.3.3   Conclusion: The Only Way

This final section has highlighted the retributive dynamics inscribed in the ecclesiastical discourse of the Church. The discussion has focused on how the discursive themes already explored – the ecclesiastical authority and the figure of the 'other' – are thoroughly enmeshed in a framework of reward and punishment, evidence for which is preserved both in textual and material sources. This relatively clear-cut framework brings together the Church and its

---

338   Ólafur Halldórsson, "Inngangur," p. lxvi.
339   Wolf, *Legends of the Saints*, p. 250.
340   *Post*, p. 817. Trans. Roughton II, p. 819.
341   *Post*, p. 816. Trans. Roughton II, p. 817.
342   *Post*, p. 815. Trans. Roughton II, p. 816.

enemies, making plain what it meant to side with either one of them, 'us' or 'them.' The message of the Church was clear for those who decided to obey the instructions of the Church and its representatives, both as regards the social order and their own, personal destiny. On the social level, it was necessary to follow the Church's directives if there was to be peace. The above examples show that in the religious discourse of the Church in medieval Iceland, peace was constructed as a phenomenon that could exclusively be reached through and within the Church. As individuals, those who heeded the Church's message were taking the only way that could lead to their salvation. The Church's message to those who chose to disregard its proclamation was equally clear: It meant risking it all.

CHAPTER 4

Rome Goes North

The fourth part of this study contains a narrative of the growth of Christianity in Iceland and the Church as an institution, while considering the material discussed in previous chapters. Surely, when it comes to showing the sociopolitical significance of the earliest religious Icelandic texts, the source analysis and its contextualization possess much value in themselves, simply through the highlighting of the most prevalent themes and explaining how they reached people around the country. Nevertheless, that discussion should to the test, as it were, by viewing it against other historical sources than those previously under inspection in this study, keeping in mind the following position of Elisabeth Schüssler Fiorenza that "all discourses about the Divine are articulated in specific sociopolitical situations, by particular people, with certain interests in mind, and for a certain audience with whom they share cultural codes and religious traditions."[1] As a concluding part of the study, this chapter should be understood as more of a synthetic discussion, in which the outcome of previous chapters is brought together with chosen episodes from the history of Christianity in the Free State Period. The main goal of this chapter is to highlight discursive similarities rarely noted in the history of scholarship so far and open them up for further interpretation. It seeks to show how prominent discursive themes from the religious source material crop up – and sometimes even predominate – the preserved evidence for some of the most important historical moments and periods in the history of the Church in Iceland. All of these historical episodes have received much scholarly attention and have a somewhat fixed place and appearance in Icelandic historiography. The most significant sources – other than the purely religious source material, of course – for the history of the Church of the period – charters, letters, bishops' sagas, and the *Sturlunga* collection – do not allow for seeking proof of the influence of each and every discursive theme. As will become clear in the course of this chapter, the source material poses a number of difficulties and its discussion will always rest to a considerable degree on probabilities. There is, however, still enough evidence to be found to shed a fresh light on important moments of the period such as the murky beginnings of Christianity in the country, Gizurr Ísleifsson's age of peace, and the long-standing conflict between *sacerdotium* and *regnum*, which

---

1 Schüssler Fiorenza, *Power of the Word*, p. 196.

in Iceland manifested itself as a conflict between the Church and the local chieftains.

4.1 In the Beginning

The sources for the first one and a half century after the official conversion of the Icelanders in the year 999 do not allow for any exact determination of when and how the religious discourses under inspection surfaced. In a general way, the following discussion is intended to throw light on the religious situation in Iceland when these religious discourses were initially making themselves heard and visible to medieval Icelanders. Medieval chroniclers like Ari Þorgilsson and the anonymous authors of the bishops' sagas set forth a relatively straightforward picture of how the Christian religion took hold in Iceland. While these medieval accounts remain subject to interpretation and, as such, hold historical value, it is more likely that the first phase of Christianity in Iceland was marked by its state of 'becoming,' as scholars Steinunn Kristjánsdóttir and Richard Cole have suggested.[2] Along such lines, the following discussion will argue for the cogency of assuming for more ruptures, discontinuities and inconsistencies than depicted by medieval historiographers.

4.1.1 Chaotic Beginnings

As discussed in the second chapter of this study, Ari *the Wise* portrays the religious situation in the 11th century as the Christian religion having settled in Iceland with relative ease under the auspices of the Haukdælir family.[3] In his opinion the first bishops were men of such excellence that there was practically no other option than for all remnants of heathendom to evaporate in a couple of winters. Ari, however, had strong ties with the family of the Haukdælir who reigned over a large part of Southern Iceland and would have painted as favourable a picture of them as possible. He was fostered by Teitr Ísleifsson in Haukadalur and in his account of the rise of Christianity in the *Book of Icelanders*, all of the major roles are played by members of the family of Haukdælir. They were among the first to be baptized on behest of the missionary King Óláfr Tryggvason; they were the first to peacefully speak on behalf of Christianity in Iceland with eventual sucess; they donated their land for the first episcopal see, Skálholt, where they also served as the first bishops. Ari also

---

2 See sections 2.1.3 and 3.2.1.2.
3 See section 2.1.3.

makes sure to frame the establishing of the other Icelandic bishopric, Hólar in the North, as a stem of Skálholt's root which could never have taken place if Gizurr would not have accepted the will of the Northerners and 'donated' a quarter of his reign for the new episcopal see. There is no reason to doubt the veracity of this course of events although Ari's loyalty to the Haukdælir might have led him to underemphasize whatever might have undermined their authority. On grounds of this version of events, scholars have come to the conclusion that since very early on, Christianity in Iceland was shaped by the interests of indigenous aristocratic families like the Haukdælir and later, many others.[4]

As successful a time it may have been for the Haukdælir in their dominion in the southern plain of Iceland, it is unlikely that the religious life was as soon as homogenous as Ari and later sources relying upon his works describe it. Christianity had been existing in Iceland for a long time before the formal conversion and it is likely that at least in some places people were practicing Christianity of the home-brewed sort.[5] Among the first settlers, many were baptized, such as Auður Ketilsdóttir (*djúpúgða*) who settled in the region of Dalir, and is recorded to have conducted religious ceremonies in a location where she also had crosses erected.[6] Helgi Eyvindarson (*magri*), who settled in Eyjafjörður, is described as a religious pragmatist, believing in Christ but calling for Þórr's protection before heading out to sea.[7] It does not seem likely that Christian practices and sentiments vanished among the following generations despite such a claim found in the *Book of Settlements*.[8] Although it is

---

4 Orri Vésteinsson, *Christianization of Iceland*, p. 24.
5 From the saga literature, two examples of such home-brewed practices are frequently mentioned. For the historian, the sagas describe ideas of 13th and 14th century people about 10th and 11th century happenings. With all such necessary precautions, these two interesting pieces of information about religious views and practices point to some kind of a freedom in religious interpretation. First, there is the rather cryptic 'creed' so-called of the sorcerer Þrándur in Gata as preserved in *Færeyinga saga*, probably composed in Iceland in the early 13th century. The creed does not remotely resemble anything that could have qualified as a creed in the Roman Church. See *ÍF* xxv, p. 115. The other example is from *Eyrbyggja saga*, an early 13th century family saga, which mentions the idea that if a farmer built a church, he had secured a place in heaven for as large a part of his household as could fit in his church. See *ÍF* IV, p. 136. Scholars have not been able to locate this idea elsewhere in medieval Catholicism. Cf. Jón Viðar Sigurðsson, *Det norrøne samfunnet*, p. 153; Sigríður Sigurðardóttir, *Skagfirska kirkjurannsóknin: Miðaldakirkjur 1000–1318*, Rit Byggðasafns Skagfirðinga I ([place missing], 2012), p. 3. See also *Kí* I, p. 67.
6 *ÍF* I, p. 139.
7 *ÍF* I, p. 250.
8 *ÍF* I, p. 396.

uncertain in which extent the Christian religion survived, it seems reasonable to assume with Hjalti Hugason that there were Christians in Iceland throughout the traditionally defined 'pagan period,' between the settlement and the official conversion, albeit in small numbers.[9] While archaeological evidence points to a predominantly pagan population, one should assume for a minimal degree of heterogeneity and syncretism, to use that problematic term, for example among the descendants of Christian settlers.[10]

Although written sources are scarce for the 11th century, archaeological research has shown how the Christian religion began to put its mark on the material landscape. Also in that regard, one should assume that there was a considerable degree of diversity in the practice of Christianity. Churches and chapels were built in great numbers around the country. At the end of the century, they even counted a greater number than at any other time during the Middle Ages.[11] At the same time, there is a considerable agreement among scholars that there was a lack of priests in the country well into the 12th century. Several reasons have been listed supporting such a conclusion. Sources seldom mention clergy of a lower ordination than a priest, which might point to a situation in which churchmen were ordained as priests as soon as possible.[12] Also speaking for the lack of priests during the early phase is the fact that time and again canonical law requirements of the minimum age of 30 for priests were broken.[13] Still another argument for the shortage of priests is provided by tales of them having served at numerous ministries over considerably short periods of time.[14] This has lead Orri Vésteinsson to surmise that "services were only given infrequently and irregularly at a church, when an itinerant priest happened by."[15] Other scholars, such as Sigríður Sigurðardóttir, have suggested the possibility, primarily on account of the great number of churches, that the

---

9   KÍ I, p. 69. See also Hermann Pálsson, *Keltar á Íslandi* (Reykjavík, 1996).
10   For an interesting example of religious syncretism, see Þór Magnússon, "Bátkumlið í Vatnsdal í Patreksfirði," *Árbók hins íslenzka fornleifafélags* 63 (1966): pp. 29–30.
11   Sigríður Sigurðardóttir, *Miðaldakirkjur*, p. 71. These churches were small in size, (c. 5m long and 3m wide), made of wood with a building technique known as stave construction, imported from Norway. In most cases, the wood was either imported or driftwood. Already in the 11th century an Icelandic version of the stavechurch-type emerged, when the wooden construction was covered with a protection layer made of turf, shielding it from strong winds. Guðbjörg Kristjánsdóttir, "Fyrstu kirkjur landsins," in *KÍ* I, p. 179.
12   KÍ I, p. 222.
13   Magnús Stefánsson, "Kong Sverre – prest og sønn av Sigurd Munn?" in *Festskrift til Ludvig Holm-Olsen på hans 70-årsdag den 9. juni 1984* (Øvre Ervik, 1984), pp. 287–307.
14   Thus, Guðmundr Arason served at least seven different ministries in Skagafjörður before he became bishop. See Orri Vésteinsson, *Christianizaton of Iceland*, p. 181.
15   Ibid., p. 54.

farmers themselves, the heads of the family, must have taken upon themselves priestly tasks, at least when none other could be found.[16] People began burying their family members according to Christian customs. Already in the 11th century and onwards, churches and cemeteries originally placed remote from the farmsite were moved closer to the location of the farmhouses.[17] Thus, before the codifying of the Old Christian Law, it seems as if there was no consistency as to whether bones were removed or not when the cemetery was discontinued. In many cases, the corpses still lie in their place, while in other cases they seem to have been relocated only in part, and still other instances, every corpse has been removed from the cemetery.[18] On these grounds, it can be assumed that laws or customs regarding bone transfers had no absolute value, or, which amounts more or less to what Jón Steffensen suggested in a 1967 article, that early Icelandic Christians simply did not care about any sort of consistency in these matters.[19]

Thus, despite the quick growth in church buildings, which might have become a trend or fashionable during the period, there are several reasons to believe that the situation was not as stable and uniform as ecclesiastical authorities might have wanted.[20] Later written sources support such a view to some degree. In the Bishops' Sagas there are indications for the bishops' struggle against an unruly population as well as unwanted religious views and practices.[21] Thus, *Hungrvaka*, a writing from c. 1200 recounting the lives of the first five bishops of Skálholt (1056–1176), tells of Bishop Ísleifr's difficulties during his

---

16 Sigríður Sigurðardóttir, *Miðaldakirkjur*, p. 72.
17 This can be established from medieval sources but also 18th and 19th century records. See Orri Vésteinsson, *Christianization of Iceland*, pp. 49–53. Recent excavations at Stóra-Seyla in Skagafjörður have even shown that cemeteries were already being discontinued and bones relocated in the 11th century. Guðný Zoëga, "Early Church Organization," 50.
18 Guðný Zoëga, "A Family Revisited," 105–128.
19 Jón Steffensen, "Ákvæði kristinna laga þáttar um beinafærslu," in *Árbók hins íslenzka fornleifafélags* (1967), 76.
20 KÍ I, p. 186.
21 With regard to the source value of the Bishops' sagas, which have been called the most formulaic of Old Icelandic literature and surely count as hagiography – some entirely, other only in part – caution is required. For long, scholars used to distinguish between secular Bishops' sagas and purely hagiographical Bishops' sagas, the latter being considered of less source quality than the former. In a 1992 article, Ásdís Egilsdóttir showed that the similarities between the writings of the two groups outweigh the differences. Ásdís Egilsdóttir, "Eru biskupasögur til?" *Skáldskaparmál* 2 (1992), 207–220. Egilsdóttir's findings have lead scholars, historians in particular, to reconsider the traditional classification of Bishops' Sagas and their differing reliability as sources. See Gunnar Karlsson, *Inngangur að miðöldum*, pp. 168–170 and KÍ I, p. 167.

episcopacy in managing the public.²² The *Saga of Bishop Jón of Hólar*, telling of the first bishop of Hólar bishopric, Jón Ögmundarson, (r. 1106–1121), originally written in Latin in the beginning of the 13th century by Gunnlaugr Leifsson of Þingeyrar-monastery, is informative particularly because of his attempts to improve the Christian religion in Iceland by abolishing undesirable practices.²³ It is also likely for Christian religious authority to have been fragmented during these first stages, particularly with regard to the fact that there were more than one bishop in the country. There are accounts of one or more missionary bishops in the country since 1030. While Bishop Ísleifr of Skálholt was in all likelihood the sole ecclesiastical authority in the South after he became bishop in 1056, there had been other missionary bishops active in different regions in the country before and during his episcopacy. Between 1030 and 1049, a missionary bishop named Hróðólfr was working in Borgarfjörður where he even founded a small monastic house before he left the country to become an abbot of Abingdon Abbey in England.²⁴ As Hjalti Hugason points out, Hróðólfr had ties to England but also, according to Adam of Bremen, the archdioecese of Hamburg-Bremen and thus brings together the most important currents of Christian thought and influence in Iceland at the time.²⁵ During the period between 1048 and 1067, a certain Bernard the Saxon was active in Northern Iceland, where he earned a reputation for his blessings of both churches and natural phenomena before he became a bishop in Selja in Norway.²⁶

All of this is not to say that Christianity's first century and a half was characterized by disorder. The examples above should however allow for the assumption that it was not as orderly as Ari and the authors of bishops' sagas describe it. Surely, there was a great number of small private churches spread all around the country and priests of various types on the move, both of which are clear indicators of the upswing of the Christian religion in Iceland. But there was still a considerable degree of uncertainty as to what was actually happening and how it was going to play out. As Orri Vésteinsson puts it: "it is easy to see that in Ari's time the Icelandic church was still far from fully developed, indeed it had only just acquired the rudiments of institutionality and

---

22   *ÍF* XVI, p. 8. On dating, see Ásdís Egilsdóttir's discussion in her introduction to *ÍF* XVI, pp. xxiv-xxvii.
23   *ÍF* XV₂, p. 207.
24   *ÍF* I, pp. 18 and 65; Adam of Bremen, *Gesta Hammaburgensis ecclesiae pontificum* II, pp. 118 and 124. See also discussion in *Kí* I, pp. 144–145 and Steinunn Kristjánsdóttir, *Leitin að klaustrunum*, pp. 71–78.
25   *Kí* I, pp. 144–145; Adam of Bremen, *Gesta Hammaburgensis ecclesiae pontificum* II, p. 125.
26   *ÍF* XVI, p. 12; Adam of Bremen, *Gesta Hammaburgensis ecclesiae pontificum* III, p. 224; IV, p. 269.

still had a long way to go before it had assumed the central place in society normally associated with the medieval Church."[27] The Church in Iceland was still getting on its feet and it is of no small importance that the emergence of the Christian religious discourses in the vernacular can be dated to this period. As already discussed, the Christian religion brought with it writing and literacy among the country's educated – and to a significant degree clerical – elite.[28] As noted, although the earliest manuscripts containing the religious discourses under inspection date to around the mid-12th century, they can be taken to be have been in existence somewhat earlier. In all likelihood, such texts were among the first things being composed in the Icelandic vernacular. The discursive themes themselves, however, were there before the advent of writing although they gained an immense momentum with the introduction of the new medium. They coincided the advent of Christianity, first primarily in Latin texts accessible only to specialists but also, as will be shown in the upcoming section, in the oral, vernacular culture.

4.1.2 Echoes from Rome

Iceland's place in the medieval Christian world was at the margins from at least two points of view: First, that of world history but the setting of medieval universal chronicles was usually located far away from the North.[29] An early Icelandic version of the history of the world is *Veraldar saga*, composed in the mid 12th century.[30] To no surprise, its course of events rotates around two geographical centers, the Holy Land on the one hand, and Rome on the other, both of which were, in differing contexts, considered by Western Europeans to be the center of the world.[31] Iceland was far removed from the scene of Christian salvation history and consequently any Christian relic or major pilgrimage site. Second, from the perspective of church politics and administration, Iceland was as far removed from the center of papal administration and bureaucracy

---

27 Orri Vésteinsson, "Formative Phase," p. 72.
28 See section 2.2.1 above.
29 Iceland's place in the world in the Middle Ages has been the subject of several studies in recent years, both from the standpoint of Icelanders themselves as a part of their world view, see in particular Sverrir Jakobsson's doctoral dissertation, *Við og veröldin*, already cited on several occasions, but also its image in other parts of the world, see Sumarliði Ísleifsson's dissertation, *Tvær eyjar á jaðrinum: ímyndir Íslands og Grænlands frá miðöldum til miðrar 19. aldar* (Reykjavík, 2015). Ísleifsson's discussion of the Middle Ages does not include references to Iceland in papal letters, however.
30 *Veraldar saga*, ed. Jakob Benediktsson, Samfund til udgivelse af gammel nordisk litteratur 61 (Copenhagen, 1944).
31 Cf. Sverrir Jakobsson, *Við og veröldin*, p. 163.

in Rome as possible. Such an opinion was for example expressed in a letter sent in 1198 by Pope Innocent III (r. 1198–1216) where he says to the incumbent Icelandic bishops, Páll Jónsson and Brandr Sæmundarson that even though "your island is far removed from the quarters of the city, you should nonetheless not consider yourselves closed off from apostolic care" and that the loving arm of papal pastoral care reaches also those who "are removed in body but truly present in spirit."[32] What follows is a standard reminder of the authoritative position of the Roman Church and the pope and by no means surprising coming from Pope Innocent III, who more than any other medieval pope strove to make his power felt: by reforming the Curia, launching Crusades, shaping doctrines of the pope's power in church and more secular affairs, and convoking and presiding over the fourth Council of the Lateran beginning in 1215.[33] In the spirit of invoking the authority of Peter's Throne, the letter goes on to describe the Roman Church as the divinely instituted mistress, supreme among all other churches in the world to which all other churches should answer like the members of the body should answer to the head. And the pope, the pastor of the Church, is charged with the task of acting on behalf of the Church, being in possession of the *plenitudo potestatis*, from which any other ecclesiastic has to receive.[34]

From the perspective of the ecclesiastical administration there is nothing exceptional about Pope Innocent III's letter to the Icelandic bishops. During Innocent's reign, the annual average of papal letters amounted to a number of around 280, many of which were dictated for the same purposes of admonishing misbehaving members of the pope's herd.[35] Even so, the letter to the bishops

---

32 "Quamvis insula vestra longo terrarum tractu ab Urbis partibus sit remota, vos tamen, qvod Apostolicæ provisionis non sitis extorres, æstimare debetis, cum ex injuncto nobis Apostolatus officio facti simus secundum Apostolum sapientibus et insipientibus debitoris, et ita pastoralem solicitudinem gerimus de propinqvis, qvod eam extendimus etiam ad remotos, qvos absentes corpore, spiritu vero præsentes, caritatis brachiis amplexamur." *DI* I, p. 299.

33 Horst Fuhrmann, *Die Päpste: Von Petrus zu Johannes Paul II.*, 2nd ed. (München, 2005), pp. 129–139.

34 "Romana Ecclesia tanqvam magistra non humana sed divina dispositione universis et singulis per orbem Ecclesiis est prælata, ut ad eam velut Caput aliæ sicut spiritualia membra respondeant, cujus pastor ita suas aliis vices distribuit, ut ceteris vocatis in partem solicitudinis solus retineat plenitudinem potestatis, ut de ipso post Deum alii dicere possint: Et nos de plenitude ipsius accepimus [...]" *DI* I, p. 300.

35 According to Richard W. Southern's calculations, the yearly average of papal letters sent under Pope Innocent was much higher than that of his predecessors but was to be largely exceeded by his 14th century successors. The annual average of letters issued under John XXII (r. 1316–1324), for instance, amounted to a number around 3.646 letters. Southern, *Western Society and the Church*, p. 109. See also section 2.1.1.2. above.

and a second one addressed to Iceland's leaders and populace, of mostly the same content, stand as the earliest surviving testimonies of the pope himself reaching out to this particular part of the fringes of the *oikoumene*, bolstering his position as the leader of the Christian world and in authority over all its members, even in Iceland. Having already been vehemently scolded by the archbishops of Niðarós in the preceding decades, it was certainly not the first time that Icelandic bishops, chieftains or the populace *in toto* were addressed and reproached by a foreign ecclesiastical office.[36]

It is likely that the letters of the pope were translated and recited to a larger number of well-to-do people, perhaps at the next general assembly of Alþingi as Gunnar F. Guðmundsson has suggested.[37] For an Icelandic populace at the periphery of the world, being addressed by the *vicarius Christi* himself must certainly have amounted to an intriguing event. Guðmundsson further speculates that such a letter might have stirred various reactions:

> Having heard the pope's message, some Icelanders might perhaps have asked themselves: When did we obligate ourselves to obey the pope in Rome? Certainly they knew that the pope was the director of the Church. But what kind of a commitment did that precisely entail? In the current Icelandic church law there was no mentioning of an archbishop or a pope. A single article mentioned the creed: "In the days of our ancestors, a law was imposed that all men in the country shall be Christian and believe in one God, father and son and Holy Spirit."[38]

It can be argued that in this passage, Guðmundsson overemphasizes the significance of the Icelandic church law for how the Christian religion was practiced in Iceland at the time. Of course, this is not to say that Guðmundsson is suggesting that the religiosity of Icelanders should be restricted to the article cited – the very first one – from the Old Christian Law section. His rich volume on Christianity in Iceland during the High and Late Middle Ages speaks otherwise. Nonetheless, the passage above could be taken to suggest a mentality of an Icelandic audience whose commitment to the pope and Peter's see is decided first and foremost by what is found in the code of Law. Such a representation of the historical reality overlooks the fact that the notion of a universal Church

---

36   For a more detailed discussion of these letters, see section 4.2.2 and 4.2.3 below.
37   *KÍ* II, p. 46. Such a practice would be in accordance with how the letters of the Niðarós-archbishops were received but they were composed in Latin and later translated into Icelandic but the only preserved versions of the Niðarós-letters exist in the vernacular.
38   *KÍ* II, p. 46. As for the reference to the Old Christian Law section, see *Grágás*, p. 1.

and its head in Rome had been a significant part of how the Christian religion had been introduced in Scandinavia since the beginning, as can be seen from early Christian Skaldic poetry.[39] In fact, it should be stressed in this context that two of the oldest fragments of Christian poetry in the Old Norse language associate Christ with Rome. Consider for example the following poem ascribed to the late 10th /early 11th century skaldic poet Eilífr Goðrúnarson:

> Setbergs kveða sitja
> sunnr at Urðar brunni;
> svá hefr ramr konungr remðan
> Róms banda sik lǫndum.[40]

> [They say that [he, Christ] sits on a seat-shaped crag
> in the south at the well of Urðr <norn>;
> thus the strong king of Rome [CHRIST]
> has strengthened himself in the lands of the gods.]

If this cryptic text is rightly ascribed to a late 10th century author, the poem counts among the very earliest Icelandic references to the Christian religion in the Old Norse language. It has been suggested that this text offers an example of syncretism in times of religious change, fusioning Old Norse mythologizing with Christian imagery. Scholars have pointed out how the image of the well of the witches of fate, Urðar brunnr, can be seen to merge with Christian depictions of *maiestas domini* or scriptural passages such as Rev. 22:1–2 where the water of life is shown to flow from the divine throne.[41] For the purposes of the present study, it is interesting to see how the poet, about whom not much is known – not even if he converted to Christianity or not – except that he was active at the court of earl Hákon Sigurðarson (937–995), frames the religious change taking place in the North in terms of a hostile overtaking. The text describes Christ as the mighty king of Rome, sitting on a hill which in medieval Scandinavian culture signified the king's elevated status where his subjects

---

39 For a classic discussion of Christian religious ideas in skaldic poetry, see Dag Strömbäck, *The Conversion of Iceland: A Survey*, Text series/Viking Society for Northern Research 6 (London, 1975), esp. pp. 55–58.
40 *Skaldic Poetry of the Scandinavian Middle Ages* III: *Poetry from Treatises on Poetics* 1, ed. Kari Ellen Gade in collaboration with Edith Marold (Turnhout, 2017), pp. 126–127. Ed. Jana Krüger, Trans. from German John Foulks. Angle brackets and square brackets in original edition.
41 *ÍB* I, p. 485. Krüger, "Fragment," p. 126.

could approach him and praise him from below.[42] According to the editor of the poem's most recent edition, "it tells of Christ supplanting the heathen *bǫnd* 'gods' in the North and taking up residence at the mythical *brunnr Urðar* 'well of Urðr.' "[43] In the poet's imagination, Christ is in the process of overcoming the heathen gods and has strengthened his position by raising for himself a throne.

Of a sligthly later date is a skaldic poem ascribed to the Icelandic lawspeaker Skapti Þóroddsson (d. 1030):

> Máttr es munka dróttins
> mestr; aflar goð flestu;
> Kristr skóp ríkr ok reisti
> Róms hǫll verǫld alla.[44]

> [The power of the lord of monks
> is greatest; God brings everything about;
> the mighty Christ created the whole world,
> and raised up the hall of Rome]

There are a few references to Skapti's efforts of introducing the Christian religion to Icelandic society in medieval sources. According to *Ólafs saga Helga* in *Heimskringla*, Skapti was part of a group of men ordered by King Ólafr Haraldsson to adapt the Icelandic law to the Christian religion[45] and according to the early 14th century *Flóamanna saga*, he built a church in gratitude for the healing of his wife's leg.[46] With all due reservations regarding the source value of these sagas, the poem can be taken to reflect the mindset of the earliest proponents of Christianity in Iceland. It is a forceful praise to the Christian God, the Lord of monks (*munka dróttinn*) and the power he possesses as the author of all things. It then proceeds to describe Christ as the creator of the entire world (a claim which has regularly sparked debates in the history of Christian theology) and specifically mentions "Róms hǫll," the palace or hall of Rome, in that context. The association of Christ with the distant city of Rome seems

---

42 Krüger, "Fragment," p. 127.
43 Krüger, "Fragment," p. 126.
44 *Skaldic Poetry of the Scandinavian Middle Ages* III: *Poetry from Treatises on Poetics* 1, ed. Kari Ellen Gade in collaboration with Edith Marold (Turnhout, 2017), pp. 355–357. Ed. and trans. Diana Whaley.
45 ÍF XXVII, p. 77.
46 ÍF XIII, pp. 325–326.

thus to have been a part of how the Christian religion was being presented in Iceland since its earliest arrival.

Interestingly, the actual founder of the Roman Church, Peter, is absent in these two fragments, which is not the case in a third text from another eleventh century Icelandic poet, Sigvatr Þórðarson. It is a stanza from a poem called *Knútsdrápa*, composed in honour of King Cnut the Great who in the early 11th century ruled over what has been termed the Danish North Sea Empire encompassing Denmark, Norway, and England. The two last stanzas of the poem are devoted to the king's pilgrimage to Rome which took place in 1027, including the following lines:

Rauf ræsir af
Rúms veg suman
kærr keisara
klúss Pétrúsi.[47]

[The leader
dear to the emperor,
close to Peter,
enjoyed some of the glory of Rome]

In these lines, Rome is described as a glorious place. As portrayed by the poet Sigvatr, the great King Cnut was able to share in that glory as he was both "dear to the emperor," and "close to Peter." Such honor, however, was not granted to everybody but only individuals of the highest standing who had the opportunity to approach such half-divine regions. Rome, as it was being introduced in Iceland and elsewhere in Scandinavia, was not primarily a geographical location, despite the considerable number of Icelandic pilgrims who took upon themselves to travel there for religious purposes.[48] Most Icelanders would never come anywhere close to Rome and to those who never visited the city, Rome was a distant yet sacred place and as such a theological construct.[49]

---

47 *Skaldic Poetry of the Scandinavian Middle Ages* I: *Poetry from the Kings' Sagas* 1, part 2, ed. Diana Whaley (Turnhout, 2012), p. 661. Ed. and trans. Matthew Townend.
48 Well-known pilgrims to Rome among medieval Icelanders include Hrafn Sveinbjarnarson and Sturla Sighvatsson.
49 The 'idea of Rome' was by no means homogenous during the Middle Ages. Thomas F. X. Noble explains well the ambiguous character of the image of Rome in the medieval mind in his article "Rome and the Romans in the Medieval Mind: Empathy and Antipathy," in *Studies on Medieval Empathies*, eds. Karl. F. Morrison and Rudolph M. Bell (Turnhout, 2013), pp. 291–315. Particularly informative is his discussion of writings by ecclesiastics, pp. 305–308.

Even though the idea or image of the city of Rome as the *caput mundi* lost much of its glory with time and was quite equivocal to the medieval mind, its position as the seat of the pope secured its position as one of Christianity's most important places, surpassed only by Jerusalem.

4.1.3 Gizurr's Age of Peace

In 1082, Gizurr Ísleifsson succeeded his father, Ísleifr Gizurarson, as bishop in Iceland. While no contemporary sources survive about Gizurr's episcopacy, there is no lack of descriptions of his time in office in later sources of predominantly ecclesiastical origin. These sources are unanimous in describing Gizurr's episcopate (1082–1122) as a period of peace and prosperity, amounting to a 'golden age' of medieval Christianity in Iceland but also in drawing up a picture of Gizurr as an ideal leader of the Church.[50] Setting the tone for later accounts is Ari Þorgilsson's *Book of Icelanders*, the earliest and most reliable source dated to the period between 1122 and 1133, in which Bishop Gizurr is described as "ástælli af ǫllum landsmǫnnum en hverr maðr annarra, þeira es vér vitim hér á landi hafa verit" [more popular with all his countrymen than any other person we know to have been in this country].[51] Commenting on Ari's description of Gizurr and his episcopacy, Orri Vésteinsson describes his account as "even by his own terse standards, unusually laudatory of Gizurr."[52] In *Hungrvaka*, composed in the beginning of the 13th century, Gizurr is said to have enjoyed great respect among his contemporaries with no man, neither learned nor unlearned, being considered as noble as he was.[53] In fact, according to the author(s) of *Hungrvaka*, he was so respected that when he died, the grief of the Icelandic population was comparable to the reaction of the Roman population after the passing of Gregory the Great.[54]

Gizurr is also described as a proponent of peace. A clear statement on the episcopacy of Gizurr as an epoch of peace is the early 13th century chronicle, *Kristni saga*, stating that "Gizurr byskup friðaði svá vel landit at þá urðu engar stórdeilur með hǫfðingjum en vápnaburðr lagðist mjǫk niðr" [Bishop Gizurr made the land so peaceful, that no great conflicts arose between chieftains, and the carrying of weapons almost ceased].[55] *Hungrvaka* also comments on

---

50   Orri Vésteinsson, *Christianization of Iceland*, pp. 58–67.
51   ÍF I, p. 22. Trans. Siân Grønlie, *Íslendingabók. Kristnisaga: The Book of the Icelanders. The Story of the Conversion* (London, 2006), p. 11.
52   Orri Vésteinsson, *Christianization of Iceland*, p. 64.
53   ÍF XVI, p. 20.
54   ÍF XVI, p. 21.
55   ÍF XV$_2$, p. 42. Trans. Grønlie, *Íslendingabók. Kristnisaga*, p. 53.

Gizurr's efforts of maintaining peace, approaching the matter from a slightly different angle by stating that the end of his episcopacy marked the beginning of a longstanding period of unrest. Two winters after Gizurr's death, a conflict arose between the most powerful chieftains in the country, Hafliði Másson and Þorgils Oddason, as is described in *Þorgils saga og Hafliða* in the *Sturlunga* collection. In the words of *Hungrvaka,* that conflict would lead to "ófriðr ok lǫgleysur ok á þat ofan manndauði sá um allt landit at engi hafði slíkr orðit síðan ⟨er⟩ landit var byggt" [war and lawlessness after that, and thereafter such a high level of mortality all across the land that the like has not been experienced since the land was settled].[56] This event, to which medieval and modern authors have ascribed great political significance, ended the period of peace which begun around 1020 and reached its heights during Gizurr's episcopacy.

Modern scholars have expressed doubts about these descriptions of events, particularly because of the silence in sources other than those of ecclesiastical origin, most importantly the annals which record strifes and killings regularly after 1120. As Gunnar Karlsson points out, the argument *ex silentio* does not suffice as evidence for a period of uninterrupted peace in this time. In fact, Karlsson asserts, it is most likely that there was a constant period of strifes and struggle in the country since the settlement.[57] Taking a similar stance, Orri Vésteinsson states that what is known about "Icelandic medieval society, or human nature in general" does by no means make a century of peace and harmony a very likely scenario.[58] While Vésteinsson does not exclude the possibility that the period was marked by "relative peace" which was then exaggerated by ecclesiastical authors, he finds more explanatory value in the development set in motion by the clash of the chieftains Þorgils and Hafliði and the contrast it posed to the preceding period. He describes the conflict as a "political watershed" because it demanded the participants to muster power and influence on an unprecedented scale. Since the settlement, the power of individual chieftains had been gradually increasing and the affair between Þorgils and Hafliði was the first exhibition of such strength. Although the conflict did not burst out in unrestrained violence, the two chieftains emerged at this point as the first political actors who were able to gather such a number of men around themselves that it was possible for them to disregard the laws and order that had been established in the country. This was the first conflict of such proportions but there were many to come in the following centuries. Explaining

---

56 *ÍF* XVI, p. 21. Trans. Camilla Basset, "Hungrvaka: Translation by Camilla Basett," Unpublished MA thesis. University of Iceland, 2013, p. 56.
57 Gunnar Karlsson, "Frá þjóðveldi til konungsríkis," p. 38.
58 Orri Vésteinsson, *Christianization of Iceland*, p. 65.

the lack of reports of earlier conflicts, Vésteinsson suggests that the political significance of this event and the changes it caused in the political landscape rendered previous conflicts so insignificant that they did not make it into historical records.[59]

In addition to such explanations of Gizurr's golden age of peace, the attention should also be directed to last chapter's analysis of how the concept of peace was constructed in ecclesiastical discourse. It is, for example, worthy of note in this context how the peace accompanying the reign of emperor Augustus is parallelled with the peace of the reign of Christ in a Christmas sermon in the *Icelandic Homily Book*.[60] According to the sermon, there was such peace around the world during the reign of Augustus that nobody had to carry arms ("engi maður bar hervopn").[61] The main characteristics of this peace were unity (*samþykki*) and one reign (*eitt ríki*). Moreover, such harmony made it possible for the authorities to collect taxes with more success than before since the world so carefully united that nobody could escape taxation.[62] According to such an understanding, the hallmarks of peace were not primarily the absence of conflict and quarreling although it was part of the program in its ideal form. Peace was first and foremost a symbol of power, marking the victory of the dominant voice and the suppression of other voices. As has been discussed previously, such an understanding of peace was prominent in the early ecclesiastical discourse and even Ari's notion of peace in the *Book of Icelanders* seems to overlap with it. In his version of the general assembly of Alþingi when Christianity was accepted, he has the lawspeaker Þorgeirr explicitly state that a prerequisite for peace is to exclude dissonance and keep one law and one custom ("ein lǫg og einn sið").[63]

Enough is known about the episcopacy of Gizurr Ísleifsson to establish that it was marked by a striving for peace, at least in the sense just outlined. During his reign as bishop, the people of Iceland saw the rise of the two episcopal seats, Skálholt (Gizurr's own family estate) and Hólar. Already in 1097, Bishop Gizurr had introduced the tithe securing the financial foundation of churches around the country, with Ari stating how remarkably obedient his countrymen were to their bishop.[64] It can also be established with considerable amount of certainty that during this time, the leaders of the Church managed to bring about

---

59 Ibid., pp. 66–67.
60 See section 3.3.1.2 above and to a lesser extent 3.1.1.1.
61 *ÍH*, p. 67.
62 *ÍH*, p. 68.
63 *ÍF* I, p. 17.
64 *ÍF* I, p. 22.

more uniformity in religious affairs than before. Thus, the *Saga of Bishop Jón of Hólar* states that in 1107 the two bishops, Gizurr and Jón, met at the Alþingi to decide, with other learned men, what to command their subjects ("hver boð þeir skyldu bjóða sínum undirmǫnnum").[65] The content of these commands cannot be known with any certainty although a list of pastoral directives found later in the saga of Bishop Jón can be taken to reflect the commands of the bishops in a general way.[66] It should also be noted how Bishop Jón, whose episcopacy lasted only three years longer than Gizurr's, is said to have countered heathen practices and other aberrant behavior with great force which had not been done "while Christianity was still young."[67] In various ways, therefore, the leaders of the Church were striving for uniformity under the reign of the Christian Church.

According to the information provided by *Hungrvaka* about Gizurr's travels before and around the time of his ordination, Gizurr was educated in Saxony, travelled much in his younger years and even all the way to Rome with his wife. He was ordained during the papacy of the reformist pope Gregory VII and seems to have taken an active stance with the pope against the emperor in the ongoing investiture controversy. Before his ordination, he travelled again to Rome for he did not want to seek the audience of the current archbishop of Hamburg-Bremen who had sided with Henry IV in the investiture controversy. As the story goes, Pope Gregory told him rather to go to Magdeburg where he was ordained by Archbishop Hartwig (r. 1079–1102). Such experiences must have made Gizurr up to date in church political affairs of the time and familiar with how churchmen around the world dealt with opposition and enemies.

It is not likely that the administrative changes and fiscal developments Gizurr ushered in during his episcopacy went through without any dispute. What is more plausible is that Gizurr managed to resolve such differences with an unseen sense of authority which stands out as one of the most characteristic traits of his career. According to *Hungrvaka*, King Haraldr Sigurðarson described him as "bezt til fallinn at bera hvert tignarnafn sem hann hlyti" [best suited to bear whichever high title he might get].[68] A little later, the same writing contains the following description: "ok var rétt at segja at hann var bæði

---

65 ÍF XV₂, p. 202. In an editorial comment on this sentence it is suggested that the word *undirmenn* corresponds to the Latin words *subjecti* or *subditi*. It further explains that the commands of a bishop were equivalent to those of a king; everyone belonging to his district were supposed to obey.
66 ÍF XV₂, pp. 207–208. See also discussion in section 3.1.1.2 above.
67 ÍF XV₂, p. 209.
68 ÍF XVI, p. 14. Trans. Basset, "Hungrvaka," p. 52.

konungr ok byskup yfir landinu meðan hann lifði" [and it was right to say that he was both a king and bishop over the land while he lived].[69] This account is preserved in an expanded version in the King's saga *Morkinskinna*:

> Svá er þat sem ér segið, en þar má gøra vel af þrjá menn. Hann má vera víkingahǫfðingi, ok er hann vel til þess fenginn. Þá má hann ok vera konungr af sínu skaplyndi ok er vel fengit. Með þriðja hætti má hann vera byskup, ok þat mun hann helzt hljóta ok mun vera inn mesti ágætismaðr.[70]
>
> [What you tell of him could be made into three men. He could be a viking chieftain, and has the makings for it. Given his temperament, he could be a king, and that would be fitting. The third possibility is a bishop, and that is probably what he will become, and he will be a most outstanding man.]

It is not likely that Gizurr's forceful character, his leadership qualitities and his experience of church politics abroad made his episcopacy void of conflict. The great amount of authority he possessed according to the medieval accounts was, however, a rich source of peace as it was understood by medieval ecclesiastics. Such a peace was not incompatible with quarreling or dispute, but was rather a sign of power; a sign of the conquest of Christian norms and customs – in this case, as defined by Gizurr and his followers – over dissenting voices. It was, after all, Gizurr who made it clear beyond doubt who would lead the Church in the coming decades and centuries. Under Gizurr, it finally became evident that those who would have the greatest say in how the Church would influence Icelandic society were the local aristocracy, led by the family of Haukdælir.

4.1.4 Conclusion: The Chieftain Church Rises

It has been maintained above that after the official conversion to Christianity around the year 999, the situation in Iceland was characterized by tension and negotiation between contending forces in the religious landscape. Eventually, it came to what seems as the almost inevitable result that the Icelandic upper class won in the race. Even though the leaders of the Church in Iceland were ordained and accepted by metropolitan bishops in Hamburg-Bremen and after 1104 in Lund, scholarship of medieval Iceland has frequently highlighted the

---

69 *ÍF* XVI, p. 16. Trans. Basset, "Hungrvaka," p. 53.
70 *ÍF* XXIII, pp. 289–290. Trans. Theodore M. Andersson and Kari Ellen Gade, *Morkinskinna: The Earliest Icelandic Chronicle of the Norwegian Kings 1030–1157*), Islandica LI (Ithaca, 2000), p. 255.

motivation of Church leaders in their own political ambition and economic interests, which certainly stands to reason. In that sense, scholars have argued that the Church did not develop a 'corporate identity,' until much later when the it came to be represented by "a body of men conscious of their special role as men of the Church, and that this role was seen as separate from the interests of secular society."[71] As noted, Bishop Gizurr and his supporters laid the foundation of their own version of the proprietary church system – the Chieftain Church – tailored to the needs and intents of the aristocracy. At the same time, however, they were cultivating a religion which to a significant degree consisted of religious discourses of domination and subordination, centering around a hierarchy which ultimately extended itself to a distant power center, the Roman See. These discourses certainly came in handy for bolstering the authority of the leaders of the nascent Chieftain Church, but how long they could be used in their favour, is another question and the subject of the ensuing section.

4.2 The Reform of Bishop Þorlákr

During the last quarter of the 12th century, there arose in Iceland a serious dispute between the leadership of the Church and some of the most powerful chieftains in the country. Shortly after Bishop Þorlákr Þórhallsson of Skálholt (1133–1193) returned back to Iceland from Norway after his episcopal ordination in 1178, he began his project of reforming the Church in Iceland.[72] As will be illustrated in what follows, Þorlákr was calling for a moral reform among the Icelanders, both laypeople and ordained, and advocating for a change of the current arrangement of church property – a local version of the proprietary church system (*Eigenkirchenwesen*).[73] With his endeavors, Þorlákr managed to provoke a strong opposition from the political elite, crystallizing in medieval sources through a stormy dispute between the bishop and Jón Loptsson (1124–1197), the wealthiest and most powerful chieftain in

---

71 Orri Vésteinsson, *Christianization of Iceland*, 4.
72 The concept of reform has been problematized by Gerd Tellenbach who points out that it has been used uncritically by scholars and in so many different ways that its meaning has become unclear and even nonexistent ("daß man geradezu von einer Leerformel sprechen könnte"). Gerd Tellenbach, *Die westliche Kirche vom 10. bis zum frühen 12. Jahrhundert*, Die Kirche in ihrer Geschichte 2, F1 (Göttingen, 1988), p. 133.
73 To date, the most thorough analysis of the proprietary church system in medieval Iceland is Magnús Stefánsson's *Staðir og staðamál: Studier i islandske egenkirkelige og beneficialrettslige forhold i middelalderen* I (Bergen, 2000).

12th century Iceland. In Icelandic historiography, the conflict is referred to as the first '*staðir*-controversy' (*Staðamál fyrri*) although scholars have problematized the precise nature of the Church's claims over property.[74] In what follows, the sources for the dispute will be examined with a focus on how discursive themes previously discussed shine through medieval depictions of the Church's first serious attempts to influence the system designed by Bishop Gizurr and other Icelandic churchmen at the end of the 11th century.

4.2.1 Libertas Ecclesiae *in Iceland*

The Icelandic controversy between Church and chieftains was by no means an isolated phenomenon. It is part of a series of reformative attempts in European church history collectively referred to under slogans such as *libertas ecclesiae*, the liberty of the Church, and *reformatio ecclesiae*, the reform of the Church, taking place during the 10th, 11th, and 12th centuries. As previously discussed, it is a manifestation of how the relationship between ecclesiastical and secular power was put to the test through a series of conflict episodes – of differing intensity – between the representatives of each sphere. The changes in the spiritual climate of Europe caused by the reform movements reached Scandinavia in the course of the 12th century. As explained above, it was a time when the power of Rome as a center of the Christian world was on the upsurge and the pope became more influential and more present than he had ever been as a leader of the Western Church both near and far.[75]

4.2.1.1 *Backdrop:* Libertas Ecclesiae *in Norway*

The 12th century was certainly an eventful time in the history of Norway which saw the rise and fall of kings in the so-called Civil Wars, the birth of the episcopal see of Niðarós and, consequently, the beginning of significant ideological and political changes, especially in respect to the understanding of kingship, that is the emergence of Christian kingship, and the relationship between Church and Crown as the former was organizing itself. This is not the place for a comprehensive account of the period but it has been extensively dealt with in scholarship.[76] For the present discussion it is of most importance to grasp the significance of the establishment of the archdiocese of Niðarós and how the archbishops, Eysteinn Erlendsson, known for his political acumen, promoted the papal policy of reform and strengthened the Church as a central institution

---

74 See Orri Vésteinsson, *Christianization of Iceland*, pp. 112–132.
75 See sections 2.1.1 and 2.1.2 above.
76 For a relatively recent treatment of the topic, see Sverre Bagge, *From Viking Stronghold to Christian Kingdom: State Formation in Norway c. 900–1350* (Copenhagen, 2010).

in Norwegian society and an active player in the political arena. This institutional consolidation of the Roman Church and the rise of the archiepiscopal office provides a necessary background for the conflicts over church property in Iceland in the context of the administrative network of the Papal empire. It was through the episcopal see of Niðarós that reformative ideas found their way to Iceland and the leaders of the Church in Iceland were inspired, influenced and supported by metropolitan bishops of Niðarós.

Since the papal reign of Gregory VII, papal emissaries – legates – had in increasing measure been travelling around the ecclesiastical empire upholding papal policy through various means such as summoning synods, visiting local churches and if necessary bothering themselves with deposing unfit bishops and abbots and installing new in their own authority. It was during one such visit of a papal legate, the Englishman Nicholas Breakspeare, (later Pope Hadrian IV (1100–1159, r. 1154–1159)), that the archdiocese was established. Before, Norway, along with Iceland, Greenland and the Northern Islands, had belonged to the administrative rule of the metropolitan of Lund, established in 1104 and given the size of the diocese, it was not possible for the church authorities to stay fully on top of things in the peripheral areas although there was always some communication ongoing between Lund and Iceland.[77] Archiepiscopal intervention in Icelandic affairs would, however, only increase with the instituting of the archbishopric in Niðarós as will become evident at a later point in this chapter.[78]

During the reign of King Magnús Erlingsson (r. 1161–1184), the relationship between Church and royal power was exceptionally amicable. Scholars have even talked about an 'alliance' between King Magnús Erlingsson and the Church, led by Archbishop Eysteinn Erlendsson.[79] In this period of peace, the archbishop established himself as a major actor in the realm of Norwegian politics with his own agenda of promoting the liberty of the Church. This he did by way of various negotiations with Erlingr Ormsson (*Skakke*), who held royal power because of his son's young age. Given that the young King Magnús could not make direct claims to the crown according to Norwegian inheritance rules

---

77 See for example, Agnes S. Arnórsdóttir, "Danske dronninger i de islandske sagaer," in *Dronningemagt i middelalderen: Festskrift til Anders Bøgh*, eds. Jeppe B. Netterstrøm and Kasper H. Andersen (Aarhus, 2018), pp. 60–61.

78 For an overview of the involvement of the archbishops of Niðarós in Icelandic affairs, see Guðrún Ása Grímsdóttir, "Um afskipti erkibiskupa af íslenzkum málefnum á 12. og 13. öld," in *Saga* 20 (1982), 28–62 and Jón Viðar Sigurðsson, "Samskipti íslenskra biskupa við útlenda yfirboðara á öldum áður," in *Saga biskupsstólanna* ([place missing], 2000), pp. 491–515, esp. pp. 492–494.

79 Bagge, *Viking Stronghold to Christian Kingdom*, p. 159.

since he was only the grandson of a king, his father and guardian Erlingr had to secure the support of the archbishop by accepting many of the Church's most important claims—most importantly, the Church's demand to stay in control over its properties.

These negotiations are reflected in several administrative documents preserved from this period, most notably Magnús Erlingsson's Coronation Oath and his Letter of privilege for the Church, dating to his coronation in 1163/64. It has been argued, that both of these documents, in addition to the Law of Succession which likely dates to the same period, are to a large extent influenced by the Church and particularly the archbishop.[80] In the coronation oath, sworn by King Magnús Erlingsson at his coronation ceremony in Bergen – the first of its kind in the Norwegian kingdom – the king promises to be faithful and obedient towards the Roman Church and its head, Pope Alexander, and that the Church will not be subject to any more taxation than it accepts itself.[81] It also brings up the issue of the Church's right (*sua iusticia*) as King Magnús proclaims that he will see to that justice will be upheld according to the laws of the country (*secundum patrias leges*) but also respect canonical law in cases when the Church so requests. This has been interpreted as a decisive step towards an independent ecclesiastical jurisdiction, an important element in the Church's fight for its *libertas*.[82] King Magnús' letter of privilege to the Church, addressed to Archbishop Eysteinn, contains an even clearer and more elaborate confirmation of what is stated in the coronation oath about the status of the king's subordination to the Church. In addition to the purely practical matters addressed by the letter relating to commerce, tariffs and taxes, it also contains a significant ideological component which has to be discussed further. In the beginning of the letter, King Magnús introduces himself as king of God's grace (*dei gracia rex Norwegie*), addressing it to the archbishop, which he describes as a legate of the apostolic seat. The king further states that he has received his kingdom from the hand of the Lord (*de manu domini*) through the archbishop's laying on of hands and that he hands "himself and his kingdom over to God." In a special act of devotion he offers the kingdom of Norway to the martyr King Ólafr, promising to guard it as the saint's viceroy (*vicarius*) and vassal (*ab eo tenens*).[83]

---

[80] Erik Gunnes, *Erkebiskop Øystein: Statsmann og kirkebygger* (Oslo, 1996), p. 108. See also Bagge, *Viking Stronghold to Christian Kingdom*, p. 167.

[81] *Latinske Dokument til Norsk Historie fram til År 1204*, ed. Eirik Vandvik (Oslo, 1959), pp. 62–65.

[82] Gunnes, *Erkebiskop Øystein*, p. 109. See also Vandvik's commentary in *Latinske Dokument til Norsk Historie*, pp. 168–170.

[83] *Latinske Dokument til Norsk Historie*, p. 60.

In this way, as Jón Viðar Sigurðsson points out, the old Norwegian farmers' church configuration came to an end.[84] It had been incorporated into the ecclesiastical hierarchy and the king had surrendered his property claims to the Church. After having secured the rights of the Church in Norway in this way, the archbishop could direct his attention to the state of affairs in Iceland.

4.2.1.2 The First Clash of Church and Chieftains

The first vocal representative of the Gregorian reform-movement in Iceland was Þorlákr Þórhallsson (1133–1193). Born in Fljótshlíð in Rangárþing, the heartland of the Oddaverjar-family, and having been schooled at Oddi itself with Eyjólfr Sæmundsson (son of Sæmundur *the Wise*), Þorlákr received a clerical ordination before the age of 20, either in 1150 or 1151.[85] Soon he went abroad for further education. He studied in Paris, possibly at the abbey of St. Victor, and in Lincoln in England, but both places, especially Paris, were known for promoting ideas of reform.[86] After six years abroad, Þorlákr returned to Iceland and, as many other Scandinavian churchmen educated in Paris and influenced by the Victorines – including the archbishops Eysteinn and Eiríkr of Niðarós – began to advance the liberty of the Church. An important venue for such activities was the order of the Augustinian canons which began to spread around the North of the Christian World in the latter half of the 12th century.[87] Þorlákr was a stringent follower of the canonical rule, and even after his ordination as bishop he kept on maintaining it strictly, also in regard to clothing.[88] In 1167/68, Þorlákr took part in founding the first house of the canons regular in Iceland at Þykkvibær in Ver and in 1174 he was elected bishop of Skálholt. For unknown reasons, possibly because of opposition among local chieftains, Þorlákr is not ordained as bishop until four years later, in the year 1178 by Archbishop Eysteinn of Niðarós.[89]

What exactly the reform of Bishop Þorlákr entailed has been subject to considerable debate. Previous scholarship assumed that Þorlákr's main aim was to acquire full control of church property, most importantly of the so-called *staðir* or church benefices. Þorlákr's reform has consequently been termed the

---

84 Jón Viðar Sigurðsson, "Samskipti íslenskra biskupa," p. 495.
85 *ÍF* XVI, p. 50.
86 *ÍF* XVI, p. 52. For discussion, see Gottskálk Jensson, "Íslenskar klausturreglur og libertas ecclesie," p. 32 and Magnús Stefánsson, "Kirkjuvald eflist," p. 96.
87 Gottskálk Jensson, "Íslenskar klausturreglur og libertas ecclesie," p. 33. Cf. Orri Vésteinsson, *Christianization of Iceland*, pp. 140–141.
88 *ÍF* XVI, p. 67.
89 *ÍF* XVI, pp. 64–66.

'*staðir*-controversy.' The main source for such an understanding of Þorlákr's reform program is a part of the younger versions (B and C) of the *Saga of Bishop Þorlákr* called *Oddaverjaþáttr* which preserves the only account of the dispute between Bishop Þorlákr and Icelandic chieftains about control over church property.[90] It describes the conflict between the bishop and his main antagonist, Jón Loptsson, who opposes the bishop's claim for absolute control over church property. In the last two decades or so, scholars have called the historical value for the events taking place in the late 12th century into question. Like Jón Böðvarsson suggested already in an article from 1968, *Oddaverjaþáttr* is in all likelihood composed during the episcopacy of Bishop Árni Þorláksson of Skálholt (r. 1269–1298) who fought adamantly for the rights of the Church in Iceland and was successful in gaining control over the Church's property.[91] Supporting Böðvarsson's dating of the source, Ásdís Egilsdóttir, Ármann Jakobsson, and Orri Vésteinsson have all pointed out that the claims made by Bishop Þorlákr according to *Oddaverjaþáttr* are suspiciously similar to the claims made by Bishop Árni a century later.[92] It is likely, therefore, that *Oddaverjaþáttr*'s version of events is strongly shaped by Bishop Árni's struggle and was composed as a piece of propaganda for the Church's case as it was being made in the late 13th century.[93] Not only was the image of Bishop Þorlákr as a saint modified so as to fit Bishop Árni's pleadings; he was also shown to have been making exactly the same claims.[94]

As regards the Church's claim over church property during the episcopacy of Bishop Þorlákr, a more likely scenario has been proposed by Orri Vésteinsson. From what can be gathered about the reform program initiated by Archbishop Eysteinn in Niðarós which in all probability influenced the agenda of Bishop Þorlákr in Iceland, it seems as if the Church was not making a claim for absolute control over church property. What Bishop Þorlákr was striving for was a change in the arrangement of church ownership in the spirit of the doctrine of lay patronage (*ius patronatus*).[95] According to this principle, laymen in possession of a church should not be understood as actual owners but rather as caretakers. Contrary to the claims of *Oddaverjaþáttr*, it seems as

90 For a detailed discussion of the different versions of the *Saga of Bishop Þorlákr*, see Ásdís Egilsdóttir's introduction to the text in *ÍF* XVI, pp. xxxi-lii.
91 Jón Böðvarsson, "Munur eldri og yngri gerðar Þorláks sögu," *Saga* 6 (1968), 81–94.
92 Ármann Jakobsson and Ásdís Egilsdóttir, "Er Oddaverjaþætti treystandi?" *Ný saga* 11 (1999), 97; Orri Vésteinsson, *Christianization of Iceland*, p. 117.
93 Orri Vésteinsson, *Christianization of Iceland*, p. 115.
94 Ármann Jakobsson and Ásdís Egilsdóttir, "Er Oddaverjaþætti treystandi?" pp. 94 and 99.
95 Orri Vésteinsson, *Christianization of Iceland*, p. 119.

if Bishop Þorlákr was not fighting for full control but only the acknowledgement among the political elite of this form of arrangement. Such an interpretation becomes even more probable considering that the *ius patronatus* made the church farmers responsible for restoring the church in case it was damaged or destroyed. Without it, it was up to the church owner alone whether he fixed his church or not. As Orri Vésteinsson points out, Bishop Þorlákr seems to have been relatively successful in establishing the arrangement around the country.[96] Furthermore, it does not look like this change in policy regarding church ownership was nearly as dramatic as the author of *Oddaverjaþáttr* would have it.

Bishop Þorlákr was, however, known for his moral stringency which he strove to implement among the Icelanders during his time in office, causing altercations between him and the most powerful men in the country. From historical sources other than *Oddaverjaþáttr* – some of which will be thoroughly analysed in the upcoming sections – it looks as if it was Þorlákr's reform in the moral sphere which caused more resistance than any changes in regard to church property. Throwing light on Þorlákr's program, is his *poenitentiale*, which in several respects counts among the strictest penitentials preserved from medieval Europe.[97] It reflects the Church's heightened claim for monitoring and interfering in the marital – and extra-marital – affairs of Icelanders which in many ways were practiced contrary to the laws and regulations of the Roman Church.[98] Prominent examples include Guðmundr Þorvaldsson (*dýri*), one of whose weaknesses was that "hann elskaði konur fleiri en þá er hann átti" [he loved other women besides his lawful wife] as well as the 12th century chieftains Gizurr Hallsson and Jón Loptsson who both kept concubines much to the dismay of the ecclesiastical authorities.[99] Jón Loptsson is even recorded to have taken Ragnheiður, Bishop Þorlákr's sister, as a concubine and conceived a child with her, Páll, who later became his uncle's successor at the episcopal see at Skálholt.[100] As will be discussed shortly, in the minds of reform-oriented bishops like Eysteinn of Niðarós and his loyal subordinate in Skálholt, such behavior amounted to nothing less than a scandal.

---

96 Ibid., pp. 121–123.
97 Sveinbjörn Rafnsson, "Þorláksskriftir og hjúskapur á 12. og 13. öld," *Saga* 20 (1982), 114–115.
98 Ibid., p. 120.
99 *Sturlunga* II, *Guðmundar saga dýra*, 137. Trans. McGrew and Thomas, *Sturlunga saga* II, p. 165. For further discussion, see Agnes S. Arnórsdóttir, *Konur og vígamenn: Staða kynjanna á Íslandi á 12. og 13. öld*, Sagnfræðirannsóknir. Studia historica 12 (Reykjavík, 1995), pp. 108–117 and Sveinbjörn Rafnsson, "Þorláksskriftir og hjúskapur," pp. 118–120.
100 *ÍF* XVI, p. 297.

As noted, before Þorlákr became bishop, the Church in Iceland was in the firm grip of the Icelandic elite. Both bishops were thoroughly involved in local affairs and not interested in the developoments taking place within the Roman Church in any way comparable to Bishop Þorlákr. The bishop of Hólar was Brandr Sæmundarson (r. 1163–1201), a member of the Oddaverjar-family and a protégé of the chieftain Jón Loptsson who accompanied him to Niðarós for his ordination. At the episcopal seat in Skálholt sat Klængr Þorsteinsson (r. 1152–1174). While Bishop Klængr had earned a reputation for his learning and poetic gifts, he was a true son of the Chieftain Church, educated at Hólar where he served as priest until he was chosen the bishop of Skálholt in 1151. According to *Hungrvaka*, he held a position as one of the chieftains, a friend of Jón Loptsson and Gizurr Hallson and in good contact with the most powerful magnates of Scandinavia.[101] In some ways at least, he seems to have behaved as such as he took up one of their lesser approved practices when he had a daughter outside of wedlock.[102] Perhaps, albeit only a matter of speculation, his extra-marital affair led to the severe ascetic practices with which he is credited in one of the Latin fragments of the *Saga of Bishop Þorlákr*.[103] Everything points to Bishop Brandr and Bishop Klængr having been perfectly comfortable with the current arrangement of the Church. As will be discussed in what follows, it was during this period that the archbishop of Niðarós began exercising his authority in Iceland for the first time.

4.2.2 The Authority of the Archbishop

The earliest source material related to the conflict between the Church and Icelandic chieftains consists of a series of letters from the archbishop in Niðarós composed during the period between 1173 and 1189. In the letters – four are ascribed to Archbishop Eysteinn until his death in 1188 and two to Archbishop Eiríkr Ívarsson (r. 1188–1205/6) – the archbishops address, both directly and indirectly, the growing tension between Icelandic local authorities and the Church. The letters were originally composed in Latin but were translated into Icelandic at an indefinite point in time.[104] They are among the earliest

---

101 *ÍF* XVI, p. 37.
102 See discussion in Philadelphia Ricketts, *High-Ranking Widows in Medieval Iceland and Yorkshire: Property, Power, Marriage and Identity in the Twelfth and Thirteenth Centuries*, The Northern World 49 (Leiden, 2010), p. 165.
103 *ÍF* XVI, p. 341.
104 See Jón Sigurðsson's introductory comments to the letters in *DI* I, pp. 220, 259, 261, 285, and 290 and further discussion in Sveinbjörn Rafnsson, "Þorláksskriftir og hjúskapur," pp. 117–118.

preserved official pieces of evidence for the relations between the Church in Iceland and the archbishopric in Niðarós and by extension the Holy See itself. Previous treatments of the letters from Niðarós have been almost exclusively concerned with philological, legal, and political aspects of the letters. What the survey of the discursive landscape of the Icelandic religious field, however, draws out is how the Church's claims were securely framed in the context of the Christian history of salvation, swirling with religious images and motives.

When the earliest preserved letter was composed, the archbishopric had been in existence for around two decades. The archbishop is, on the one hand, preoccupied with introducing the idea of a non-Icelandic institution being capable of making claims to authority over Icelanders, their behavior and their property.[105] Iceland was certainly a part of the Christian *oikoumene*, and it should be assumed that ecclesiastics in monasteries and church centers around the country were informed about church political developments in Europe. On the administrative, economic level, however, the Church in Iceland was shaped by the interests of local magnates, who had the deciding word when it came to appoint individuals for episcopal office. Neither of the incumbent bishops, Klængr and Brandr, was likely to promote a papal policy bound to have unsettling political and economic consequences for the ruling classes in Iceland. Both bishops were active participants in political strifes and quarrels of the day – not only as reconcilers – as can be seen from their frequent occurrence in the pages of the *Sturlunga* collection. Words such as 'authority' (*vellde*) and 'obedience' (*hlydne*) frequently occur in the archbishop's message as he strives to make plain the logic of the ecclesiastical hierarchy as it should appropriately operate - descending ultimately from God through the pope in Rome, and through the metropolitan bishop in Niðarós to the bishops in Iceland. Furthermore, as Guðrún Ása Grímsdóttir has pointed out, it is likely that the Icelandic bishops were bound by an oath of obedience to the archbishop as can be surmised from a statute of Pope Anastasius IV (r. 1153–1154) in which he confirms the founding of Niðarós archbishopric.[106]

On the other hand, the archbishop expresses his grave concerns about the behavior of the Icelanders, admonishing and forthright scolding various kinds of wrongdoings, primarily in the field of sexual morality as well as the behavior of and towards clerics. All of these concerns had been frequent topics in the clerical discourse of Continental Europe over the preceding two centuries and

---

105   There had been contact between Iceland and Niðarós, bishop Brandr Sæmundarson (r. 1163–1201) of Hólar had for instance been ordained in Niðarós by Archbishop Eysteinn in 1163, the first Icelandic bishop to receive his ordination from the new archsee. *ÍF* XVI, p. 35.
106   Guðrún Ása Grímsdóttir, "Um afskipti erkibiskupa," p. 32.

as has been systematically noted by historians discussing these letters through the years, their arrival clearly marks the heralding of the papal reform policy in Iceland.

The first preserved letter has been dated to 1173.[107] According to the testimony of the bishops' chronicle *Hungrvaka*, the reason for Archbishop Eysteinn's letter is the request of Bishop Klængr of Skálholt for a permission to withdraw from the bishop's office for health reasons and for a new bishop to be appointed before the death of Bishop Klængr.[108] The letter itself shows, however, that the archbishop had more on his mind than the installment of a new bishop in Skálholt. It is addressed to the bishops, all other excellent men in the country ("ollum odrum agætis monnum") as well as the general public ("allri alþydu"). The letter opens on a pastoral note with the archbishop reminding the recipients of his pastoral responsibility towards the Icelanders which might also be interpreted, as scholars have done, as stressing the archbishop's authority over them.[109]

> Eg veitt at ydur mon kvnnigt vera. at ek ǻ ydvars mals at gæta til vardveislv af gvdz alfv. og vere mer fagnadur ǻ. ef ek gæta so til gætt at gudi þætti vel. og oss væri ollvm gagn j.[110]
>
> [I know that you are aware that I am responsible for overseeing your matters on behalf of God and I would rejoice if I could carry that task out in a manner pleasing to God and of use for all of us.]

Archbishop Eysteinn then addresses the situation in Iceland. Without providing any specifics, he brings up the issue that Icelanders had been suffering from a battle (*bardagi*) for a while (*vm hrider*). The archbishop might be referring to the disputes and the occasional open conflicts beginning in 1159 between the chieftains Einar Þorvarðarson and Sturla Þórðarson of Hvammur but he chooses to keep his discussion on a general level.[111] From the point of view of a medieval ecclesiast, and certainly many other people at the time,

---

107 This is the only letter of the six of which there exists a Latin version as well, printed in Finnur Jónsson's ecclesiastical history. *Historia Ecclesiastica Islandiæ* I, pp. 236–239. That version is a translation of the original Old Icelandic translation, made by either Finnur or, what is more likely, his son Hannes Finnsson (1739–1796).
108 *ÍF* XVI, p. 39.
109 Magnús Stefánsson, "Kirkjuvald eflist," pp. 94–95.
110 *DI* I, p. 221.
111 *Sturlunga* I, pp. 60–90. Archbishop Eiríkr begins his letter to bishops Þorlákr and Brandr dated to 1190 by telling them about the 'battle' raging in his own country, Norway. *DI* I, p. 290.

the specifics of particular conflicts are also only characteristics of a battle of infinitely greater proportions, i.e. the cosmic struggle between God and the Devil, good and evil, angels and demons, saints and sinners, cutting through all planes of existence. But even so, the havoc of this battle is not always and perhaps rarely visible to the naked eye and in the face of persistent pain and suffering it is easy to come to the conclusion that one is fighting on the wrong side of the battle. Eysteinn reminds his recipients that despite the high number of good men in Iceland, "in this world, one cannot distinguish between the good and the bad, and many good men have to suffer bad things."[112] But this condition is simply the cost of belonging to a fallen human race, exiled from paradise into the struggles of this sinful state of existence. This theological worldview provides the backdrop against which the archbishops' letters need to be read, both in terms of how they establish their own authority and that of the Icelandic local bishops such as Þorlákr, but also, as will be addressed shortly, their treatment of the moral situation among the Icelandic population, especially the chieftains, which they systematically condemn.

4.2.3 Enemies of the Church

A central theme in the archbishops' letters is their complaints about the behavior of the Icelandic population, particularly from the upper layer of society. The charges they make are both directed towards moral offenses but also direct disobedience, that is the apparently frequent occurrence of disregard for ecclesiastical and in particular episcopal authority. In the moral realm, the archbishops express their strong disapproval of what they have heard about Icelanders beating, hurting and killing clergymen. Furthermore, "some men have left their wives and taken mistresses instead. Some keep both their wives and mistresses under their roof and live such unholy lives that it tempts all Christian men to sin."[113] And in a later letter from 1180, addressed to the Icelandic bishops and a group of named chieftains, Archbishop Eysteinn laments how professed Christian chieftains such as Jón Loptsson and Gizurr Hallsson – whose behavior should ideally have been exemplary for others – have been found severely lacking in matters considered Christian.[114] The most

---

112 "Eigi verdur þessa heims grein gior medal ens goda og illa. þa giallda idolega. marger goder ens jlla." *DI* I, p. 221.
113 *DI* I, p. 221. Translation of citation by Jochens in Agnes S. Arnórsdóttir, *Property and Virginity*, p. 80.
114 "At þui. at vier hofum heyrtt. þa er margs med ydr [á] fatt þat er kristnir menn adrir fylgja." *DI* I, p. 262.

serious fault is the indecency and uncleanliness of the life they are leading which the archbishop compares to the behavior of livestock.[115]

The leaders of the Icelanders had been found lacking both in regard to sexual morality and obedience. What is more, after Bishop Þorlákr Þórhallsson assumed office, the first real proponent of the Gregorian reform movement in Iceland, they ignored and possibly even actively opposed his regulations and decrees. Taking a closer look on how these offenses and the perpetrators are described, it can be seen how the behavior criticized in the letter is described as "neither correct belief nor Christendom"[116] and "against God and holy decrees"[117] The Icelanders are said to have committed "great crimes,"[118] walking the "wrong course,"[119] taking "ill advice,"[120] as opposed to the good advice leading to salvation.[121] This is of course quite basic polemical rhetoric but elsewhere in the letters it appears how the archbishops make use of the traditional image of the opponent, as they refer to their adversaries as "stupid,"[122] "stubborn,"[123] and of "hardened mind"[124] and wallowing in the error of older times.

As noted, in the wider European context of the Western Church, there was no lack of statutes and regulations addressing relating to the above-mentioned offenses In terms of laws and regulations regarding sexual morals and marital affairs the archiepiscopal letters have been analysed by Agnes S. Arnórsdóttir.[125] In the case of clerical violence, Sverrir Jakobsson has placed the archbishop's letters, although he is more preoccupied with 13th century events as described in *Sturlunga*, in the context of the *Pax dei* movement.[126] Both the reform of

---

115 "lifit bufiar life." *DI* I, p. 262.
116 "hvorke [...] rett trva ne kristne," *DI* I, p. 221.
117 "j mote gudj. Og helgvm settningvm," *DI* I, p. 222.
118 "j storglæpvm standa," *DI* I, p. 222.
119 "Ovegur," *DI* I, p. 233.
120 "draga menn fra orade," *DI* I, p. 263.
121 "ef eigi uilia menn vikiast til hialprada þessara," *DI* I, p. 223.
122 "hugar herda og oþiarft sialfræde." *DI* I, p. 259.
123 "En ef menn vilia þra sitt vit leggia," *DI* I, p. 222.
124 "ef stadfesta kemur æ mot. þra heimskra manna." *DI* I, p. 289.
125 Agnes S. Arnórsdóttir, *Property and Virginity*, pp. 77–86.
126 Sverrir Jakobsson, "Friðarviðleitni kirkjunnar á 13. öld," *Saga* XXXVI (1998), 17–18. The Peace of God movement emerged in Southern France (in the province of Auvergne) from where it spread around Europe in several phases in the course of the tenth and eleventh centuries. In the late tenth and early eleventh century it is referred to as the *pax*, *pactum pacis*, *restauratio pacis et iustitiae*, and *convenientia pacis* and after 1027 it frequently expanded into the *pactum sive treuga* or *treuga Dei* (the Truce of God). *Lexikon des Mittelalters*, s.v. "Gottesfrieden." Through the years, scholars from different fields of historical research – legal, social and religious in particular – have debated the reasons behind the rise of the movement, whether it was the "religious enthusiasm generated

sexual morals and clerical violence constituted a part of the broader movement of the reform of the Church. The emphasis here, however, lies more on bringing out how these offenses might have served to illustrate the position of the Icelanders in the dualistic framework of the medieval Christian worldview.

To such ends, it is important to pay attention to how the archbishops' message of disciplining and reproach was formulated within the broader ecclesiastical discursive frame of the fight against the Church's enemies. Surely, important analysis has been carried out, identifying which conciliar statutes provide the legal background for the claims made in the letters and statutes issued by the archbishops of Niðarós.[127] However, although much of the source material ascribed to named churchmen, such as archbishops and other high-ranking church officials, pertains largely to ecclesiastical laws and regulations, it is important to avoid painting an overly bureaucratic and legalistic a picture of the Church and the concerns of ecclesiastics. In the Middle Ages, the Church was *the* channel of grace into the world. Institutional structures like canon law were the necessary means through which the Church could operate in a fallen world without which it would never have been able to establish and consolidate its position in society. But such structures were only worldly representations for achieving goals which were ultimately religious. Ideally, they were never the goal in and of themselves, the struggle for the implementation of church policy, bishop's authority, and implementation of church law was always a part of a much larger fight, taking place on all levels of reality, within the individual, in society, and on the cosmic plane.

The archbishops' letters clearly portray the religious worldview of the medieval ecclesiast. In a world marked by ongoing struggle between the forces of

---

by the one thousandth anniversary of Christ's life on earth, the profound social adjustments brought on by the devolution of power and the emergence of the *milites* as a distinct group, the traditions of episcopal jurisdiction over church lands, the shared administrative and family histories of the prelates and nobles, [or] the desires of monks to promote their cult centers and protect the pilgrims who flocked to them," Frederick S. Paxton's "History, Historians, and the Peace of God," in *The Peace of God: Social Violence and Religious Response in France around the Year 1000*, eds. Thomas Head and Richard Landes (Ithaca, 1992), p. 40. For the present purposes, it suffices to resort to Hans-Werner Goetz's general observation that the Peace of God movement was a movement of restoration which, driven by a religious impulse and looking to the aims of the Church reform, sought to bring back law and order. Hans-Werner Goetz, "Die Gottesfriedensbewegung im Licht neuer Forschungen," in *Landfrieden: Anspruch und Wirklichkeit*, Rechts- und Staatswissenschaftliche Veröffentlichungen der Görres-Gesellschaft, Neue Folge 98, eds. Arno Buschmann and Elmar Wadle (Paderborn, 2002), pp. 42–43.

127 See for example Lára Magnúsardóttir's analysis of letters and statutes from Niðarós in her doctoral dissertation, *Bannfæring og kirkjuvald*, pp. 120–124, 241, and 266–267.

good and evil, there was much more at stake than worldly interests. The archbishops consistently render their claims to the Icelanders into the terms of the struggle between right and wrong belief. The battle against unbelievers was still ongoing. The people they were criticizing were still flirting with ancient habits which the archbishops opposed to the right teaching carried out by the Church.

In a letter dated to 1179, the year after Þorlákr had been ordained as bishop of Skálholt, addressed both to him but also the Icelandic population in general, Archbishop Eysteinn addresses the issue of Þorlákr's efforts for reforming the Church in Iceland. In the letter, the archbishop both expresses his contentment about the extent to which Þorlákr's decrees had been received without difficulties but also a serious warning to those who might have disregarded it, framing it in the context of the original introduction of Christianity and its confrontation with ancient pagan customs:

> En ef nockurer varda vor bodord. eda hans. fyri þui at helldur til nymælis. at forn og onyt siduenia þuerr er hier til hefur þeim afskeidis hrvndit og haf[a] menn eigi þa vit tôku veitta ne geslu sem vergdvkt vere. þa felle menn þat ur skape sier. og se hvat er satt er. og engi mundi vit kristne tekit hafa. hier ne j odrum stad. ef engi skyllde vit þa osidv skiliast er fyrnska hellt. eda forelldrar fagodv.[128]
>
> [But if some disregard our commands or his [Þorlákr's] as novelties, and because that ancient and useless custom which hitherto has lead them astray [...] then they should dismiss it from their minds and see what is true, that nobody would have accepted Christianity, nor here nor elsewhere, if nobody would have departed from the bad habits of antiquity or cultivated by ancestors.]

There is an interesting parallel to this kind of argument in the *Saga of the Apostle Peter*, preserved in an early 13th century manuscript, where the apostle Peter is giving a speech in front of a pagan audience in the Greek city of Tripolis.

> [Þetta mællta ek eigi af þvi, at þer munut nu vilia slika villu faga, helldr fyrir þvi at þer munut nu vilia hafna sem fyrst villu þeiri, er frændr yðrir kendu yðr i ØSku, þviat morgum er trautt at hafna veniu sinni ok frænda

---

128 *DI* I, p. 259.

sinna [...] að trua yður megi magnaz, sva at engi ef se eptir hinnar fornu villu.]¹²⁹

I do not say this so that you would wish now to cultivate such error, but rather so that you would now wish to reject as soon as possible the heresies that your kinsmen taught you in your youth, for many are unwilling to abandon their customs or their kinsmen [...] so that your faith might be magnified and so that no doubt will remain concerning your old heresy.

If the archbishop's letter is read over against the passage from the *Saga of the Apostle Peter*, which most certainly was already familiar to the 12th century audience, it becomes even clearer how the archbishop was framing his warning within a discursive framework centering on the struggle against ancient error and heresy.

In a letter dated a year later, to 1180, the archbishop writes again to Bishop Þorlákr, but in his salutation, he also mentions a number of chieftains, the best known of whom were Jón Loptsson and Gizurr Hallsson. In his letter, the archbishop severely scolds the chieftains for their immoral lifestyle and stubbornness which he explicitly refers to as "ancient customs":

> Nv styrkit þier rad biskupa og setid eigi so fyrnskv ydra. at eigi takid þier vit hialp rade. er þier vitód sialfer Gitzor og Jon at engi er fyrir þvi at helldur nymæle. er hier þycke nytt at heyra. Er meir hefur riktt sialfræde en sanninde. Nv giorit nockrra þa skipan áá mote fiandans vellde. Med þvi alite sem gvd mvn til setia med yckur og biskupa áá syn.¹³⁰
>
> [Now you should support the deliberation of bishops and not regard your ancient customs so highly that you do not accept redemptive advice since you know yourselves, Gitzor and Jon, that nothing is necessarily a novelty if it sounds new to your ears, when audacity has been in charge rather than truth. Now arrange your matters against the Devil's reign, as orderered by God and approved by the bishops.]

After Archbishop Eysteinn's death in 1188, he was succeeded by Eiríkr Ívarsson who continued his predecessor's involvement in Icelandic church politics. He also seems to have made use of similar rhetorical strategies of describing his opponents' customs as ancient.

---

129 *Post*, p. 178. Trans. Roughton II, p. 521.
130 *DI* I, p. 263–264.

> Nv med þvi at ec em til bodorda settur yfer badum. þa so sem þid eigvd gvdj hlydnj at uieta. og hinum helga petro og mier so tacid tid vit þeim bodordum. og teiz at bader. En ef so er at menn rise med ollv a̋ mote. og vilia so aa fyrnsku hallda at bodord ydur eiga ongvan stad. þa sækist helldur aa fund minn.[131]
>
> [Now since I have been placed in command over both of you, in the same way as you are expected to obey God, the Holy Peter and me, accept these commands [...] But in the event that men will rise up against you and persist in their ancient customs ignoring your commands, rather seek my audience.]

The above lines of Eiríkr's statute show an important link between the discourse of the heretical enemy and the construction of episcopal authority in medieval Icelandic society. As frequently mentioned, the letters of the archbishops draw up a picture of Icelandic society as plagued by moral corruption and disobedience. The bishops consistently place the individuals at fault in opposition to Christian behavior, correct doctrine, and the Church. Eysteinn frankly explains to Icelandic chieftains that "you are lacking in many things which other Christians duly practice."[132] The way out of this sinful condition, is to grab on to the only available safety line which is the one thrown into the darkness by the Church and manifests itself in teachings and commands of ecclesiastics of all ranks, allowing Archbishop Eysteinn to modestly refer to his commands as "council of deliverance" (*hialprad*).[133] Those who do not grasp the gravity of the situation and follow the appropriate ways to react to it - show remorse with concrete acts as administered by the archbishop - do not have correct faith and cannot be counted among Christians. And as the survey of early ecclesiastical discourse in Iceland has shown, they have joined some dubious company and what is more, the eternal welfare of their soul is at grave risk.

> En hvorke er rett trva ne kristne. og eigi þav verk er til hialpar mecgi draga. nema snn trv bve vnder. Nv veitt eg. at þat mvnv aller seigia. er at ero spurder. at retta kristne fae. En hverr er sa. er tvi tryde. at epter god verk. skyllde eilifan fagnad taka. En epter jll verck elld brennanda. ok kvol eilifa. at hann skyllde eigi hirtast orada sinna. Ef hann vere aa minntur vm þav verk er til eilifs dauda draga.[134]

---

131   *DI* I, p. 286.
132   "Þa er margs med ydr åa fatt þat er kristnir menn adrir fylgia," *DI* I, p. 262.
133   *DI* I, p. 222.
134   *DI* I, p. 221.

[But it is neither correct belief or Christianity, and not deeds capable of bringing one to salvation, unless there is a true belief underlying. I know that everybody will say, when asked, that they have received the correct faith. But who believes that he is to receive eternal rejoice after good deeds but burning and eternal torture after the bad if he does not repent his wicked actions when admonished about those deeds that lead to eternal death.]

Of course, the Church was concerned with getting its demands through, but they should not be dehistoricized so as to treat them as purely aimed at the political expansion and economic growth of the Church as an institution. The claims for authority and for the implementation of particular regulations was firmly rooted in the religious discursive context of the time, without which it will not be fully understood. It has become somewhat of a truism in the scholarship of medieval history, especially in Iceland, that the bishops, particularly during the Catholic era, were cold-hearted and greedy individuals who would go at any length to increase their wealth and property and one of the ways most frequently cited is the threat of eternal damnation.[135] It is important to keep in mind that the bishops' discourse of eternal death and damnation was not a 'trick' they invented but an inherent part of the Christian religion at the time.

4.2.4 Conclusion: On the Other Side

When the first letters from Niðarós started to arrive in Iceland it must have caused a great deal of distress – a crisis even – for the recipients. Home-grown bishops like Klængr and Brandr, Christian magnates and the clergy of the Chieftain Church had until then been on the safe side in the ongoing cosmic struggle, fighting the good fight of the Church alongside apostles and other saints. There is no reason to assume otherwise than they had identified with religious discourses cut from the same cloth as the ones found in the *Icelandic Homily Book* and the hagiographic literature preserved from the 12th and 13th century, aligning themselves to the power structures inscribed in them. Now, however, they were confronted with a new reality as they came into the disfavour of the archbishop of Niðarós, an ecclesiastical authority which they acknowledged – theoretically at least – and had been implicitly promoting through their use of the religious discourses accompanying the Christian religion since its arrival on the island. All of a sudden, they found themselves on

---

135 See Lára Magnúsardóttir's discussion of the representation of the bishop in Icelandic historiography, *Bannfæring og kirkjuvald*, pp. 160–187.

the other side, – forced by their own hand, as it were – grouped with the enemies of the Church and, consequently, in grave peril. In such light, it can be argued that the corporate identity of the Church as an institution should not be restricted to the administrative structures and the professional identity of the institution's elite and specialists. An important element of the corporate identity of the Church was constituted by its religious discourses, making it possible for the local aristocracy who had taken it upon themselves to get the Church on its feet in the first place to be overridden by an authority representing the ecclesiastical empire of the Roman Church.

4.3 Reform and Violence: The Rule of Bishop Guðmundr

A more heated conflict between Church and chieftains arose several decades later, but then in the Northern diocese of Hólar. In 1201, a man was elected to the episcopacy by the magnates of the North whom they believed would not be a great source of trouble for the ruling class. His name was Guðmundr Arason (r. 1203–1237) who, contrary to the expectations of those who elected him, would soon become one of the most controversial figures in Icelandic politics. Compared to the conflict previously discussed between Bishop Þorlákr and Jón Loptsson, Guðmundr's conflict with the Northern chieftains became much more violent and resulted in a number of casualties, including that of Kolbeinn Tumason, one of the most powerful chieftains at the time. Ultimately, the strife was grounded in the same ecclesiological and religiopolitical developments as the first clash between Church and chieftains and brought to the fore some of the discursive themes discussed in the course of this study. The following discussion will explore the religious context of this most heated conflict between the Church and country's political elite and with a particular focus on how the discourses under analysis came into play, not only in verbal discourse but also in material artefacts such as episcopal and clerical dress.

4.3.1 *Guðmundr's Rise to the Episcopacy*
The most informative source for the course of events playing out in the early 13th century is the *Sturlunga* collection. It should be noted that the *Sturlunga* collection cannot be taken as a source for how certain things were exactly uttered or how particular events took place. Nonetheless, although they the are written in the same time as most of the sagas of the Icelanders, in the course of the 13th century that is, the sagas of the *Sturlunga* collection stand much closer in time to the events which they describe. Most historians of medieval Iceland, therefore, take the texts as a reliable source for the spirit of the age, throwing

light on courses of events that could very well have taken place as they are described and recounting dialogues that could very well have been uttered.[136]

As soon as he assumed office, Bishop Guðmundr showed himself to be more domineering and less conforming to the will of the ruling magnates than they had expected.[137] Kolbeinn Tumason, the most powerful chieftain in Northern Iceland at the beginning of the 13th century, had been on amicable terms with Guðmundr before he became bishop at Hólar.[138] Guðmundr, who also was first cousin with Kolbeinn's wife, spent the winter of the year 1200 at his farmstead, Víðimýri in Skagafjörður, and was treated there with respect and affection. After that winter, Kolbeinn came to the conclusion that Guðmundr was truly a saintly man ("að sönnu sannhelgr maðr").[139] When Guðmundr's predecessor at Hólar, Brandr Sæmundarson, died in 1201, Kolbeinn is said to have consulted with his friends and elected Guðmundr as bishop, although the decision was made on other grounds than his sanctity. According to *Íslendinga saga*, Guðmundr's reputation as a popular and modest man made him a feasible option for Kolbeinn's intention of maintaining control over the Church.

---

136 See for example the view of Agnes S. Arnórsdóttir, *Konur og vígamenn*, pp. 20–25. See also Guðrún Nordal who describes *Sturlunga* as an important source "not only about historical events but also giving a precious insight into the thought world and the life views of 13th century Icelanders." *ÍB* 1, p. 309. Similarly, in his assessment of the historical value of *Sturlu saga*, Orri Vésteinsson expresses the opinion that "these were considered by the author to be realistic attitudes which must therefore have been current in the first two decades of the thirteenth century when the saga was written." Orri Vésteinsson, *Christianization of Iceland*, p. 211. A voice of skepticism towards the source value of the *Sturlunga* sagas is that of literary scholar Úlfar Bragason who has criticized the uncritical attitude of historians of medieval Iceland towards *Sturlunga* as a historical source. In his writings on the subject, he has emphasized the importance of assessing the narrative principles of the sagas of the collections before they are used as sources. Such an approach, he contends, will reveal that the *Sturlunga* sagas belong to the same narrative system as the Sagas of the Icelanders and should therefore be taken with the same degree of skepticism when it comes to using them as historical sources. See Úlfar Bragason, *Ætt og saga: Um frásagnarfræði Sturlungu eða Íslendingasögu hinnar miklu* (Reykjavík, 2010), for example pp. 67–91 and pp. 263–268. While acknowledging the importance of being aware of the *Sturlunga* accounts as literary constructions, the historians Helgi Þorláksson and Gunnar Karlsson have responded to Bragason's skepticism by pointing out that the narrative patterns he identifies in the *Sturlunga* collection correspond to historically verifiable social conventions, such as feuding and peace-making. See Helgi Þorláksson, "Úlfar Bragason. Ætt og saga: Um frásagnarfræði Sturlungu eða Íslendinga sögu hinnar miklu," *Saga* 49 (2011), 227 and Gunnar Karlsson, *Inngangur að miðöldum*, pp. 204–205.
137 *Sturlunga, Íslendinga saga*, p. 213.
138 Ibid., p. 195.
139 Ibid., p. 177.

Mæltu það margir að Kolbeinn vildi því Guðmund til biskups kjósa að hann þóttist þá ráða bæði leikmönnum og kennimönnum fyrir norðan land.[140]

[Many men commented that Kolbein had wanted Guðmund chosen bishop because he thought he himself would thus control both laymen and clergy in the north.]

When describing Guðmundr's reaction to his election as bishop of Hólar, the sources describe him accepting the office with great reluctancy. After he heard that he was a candidate for the episcopacy he became so afraid that he could not sleep nor eat. Upon hearing of his election he was overcome with sadness and could not speak for some time. Later, he tries to get other clergymen to release him from his burden and take on the bishop's office in his stead. Although this account is to some degree influenced by the hagiographic topos of the 'reluctant bishop,' some scholars have taken the elaborate description of the involvement of Guðmundr's kinsmen in his decision-making as an indicator that it is based on historical events.[141] It should also not be excluded that hagiographic topoi could have influenced the decisions and practices of well-read ecclesiastics like Guðmundr. Of particular interest, is Guðmundr's response to his cousin Ögmundr Þorvarðsson when he asks why he does not want to become bishop. At that point, Guðmundr expresses his concern about having to deal with "marga menn óhlýðna og öfundarfulla" [many disobedient and envious men].[142] As has been repeatedly stressed, disobedience and envy were central characteristics of the opponents of the apostles and the saints in ecclesiastical discourse in Iceland at the time. So already before he accepted the office, his attitude towards his opponents is framed in terms of the religious discourse of the Church.

Eventually, Guðmundr agrees to become the bishop of Hólar and in the year 1202 he sails to Norway. At that point, a civil war had been raging in Norway for decades and had reached extreme heights after the emergence of the Faroese priest Sverrir Sigurðsson as the leader of the opposition against King Magnús Erlingsson. After the battle at Fimreite in Sognefjord in 1184, where King Magnús was killed, Sverrir became the king of Norway although he did not

---

140 Ibid., p. 196. Trans. McGrew, *Sturlunga saga* I, p. 128.
141 Bernadine McCreesh, "Saint-Making in Early Iceland," *Scandinavian-Canadian Studies* 17 (2006–2007), 21, n. 11. In his discussion of Þorvarðr Þorgeirsson attempt to convince Guðmundr to accept the bishop's office, Orri Vésteinsson makes no reservation about the historical value of the account. Orri Vésteinsson, *Christianization of Iceland*, p. 204.
142 *Sturlunga, Prestssaga*, p. 200.

manage to suppress the opposition against him. The Church had stood firmly behind King Magnús and remained a powerful force of opposition throughout Sverrir's reign. After a series of altercations, Archbishop Eiríkr had to flee from Norway and, in the end, Sverrir was excommunicated by the pope. On his way to Norway, during a layover in the Hebrides, Guðmundr and his fellowship learn that King Sverrir had died.[143] As noted at the very end of the *Prestssaga Guðmundar Arasonar*, the bishop-elect first meets King Hákon Sverrisson, the son of King Sverrir, in Bergen, who received him amicably and then he sails north to Niðarós where he is ordained by Archbishop Eiríkr Ívarsson, who had returned from his exile.[144]

This information is by no means unimportant for the present study. At the archbishop's court in Niðarós, Guðmundr came into contact with people who had been involved in the hefty and longstanding church political disputes in which the discursive themes under inspection had been employed with a high degree of sophistication.[145] In the conflict between the Church and King Sverrir, the conflict potential of the religious discourses under inspection was being mobilized on both sides. While the archbishop of Niðarós and his clergy made what use they could of their position as the legitimate representatives of the apostolic seat, King Sverrir rejected their entire message straight out as false threats procured by treacherous priests of error. A very enlightening source for the king's argumentation is his speech against the bishops, composed towards the very end of the 12th century.[146] Interestingly enough, although King Sverrir had been excommunicated by the pope he did not reject the ultimate authority of Rome, claiming only that the pope was misinformed, unable to get the correct information about state of affairs so far away. Thus, realizing how much was at stake, King Sverrir and his advisors challenged the church administration on the rightful claim for the Church's ecclesiastical discourse.

---

143   Ibid., p. 208.
144   Ibid., p. 209.
145   See section 4.2.2.1 above.
146   In addition to King Sverrir himself, several clerics from his court have been suggested as main authors of the speech. As pointed out by Erik Gunnes, the only certainty about the speech's authorship is that he must have had a thorough knowledge of the Bible, theology, rhetoric and been well oriented in the religio-political discourse of the time, all of which is likely that he acquired abroad. The arguments employed bear most resemblance to what one would encounter in England and Germany. Gunnes's conclusion is that the speech was produced in an intellectual environment related to the courts of Henry II and Frederick Barbarossa. Erik Gunnes, *Kongens ære: kongemakt og kirke i "En tale mot biskopene,"* (Oslo, 1971), pp. 351–352.

Nothing can be said with certitude about how this situation came to influence the decisions and actions of Guðmundr as bishop of Hólar. What can be surmised from Guðmundr's reaction when he was elected bishop is that he was already leaning towards the reformist stance. He dreaded coming into conflict with the "disobedient and envious men," which was bound to happen if he would keep to the reformist agenda. If anything, it seems likely that Guðmundr's stay at the court of Archbishop Eiríkr would have strengthened such a conviction. After the death of Bishop Þorlákr, there had not been any serious endorsement of reform in the country and one could not expect any such efforts from Niðarós while the archbishop's court was in crisis-mode. With Guðmundr's rise to the episcopacy and with the archbishop back in Niðarós, this was about to change. In the following years, the program of reform would be carried out with unseen religious fervour and severity.

4.3.2   Religious Fervour and Armed Battles

As soon as Guðmundr had returned from Norway and assumed the "governance of Christianity" (*stjórn kristni*) in the North, the dissonance between him and the chieftain Kolbeinn Tumason became increasingly manifest.[147] The first major conflict between the two revolved around jurisdictional boundaries – a central bone of contention between *sacerdotium* and *regnum* during the High Middle Ages – regarding the case of a certain priest whom Kolbeinn was charging for old money affairs (*fornt fémál*). The priest seeks the support of the bishop who refuses to accept Kolbeinn's say in the case who persists and calls for the priest to be sentenced as an outlaw. The case is taken up at the next assembly where Bishop Guðmundr shows up and attempts to make an influence with the means available to him, mustering whatever authority the episcopal attire could provide him with: "þá gekk biskup til dóms við staf og stólu og fyrirbauð þeim að dæma prestinn en þeir dæmdu eigi að síður" [the bishop came with his staff and his stole and forbade them to pass sentence on the priest. But they passed sentence on him all the same.].[148] From what

---

147   *Sturlunga* I, *Íslendinga saga*, p. 213.
148   Ibid., p. 214. Trans. McGrew, *Sturlunga saga* I, p. 134. This is not the only instance recorded in *Íslendinga saga* of bishops attempting to influence urgent matters in their ceremonial dress. When Órækja Snorrason came after Gizurr Þorvaldsson at Skálholt, bishop Sigvarðr Þéttmarsson (r. 1238–1268) promises Gizurr his support and all his clerics against Órækja in the following words: "Hann kveðst og vega skyldu með þeim vopnum sem hann hafði til" [He said that he would fight with any weapons he could lay hand on]. *Sturlunga* I, *Íslendinga saga*, p. 447. Trans. McGrew, *Sturlunga saga* I, p. 366. Later, when the fight between the two chieftains has begun, the bishop emerges from beyond the defense wall in ceremonial apparel with mitre, crozier, books and candles, fully equipped for the

is known about liturgical clothing of bishops and the episcopal emblems in the Icelandic Free State, it seems reasonable to assume that it was thoroughly grounded in the discursive framework explored in the third chapter of this book and according to *Sturlunga*, Bishop Guðmundr was willing to use that symbolic power in the conflicts in which he participated.[149]

This encounter and the assembly's verdict set in motion a course of events leading to the excommunication of Kolbeinn. When Kolbeinn came to summon the bishops' men to be tried at the assembly of Hegranes, the bishop found himself compelled to recapitulate Kolbeinn's excommunication in a ceremonious manner:

> Biskup og hans men voru á húsum uppi og var hann skrýddur og las hann bannsetning á norræna tungu svo að þeir skyldu skilja. Og ef Kolbeinn hefði verið verr stilltur í því sinni þá hefði þar bardagi orðið.[150]
>
> [The bishop and his men were up on the house; he was in his robes, and read out the sentence of excommunication in the Icelandic tongue so that they would understand it. If Kolbein had been less restrained on that occasion there would have been a battle.]

It should be noted at this point that underlying these events and those that followed was a fervent religious atmosphere which was to no small degree associated with the persona of Guðmundr himself. Scholars have often ascribed the intensity of the conflict between Bishop Guðmundr and the chieftains in the North to Guðmundr's passionate and uncompromising character.[151] It seems, however, that the heat of the conflict can be sufficiently accounted for without resorting to psychological interpretations although they can be taken to hold complementary explanatory value. The capability of religious

---

excommunication ritual he was about to initiate. In her English translation, McGrew seems to assume that the bishop and his clerics had actually taken arms to engage in a physical fight while it seems more accurate that by the words 'weapons' bishop Sigvarðr meant spiritual weapons the most powerful of which was the ritual of excommunication.

149 See section 3.3.2.3 above.
150 *Sturlunga* I, *Íslendinga saga*, p. 215. Trans. McGrew, *Sturlunga saga* I, p. 135.
151 Emphasizing the effect of a series of traumas Guðmundr went through in his early years, Hjalti Hugason has attempted to analyse Guðmundr's character from the perspective of modern therapeutic approaches. Thus he seeks to throw light on the contradictory tension characterizing Guðmundr's actions which in his opinion cannot be exclusively explained with reference to the conflicts in which he was engaged. Hjalti Hugason, "Áfallatengt álagsheilkenni á miðöldum? Ráðgátan Guðmundur Arason í ljósi meðferðarfræða nútímans," *Skírnir* 186 (spring, 2012): 98–124.

ideas to incite and escalate in times of unrest is well-known and it seems as if the athmosphere in the late 12th century and at the beginning of the 13th was already fraught with tension capable of producing such effects. As an example, the author of the *Prestssaga* describes how just over a decade before Guðmundr was elected bishop, people interpreted current events like Saladin's capture of Jerusalem in 1187 and natural occurrences like a solar eclipse and the exceptionally hard winter of that year in apocalyptic terms: "margir vitrir menn ætluðu verða mundu heimsslit" [many wise man believed that the end of the world was nigh].[152] A few years later, rumours of Guðmundr's sanctity and miraculous deeds were circulating and some of them were recorded by the author of the *Prestssaga*.[153] At one point, the same author even states that there were so many extraordinary happenings surrounding Guðmundr's religious ceremonies during his travels around the country, that it was impossible for him to recount all of them in his work. In 1198, Guðmundr was the only cleric apart from bishops who participated in the *translatio* ceremony of Bishop Þorlákr's relics in which he served an important role.[154] According to the text of the *Prestssaga*, it was the opinion of many people before and during Guðmundr's episcopacy, including Kolbeinn Tumason who was to become his archenemy, that Guðmundr was a holy man.[155] Despite the unmistakable hagiographical elements of that particular work, it can nonetheless be suggested that already before Guðmundr's election, he enjoyed a high degree of popular respect and sanctity, which was bound to spill over into any conflict he would become involved in.[156]

It is important to keep this background in mind as well as the discursive landscape explored above when considering the violent conflicts which first broke out in open battle in 1208. At that point, the disagreement between Bishop Guðmundr and the Northern chieftains surrounding their contending claims for jurisdiction and authority had reached a high point. The disputation

---

152 *Sturlunga* I, *Prestssaga*, p. 119.
153 There are descriptions of the fire of the Holy Spirit surrounding him and birds sitting on his shoulders. Ibid., p. 122.
154 Ibid., pp. 176–177.
155 Ibid., p. 206.
156 This is evident from many passages of the *Prestssaga* but also reflected in a letter from the Oddaverjar-chieftain Sæmundur Jónsson to his brother bishop Páll of Skálholt (which is only preserved in *Prestssaga* and versions of the sagas of Guðmundr). Despite the fact that Guðmundr had sided with Sigurðr Ormsson in a dispute with Sæmundr on inheritance matters, Sæmundur described Guðmundr as "leyfður af mönnum" [praised by men] and that his election in the bishop's office in all likelihood God's will. Ibid., p. 206. See also *DI* I, pp. 333–337.

crystallized in the chieftains and their supporters disregarding Guðmundr's excommunication completely while the bishop treated the men sentenced by the chieftains to outlawry as free men. The bishop, who had gathered around himself many men, removed a shrine, holy relics, and books from Möðruvellir, the farmstead of the chieftain Sigurðr Ormsson, for he did not want such sacred things to be in the care of banished men. Claiming that the bishop had now begun stealing and warring against them, they begin gathering their forces and surround the episcopal seat of Hólar, preparing for the battle which would take place at Víðines, a few kilometers northeast of the episcopal seat itself. Before the battle broke out, there had been attempts at reconciling the two parties, but Kolbeinn Tumason rejected all such efforts. The fight cost several men their lives, including Kolbeinn who was struck by a rock in the forehead.[157]

The battle at Víðines in 1208 was the first case of the Church's fight for liberty in Iceland breaking out in an armed battle. The only surviving source about how it was discursively framed is Sturla Þórðarson's *Íslendinga saga* and the hagiographic sagas on Bishop Guðmundr, which unfortunately are limited and relatively far removed in time. However, enough is known about how such conflicts were being discursively constructed before – for example in the first clash between Church and chieftains and in the struggle between King Sverrir and the Norwegian bishops – to hypothesize about how it might have been in this case. It is even possible that such discourses might have shaped Sturla Þórðarson's description of the events leading up to the battle when he wrote about them decades later. In that description, the archenemy of the bishop, Kolbeinn, is described as "þver" [stubborn] and "óleiðingasamur" [intractable].[158] Furthermore, since it was the feast of the nativity of Mary, every church bell of the see was rung out for evensong but Kolbeinn and his men did not hear. In the Stave Church Homily from the *Icelandic Homily Book*, church bells are understood to allegorically represent the Christian teaching, calling people to do good deeds. The failing of Kolbeinn and his men to hear the church bells might have been taken as a symbol for their deafness towards the Christian teaching and consequently their antagonistic position.[159] Whether or not this

---

157 *Sturlunga* I, *Íslendinga saga*, p. 219.
158 *Sturlunga* I, *Íslendinga saga*, p. 218.
159 "Klukkur merkja kennimenn þá, er fagurt hljóð gjöra fyr Guði og mönnum í bænum sínum og kenningum" [Bells denote those clerics who make sweet sound before God and men in their prayers and teachings], *ÍH*, p. 150."Klukkur merkja kenningar þær, er oss vekja til góðar verka" [Bells denote the teachings which awake us to carry out good deeds.], *ÍH*, p. 151. For discussion and more examples of the meaning of churchbells from medieval Europe, see John H. Arnold and Caroline Goodson, *Viator* 43 (2012): 99-130.

was the way these events were understood and interpreted as they were taking place is impossible to ascertain, but as shown, the discourses were there, ready and accessible.

The dispute was not settled with the battle of Víðines and the descriptions of the following events make it possible to move the discussion beyond the level of the merely hypothetical. In the battle of Hólar, taking place in the spring of 1209, seven of the most powerful chieftains of the country had gathered large forces to go against the bishop at Hólar where he resided with a much smaller number of men. Having subdued the resistance of the bishops' men, the chieftains removed the bishop from his see, ransacked it and executed a few of the bishops' followers. Illustrative of the religious heat underlying the motivations of some of the participants in the struggle is the execution of a member of the bishop's team, a certain Sveinn Jónsson, the description of which deserves to be quoted in full:

> En er biskup var í brottu gengu þeir Arnór inn í kirkju með vopnum og eggjuðu út þá er inni voru og þeir þóttust mestar sakir við eiga ella kváðust þeir mundu sækja þá eða svelte þá í kirkjunni. Þá mælti Sveinn Jónsson: "Gera má eg kost á út að ganga." Þeir spurðu hver sá væri. "Ef þér limið mig að höndum og fótum áður en þér hálshöggvið mig." Og þessu var honum játað. Gekk hann þá út og allir þeir því að þeir vildu eigi að kirkjan saurgaðist af þeim eða blóði þeirra. Allir gengu slyppir út. Var Sveinn þá limaður og söng meðan Ave María. Síðan rétti hann hálsinn undir höggið og var allmjög lofuð hans hreysti sem guð hjálpi honum.[160]
>
> [When the bishop had gone, Arnór and his men went up to the church with their weapons and urged those who were inside, and who they thought had given them the most offense, to come out. Otherwise, they said, they would attack them or starve them out in the church. Then Svein Jónsson said: "I make one condition if I come out." They asked what that might be. "That you cut off my hands and feet before you strike of my head." This was granted him. He came out then, and all the others, because they did not want the church to be defiled by them or their blood; they all came out unarmed. Then Svein was dismembered and throughout this he sang an *Ave Maria*. After that he stretched out his neck for the blow; his courage was much praised.]

---

160 *Sturlunga* I, *Íslendinga saga*, p. 223. Trans. McGrew, *Sturlunga saga* I, p. 144.

Nothing is known about Sveinn other than his participation in the two battles between Bishop Guðmundr's men and his opponents; first, at Víðines where he is said to have made good use of a sword called Brynjubítr which had been acquired by a certain Sigurðr the Greek (*grikkr*) in Constantinople, and then, at Hólar after which he requested dying a martyr's death.[161] The episode clearly reflects the religious elements inherent to the conflict. Sturla Þórðarson's depiction of the event in *Íslendinga saga* is characteristically unemotional. He makes no mention of the religious motivation of Sveinn's actions, stating only that he was much admired for his actions. There can, however, be no doubt that Sveinn's request for being dismembered before his execution was supposed to underline that his gruesome death should be understood as that of a martyr and that he was fighting for God's good cause. Singing *Ave Maria* while undergoing such torments would only have strengthened such an understanding. Although Sveinn's death is the only recorded case of such conduct in medieval Iceland, it can well be interpreted as the radical manifestation of how fighting for the bishop and the Church was being framed in general, at least within the bishop's camp. Alongside the apostles and other saints, martyrs and confessors, about whom they had heard so much in sermons and other readings of the Church's religious writings, the bishop's men were fighting against the age-old enemy of the Church.

4.3.3 Iceland's Salvation

The discursive themes under analysis shine through in the only surviving evidence for the involvement of the current archbishop of Niðarós in this conflict. At that point, the crisis in the relationship between Church and the Icelandic chieftains had never been worse. Two magnates, Arnór Tumason, Kolbeinn's brother, and Sigurðr Ormsson, had taken over Hólar episcopal seat and begun collecting the bishop's tithe as well as forcing priests to give their services in the cathedral against the will of the bishop. Bishop Guðmundr, who had accepted Snorri Sturluson's offer of staying with him in Reykholt in Borgarfjörður in the winter of 1210–1211, had banned all clerics who had sung masses in the cathedral while he himself carried out all his services in tents because no church could be considered fit while the head church had not been cleaned after the defilement it suffered in the battle at Hólar. In the grieving words of Sturla Þórðarson, it was a state of "aumleg og hörmuleg kristni" [miserable and sorrowful Christianity] as everybody behaved according to their own will

---

161 *Sturlunga* I, *Íslendinga saga*, pp. 219, 223, and 246. For a discussion of the sword from Constantinople, see Sverrir Jakobsson, *Auðnaróðal*, pp. 129–134.

and nobody was there to give guidance or speak the truth.¹⁶² In this state of affairs, the seven chieftains who had gone against Bishop Guðmundr at Hólar received a letter from the archbishop of Niðarós, who at that point was Þórir Guðmundsson (r. 1206–1214).¹⁶³

The archbishop begins his letter by reminding the chieftains of who they are dealing with, namely a representative of God. Citing Luke 10:16, he points out that obedience to God's representative equals obedience to God and contempt towards them is contempt towards God. By reference to Psalm 45:17, he emphasizes the continuation of the Church's teaching: "Þá kenning kennum vér er þeir lærðu oss" [We teach the doctrine which they taught us]. On such grounds, he finds himself compelled to speak out and reprimand the recipients of his letter, both for their sake and his own since ultimately, he was responsible for their fate if he fails to admonish them for their crimes.¹⁶⁴ Archbishop Þórir then proceeds to summarize what he has heard about the situation: Unlearned men have taken the power to hold the bishop in contempt which he describes as "hörmulegur grimmleikur og fátíður, guði og öllum guðs lögum gagnstaðlegur" [deplorable and extraordinary cruelty, contrary to God and all God's laws] for nobody is allowed to judge a bishop except the pope and by extension he himself as the holder of the archbishop's office. The perpetrators have furthermore become guilty of committing crimes which only the pope can acquit: deposing the bishop, killing many of his men and endangering the souls he is responsible for. Until that point, alhtough the archbishop seems to have sent other messages before, none of them has shown any sign of remorse, which the archbishop blames on their "vansi trúar, ofkapp og þrályndi þeirra er í illu þrályndast" [lack of belief, the stubbornness, and the obduracy of those who obstinately persevere in their evil courses].¹⁶⁵ Therefore, he sees no other way possible than to summon them to Niðarós, threatening longstanding harm as prescribed by God ("til langra meina mun standa eftir því sem guð kennir oss") in case the chieftains choose to ignore his commands, which cannot be interpreted otherwise.

> Það bjóðum vér og undir hlýðni guði til þakka, heilagri kristni til frelsis, syndum yðrum til lausnar og öllum landslýð til þurftar að þér sækið að sumri á vorn fund en vér skulum alla stund á leggja að ósætt falli, sætt rísi, sálur hjálpist og langær friður standi í þessu landi.¹⁶⁶

---

162 Sturlunga I, Íslendinga saga, p. 224.
163 Ibid., pp. 225–226. See also DI I, pp. 355–369.
164 Sturlunga I, Íslendinga saga, p. 226. Trans. McGrew, Sturlunga saga I, p. 147.
165 Sturlunga I, Íslendinga saga, p. 226. Trans. McGrew, Sturlunga saga I, p. 148.
166 Sturlunga I, Íslendinga saga, p. 226. Trans. McGrew, Sturlunga saga I, p. 148.

> [In this we command you – for the sake of the protection found in obedience to God, the freedom found in [Holy Christianity], for the remission of your sins, and as a benefit for the whole nation – that you come into our presence next summer, and we shall all strive as hard as we can that harmony may grow and enmity may diminish, that souls may be saved and enduring peace be established in this land.]

As this passage shows, which brings together many of the discursive themes under analysis in this study, the urgency of the letter is great. It is not only the salvation of many souls which is at stake, but the welfare of the entire country. And it is only through the Church and by heeding the bishops' and archbishop's words, that enduring peace and harmony will be established on the island.

Although it did not mark any clear watershed in the conflict, the significance of the archbishop's letter should not be underestimated.[167] It was, after all, written with an authority descending directly from the pope, a point which the archbishop asks the Icelandic chieftains to bear in mind. As should be clear by now, the letter makes distinct use of other significant discursive themes explored above. He scolds them for their stubbornness and lack of faith and threatens them with judgment of God. Finally, he promises the chieftains peace if they heed his words. According to *Íslendinga saga*, the archbishop's letter calmed Arnór and the other chieftains ("kyrrast þeir Arnór við bréfin").[168] Guðmundr was allowed to return to his see and although it seems that he did not assume full control of the seat's properties, he remained there in peace until 1214 when he went to Norway to meet with the archbishop. Those of the chieftains who reacted to the archbishop's letter, Arnór Tumason and Þorvaldr Gizurarson, had already departed to Niðarós in 1213 but the outcome of that meeting remains unclear. Scholars agree that after the battle of Hólar in 1209, Guðmundr never possessed enough power and authority to advance the cause of the Church's liberty in any significant way.[169]

4.3.4 Conclusion: Framing Violence

The discussion above proposes a reading of the extant sources for the episcopacy of Guðmundr Arason as a rare example from the Icelandic Free State of how religion can incite and legitimize the use of physical force and violence in battle. As noted, scholars have often explained the heat of the conflict with

---

167 See for example commentary in *DI* I, p. 360.
168 *Sturlunga* I, *Íslendinga saga*, p. 226.
169 Jón Jóhannesson, *Íslendinga saga* I, p. 245; Orri Vésteinsson, *Christianization of Iceland*, pp. 174 and 177; Sverrir Jakobsson, *Auðnaróðal*, pp. 128–129.

regard to Bishop Guðmundr's aggressive character and obstinate frame of mind which can certainly be shown to have played a role in the course of events. As suggested above, however, the conflict between Guðmundr and the Northern chieftains will not be sufficiently explained without reference to the religious context in which it played out. Unfortunately, no contemporary records survive from Guðmundr himself or any of his supporters but from what can be gathered from the surviving records, it looks as if the conflict was being carried out within the discursive parameters outlined above. Already before he was ordained by the archbishop of Niðarós, who had himself been heavily involved in a no less violent conflict, Guðmundr was considered as a holy man during his episcopacy – a friend of God and his emissaries, fighting disobedient and envious opponents. He had gathered around himself a staunch group of supporters, some of whom were willing to suffer a martyr's death for the cause. The letter from Archbishop Þórir frames the conflict in the same discursive terms. Surely, there is no lack of violent encounters between armed forces in historical records from the Free State Era but only rarely they are motivated by religion. Interestingly enough for the purposes of the present study, Christian religious discourses seem to have played a significant role in the battle of Víðines and other related conflicts when the interests of the local elite and the Roman Church became irreconcilable.

CHAPTER 5

Conclusion

As noted at the outset of this study, the history of the rise of Christianity and the Church in the Icelandic Free State has been marked by a research paradigm traditionally referred to with the phrase 'Chieftain Church.' This paradigm assumes that the political elite in Iceland had all the say in matters relating to the organization of the Christian Church. To all intents and purposes, it was the Icelandic chieftains who 'allowed' the Christian religion to thrive in the country as long as it benefited the interests of the ruling class. The latest proponent of this view, Orri Vésteinsson, has even gone as far as to conclude that until the 13th century, the Church was not an actual church in the sense of an organized institution with its own corporate identity but 'simply one aspect of life' in the dealings of the Icelandic magnates.[1] While it accepts the general assumptions of this paradigm regarding the major role played by the Icelandic magnates in the political sphere, this study has stressed that there were other forces at play than the social, political, and economic interests of the chieftain class, moving the attention towards the content of the Christian religion itself. In more technical terms, it has sought to bring the social and political agency of the Christian religion to the fore which has all too often been regarded as closed off in the world of ecclesiastics. Central to its course of inquiry has been to ask what this aspect of life entailed and how it became a part of the life of medieval Icelanders.

Unlike most other studies of this period of Icelandic history, the vantage point of this research project has been the extant source material for the Christian religion as it manifested itself in 11th, 12th, and 13th century Iceland. Most prominent among the preserved religious material and consequently the most important sources for this study are texts in the Icelandic vernacular, containing material of hagiographic and homiletic nature. The limited degree to which these sources have been used for understanding the history of the Church in Iceland is an interesting glitch in the historiography of the period. They have mostly been the subject of research amongst literary scholars and philologists who have not made strong efforts to think of the social presence of the ideas found in these texts which, as stated, is an important goal of this study.

---

1   Orri Vésteinsson, *Christianization of Iceland*, p. 4.

An important premise for this study has been that these texts are essentially communicative texts, in the sense that their content was not restricted to a group of religious specialists, in this case the clerical caste, although they were certainly most familiar with it and responsible for spreading it around the country. In such light, it has proven fruitful to view these texts as sources for 'religious discourse' and thus suggested that the hagiographic and sermonic sources should not be seen in isolation from the society they belonged to but as actively shaping it. Such discourse made itself heard and felt all around the country, not only in the verbal interaction between priests and their flocks, but also manifesting itself in the material world, in wood carvings, textile ornamentation, and liturgical objects. In this way, it is made possible to take the religious aspect of life in the Icelandic Free State seriously as a significant part of the society and culture in which the Icelandic chieftains made their decisions.

Acknowledging the fact that the Christian religion would never have taken as firm a hold in Icelandic society without the support and acceptance of the local aristocracy, this study has placed a great weight on the rise of the Church in Iceland as a part of a broad and consistent expansion of a large-scale institution, namely the Western Church with an administrative center in the papal see in Rome. This has not only been done by explaining how the first Christian institutions of the Church in Iceland grew and came to be incorporated into the administrative hierarchy of the Roman Church nor through an emphasis on the relations with higher ecclesiastical authorities like the archbishoprics of Lund and in particular that of Niðarós, although both points provide important background material for the source analysis taking place. As stated, the main field of inquiry has been the content of the Christian religion and how it can be understood to have played a role in the social and political developments accompanying the growth of Christianity and the rise of the Church as an institution. Its main objective of analysis has been those layers of the religious discourse which were defined at the beginning of this study as constituting the Church's 'ecclesiastical discourse' because of its consistent references to the Church as an insitutiton and a large-scale organization extending itself around the world, for example its offices, its institutional structures, means of aedificiation, and retributive mechanisms. Thus, through the employment of the so-called 'imperial framework,' it has highlighted the structures of domination and subordination incorporated in these discourses as it has striven to show how the Church as an international institution was present in Icelandic society from its earliest phase.

Priests of differing standing – ranging from ordained chieftains to servile priests – whose primary concern was either their own success in the political

CONCLUSION

affairs of the day or that of their overlord, were using and diffusing religious discourses which might at first look as if they were exclusively preoccupied with the divine, but were in actuality bolstering the authority of a distant power center, establishing friends and foes of the Church and dealing out reward and punishment accordingly. Although it stands to reason that the Icelandic upper class shaped the Church according to their own needs and interests, they were at the same time internalizing and reproducing the ecclesiastical discourse and thereby corroborating the power structures which would come to override their own authority and, eventually, remove control of the Church from their hands. Such a development is reminiscent of how large-scale empires from all periods in history gradually infiltrate the elites – the so-called interpretative elites – at the margins of their dominions with what has been termed imperial discourses which, in turn made it easier for them to maintain control over their territories. Of course, one should not take such a comparison too far, but the similarities are unmistakable.

It was of course never a question whether the Icelandic chieftains would make use of such discourse. By accepting the Christian religion, one accepts its religious discourses. The earliest churches in Iceland were dedicated to apostles and other saints. In some cases they may have contained powerful images of these figures and as time passed, many would be in the possession of religious texts telling of their deeds and martyrdoms. In the beginning, such imagery and accounts certainly contributed to the authority of the owners of the churches, but ultimately, the force of these discourses would not support their local interests. As time passed, and the Church as an institution made claims to more power and influence in the Icelandic religious landscape, it linked directly into the very same discourses that the local churchlords had used to build up their church order in the 11th and early 12th centuries. As shown in the synthetic discussion of the fourth chapter of this book, this is visible from the earliest intervention by a non-Icelandic ecclesiastical authority, that is, the first letters stemming from the archbishop in Niðarós. By exploring such moments and others in the history of the Church in the Free State, it has been shown how the ecclesiastical discourse, already present in the church of the Icelandic chieftains, came to be consistenly used against them as the Roman Church strenghtened its position still further as the sole power in the religious landscape at the margins of its rule.

APPENDIX

Manuscript Sources

What follows is a chronologically arranged list of the manuscript corpus of this study with a short content description of each. In several cases, the manuscripts contain the same text. As noted, they represent a very limited portion of the texts that actually existed, even though there is no way to establish how much it actually was. It can be safely assumed, however, that the corpus under inspection provides this research with a sample illustrative of Christian religious discourse diffused during the first centuries of Christianity in Iceland.[1]

AM 237 a fol.
Considered among the very oldest Icelandic manuscripts (dated to 1140–1160), AM 237 fol contains fragments of two homilies. One of them is the widely discussed "Stave-Church Homily" or "Dedication Homily," an allegorical interpretation of the church building. The other one has been identified as a translation of Pope Gregory's *Homilia in Evangelia* 34 on Michael and all angels. Full versions of these sermons are found both in the *Icelandic Homily Book* (Stock. Perg. 15 4to) and the *Norwegian Homily Book* (AM 619 4to). The manuscript is written with a Carolingian script, in two columns, with

---

[1] The dating of several of the earliest Old Icelandic manuscripts, of which a large part survives only in fragments, rests on the work of the Danish philologist Kristian Kålund who edited a catalogue of the entire Arnamagnæan collection (Árni Magnússon's collection of Icelandic manuscripts), published in 1888–1894. *Katalog over Den Arnamagnæanske Håndskriftsamling*, 2. vols (Copenhagen, 1888–1894). Most manuscripts have been revisited by later scholars but often only to confirm Kålund's dating or give a more precise dating within a broader time frame provided by him. Rarely does the discrepancy exceed more than a few decades. Philologist Stefán Karlsson was one of the most productive scholars in such endeavors. For a complete list of his publications,, see "Ritaskrá" in *Gripla* XVII (2006), 208–215. Other important works on the dating of Icelandic manuscript from the period are Hreinn Benediktsson's *Early Icelandic Script* and - admittedly rather dated but still cited in scholarly discussion - Konráð Gíslason's *Um frumparta íslenzkrar tungu í fornöld* (Copenhagen, 1846). A comprehensive overview of manuscripts, their dating and relevant scholarly discussion can be found on the website of the "Dictionary of Old Norse Prose," a dictionary project run by the Department of Scandinavian Research at the University of Copenhagen. *Ordbog over det norrøne prosasprog*. For the date of manuscripts outside the Arnamagnæan collection, Kirsten Wolf's handbook has been consulted. Kirsten Wolf, *The Legends of the Saints in Old Norse-Icelandic Prose*, TONIS (Toronto, 2013).

a heading and an initial in red ink. It is believed to have been a part of a considerably large homiliary.[2]

AM 655 IX 4to

Fragment AM 655 IX 4to[3] counts three sheets with hagiographic material, parts of the *vitae* of the apostle Matthew and the saints Blaise (Blasius) and Placidus (later called Eustace). It is the oldest fragment from a compound of 32 manuscript fragments (counting fragments no. XII–XIII as one) with the shelfmark AM 655 4to, many of which remain the oldest within the corpus of religious documents and will therefore figure prominently in this list. Palaeographic and orthographical investigations of this particular fragment suggests that it was written by a Norwegian but the relationship to other manuscripts indicates that the scribe was probably located in Iceland at the time.[4] It is one of the earliest preserved manuscript of the Arnamagnæan corpus (dated to the period between 1150–1199) and is believed to be the oldest preserved fragment written by a Norwegian.[5]

AM 655 III 4to

Fragment III contains two sheets with the saga of Nicholas, bishop of Myra.[6] Nicholas was popular in medieval Iceland and stories about him were translated into Old Icelandic at least as early as 1200 when the manuscript fragment AM 655 III 4to was composed (1175–1225).[7] It counts three sheets with miracles, the account of the *translatio* of Nicholas' bones and a conclusion where Nicholas is praised.

AM 655 VII and VII 4to

These two fragments, two sheets each, contain the earliest manuscript fragments of an Icelandic world chronicle (*Weltchronik*), called *Veraldar saga* by its late 19th century editor, Konráð Gíslason.[8] The two manuscript fragments both contain the

---

2 See David McDougall, "Homilies (West Norse)" in *Medieval Scandinavia: An Encyclopedia*, ed. Phillip Pulsiano (New York, 1993), p. 290.
3 Edited in Unger, *HMS* I, pp. 269–271; Unger *HMS* II, pp. 207–209; *Post*, pp. 823–825. Plácíduss saga also in *Plácidus saga: With an Edition of Plácitus drápa by Jonna Louis-Jensen*, ed. John Tucker (Copenhagen: Reitzel, 1998). Mattheuss saga also in *Mattheus saga postula*, ed. Ólafur Halldórsson (Reykjavík: Stofnun Árna Magnússonar á Íslandi, 1994).
4 Ólafur Halldórsson, "Inngangur," p. lxvi.
5 Ibid., p. lxiv.
6 Edited in Gustav Morgenstern, *Arnamagnæanische Fragmente (Cod. AM. 655 4to III-VIII, 238 fol. II, 921 4to IV 1.2: Ein Supplement zu den Heilagra manna sögur nach den Handschriften* (Leipzig, 1893), pp. 1–7.
7 Sverrir Tómasson, "Bergur Sokkason og íslenskar Nikulás sögur," in *Tækileg vitni: Greinar um bókmenntir*, ed. Guðvarður Már Gunnlaugsson (Reykjavík, 2011), p. 323. See also Turville-Petre, *Origins of Icelandic Literature*, p. 133.
8 The fragments are printed separately in Morgenstern, *Arnamagnæanische Fragmente*, pp. 35–44.

text of one of two versions preserved in medieval manuscripts, the B-version which is richer in allegorical interpretations than is the A-version.[9] The text ends by telling of the emperors of the German empire, ending with Frederick I ("En nv er Fridrekr" [But now is Frederick]) who died in 1190, so the text must have been written before that date. Many scholars look to Skálholt episcopal seat as a place for the text's composition and even speculated about the chieftain Gizurr Hallsson as the text's author.[10]

AM 673 a I and II 4to

The two manuscripts grouped together under the siglum AM 673 a 4to, 11 sheets in total, contain primarily allegorical material. Most of the scholarly discussion has been concerned with a translation of an illustrated bestiary called *Physiologus* occupying the greater part (7 of the total 11).[11] Originally composed in the 4th century, the *Physiologus* had become a widely used school-text in 12th century Western Europe and would retain that position throughout the Middle Ages.[12] The manuscript contains the moral or allegorical interpretation of animals or other creatures, some of which are bordering on the supernatural.[13] The two last sheets contain what appears to be parts of sermons but would, according to Thomas N. Hall, "be more accurately described as allegorical exempla."[14] The first one is a ship-allegory but the other is a piece from an allegorical sermon on the rainbow. Both of these sermon fragments have been recently edited by Carla Cucina.[15]

AM 655 II 4to

A manuscript fragment consisting of 4 sheets.[16] It was dated by Unger and Kålund to the beginning of the 13th century.[17] The fragment contains part of the legend of a certain general named Romaldus to whom the virgin Mary appears along with the saints Agatha and Thecla.

---

9   *ÍB* I, p. 403.
10 *ÍB* I, pp. 405–406.
11 For a detailed description of the codex see Cucina, "Rainbow Allegory," pp. 63–67.
12 Willene B. Clark, *A Medieval Book of Beasts: The Second-Family Bestiary. Commentary, Art, Text and Translation* (Woodbridge, 2006), p. 9.
13 Sheet 2, which shows only illustrations and no text, has been identified as an iconographic cycle based on Isidore's *Etymologies*, a chapter on Portents (De Portentis). See Cucina, "Rainbow Allegory," p. 65.
14 Thomas N. Hall, "Old Norse-Icelandic Sermons," p. 694.
15 Carla Cucina, "*En kjǫlrinn jarteinir trú rétta.* Incidenza di tropi classici e cristiani sulle tradizioni anglosassone e scandinava." *Rivista Italiana di Linguistica e di Dialettologia* XII (2010), 25–93. Semi-diplomatic edition on pp. 53–56. Cucina, "Rainbow Allegory". Semi-diplomatic edition on pp. 69–74.
16 Printed in *Mariu saga*, pp. XXXII-XXXVIII.
17 Unger, *Mariu saga*, p. xxxiv; Kålund, *Katalog* II, p. 58.

AM 655 IV 4to

Two sheets of a defect manuscript containing the *vita* of Pope Silvester. Dated by Kålund to the first quarter of the 13th century.[18] Stefán Karlsson has argued that *Silvesters saga* was used by the author of *Veraldar saga* which was composed as early as 1138–1152.[19]

AM 655 V 4to

Another two sheets dating to the first quarter of the 13th century containing parts of a life of Silvester and a portion from the saga of Erasmus of Antioch or Elmo as he is sometimes called.[20] There is not much evidence for the veneration of Erasmus who is only mentioned in one Icelandic calendar, in AM 249 l fol., dating to 1175–1200.[21]

AM 686 b 4to

Five leaves dating to the early 13th century containing homilies on the annunciation to the virgin Mary, the nativity of Mary, and the resurrection.[22] The *Icelandic Homily Book* preserves all these homilies entirely.

AM 686 c 4to

One leaf, dated to around 1200–1225, containing a sermon on the resurrection based on Gregory's 25th *Homilia in Evangelia*.[23]

AM 655 VI 4to

The fragment consists of two leaves dating to the beginning of the 13th century containing part of the life of Basil of Caesarea.[24] Two of these leaves are so defect that they could not be edited. There exists one leaf (Lbs fragm 74) from a thirteenth century Latin version of *Vita Basilii*, written by an Icelandic scribe in the 13th century, but since the Latin and Icelandic versions do not contain the same parts of the vita it

---

18 Printed in Morgenstern, *Arnamagnæanische Fragmente*, pp. 14–24 and in HMS II, pp. 281–286.
19 Stefán Karlsson, "Inventio Crucis, cap 1, og Veraldar saga." In *Opuscula Septentrionalia: Festskrift til Ole Widding 10.10.1977* (Copenhagen, 1977), pp. 127–130.
20 Printed in Morgenstern, *Arnamagnæanische Fragmente*, pp. 14–24. Sheet 2v also printed in HMS II, pp. 280–281; the fragment from *Erasmus saga* printed in HMS I, pp. 363–368.
21 Cormack, *Saints in Iceland*, p. 38. For the dating of AM 249 l fol. See Kålund, *Katalog* I, p. 230.
22 The fragment is printed in *Leifar*, pp. 175–179.
23 Printed in Konráð Gíslason, *Um frum-parta*, pp. c-ciii.
24 Printed in Morgenstern, *Arnamagnæanische Fragmente*, pp. 14–24. Immediately following AM 655 VI 4to in Morgenstern's edition is AM 238 II fol., which also contains fragments of the the *vita* of Basil. A facsimile and an edition of leave 2r of AM 655 VI 4to is also found in Hreinn Benediktsson's *Early Icelandic Script*, plate 21 and p. xvi.

is impossible to establish whether that particular manuscript served as a source for the Icelandic translation.[25] Basil was, in all probability, not venerated as a patron saint at any Icelandic church or monastery despite vague hints in later church registers.[26]

AM 655 XIX 4to

These two leaves, dated to the first half of the 13th century, contain a fragment of one of the best-known Marian miracles, the legend of Theophilus.[27]

AM 645 4to

AM 645 4to is the oldest preserved Icelandic collection of saints' lives, dating to the first half of the thirteenth century. The manuscript consists in fact of two separate codices: Codex I being older and numbering 42 sheets and Codex II, dated a little later counting 24 sheets. Codex I contains the sagas of Clement, James the Greater, Matthew, in part the sagas of Bartholomew, Peter, and Andrew and a large part of a text recounting the miracles of Bishop Þorlákr. In Codex II one can find parts of Andrew's saga, complete versions of the sagas of Paul and Martin of Tours and a text called *Niðrstigningar saga* (an Icelandic version of *Descensus Christi ad Inferos*). The 19th century philologist Ludvig Larsson suggested a date between 1225–1250 but in her introduction to the facsimile edition of the manuscript, Anne Holtsmark argued for an earlier dating. Concerning the texts in both codices, Anne Holtsmark states that "all the texts are copies, many of them at second or third hand."[28] On grounds of her palaeographical analysis, she suggests that the older codex was written by a single scribe while the younger is believed to exhibit at least three hands. She furthermore argues, as suggested by Ludvig Larsson, that the manuscript shows affinities with the *Icelandic Homily Book*, both of which belong to "a group of manuscript which we may call the school of The First Grammatical Treatise," that is to say that they know and to an extent follow, albeit not very stringently, the rules set forth by the first grammarian.[29] On grounds of the content of the miracle book of Þorlákr, contained in Codex I, it has been suggested that the manuscript was composed at the episcopal seat of Skálholt. The text seems to be modelled after the original version collected by Þorlákr's successor, Páll Jónsson, to support the formal institution of a mass for Þorlákr which, according to annals, took place in 1199. All of the miracles described in this collection

---

25 The Latin version shows strong resemblance to a so-called "17-chapter version" of Euphemius' ninth-century translation of a Greek version attributed to Pseudo-Amphilochios. Peter Jorgensen, "The *Life of St. Basil* in Iceland," *Gripla* 26 (2015), 58.
26 Cormack, *Saints in Iceland*, p. 76.
27 The fragment is printed in the introduction in Unger, *Mariu saga*, pp. XXXI–XXXII.
28 Anne Holtsmark, "Introduction," in *A Book of Miracles: MS No. 645 4to of the Arna-Magnæan Collection in the University Library of Copenhagen* (Copenhagen, 1938), p. 11.
29 Holtsmark, "Introduction," p. 10.

take place in Iceland's southern part and most of them in the immediate vicinity of Skálholt. Hreinn Benediktsson dated codex I to around 1220 and codex II to the second quarter of the 13th century.

Stock. Perg. 15 4to. The Icelandic Homily Book

The manuscript Stock. Perg. 15 4to, is doubtless the most important source for how the Christian message was mediated in Iceland during Christianity's early stages and has been the subject of a thorough discussion earlier in this study.[30] The manuscript is usually dated to around 1200. Amounting to a total number of 102 sheets which contain 62 texts or fragments of texts, it remains by far the largest manuscript containing religious material dating to the formative years of the Church in Iceland. The largest part of the text it contains are sermons.

AM 677 4to,

AM 677 4to counts 41 leaves and has been dated to the early 13th century.[31] The content of the manuscript is predominated by Pope Gregory the Great. 17 leaves contain 10 of Gregory's 40 *Homilliae in Evangelia*, while the other 12 contain parts of Gregory's *Dialogi*. The remaining seven leaves contain primarily *Prosper's epigrams* and a small fragment of *De XII abusivis saeculi*. Given Gregory's enormous popularity in the middle ages, his early literary presence in Iceland is of no surprise.[32]

---

30   See discussion in section 2.2.2.3 above.
31   In his *Katalog*, Kålund dated the manuscript to c. 1200 and in both Hreinn Benediktsson, *Early Icelandic Script*, 11 and in the manuscript register to the *Ordbog over det norrøne prosasprog* (Copenhagen, 1989), p. 46 it is dated to the first quarter of the 13th century. For a recent critical edition of the manuscript see AM 677 4°. *Four Early Translations of Theological Texts: Gregory the Great's Gospel Homilies, Gregory the Great's Dialogues, Prosper's Epigrams, De XII Abusivis Saeculi*, Rit 100, ed. Andrea de Leeuw van Weenen (Reykjavík, 2018).
32   There is evidence that several of Gregory's works existed in Iceland during the middle ages. In addition to the two works already mentioned, the *Homiliae in Evangelia* and the *Dialogi*, inventories of monasteries show the possession of *Regula pastoralis*, *Homiliae in Hiezechihelem*, *Moralia in Job*, and *Expositio in Canticis canticorum*. It is not, however, known how many, if any, of these were translated into Old Icelandic nor is it known when the monasteries came into the possession of them. Of these four writings, the only preserved fragments are written in Latin. Régis Boyer, "The Influence of Pope Gregory's *Dialogues* on Old Icelandic Literature," in *Proceedings of the First International Saga Conference*, eds. Peter Foote, Hermann Pálsson, and Desmond Slay (London, 1973), p. 2; Kirsten Wolf, "Gregory's Influence on Old Norse-Icelandic Religious Literature," in *Rome and the North: The Early Reception of Gregory the Great in Germanic Europe*, Mediaevalia Groningiana New Series 4, eds. Rolf H. Bremmer Jr., Kees Dekker and David F. Johnson (Paris, 2001), pp. 266–269.

AM 652/630 4to

AM 652 4to has been variously dated by scholars from the middle to the end of the 13th century.³³ The manuscript is defect but is preserved in full in the 17th century copy AM 630 4to.³⁴ In what follows it will be referred to as AM 652/630 4to. The defect AM 652 4to contains fragments of the lives of the apostle John, James the Greater, Bartholomew, Andrew, and Matthew but AM 630 4to contains these same texts in addition to the lives of the apostles Peter, Philip and James the Less, Simon and Jude, Thomas, and Matthias. Not much is known about the origin of AM 652 4to. The 17th century copy was made by Steindór Ormsson (1626–1700) who, according to a note by Árni Magnússon attached to the manuscript, copied it after a book owned by Sigmundur Guðmundsson from Seljaland in Skutulsfjörður in Iceland's northwestern part. The name Sigmundur Guðmundsson, as well as the names of his children Halldór and Sigríður, appear on the margins of AM 652 4to which indicates that AM 630 4to was copied directly after that particular book. Nothing else is known about Sigmundur or his children other than the affiliation with Seljaland in Skutulsfjörður.

AM 696 XXIV 4to

Two leaves, dated to the early 13th century, with a fragmentary exegetical treatise on two of the Penitential Psalms, number 32 and 38.³⁵

AM 655 XXI 4to

AM 655 XXI 4to, dated to the first half of the 13th century, has been described by Hans Bekker-Nielsen as a homiletic handbook.³⁶ The manuscript consists of six sheets containing lections to be read at the feasts of Gregory the Great, Cuthbert, Benedict as well as the ending of a homily centering on Jesus's saying on a kingdom divided against itself (Mark 3:24, Matt. 12:22–28).

AM 655 XVII 4to

Three leaves, dating to the mid 13th century, from the *Saga of Paul* (II), a *vita* of the apostle Paul, based on the *Historia Actuum Apostolorum*, attributed to Peter of Poitiers,

---

33 Both Kristian Kålund and Hreinn Benediktsson dated it to the second half of the 13th century. Unger to the end of the 13th century but most recently Ólafur Halldórsson dates it to not many decades older than 1270. On such grounds, Roughton is comfortable with dating it to "the middle of the thirteenth century." Roughton 1, 3. See also his article, "Stylistics and Sources of the Postola sögur in AM 645 4to and AM 652 4to", *Gripla* XVI (2005), 7.

34 A modern edition of the complete manuscript is only available in Unger's *Postola sogur*.

35 Unpublished.

36 Published in *Leifar*, pp. 167–172.

a commentary on Paul's epistles and Pauline hagiography.[37] An entire version of the text is preserved in *Codex Scardensis*.[38]

AM 655 XXIII 4to

A single leaf, dating to the second quarter of the 13th century, from what might have been, like Kålund originally suggested, a homily on the fourth penitential psalm, Psalm 50.[39] As James W. Marchand has argued, the manuscript might more aptly be described as a commentary speculating further about the existence of an extensive commentary on the Psalter in Icelandic at the time.[40] On the basis of notes accompanying the manuscript, it is likely that it was written in Önundarfjörður in Northwestern Iceland. The verso side of the leave, which remains unpublished, contains a prayer in Latin.

AM 655 I 4to

A single leaf containing a fragment of a homily on the efficacy of baptism, dated to the second quarter of the 13th century.[41] The leaf had been used as a cover for a book, owned by Þórður Jónsson (1609–1670), a pastor in Hítardalur in Mýrar, and later by Guðmundur Þorleifsson (1658–1720) from whom Árni Magnússon acquired the fragment.

AM 655 XV 4to

One leaf containing a part of the *Saga of Benedict*. Originally dated to the thirteenth century but Hreinn Benediktsson suggested a more specific date of the latter half of the 13th century.[42]

AM 655 XXVII

AM 655 XXVII 4to was written by an Icelander in the latter half of the 13th century.[43] Consisting of 14 sheets (12 intact and 2 defect), the manuscript is by far the largest

---

37 Wolf, *Legends of the Saints*, 304. Kålund dated the fragment to the 13th century but Birgit Christensen later dated to the middle of the thirteenth century. For a more detailed discussion of the sources of this version see Collings, *Codex Scardensis*, pp. 31–52.
38 Edition of AM 655 4to XVII in *Post*, pp. 266-263, 271–274, and 276–278.
39 Hreinn Benediktsson, *Early Icelandic Script*, p. xxv. The fragment of the text was published by Konráð Gíslason in *Um frum-parta*, pp. lxxxii-lxxxii and again with an English translation by James W. Marchand, "An Old Norse Fragment of a Psalm Commentary," *Maal og minne* (1976), 25–26.
40 Marchand, "An Old Norse Fragment," pp. 25–28.
41 Edited in Konráð Gíslason, *Um frum-parta*, lxvii-lxix. Regarding the dating of the manuscript, see Gustav Lindblad, *Det isländska accenttecknet: En historisk-ortografisk studie* (Lund, 1952), p. 92.
42 Hreinn Benediktsson, *Early Icelandic Script*, p. xliv.
43 The manuscript has not been published in its entirety. An edition of the complete manuscript with a detailed introduction can be found in Hallgrímur Ámundason's BA thesis.

of the manuscript compound AM 655 4to. It contains 11 texts or fragments of texts containing theological and homiletic material: An enumeration of Christian virtues, Mariological texts which have been shown to be related to Kygri-Björn Hjaltason's *Maríu saga*, a translation of the *Gospel of Nicodemus* (the story of Joseph of Arimathea in prison), homily on Peter and Paul, the ending of a homily on All Saints Day, homily on the importance of crying, and a homily on the annunciation. As summarized by Stephen Pelle, most of the texts in the manuscripts "are either homilies or could easily be adapted for preaching."[44]

AM 655 XXVIII a 4to

The fragment contains parts of the *vitae* of Ambrose and Clement.[45] Dated to the first half of the thirteenth century by Unger and to the second half by Hreinn Benediktsson and later by Hofmann.[46] The version of the saga of Ambrose is a translation of BHL 377.[47] The translation of the saga of Clement is a copy of the same translation of the version of the saga that is preserved in its entirety in AM 645 4to.[48]

AM 655 X 4to

Two badly damaged leaves, written in the third quarter of the 13th century, containing the end of the vita of Maurice and the beginning of the *vita* of Placidus (Eustace).[49]

Hallgrímur Ámundason, "AM 655 XXVII 4to: Útgáfa, stafagerð, stafsetning" (B.A. thesis, University of Iceland, 1994). More recently, parts of the manuscript have been studied and published, see Pelle, "Twelfth-Century Sources," pp. 45–75 and Dario Bullitta, "Story of Joseph," pp. 47–74. On the dating and provenance of the manuscript, see Hallgrímur Ámundason, "AM 655 XXVII 4to," p. 26. Hreinn Benediktsson also included the manuscript in his *Early Icelandic Script* while Ole Widding had earlier assessed it of Norwegian origin. Ole Widding, "Håndskriftanalyser," *Bibliotheca Arnamagnæana* 1; *Opuscula* II (1961), 69. Ámundason's findings have not been disputed by recent treatments of the manuscript, cf. Pelle, "Twelfth-Century Sources," p. 51 and Bullitta, "Story of Joseph," p. 51.

44 Pelle, "Twelfth-Century Sources," p. 52.
45 The fragment of the saga of Ambrose is printed in *HMS* I, pp. 52–54 and the fragment of Clement is printed in Dietrich Hofmann, *Die Legende von Sankt Clemens in den skandinavischen Länder im Mittelalter* (Frankfurt a. M., 1997), pp. 277–282.
46 *HMS* I, p. IX; Hreinn Benediktsson, *Early Icelandic Script*, pp. xlviii-xlix; Hofmann, *Legende von Sankt Clemens*, p. 112.
47 Wolf, *Legends of the Saints*, p. 24.
48 Hofmann, *Legende von Sankt Clemens*, p. 112.
49 For dating see John Tucker, "Scribal Hands in AM 655 4to X," *Opuscula* 6 (1979), 124–125. The manuscript has undergone three palaeographic studies, with Ole Widding and Hreinn Benediktsson coming to the same conclusion of the manuscript having been written by two scribes. Widding, "Håndskriftanalyser," p. 84–85; Hreinn Benediktsson, "Tvö handritsbrot," *Íslenzk tunga* 5 (1964), 142–144. The entire fragment is printed in *HMS* I, pp. 656–658 and *HMS* II, pp. 204–207.

The manuscript is in all probability a copy but not after the version preserved in AM 655 IX 4to.[50] While the cult of Placidus has been studied relatively thoroughly, less can be found about Maurice, the martyr leader of the Theban legion.[51]

AM 655 XIV 4to

The fragment consists of two leaves, both dating to the third quarter of the 13th century.[52] The first leaf contains the *vita* of the apostle John and the second a part from the legend of how the relics of Stephen protomartyr were discovered, the *Inventio S. Stephani*. The text of John's *vita* is an abridged version of the text which is preserved in AM 652/630 4to.[53] The text of Stephen's *vita* is a sermonic text, related to the version of the sermon on Stephen found in the *Icelandic Homily Book* as well as AM 655 XXII 4to and might stem from copies of the same original translation.[54] The manuscript bears the mark of having been written in a scribal context under Norwegian influence, and might have been written by the same scribe as AM 655 XII-XIII 4to and AM 310 4to.[55]

AM 655 XXII 4to

Two leaves (late 13th century), like AM 655 XIV 4to, from the *Inventio* of Stephen protomartyr, somewhat fuller than the version in AM 655 XIV 4to but, as noted, ultimately derived from the same translation.[56]

AM 655 XVI 4to

Four leaves dating to the late 13th century containing parts of the sagas of apostles Peter and Paul. Text also found in AM 645 4to.

---

50 Tucker, "Introduction," p. xxx.
51 First and foremost in the introduction to *Plácidus saga*. For an introduction to the martyr Maurice, see Bengt Ingmar Kilström, "Martyrer, 10.000" in *KLNM* XI, cols. 477–478.
52 For dating, see Ole Widding, "Et fragment af Stephanus saga (AM 655, 4° XIV B), tekst og kommentar," *Acta Philologica Scandinavica* 21 (1952), 163–164. Widding's article contains the only available edition of the manuscript to date.
53 Simonetta Battista, "Old Norse Hagiography and the Question of the Latin Sources," in *Scandinavia and Christian Europe in the Middle Ages: Papers of the 12th International Saga Conference Bonn/Germany, 28th July-2nd August 2003*, eds. Rudolf Simek and Judith Meurer (Bonn, 2003), p. 28. This text of the *vita* of John remains unpublished.
54 Widding, "Et fragment af Stephanus saga," p. 171.
55 Stefán Karlsson, "Om norvagismer i islandske håndskrifter," in *Stafkrókar*, ed. Guðvarður Már Gunnlaugsson (Reykjavík, 1992), p. 181.
56 For dating, Kålund, *Katalog* II, p. 64; Wolf, *Legends of the Saints*, p. 338. The fragment remains unedited but corresponds to the following parts of *HMS* II, pp. 302 (line 24) 303 (line 2); 303 (line 11) 304 (line 2); 305 (line 33) – 306 (line 26); 307 (lines 8–34). Marianne E. Kalinke, "Stefanus saga in Reykjahólabók," *Gripla* IX (1995), 133.

AM 655 XXXIII 4to

The manuscript fragment was dated to the second half of the 13th century by Hreinn Benediktsson. It consists of two sheets and contains short segments from a text on the Forty Armenian Martyrs (Latin title: *Passio quadraginta militum*; Icelelandic title: *XL riddara saga*) and the saga of Mary of Egypt.[57] Hreinn Benediktsson has suggested that the fragment originally belonged to the same codex as AM 655 X 4to.[58]

AM 655 XVIII 4to

A single leaf from a homily on All Saints which is found complete in the *Icelandic Homily Book*. It has been dated to the second half of the 13th century. Based on paleographic similarities, both Konráð Gíslason and later Hreinn Benediktsson have speculated whether it might originally have belonged to the same manuscript as AM 655 XXVIII.[59]

AM 655 XII-XIII 4to

Originally counted as two fragments, the fragment XII-XIII counts six leaves with fragments from five different *vitae* of apostles: Peter, James the Greater, Bartholomew, Matthew, and a joint account of apostles Simon and Jude.[60] The saga of Peter is an abbreviated version of the version found in AM 652/630 4to.[61] The saga of James is an independent translation of the same source as the one found in AM 645 4to and AM 652/630 4to.[62] The saga of Matthew is the same as the one found in AM 655 IX 4to, AM 645 4to, AM 652/630 4to. The sagas of Bartholomew and Simon and Jude are independent translations.[63] The fragment has been dated to the third quarter of the 13th century.[64] It has been the subject of palaeographic and phonetic debate concerning Norwegian influence on the Icelandic language but it has been argued that the fragment was written by an Icelandic scribe in a scribal context under strong Norwegian influence. According to notes accompanying the manuscript, it was originally a part

---

57   The text on the Forty Armenian Martyrs was published by Unger in *HMS* 2, pp. 219–221; the part of the *Life of Mary of Egypt* has not been published in full but only as variations to a younger version of the text, also in Unger, *HMS* 1, pp. 495, 504–505, and 506–507.

58   Hreinn Benediktsson, "Tvö handritsbrot," pp. 147–148.

59   The manuscript has been edited by Hallgrímur Ámundason in his BA-thesis. Hallgrímur Ámundason, "AM 655 XXVII 4to," pp. 1–3. Also in Konráð Gíslason, *Um frum-parta*, pp. lxxviii-lxxxi. The homily in its entirety can be found in *ÍH*, pp. 56–64. A similar but abbreviated version is also preserved in the *Norwegian Homily Book*. For dating, Kålund, *Katalog* II, p. 63.

60   The text of the manuscript is printed in *Post*, pp. 211–216 (Peter), 529–533 (James), 762–766 (Bartholomew), 791–797 (Simon and Jude), and 834–841 (Matthew).

61   Wolf, *Legends of the Saints*, p. 310.

62   Ibid., p. 156.

63   Wolf, *Legends of the Saints*, pp. 54 and 335.

64   Widding, "Et fragment af Stephanus saga," 164; Stefán Karlsson, "Om norvagismer," p. 182.

of a codex named Höskuldsstaðabók which belonged to the church at Höskuldsstaðir in Húnavatnssýsla, not far from the Benedictine monastery at Þingeyrar which Stefán Karlsson suggested as the manuscript's writing place.[65] There were Norwegian bishops both in Skálholt and Hólar from 1238 into the 1260s.

AM 240 fol. XI; NRA 78

The earliest fragments of a *vita* of the virgin Mary, both dating to the second half of the 13th century. On the basis on a short clause at the end of the mid-14th century *Guðmundar saga* written by the monk Arngrímr Brandsson, *Maríu saga* was composed by a cleric named Kygri-Björn Hjaltason. The relatively scarce information available on Kygri-Björn depict him as a distinguished cleric who had travelled much abroad and was probably present at the Lateran Council of 1215.[66] The Icelandic version of the *vita* has been described as unique on grounds of its wide range of source material, both hagiographic as well as exegetical patristic works, and how it weaves its theological commentary into the narrative.[67] The identified sources for the work are the canonical gospels of Matthew and Luke, the *Gospel of Pseudo-Matthew*, the *Trinubium Annae*, books 16 and 17 of Josephus' *Antiquitates*, patristic works by Augustine, Jerome, John Chrysostom, and Gregory the Great.[68]

AM 238 XXVIII fol.

Consisting only of a single leaf, this manuscript fragment has been dated to the last quarter of the 13th century.[69] It has also been argued that it might have been written by a Norwegian located in Iceland, perhaps a cleric accompanying one of the Norwegian bishops sitting in Skálholt and Hólar around the mid-13th century.[70] It contains a vivid description of the tortures of hell and the joys of heaven which originally was part of a writing on the martyr Sebastian, *Acta Sebastiani*. The text is a part of speech given by the martyr Sebastian found in the *Acta Sebastiani*, a translation of which is found in

---

65 Karlsson's reasoning was partly based on the writing location but also on the palaeographic and orthographic similarities to the manuscript AM 279 a 4to which was definitely written at Þingeyrar as well on his findings that AM 655 XII–XIII 4to was written by the same Icelandic scribe as the manuscripts AM 655 XIV 4to and AM 310 4to. AM 310 4to contains a copy of the Icelandic version of *Ólafs saga* by Oddr Snorrason, monk at Þingeyrar. Stefán Karlsson, "Om norvagismer," p. 182.

66 Gabrielle Turville-Petre, *Nine Norse Studies* (London, 1972), p. 106.

67 Wilhelm Heizmann, "Maríu saga," in *Medieval Scandinavia: An Encyclopedia*, p. 408.

68 Ibid.

69 Stefán Karlsson, "Om himmel og helvede på gammelnorsk: AM 238 XXVIII fol," in *Festskrift til Ludvig Holm-Olsen på hans 70-årsdag den 9. Juni 1984* (Øvre Ervik, 1984), p. 193.

70 Ibid., p. 194.

the manuscript compound AM 238. It is, as pointed out by Stefán Karlsson, uncertain if this text was originally part of Sebastian's *vita* or as an independent homily.[71] Karlsson furthermore suggests that the text of AM 238 XXVIII fol. is based on the same source text as a sermon in the *Icelandic Homily Book*.[72]

AM 655 XI 4to

Two leaves from a sermon to be delivered on Ash Wednesday, dated to the late 13th century or early 14th century.[73]

AM 655 XXVIII b 4to

Two damaged leaves, dated to around 1300 by Jón Helgason. These are the oldest Icelandic manuscripts with the Old Norse *Konungs skuggsjá* (Speculum Regale; Fürstenspiegel).[74]

---

71 Ibid., p. 186.
72 *ÍH*, pp. 204–208.
73 See Eva Rode, "Et fragment af en prædiken til askeonsdag: AM 655 XI, 4to" *Opuscula* 7 (1979), 44–61.
74 Edited by Jón Helgason in "Et fragment av Kongespeilet," in *Festskrift til Ludvig Holm-Olsen på hans 70-årsdag den 9. Juni 1984* (Øvre Ervik, 1984), pp. 124–141.

Bibliography

The bibliography does not include works in the list of abbreviations on pp. XI–XII.

Addams, Jane. *Newer Ideals of Peace: The Moral Substitutes for War*. Chester: Quanterness Press, 2005.

Aðalsteinsson, Jón Hnefill. *Under the Cloak: The Acceptance of Christianity in Iceland with Particular Reference to the Religious Attitudes Prevailing at the Time*. Uppsala: Almqvist and Wiksell, 1978.

Althoff, Gerd. *Selig sind, die Verfolgung Ausüben*. Darmstadt: WBG, 2013.

AM 677 4°. *Four Early Translations of Theological Texts: Gregory the Great's Gospel Homilies, Gregory the Great's Dialogues, Prosper's Epigrams, De XII Abusivis Saeculi*. Rit 100. Edited and morphologically analysed by Andrea de Leeuw van Weenen. Reykjavík: Stofnun Árna Magnússonar, 2018.

Angenendt, Arnold. *Geschichte der Religiosität im Mittelalter*. 4th edition. Darmstad: Primus Verlag, 2009 [1997].

Antonsson, Haki. *Damnation and Salvation in Old Norse Literature*, Studies in Old Norse Literature. Woodbridge: D.S. Brewer, 2018.

Antonsson, Haki. "The Construction of Auðunar þáttr vestfirzka: A Case of Typological Thinking in Early Old Norse Prose," *Scandinavian Studies* 90 (2018): 485–508.

Arnórsdóttir, Agnes S. *Konur og vígamenn: Staða kynjanna á Íslandi á 12. og 13. öld*, Sagnfræðirannsóknir. Studia historica 12. Reykjavík: Sagnfræðistofnun; Háskólaútgáfan, 1995.

Arnórsdóttir, Agnes S. *Property and Virginity: The Christianization of Marriage in Medieval Iceland 1200–1600*. Aarhus: Aarhus University Press, 2009.

Arnórsdóttir, Agnes S. "Cultural Memory and Gender in Iceland from Mediveal to Early Modern Times." *Scandinavian Studies* 85 (2013): 378–399.

Arnórsdóttir, Agnes S. "Danske dronninger i de islandske sagaer." In *Dronningemagt i middelalderen: Festskrift til Anders Bøgh*. Edited by Jeppe B. Netterstrøm and Kasper H. Andersen, 53–82. Aarhus: Aarhus Universitetsforlag, 2018.

Assmann, Jan. *Das kulturelle Gedächtnis: Schrift, Erinnerung und politische Identität in frühen Hochkulturen*. 6th edition. Beck'sche Reihe 1307. München: Beck, 2007.

Auerbach, Erich. " 'Figura.' " In *Scenes from the Drama of European Literature*. Foreword by Paolo Valesio. Theory and History of Literature 9. Minneapolis. University of Minnesota Press, 1984.

Ágústsson, Hörður. *Dómsdagur og helgir menn á Hólum: Endurskoðun fyrri hugmynda um fjalirnar frá Bjarnastaðahlíð og Flatatungu*. Staðir og kirkjur II. Reykjavík: Hið íslenska bókmenntafélag, 1989.

Ámundason, Hallgrímur. "AM 655 XXVII 4to: Útgáfa, stafagerð, stafsetning." BA thesis, University of Iceland, 1994.

Bagge, Sverre. *From Viking Stronghold to Christian Kingdom: State Formation in Norway c. 900–1350*. Copenhagen: Museum Tusculanum Press, 2010.

Bakhtin, Mikhail M. "Discourse in the Novel." In *The Dialogic Imagination: Four Essays by M. M. Bakhtin*. Edited by Michael Holquist, translated by Caryl Emerson and Michael Holquist, 259–422. University of Texas Press Slavic Series 1. Austin: University of Texas Press, 1981.

Basset, Camilla. "Hungrvaka: Translation by Camilla Basett." MA thesis, University of Iceland, 2013.

Bataillon, Louis J. "Approaches to the Study of Medieval Sermons." *Leeds Studies in English* 11 (1980): 19–35.

Battista, Simonetta. "Interpretations of the Roman Pantheon in the Old Norse Hagiographic Sagas." In *Old Norse Myths, Literature and Society*. Edited by Margaret Clunies Ross, 175–197. The Viking Collection 14. Odense: University Press of Southern Denmark, 2003.

Battista, Simonetta. "Old Norse Hagiography and the Question of the Latin Sources." In *Scandinavia and Christian Europe in the Middle Ages: Papers of the 12th International Saga Conference Bonn/Germany, 28th July-2nd August 2003*. Edited by Rudolf Simek and Judith Meurer, 26–33. Bonn: Universität Bonn, 2003.

Bäuml, Franz H. "Varieties and Consequences of Medieval Literacy and Illiteracy." *Speculum* 55 (1980): 237–265.

Bell, L. Michael. ""Hel our Queen": An Old Norse Analogue to an old English Female Hell." *Harvard Theological Review* 76/2 (1983): 263–268.

Benediktsson, Hreinn. "Tvö handritsbrot," *Íslenzk tunga* 5 (1964): 139–149.

Benediktsson, Hreinn. *Early Icelandic Script: As Illustrated in Vernacular Texts from the Twelfth and Thirteenth Centuries*. Series in Folio II. Reykjavík: Manuscript Institute of Iceland, 1965.

Benediktsson, Hreinn. *The First Grammatical Treatise: Introduction, Text, Notes, Translation, Vocabulary, Facsimiles*. University of Iceland publications in linguistics. Reykjavík: Institute of Nordic Linguistics, 1972.

Benediktsson, Jakob, ed. *Veraldar saga*. Samfund til udgivelse af gammel nordisk litterature 61. Copenhagen: B. Lunos bogtr., 1944.

Berend, Nora. "The Concept of Christendom: A Rhetoric of Integration or Disintegration?" In *Hybride Kulturen in mittelalterlichen Europa/ Hybrid Cultures in Medieval Europe*. Edited by Michael Borgolte, 51–62. Europa im Mittelalter 16. Berlin: Akademie Verlag, 2010.

Berg, Kirsten M. "Homilieboka – for hvem og til hva?" In *Vår eldste bok: Skrift, miljø og biletbruk i den norske homilieboka*. Edited by Odd Einar Haugen and Åslaug Ommundsen, 131–150. Bibliotheca Nordica 3. Oslo: Novus forlag, 2010.

Bernharðsson, Haraldur. "Kirkja, klaustur og norskublandið ritmálsviðmið." In *Íslensk klausturmenning á miðöldum*. Edited by Haraldur Bernharðsson, 149–172. Reykjavík: Miðaldastofa Háskóla Íslands, 2016.

Beutel, Albrecht. "Vom Nutzen und Nachteil der Kirchengeschichte: Begriff und Funktion einer theologischen Kerndisziplin." In *Protestantische Konkretionen: Studien zur Kirchengeschichte*. 1–27. Tübingen: Mohr Siebeck, 1998.

Birkeli, Fridtjov. *Norske steinkors i tidlig middelalder: Et bidrag til belysning av overgangen fra norrøn religion til kristendom*. Oslo: Universitetsforlaget, 1973.

Bhabha, Homi K. *The Location of Culture*. London: Routledge, 1994.

Borgolte, Michael. *Europa endeckt seine Vielfalt 1050–1250*. Handbuch der Geschichte Europas 3. Verlag Eugen Ulmer: Stuttgart, 2002.

Bourdieu, Pierre. "Genesis and Structure of the Religious Field." *Comparative Social Research* 13 (1991): 1–44.

Boyer, Régis. "The Influence of Pope Gregory's *Dialogues* on Old Icelandic Literature." In *Proceedings of the First International Saga Conference*. Edited by Peter Foote, Hermann Pálsson, and Desmond Slay, 1–27. London: The Viking Society for Northern Research, University College London, 1973.

Boyer, Régis. *La vie religieuse en Islande (1116–1264) d'après la Sturlunga Saga et les Sagas des Évêques*. Paris: Fondation Singer-Polignac, 1979.

Boyer, Régis. "Were the Icelanders Good Christians according to Samtidarsogur?" In *Samtíðarsögur: The Contemporary Sagas* I. The Ninth International Saga Conference, 111–122. Akureyri: [s.n], 1994.

Bragason, Úlfar. *Ætt og saga: Um frásagnarfræði Sturlungu eða Íslendingasögu hinnar miklu* (Reykjavík: Háskólaútgáfan, 2010.

Bremen, Adam of. *Magistri Adam Bremensis Gesta Hammaburgensis Ecclesiae Pontificum*. 3rd ed. Hannover and Leipzig: Impensis Bibliopolii Hahniani, 1917.

Brink, Stefan. "Early Ecclesiastical Organization of Scandinavia, Especially Sweden." In *Medieval Christianity in the North*. Edited by Kirsi Salonen, Kurt Villads Jensen and Torstein Jørgensen, 23–39. Acta Scandinavica 1. Brepols: Turnhout, 2013.

Buc, Philippe. *Holy War, Martyrdom, and Terror: Christianity, Violence, and the West, ca. 70-C.E. to the Iraq War*. Philadelphia: University of Pennsylvania Press, 2015.

Bullitta, Dario. "The Story of Joseph of Arimathea in AM 655 XXVII 4to." *Arkiv för nordisk filologi* 131 (2016): 47–74.

Burke, Peter. *What is Cultural History?* Cambridge: Polity, 2008.

Bynum, Caroline Walker. *Holy Feast and Holy Fast: The Religious Significance of Food to Medieval Women*. New Historicism. Berkeley: University of California Press, 1987.

Bynum, Caroline Walker. *The Resurrection of the Body in Western Christianity, 200–1336*. New York: Columbia University Press, 1995.

Byock, Jesse L. "History and the Sagas: The Effect of Nationalism." In *From Sagas to Society: Comparative Approaches to Early Iceland*. Edited by Gísli Pálsson, 43–59. Enfield Lock, Middlesex: Hisarlik Press, 1992.

Böðvarsson, Jón. "Munur eldri og yngri gerðar Þorláks sögu." *Saga* 6 (1968): 81–94.

Canning, Joseph. *History of Medieval Political Thought 300–1450*. London and New York: Routledge, 2005 [1996].

Carruthers, Mary. *The Craft of Thought: Meditation, Rhetoric, and the Making of Images.* Cambridge: Cambridge University Press, 1998.
Carter, Warren. *Matthew and Empire: Initial Explorations.* Harrisburg: Trinity Press, 2001.
Chakrabarty, Dipesh. *Provincializing Europe: Postcolonial Thought and Historical Difference.* Princeton: Princeton University Press, 2000.
Chazelle, Celia M. "Pictures, Books, and the Illiterate: Pope Gregory I's Letters to Serenus of Marseilles." *Word & Image* 6 (1990): 138–153.
Clanchy, Michael T. *From Memory to Written Record: England 1066–1307.* 2nd edition. Oxford: Blackwell, 1993.
Clark, Willene B. *A Medieval Book of Beasts: The Second-Family Bestiary. Commentary, Art, Text and Translation.* Woodbridge: Boydell Press, 2006.
Clayton, Mary. "Preaching and Teaching." In *The Cambridge Companion to Old English Literature.* Edited by Malcolm Godden and Michael Lapidge, 159–179. Cambridge: Cambridge University Press, 2013.
Cohen, Jeremy. *Living Letters of the Law: Ideas of the Jew in Medieval Christianity.* Berkeley: University of California Press, 1999.
Colás, Alejandro. *Empire.* Key Concepts. Cambridge: Polity, 2007.
Cole, Andrew. "What Hegel's Master/Slave Dialectic Really Means." *Journal of Medieval and Early Modern Studies* 34/3 (2004): 577–610.
Cole, Richard. "*Kyn / Fólk / Þjóð / Ætt*: Proto-Racial Thinking and its Application to Jews in Old Norse Literature." In *Fear and Loathing in the North: Jews and Muslims in Medieval Scandinavia and the Baltic Region.* Edited by Cordelia Heß and Jonathan Adams, 239–268. Berlin: Walter de Gruyter, 2015.
Cole, Richard. "Homotopia, or, Reading Sagas on an Industrial Estate." *Exemplaria* 30/2 (2018): 105–128.
Collings, Lucy Grace. "The Codex Scardensis: Studies in Icelandic Hagiography." Doctoral thesis, Cornell University, 1969.
Congar, Yves M.-J. "Der Platz des Papsttums in der Kirchenfrömmigkeit der Reformer des 11. Jahrhunderts." In *Sentire Ecclesiam: Das Bewusstsein von der Kirche als gestaltende Kraft der Frömmigkeit.* Edited by Jean Daniélou and Herbert Vorgrimer, 196–217. Freiburg i. B.: Herder, 1963.
Conti, Aidan. "Gammelt og nytt i Homiliebokens Prekenunivers." In *Vår eldste bok: Skrift, miljø og bilethruk i den norske homilieboka.* Edited by Odd Einar Haugen and Åslaug Ommundsen, 165–186. Bibliotheca Nordica 3. Oslo: Novus Forlag, 2010.
Cormack, Margaret. *The Saints in Iceland: Their Veneration from the Conversion to 1400.* Subsidia hagiographica 78. Brussels: Société des Bollandistes, 1994.
Cormack, Margaret. "Irish and Armenian ecclesiastics." In *West over Sea: Studies in Scandinavian Sea-Borne Expansion and Settlement before 1300.* Edited by Barbara Crawford et al., 227–234. Northern World 31. Leiden: Brill, 2006.
Cormack, Margaret. *Saints and their Cults in the Atlantic World.* Columbia: University of South Carolina Press, 2007.

Cormack, Margaret. *Muslims and Others in Sacred Space*. Oxford: Oxford University Press, 2012.

Crossley, Paul. "Ductus and memoria: Chartres Cathedral and the Workings of Rhetoric." In *Rhetoric Beyond Words: Delight and Persuasion in the Arts of the Middle Ages*. Edited by Mary Carruthers, 214–249. Cambridge: Cambridge University Press, 2010.

Cucina, Carla. "The Rainbow Allegory in the Old Icelandic Physiologus Manuscript." *Gripla* 22 (2011): 63–118.

Cucina, Carla. "*En kjǫlrinn jarteinir trú rétta*. Incidenza di tropi classici e cristiani sulle tradizioni anglosassone e scandinava." *Rivista Italiana di Linguistica e di Dialettologia* XII (2010): 25–93.

de Leeuw van Weenen, Andrea. "Part 1: Introduction." In *The Icelandic Homily Book: Perg 15 4to in the Royal Library, Stockholm*. Icelandic Manuscripts: Series in Quarto 3. 5–20. Reykjavík: Stofnun Árna Magnússonar, 1993.

Dressler, Markus. "*The Social Construction of Reality* (1966) Revisited: Epistemology and Theorizing in the Study of Religion." *Method and Theory in the Study of Religion* (2018): 1–32.

Driscoll, Matthew. "The Words on the Page: Thoughts on Philology Old and New." In *Creating the Medieval Saga: Versions, Variability, and Editorial Interpretations of Old Norse Saga Literature*. Edited by Judy Quinn and Emily Lethbridge, 87–104. The Viking Collection 18. Odense: University Press of Southern Denmark, 2010.

Duggan, Charles. *Twelfth-Century Decretal Collections and Their Importance in English History*. University of London Historical Studies 12. London: The Athlone Press, 1963.

Duggan, Lawrence G. "Was Art Really the "Book of the Illiterate"?" In *Reading Images and Texts: Medieval Images and Texts as Forms of Communication*. Edited by Mariëlle Hageman and Marco Mostert, 63–108. Utrecht Studies in Medieval Literacy 8. Turnhout: Brepols, 2005.

Duindam, Jeroen. "Pre-modern Power Elites: Princes, Courts, Intermediaries." In *The Palgrave Handbook of Political Elites*. Edited by Heinrich Nest and John Higley, 161–179. London: Palgrave Macmillan, 2018.

Ebel, Uwe. "Ex oriente lux: Zum Problem theologischer Sinngebung in der Heiðarvíga saga." In *International Scandinavian and Medieval Studies in Memory of Gerd Wolfgang Weber*. Edited by Michael Dallapiazza et al. Trieste: Edizioni Parnaso, 2000.

Eco, Umberto. "Inventing the Enemy." In *Inventing the Enemy and Other Occasional Writings*. Translated by Richard Dixon. Boston and New York: Houghton Mifflin Harcourt, 2012.

Eco, Umberto. "Auf dem Wege zu einem Neuen Mittelalter." In *Über Gott und die Welt: Essays und Glossen*. Translated by Burkhart Kroeber, 8–32. München: DTV, 2013.

Egilsdóttir, Ásdís. "Eru biskupasögur til?" *Skáldskaparmál* 2 (1992): 207–220.

Egilsdóttir, Ásdís. "Klausturreglur og bókmenntir." In Gunnar F. Guðmundsson, *Íslenskt samfélag og Rómakirkja*. 241–245. Vol. II of *Kristni á Íslandi*. Reykjavík: Alþingi, 2000.

Egilsdóttir, Ásdís. *Fræðimæmi: Greinar gefnar út í tilefni 70 ára afmælis Ásdísar Egilsdóttur*. Reykjavík: Hið íslenska bókmenntafélag, 2016.

Egilsdóttir, Ásdís. "Að kunna vort mál að ráða." In *Fræðinæmi: Greinar gefnar út í tilefni 70 ára afmælis Ásdísar Egilsdóttur*. 249–261. Reykjavík: Hið íslenska bókmenntafélag, 2016.

Egilsdóttir, Ásdís. "From Orality to Literacy: Remembering the Past and the Present in *Jóns saga helga*." In *Fræðinæmi: Greinar gefnar út í tilefni 70 ára afmælis Ásdísar Egilsdóttur*. 235–48. Reykjavík: Hið íslenska bókmenntafélag, 2016.

Egilsdóttir, Ásdís. "The Beginnings of Local Hagiography in Iceland: The Lives of Bishops Þorlákr and Jón." In *Fræðinæmi: Greinar gefnar út í tilefni 70 ára afmælis Ásdísar Egilsdóttur*. 31–43. Reykjavík: Hið íslenska bókmenntafélag, 2016.

Einarsdóttir, Ólafía. *Studier i kronologisk metode i tidlig islandsk historieskrivning*. Bibliotheca historica Lundensis 13. Stockholm: Natur och kultur, 1964.

Eliade, Mircea. *Cosmos and History: The Myth of the Eternal Return*. Translated by Williard R. Trask. New York: Harper and Brothers, 1959.

Epp, Eldon Jay. *Junia: The First Woman Apostle*. Minneapolis: Fortress, 2005.

Eyjólfsson, Sigurjón Árni. "Kristni á Íslandi: umfjöllun um tímamótaverk." *Kirkjuritið* 68/2 (2001): 38–48.

Fahn, Susanne Miriam and Gottskálk Jensson. "The Forgotten Poem: A Latin Panegyric for Saint Þorlákr in AM 382 4to." *Gripla* 21 (2010): 19–60.

Fairclough, Norman. *Language and Power*, 3rd ed. Abingdon: Routledge, 2015.

Fanon, Frantz. *Black Skin, White Masks*. London: Pluto Books, 1986 [1952].

Finlay, Alison. "Interpretation or Over-Interpretation? The dating of two *Íslendingasögur*." *Gripla* XIV (2003): 61–91.

Fitzgerald, Tim. "Bruce Lincoln's "Theses on Method": Antitheses." *Method and Theory in the Study of Religion* 18 (2006): 392–423.

Flohr, Anne Katrin. *Feindbilder in der internationalen Politik: Ihre Entstehung und ihre Funktion*. Bonner Beiträge zur Politikwissenschaft 2. Münster: LIT, 1991.

Franke, Otto. *Geschichte des chinesischen Reiches: Eine Darstellung seiner Entstehung, seines Wesens und seiner Entwicklung bis zur neuesten Zeit*. 5 vols. Berlin: De Gruyter, 1939–1952.

Froehlich, Karlfried. "Saint Peter, Papal Primacy, and the Exegetical Tradition, 1150–1300." In *The Religious Roles of the Papacy: Ideals and Realities, 1150–1300*. Edited by Christopher Ryan, 3–43. Papers in Mediaeval Studies 8. Toronto: Pontifical Institute of Mediaeval Studies, 1989.

Foucault, Michel. *The Archaeology of Knowledge. And the Discourse on Language*. Translated by A. M. Sheridan Smith. New York: Vintage Books, 2010 [1972].

Fuery, Patric. *The Theory of Absence: Subjectivity, Signification, and Desire*. Contributions in Philosophy 55. London: Greenwood Press, 1995.

Fuhrmann, Horst. *Die Päpste: Von Petrus zu Johannes Paul II*. München: C. H. Beck, 2005.

Fürst, Alfons, Harutyun Harutyunyan, Eva-Maria Schrage et al., eds. *Von Ketzern und Terroristen: Interdisziplinäre Studien zur Konstruktion und Rezeption von Feindbildern*. Münster: Aschendorff Verlag, 2012.

Gade, Kari Ellen, ed. (in collaboration with Edith Marold). *Poetry from Treatises on Poetics*. Vol. III of *Skaldic Poetry of the Scandinavian Middle Ages*. Turnhout: Brepols, 2017.

Gibbon, Edward. *The History of the Decline and Fall of the Roman Empire*. 8 vols. London: Folio Society, 1984–1990.

Gillmann, Franz. "Zur scholastischen Auslegung von Mt 16, 18." *Archiv für katholisches Kirchenrecht* 104 (1924): 41–53.

Gíslason, Konráð. *Um frumparta íslenzkrar tungu í fornöld*. Copenhagen: Hið íslenska bókmenntafélag, 1846.

Gjerløw, Lilli. *Liturgica Islandica I Text*. Bibliotheca Arnamagnæana xxxv. Copenhagen: C. A. Reitzels Boghandel, 1980.

Goetz, Hans-Werner. "Die Gottesfriedensbewegung im Licht neuer Forschungen." In *Landfrieden: Anspruch und Wirklichkeit*. Edited by Arno Buschmann and Elmar Wadle, 31–45. Rechts- und Staatswissenschaftliche Veröffentlichungen der Görres-Gesellschaft, Neue Folge 98. Paderborn: Ferdinand Schöningh, 2002.

Goetz, Hans-Werner. *Geschichtschreibung und Geschichtsbewußtsein im hohen Mittelalter*. 2nd edition. Orbis mediaevalis. Vorstellungswelten des Mittelalters 1. Berlin: Akademie Verlag, 2008.

Goez, Werner. *Kirchenreform und Investiturstreit 910–1122*, 2nd edition. Stuttgart: Kohlhammer, 2008.

Gramsci, Antonio. *Selection from the Prison Notebooks*. Edited and translated by Quentin Hoare and Geoffrey Nowell Smith. New York: International Publishers, 1971.

Grágás: lagasafn íslenska þjóðveldisins. Edited by Gunnar Karlsson, Kristján Sveinsson and Mörður Árnason. Reykjavík: Mál og menning, 2001.

Green, Dennis Howard. *Medieval Listening and Reading: The Primary Reception of German Literature 800–1300*. Cambridge: Cambridge University Press, 1994.

Grimes, Donald J. "Petrine Primacy: Perspectives of two Insular Commentators (A.D. 600–800)." *Proceedings of the PMR Conference* 12/13 (1987–1988): 149–158.

Grímsdóttir, Guðrún Ása. "Um afskipti erkibiskupa af íslenzkum málefnum á 12. og 13. öld." *Saga* 20 (1982): 28–62.

Grundmann, Herbert. "Der Typus des Ketzers in Mittelalterlicher Anschauung." In *Kultur- und Universalgeschichte: Walter Goetz zu seinem 60. Geburtstage*. 91–107. Teubner: Leipzig/Berlin, 1927.

Grundmann, Herbert. "Litteratus – illiteratus." *Archiv für Kulturgeschichte* 40 (1958): 1–65.

Grønlie, Siân E. *The Saint and the Saga Hero: Hagiography and Early Icelandic Literature*. Studies in Old Norse Literature. Woodbridge: D. S. Brewer, 2017.

Grønlie, Siân E. *Íslendingabók. Kristnisaga: The Book of the Icelanders. The Story of the Conversion.* London: Viking Society for Northern Research, University College London, 2006.

Guðjónsson, Elsa E. *Reflar í íslenskum miðaldaheimildum fram til 1569.* Reykjavík: [s.n.], 1991.

Guðjónsson, Elsa E. *Traditional Icelandic Embroidery.* Kópavogur: Elsa E. Guðjónsson, 2003.

Guðnason, Bjarni. *Túlkun Heiðarvígasögu.* Studia Islandica 50. Reykjavík: Bókmenntaf ræðistofnun Háskóla Íslands, 1993.

Guðmundsson, Guðmundur J. "Tíu páfabréf frá 15. öld." *Saga* XLVI:1 (2008): 56–75.

Gullick, Michael. "Skriveren og kunstneren bak homilieboken." In *Vår eldste bok: Skrift, miljø og biletbruk i den norske homilieboka.* Edited by Odd Einar Haugen and Åslaug Ommundsen, 77–100. Bibliotheca Nordica 3. Oslo: Novus forlag, 2010.

Gunn, Simon. *History and Cultural Theory.* London: Routledge, 2006.

Gunnes, Erik. *Kongens ære: kongemakt og kirke i "En tale mot biskopene."* Oslo: Gyldendal, 1971.

Gunnes, Erik. *Erkebiskop Øystein: Statsmann og kirkebygger.* Oslo: Aschehoug, 1996.

Gunnlaugsson, Guðvarður Már. "Iceland." In *The Beginnings of Nordic Scribal Culture, ca 1050–1300: Report from a Workshop on Parchment Fragments, Bergen 28–30 October 2005.* Edited by Åslaug Ommundsen, 32–35. Bergen: Centre for Medieval Studies, 2006.

Gunnlaugsson, Guðvarður Már. "Ritaskrá: Útgáfur og fræðilegar greinar 1960–2006." *Gripla* XVII (2006): 208–215.

Gunnlaugsson, Guðvarður Már. "Voru scriptoria í íslenskum klaustrum?" In *Íslensk klausturmenning á miðöldum.* Edited by Haraldur Bernharðsson, 173–199. Reykjavík: Miðaldastofa Háskóla Íslands, 2016.

Hall, Thomas N. "Old Norse-Icelandic Sermons" In *The Sermon.* Edited by Beverly Mayne Kienzle, Typologie des Sources du Moyen Âge Occidental, 661–709. Turnhout: Brepols, 2000.

Hall, Thomas N. "The Early Medieval Sermon." In *The Sermon.* Edited by Beverly Mayne Kienzle, 203–269. Typologie des Sources du Moyen Âge Occidental. Turnhout: Brepols, 2000.

Hallberg, Peter. "Imagery in Religious Old Norse Prose Literature: An Outline." *Arkiv för nordisk filologi* 102 (1987): 120–170.

Halldórsson, Ólafur. "Inngangur." In *Mattheus saga postula.* Edited by Ólafur Halldórsson, i-cxlviii. Rit 41. Reykjavík: Stofnun Árna Magnússonar á Íslandi, 1994.

Harðarson, Gunnar. "Inngangur." In *Þrjár þýðingar lærðar frá miðöldum. Elucidarius. Um kostu og löstu. Um festarfé sálarinnar.* 7–42. Íslensk heimspeki III. Reykjavík: Hið íslenska bókmenntafélag, 1989.

Harðarson, Gunnar. "Viktorsklaustrið í París og norrænar miðaldir." In *Íslensk klausturmenning á miðöldum*. Edited by Haraldur Bernharðsson, 119–148. Reykjavík: Miðaldastofa Háskóla Íslands, 2016.

Harting-Correa, Alice L. *Walahfrid Strabo's Libellus de exordiis et incrementis quarundam in observationibus ecclesiasticis rerum: A Translation and Liturgical Commentary*. Mittellateinische Studien und Texte XIX. Leiden: Brill, 1996.

Hartl, Ingrid. *Das Feindbild der Kreuzzugslyrik: Das Aufeinandertreffen von Christen und Muslimen*. Wiener Arbeiten zur germanischen Altertumskunde und Philologie 40. Lang: Bern, 2009.

Hauglid, Roar. *Norse stavkirker: Dekor og utstyr*. Oslo: Dreyer, 1973.

Hálfdanarson, Guðmundur. "Interpreting the Nordic Past: Icelandic Medieval Manuscripts and the Construction of a Modern Nation." In *The Uses of the Middle Ages in Modern European States: History, Nationhood, and the Search for Origins*. Edited by Robert J. W. Evans and Guy P. Marchal, 52–71. Basingstoke: Palgrave Macmillan, 2011.

Hehl, Ernst-Dieter. "Das Papsttum in der Welt des 12. Jahrhunderts. Einleitend Bemerkungen zu Anforderungen und Leistungen." In *Das Papsttum in der Welt des 12. Jahrhunderts*. Edited by Ernst D. Hehl and Ingrid H. Ringel, 9–23. Mittelalter-Forschungen 6. Stuttgart: Jan Thorbecke Verlag, 2002.

Helgason, Jón. "Et fragment av Kongespeilet." In *Festskrift til Ludvig Holm-Olsen på hans 70-årsdag den 9. Juni 1984*, 124–141. Øvre Ervik: Alvheim og Eide, 1984.

Hellström, Jan Arvid. *Vägar till Sveriges kristnande*. Stockholm: Atlantis, 1996.

Hirsch, Emanuel. Review of *Islands Kirke fra dens Grundlæggelse til Reformationen*, by Jón Helgason. *Theologische Literaturzeitung* 23 (1927): 541.

Hermann, Pernille. *Literacy in Medieval and Early Modern Scandinavian Culture*. Odense: University Press of Southern Denmark, 2005.

Hermann, Pernille. "The Mind's Eye: The Triad of Memory, Space and the Senses in Old Norse Literature." *European Journal of Scandinavian Studies* 47 (2017): 203–217.

Hermann, Pernille. "Literacy." In *Routledge Research Companion to the Medieval Icelandic Sagas*. Edited by Ármann Jakobsson and Sverrir Jakobsson, 34–47. London and New York: Routledge, 2018.

Higely, John. "Continuities and Discontinuities in Elite Theory." In *The Palgrave Handbook of Political Elites*. Edited by Heinrich Nest and John Higley, 25–39. London: Palgrave Macmillan, 2018.

Hjelm, Titus. "Theory and Method in Critical Discursive Study of Religion: An Outline." In *Making Religion: Theory and Practice in the Discursive Study of Religion*. Edited by Frans Wijsen and Kocku von Stuckrad, 15–34. Leiden, Boston: Brill, 2016.

Hofmann, Dietrich. *Die Legende von Sankt Clemens in den skandinavischen Länder im Mittelalter*. Frankfurt a. M.: Peter Lang, 1997.

Holtsmark, Anne. "Introduction." In *A Book of Miracles: MS No. 645 4to of the Arna-Magnæan Collection in the University Library of Copenhagen*. Copenhagen: Einar Munksgaard, 1938.

Hugason, Hjalti. "Átök um samband ríkis og kirkju: Deilur Guðmundar Arasonar og Kolbeins Tumasonar í kirkjupólitísku ljósi." *Saga* XLVII/1 (2009): 122–148.

Hugason, Hjalti. "Áfallatengt álagsheilkenni á miðöldum? Ráðgátan Guðmundur Arason í ljósi meðferðarfræða nútímans." *Skírnir* 186 (spring, 2012): 98–124.

Hunt, Lynn, ed. *The New Cultural History: Essays*. Berkeley: University of California Press, 1989.

Illich, Ivan. "Peace vs Development." *Democracy* 2 (January, 1981): 53–68.

Ísleifsdóttir, Vilborg Auður. "Öreigar og umrenningar: Um fátækraframfærslu á síðmiðöldum og hrun hennar." *Saga* XLI/2 (2003): 91–126.

Ísleifsson, Sumarliði. *Tvær eyjar á jaðrinum: ímyndir Íslands og Grænlands frá miðöldum til miðrar 19. aldar*. Reykjavík: Háskólaútgáfan, Sagnfræðistofnun Háskóla Íslands, 2015.

Jakobsson, Ármann and Ásdís Egilsdóttir. "Er Oddaverjaþætti treystandi?" *Ný saga* 11 (1999): 91–100.

Jakobsson, Ármann. "Hinn fullkomni karlmaður: Ímyndarsköpun fyrir biskupa á 13. öld." *Studia theologica islandica* 25 (2007): 119–130.

Jakobsson, Ármann. "The Fearless Vampire Killers: A Note about the Icelandic Draugr and Demonic Contamination in Grettis Saga." *Folklore* 120 (2008): 307–316.

Jakobsson, Ármann. " 'Er Saturnús er kallaðr en vér köllum Frey': The Roman Spring of the Old Norse Gods." In *Between Paganism and Christianity in the North*. Edited by Leszek P. Słupecki and Jakub Morawiec, 158–164. Rzeszów: Rzeszow University Press, 2009.

Jakobsson, Ármann. "Fötlun á Íslandi á miðöldum: svipmyndir." In *Fötlun og menning: Íslandssagan í öðru ljósi*. Edited by Hanna Björg Sigurjónsdóttir, Ármann Jakobsson, and Kristín Björnsdóttir, 51–69. Reykjavík: Félagsvísindastofnun HÍ, Rannsóknarsetur í fötlunarfræðum, 2013.

Jakobsson, Sverrir. "Friðarviðleitni kirkjunnar á 13. öld." *Saga* 36 (1998): 7–46.

Jakobsson, Sverrir. *Við og veröldin: Heimsmynd Íslendinga 1100–1400*. Reykjavík: Háskólaútgáfan, 2005.

Jakobsson, Sverrir. "Heaven is a Place on Earth: Church and Sacred Space in Thirteenth-Century Iceland." *Scandinavian Studies* 82 (2010): 1–20.

Jakobsson, Sverrir. *Auðnaróðal: Baráttan um Ísland 1096–1281*. Reykjavík: Sögufélag, 2016.

Jambeck, Karen K. "Discourse." In *Handbook of Medieval Studies: Terms, Methods, Trends*. Edited by Albrecht Classen, 1488–1499. Vol. 1. Berlin: de Gruyter, 2010.

Jensson, Gottskálk Þór. "Lost Latin Literature of Medieval Iceland: The Fragments of the *Vita sancti Thorlaci* and Other Evidence." *Symbolae Osloenses* 79 (2004): 150–170.

Jensson, Gottskálk Þór. "Nokkrar athugasemdir um latínubrotin úr *Vita sancti Thorlaci episcopi et confessoris*." In *Pulvis Olympicus. Afmælisrit tileinkað Sigurði Péturssyni*. Edited by Jón Ma. Ásgeirsson, Kristinn Ólason and Svavar Hrafn Svavarsson, 97–109. Háskólaútgáfan: Reykjavík, 2009.

Jensson, Gottskálk Þór. "*Revelaciones Thorlaci Episcopi* – Enn eitt glatað latínurit eftir Gunnlaug Leifsson munk á Þingeyrum." *Gripla* 23 (2012): 133–175.

Jensson, Gottskálk Þór. "Íslenskar klausturreglur og libertas ecclesie á ofanverðri 12. öld." In *Íslensk klausturmenning á miðöldum*. Edited by Haraldur Bernharðsson, 9–57. Reykjavík: Miðaldastofa Háskóla Íslands, 2016.

Johrendt, Jochen and Harald Müller. "Zentrum und Peripherie: Prozesse des Austausches, der Durchdringung und der Zentralisierung der lateinischen Kirche im Hochmittelalter." In *Römisches Zentrum und kirchliche Peripherie: Das universale Papsttum als Bezugspunkt der Kirchen von den Reformpäpsten bis zu Innozenz III*. Edited by Jochen Johrendt and Harald Müller, 1–18. Neue Abhandlungen der Akademie der Wissenschaften zu Göttingen. Philologisch-Historische Klasse. Neue Folge 2. Berlin: de Gruyter, 2008.

Jorgensen, Peter. "The *Life of St. Basil* in Iceland." *Gripla* 26 (2015): 57–79.

Jørgensen, Marianne W. J and Louise J. Phillips. *Discourse Analysis as Theory and Method*. Los Angeles: Sage, 2010.

Jóhannesson, Jón. "Tímatal Gerlands." *Skírnir* 126 (1952): 76–93.

Jóhannesson, Jón. *Íslendinga saga* I. *Þjóðveldisöld*. Reykjavík: Almenna bókafélagið, 1956.

Jónsdóttir, Selma. *An 11th Century Byzantine Last Judgment in Iceland*. Reykjavík: Almenna bókafélagið, 1959.

Jónsson, Finnur. *Historia Ecclesiastica Islandiæ, ex historiis, annalibus, legibus ecclesiasticis, aliisqve rerum septentrionalium monumentis congesta, et constitutionibus regum, bullis pontificum romanorum, statutis conciliorum nationalium et synodorum provincialium, nec non archiepiscoporum et episcoporum epistolis, edictis et decretis magistratuum, multisqve privatorum litteris et instrumentis, maximam partem hactenus ineditis, illustrata*. 4 vols. Copenhagen: Gerhardus Giese Salicath, 1772–1778.

Kalinke, Marianne E. "Stefanus saga in Reykjahólabók." *Gripla* IX (1995): 133–187.

Karlsdóttir, Gunnvör S. *Guðmundar sögur biskups: Þróun og ritunarsamhengi*. Doctoral thesis, University of Iceland, 2017.

Karlsson, Gunnar. "Frá þjóðveldi til konungsríkis." In *Saga Íslands* II. Edited by Sigurður Líndal, 3–54. Reykjavík: Hið íslenska bókmenntafélag, Sögufélagið, 1975.

Karlsson, Gunnar. "Verkið sem tókst að vinna: Um Kristni á Íslandi I-IV." *Ný saga* 12 (2000): 21–28.

Karlsson, Gunnar. *Goðamenning: Staða og áhrif goðorðsmanna í þjóðveldi Íslendinga*. Reykjavík: Heimskringla, Háskólaforlag Máls og menningar, 2004.

Karlsson, Gunnar. *Inngangur að miðöldum: Handbók í íslenskri miðaldasögu*. Reykjavík: Háskólaútgáfan, 2007.

Karlsson, Stefán. "Inventio Crucis, cap 1, og Veraldar saga." In *Opuscula Septentrionalia: Festskrift til Ole Widding 10.10.1977*. 127–130. Copenhagen, Reitzel, 1977.

Karlsson, Stefán. "Om himmel og helvede på gammelnorsk AM 238 XXVIII fol." In *Festskrift til Ludvig Holm-Olsen*. 185–195. Øvre Ervik: Alvheim og Eide, 1984.

Karlsson, Stefán. "Drottinleg bæn á móðurmáli." *Studia theologica islandica* 4 (1990): 145–174.

Karlsson, Stefán. "Islandsk bogeksport til Norge i middelalderen." In *Stafkrókar: Ritgerðir eftir Stefán Karlsson gefnar út í tilefni sjötugsafmælis hans 2. desember 1998*. Edited by Guðvarður Már Gunnlaugsson, 188–205. Reykjavík: Stofnun Árna Magnússonar á Íslandi, 2000.

Karlsson, Stefán. "Íslensk bókagerð á miðöldum." In *Stafkrókar: Ritgerðir eftir Stefán Karlsson gefnar út í tilefni sjötugsafmælis hans 2. desember 1998*. Edited by Guðvarður Már Gunnlaugsson, 225–241. Reykjavík: Stofnun Árna Magnússonar á Íslandi, 2000.

Karlsson, Stefán. "Om norvagismer i islandske håndskrifter." In *Stafkrókar: Ritgerðir eftir Stefán Karlsson gefnar út í tilefni sjötugsafmælis hans 2. desember 1998*. Edited by Guðvarður Már Gunnlaugsson, 173–187. Reykjavík: Stofnun Árna Magnússonar á Íslandi, 2000.

Keller, Reiner. "The Sociology of Knowledge Approach to Discourse (SKAD)." *Human Studies* 34 (2011): 43–65.

Kéry, Lotte. "Dekretalenrecht zwischen Zentrale und Peripherie." In *Römisches Zentrum und kirchliche Peripherie: Das universale Papsttum als Bezugspunkt der Kirchen von den Reformpäpsten bis zu Innozenz III*. Edited by Jochen Johrendt and Harald Müller, 19–45. Neue Abhandlungen der Akademie der Wissenschaften zu Göttingen. Philologisch-Historische Klasse. Neue Folge 2. Berlin: de Gruyter, 2008.

Kienzle, Beverly Mayne. "Introduction." In *The Sermon*. Edited by Beverly Mayne Kienzle, 143–174. Typologie des Sources du Moyen Âge Occidental 154. Turnhout: Brepols, 2000.

King Jr., Martin Luther. *Letter from Birmingham Jail*. Penguin Modern. New York: Penguin Random House, 2018.

Kohn, Margaret. "Post-colonial theory." In *Ethics and World Politics*. Edited by Duncan Bell, 200–218. Oxford: Oxford University Press, 2010.

Kristjánsdóttir, Guðbjörg. "Dómkirkjur." In Gunnar F. Guðmundsson, *Íslenskt samfélag og Rómakirkja*. 154–164. Vol. II of *Kristni á Íslandi*. Reykjavík: Alþingi, 2000.

Kristjánsdóttir, Guðbjörg. "Sóknarkirkjur og búnaður þeirra." In Gunnar F. Guðmundsson, *Íslenskt samfélag og Rómakirkja*. 190–202. Vol. II of *Kristni á Íslandi*. Reykjavík: Alþingi, 2000.

Kristjánsdóttir, Guðbjörg. "Fyrstu kirkjur landsins." In Hjalti Hugason, *Frumkristni og upphaf kirkju*. 175–184. Vol. I of *Kristni á Íslandi*. Reykjavík: Alþingi, 2000.

Kristjánsdóttir, Guðbjörg. "Dómsdagsmynd frá Bjarnastaðahlíð." In Hjalti Hugason, *Frumkristni og upphaf kirkju.* 274–277. Vol. 1 of *Kristni á Íslandi.* Reykjavík: Alþingi, 2000.

Kristjánsdóttir, Guðbjörg. "Messuföng og kirkjulist: Búnaður kirkna í kaþólskum sið." In *Hlutavelta tímans: menningararfur á Þjóðminjasafni.* Edited by Árni Björnsson and Hrefna Róbertsdóttir, 246–259. Reykjavík: Þjóðminjasafn Íslands, 2004.

Kristjánsdóttir, Steinunn. "Kristnitakan. Áhrif tilviljanakennds og skipulegs trúboðs." *Saga* XLV/1 (2007): 113–130.

Kristjánsdóttir, Steinunn. *Sagan af klaustrinu á Skriðu.* Reykjavík: Sögufélag, 2012.

Kristjánsdóttir, Steinunn. "Becoming Christian: A Matter of Everyday Resistance and Negotiation." *Norwegian Archaeological Review* 48 (2015): 27–45.

Kristjánsdóttir, Steinunn. *Leitin að klaustrunum: Klausturhald á Íslandi í fimm aldir.* Reykjavík: Sögufélag, 2017.

Kristjánsson, Jónas. "Learned Style or Saga Style?" In *Speculum Norroenum: Norse Studies in Memory of Gabrielle Turville-Petre.* Edited by Ursula Dronke et al., 260–292. Odense: Odense University Press, 1981.

Kristjánsson, Jónas. *Eddas and Sagas: Iceland's Medieval Literature.* Reykjavík. Hið íslenska bókmenntafélag, 1988.

Kristjánsson, Jónas. "Sagas and Saints' Lives." In *Cultura classica e cultura germanica settentrionale: atti del Convegno internazionale di studie, Università di Macerata, Facoltà di lettre e filosofia: Macerata-S. Severino Marche, 2–4 maggio 1985.* Edited by Pietro Janni, Diego Poli and Carlo Santini, 125–143. Quademi linguistici e filologici 3. Macerate: Università de Macerate, 1988.

Kålund, Kristian, ed. *Katalog over Den Arnamagnæanske Håndskriftsamling.* 2. Vols. Copenhagen: Gyldendal, 1888–1894.

Lachmann, Richard. "Hegemons, Empires, and Their Elites." *Sociologia, Problemas e Práticas* 75 (2014): 9–38.

Laclau, Ernesto and Chantal Mouffe. *Hegemony and Socialist Strategy: Towards a Radical Democratic Politics,* 2nd ed. London: Verso, 2001.

Landwehr, Achim. *Historische Diskursanalyse.* Historische Einführungen 4. Frankfurt: Campus Verlag, 2008.

Larson, Atria A. "Popes and Canon Law." In *A Companion to the Medieval Papacy: Growth of an Ideology and an Institution.* Edited by Keith Sisson and Atria A. Larson, 135–157. Brill's Companions to the Christian Tradition 70. Leiden and Boston: Brill, 2016.

Larson, Atria A. and Keith Sisson. "Papal Decretals." In *A Companion to the Medieval Papacy: Growth of an Ideology and an Institution.* Edited by Keith Sisson and Atria A. Larson, 158–173. Brill's Companions to the Christian Tradition 70. Leiden, Boston: Brill, 2016.

Laugerud, Henning. "To See with the Eyes of the Soul: Memory and Visual Culture in Medieval Europe." *Arv: Nordic Yearbook of Folklore* 66 (2010): 43–68.

Laxness, Halldór. "Tímatalsrabb: Dr. Ólafía Einarsdóttir brýtur í blað." *Tímarit Máls og menningar* 27/1 (1966): 31–42.

Lárusson, Magnús Már. "On the so-called "Armenian" bishops." *Studia Islandica* xviii (1960): 23–38.

Lárusson, Magnús Már. *Fróðleikspættir og sögubrot*. Hafnarfjörður: Skuggsjá, 1967.

Le Goff, Jacques. *The Medieval Imagination*. Translated by Arthur Goldhammer. Chicago and London: The University of Chicago Press, 1992.

Lentes, Thomas. "Textus Evangelii: Materialität und Inszenierung des *textus* in der Liturgie." In *'Textus' im Mittelalter: Komponenten und Situationen des Wortgebrauchs im schriftsemantischen Feld*. Edited by Ludolf Kuchenbuch and Uta Kleine, 133–148. Veröffentlichungen des Max-Planck-Instituts für Geschichte 216. Göttingen: Vandenhoeck & Ruprecht, 2016.

Lincoln, Bruce. *Discourse and the Construction of Society: Comparative Studies of Myth, Ritual, and Classification*. Oxford: Oxford University Press, 1989.

Lincoln, Bruce. *Authority: Construction and Corrosion*. Chicago: University of Chicago Press, 1994.

Lincoln, Bruce. *Theorizing Myth: Narrative, Ideology, and Scholarship*. Chicago and London: The University of Chicago Press, 1999.

Lincoln, Bruce. *Gods and Demons, Priests and Scholars: Critical Explorations in the History of Religions*. Chicago: The University of Chicago Press, 2012.

Lincoln, Bruce. "Theses on Method." In *Gods and Demons, Priests and Scholars: Critical Explorations in the History of Religions*, 1–3. Chicago: University of Chicago Press, 2012. First published in *Method & Theory in the Study of Religion* 8, no. 3 (1996): 225–27.

Lincoln, Bruce. "How to Read a Religious Text." In *Gods and Demons, Priests and Scholars: Critical Explorations in the History of Religions*, 1–3. Chicago: University of Chicago Press, 2012.

Lindblad, Gustav. *Det isländska accenttecknet: En historisk-ortografisk studie*. Lund: C. W. K. Gleerup, 1952.

Luz, Ulrich. *Matthew 8–20*. Hermeneia. Minneapolis: Fortress Press, 2001.

Lönnroth, Lars. "Thesen om de två kulturerna: Kritiska studier i den isländska sagaskrivningens sociala förutsättningar." *Scripta islandica* 15/3 (1964): 3–97.

Lönnroth, Lars. "The Noble Heathen: A Theme in the Sagas." *Scandinavian Studies* 41 (1969): 1–29.

Madigan, Kevin. *Medieval Christianity: A New History*. New Haven and London: Yale University Press, 2014.

Magnúsardóttir, Lára. *Bannfæring og kirkjuvald á Íslandi 1275–1550: Lög og rannsóknarforsendur*. Reykjavík: Háskólaútgáfan, 2007.

Magnússon, Þór. "Bátkumlið í Vatnsdal í Patreksfirði." *Árbók hins íslenzka fornleifafélags* 63 (1966): 5–32.

Mann, Michael. *The Sources of Social Power*. Vol. 1 of *A History of Power from the Beginning to A.D. 1760*. Cambridge: Cambridge University Press, 1986.

Marchand, James W. "An Old Norse Fragment of a Psalm Commentary." *Maal og minne* (1976): 24–29.

Mastnak, Tomaž. *Crusading Peace: Christendom, the Muslim World, and Western Political Order*. Berkeley and Los Angeles: University of California Press, 2002.

Mattheus saga postula. Ed. Ólafur Halldórsson. Reykjavík: Stofnun Árna Magnússonar á Íslandi, 1994.

McCreesh, Bernadine. "Saint-Making in Early Iceland." *Scandinavian-Canadian Studies* 17 (2006–2007): 12–23.

McDougall, David. "Homilies (West Norse)." In *Medieval Scandinavia: An Encyclopedia*. Edited by Phillip Pulsiano, 290–292. New York and London: Garland, 1993.

McKitterick, Rosamund. *The Uses of Literacy*. Cambridge: Cambridge University Press, 1990.

Messuskýringar: Liturgisk symbolik frå den norsk-islandske kyrkja i millomalderen. Edited by Oluf Kolsrud. Oslo: Dybwad, 1952.

Metzler, Irina. *Disability in Medieval Europe: Thinking about Physical Impairment During the High Middle Ages, c. 1100–1400*. Routledge Studies in Medieval Religion and Culture 5. London, Routledge, 2006.

Moore, R. I. *The Formation of a Persecuting Society: Authority and Deviance in Western Europe 950–1250*. 2nd ed. Oxford: Blackwell, 2007.

Moore, Stephen D. *Empire and Apocalypse: Postcolonialism and the New Testament*. The Bible in the Modern World 12. Sheffield: Sheffield Phoenix Press, 2006.

Morgenstern, Gustav. *Arnamagnæanische Fragmente (Cod. AM. 655 4to III-VIII, 238 fol. II, 921 4to IV 1.2: Ein Supplement zu den Heilagra manna sögur nach den Handschriften*. Leipzig and Copenhagen: Emil Gräfes Buchhandlung and Skandinavisk Antiquariat, 1893.

Morkinskinna: The Earliest Icelandic Chronicle of the Norwegian Kings 1030–1157. Translated by Theodore M. Andersson and Kari Ellen Gade. Islandica LI. Ithaca and London: Cornell University Press, 2000.

Mortensen, Lars Boje. "Den formative dialog mellem latinsk og folkesproglig litteratur ca 600–1250." In *Reykholt som makt- og lærdomssenter i den islandske og nordiske kontekst*. Edited by Else Mundal, 229–71. Reykholt: Snorrastofa, 2006.

Muessig, Carolyn. "Audience and Preacher: *Ad status* Sermons and Social Classification." In *Preacher, Sermon and Audience in the Middle Ages*. Edited by Carolyn Muessig, 255–276. Leiden: Brill, 2002.

Müller, Harald. "The Omnipresent Pope: Legates and Judges Delegate." In *A Companion to the Medieval Papacy: Growth of an Ideology and an Institution*. Edited by Keith Sisson and Atria A. Larson, 199–219. Brill's Companions to the Christian Tradition 70. Leiden and Boston: Brill, 2016.

Münkler, Herfried and Grit Straßenberger. *Politische Theorie und Ideengeschichte: Eine Einführung*. München: C.H. Beck, 2016.

Münkler, Herfried. *Empires: The Logic of World Domination from Ancient Rome to the United States*. Translated by Patrick Camiller. Cambridge: Polity, 2007.

Nakashian, Craig M. *Warrior Churchmen of Medieval England 1000–1250: Theory and Reality*. Suffolk: Boydell and Brewer, 2016.

Nasrallah, Laura Salah. *Christian Responses to Roman Art and Architecture: The Second-Century Church Amid the Spaces of Empire*. Cambridge: Cambridge University Press, 2010.

Nedkvitne, Arnved. *The Social Consequences of Literacy in Medieval Scandinavia*. Utrecht Studies in Medieval Literacy 11. Turnhout: Belgium, 2004.

Nedkvitne, Arnved. *Lay Belief in Norse Society, 1000–1350*. Copenhagen: Museum Tusculanum Press, University of Copenhagen, 2009.

Nirenberg, David. *Anti-Judaism: The History of a Way of Thinking*. London: Head of Zeus, 2013.

Noble, Thomas F. X. "Rome and the Romans in the Medieval Mind: Empathy and Antipathy." In *Studies on Medieval Empathies*. Edited by Karl. F. Morrison and Rudolph M. Bell, 291–315. Turnhout: Brepols, 2013.

Nordal, Guðrún. *Ethics and Action in Thirteenth-Century Iceland*. Odense: Odense University Press, 1998.

Nordal, Sigurður. "Samhengið í íslenzkum bókmenntum." In *Íslenzk lestrarbók 1400–1900*, ix–xxxii. Reykjavík: Bókaverzlun Sigfúsar Eymundssonar, 1924.

Nordal, Sigurður. *Íslensk menning* 1. Reykjavík: Mál og menning, 1942.

Oediger, Friedrich Wilhelm. *Über die Bildung der Geistlichen im späten Mittelalter*. Studien und Texte zur Geistesgeschichte des Mittelalters. Leiden: Brill, 1953.

Ohly, Friedrich. "Typologie als Denkform der Geschichtsbetrachtung." In *Natur, Religion, Sprache, Universität: Universitätsvorträge 1982/1983*. Schriftenreihe der Westfälischen Wilhelms-Universität Münster 7. Münster: Aschendorff, 1983.

Ommundsen, Åslaug. "The Word of God and the Stories of Saints: Medieval Liturgy and its Reception in Norway." In *The Performance of Christian and Pagan Storyworlds*. Edited by Lars Boje Mortensen and Tuomas M. S. Lehtonen, 45–66. Medieval Identities: Socio-Cultural Spaces 3. Turnhout: Brepols, 2013.

Ordbog over det norrøne prosasprog. Registre. Copenhagen: Arnamagnæanske commission, 1989.

Óskarsdóttir, Svanhildur. "Universal history in fourteenth-century Iceland: Studies in AM 764 4to." Doctoral thesis, University of London, 2000.

Óskarsdóttir, Svanhildur. "Prose of Christian Instruction." In *A Companion to Old Norse-Icelandic Literature and Culture*. Edited by Rory McTurk, 338–353. Oxford: Blackwell, 2005.

Paasche, Fredrik. *Homiliu-bók (Icelandic Sermons). Perg. 4to No. 15 in the Royal Library Stockholm.* Corpus Codiscum Islandicorum Medii Aevi 8. Copenhagen: Levin & Munksgaard, 1935.

Padberg, Lutz E. *Die Christianisierung Europas im Mittelalter.* 2nd edition. Stuttgart: Reclam, 2009.

Palazzo, Eric. *A History of Liturgical Books from the Beginning to the Thirteenth Century.* Translated by Madeleine Beaumont. Collegeville: The Liturgical Press, 1998.

Patschovsky, Alexander. "Heresy and Society: On the Political Function of Heresy in the Medieval World" in *Texts and the Repression of Medieval Heresy.* 23–41. Edited by Caterina Bruschi and Peter Biller. York Studies in Medieval Theology IV. Suffolk: York Medieval Press, 2003.

Paxton, Frederick S. "History, Historians, and the Peace of God." In *The Peace of God: Social Violence and Religious Response in France around the Year 1000.* Edited by Thomas Head and Richard Landes, 21–40. Ithaca: Cornell University Press, 1992.

Pálsson, Gísli, ed. *From Sagas to Society: Comparative Approaches to Early Iceland.* Enfield Lock, Middlesex: Hisarlik Press, 1992.

Pálsson, Hermann. *Art and Ethics in Hrafnkel's saga.* Copenhagen: Munksgaard, 1971.

Pálsson, Hermann. *Keltar á Íslandi.* Reykjavík: Háskólaútgáfan, 1996.

Pelikan, Jaroslav. *The Growth of Medieval Theology.* Chicago: University of Chicago Press, 1978.

Pelinka, Anton, ed. *Feindbilder in Europa: Analysen und Perspektiven,* Studienreihe Konfliktforschung 23. Vienna: Braumüller, 2008.

Pelle, Stephen. "Twelfth-Century Sources for Old Norse Homilies: New Evidence from AM 655 XXVII 4to." *Gripla* XXIV (2013): 45–75.

Plácidus saga: With an Edition of Plácitus drápa by Jonna Louis-Jensen. Edited by John Tucker. Copenhagen: Reitzel, 1998.

Pomarici, Francesca. "Papal Imagery and Propaganda: Art, Architecture, and Liturgy." In *A Companion to the Medieval Papacy: Growth of an Ideology and an Institution.* Edited by Keith Sisson and Atria A. Larson, 85–120. Brill's Companions to the Christian Tradition 70. Leiden and Boston: Brill, 2016.

Prakash, Gyan. "Introduction." In *After Colonialism: Imperial Histories and Postcolonial Displacements.* Edited by Gyan Prakash, 3–18. Princeton Studies in Culture/Power/History. Princeton: Princeton University Press, 1994.

Quast, Bruno. "Literarische Inkulturation. Zur Einleitung." In *Inkulturation. Strategien bibelepischen Schreibens in Mittelalter und Früher Neuzeit.* Edited by Bruno Quast und Susanne Spreckelmeier, 1–13. Literatur - Theorie - Geschichte 12. Berlin and Boston: de Gruyter, 2017.

Rafnsson, Sveinbjörn. Review of *Saga Íslands* I-II by Magnús Stefánsson et al. *Skírnir* 149 (1975): 210–222.

Rafnsson, Sveinbjörn. Review of *Saga Íslands* III by Magnús Stefánsson et al. *Skírnir* 153 (1979), 206–214.

Rafnsson, Sveinbjörn. "Þorláksskriftir og hjúskapur á 12. og 13. öld." *Saga* 20 (1982): 114–129.

Rafnsson, Sveinbjörn. *Páll Jónsson Skálholtsbiskup: Nokkrar athuganir á sögu hans og kirkjustjórn*. Ritsafn sagnfræðistofnunar 33. Reykjavík: Sagnfræðistofnun Háskóla Íslands, 1993.

Resnick, Irven M. "Lingua dei, lingua hominis: Sacred Language and Medieval Texts." *Viator* 21 (1990): 51–74.

Reuter, Timothy. "The 'Imperial Church System' of the Ottonian and Salian Rulers: a Reconsideration." *Journal of Ecclesiastical History* 33 (1982): 347–374.

Ricketts, Philadelphia. *High-Ranking Widows in Medieval Iceland and Yorkshire: Property, Power, Marriage and Identity in the Twelfth and Thirteenth Centuries*, The Northern World 49. Leiden: Brill, 2010.

Robinson, Ian S. *The Papacy, 1073–1198: Continuity and Innovation*. Cambridge: Cambridge University Press, 1990.

Rode, Eva. "Et fragment af en prædiken til askeonsdag: AM 655 XI, 4to." *Opuscula* 7 (1979): 44–61.

Rose, Els. "*Virtutes apostolorum*: Editorial Problems and Principles." *Apocrypha* 23 (2012): 11–45.

Rose, Els. "*Virtutes apostolorum:* Origin, Aim, and Use." *Traditio* 68 (2013): 68–96.

Rose, Els. "*Abdias Scriptor Vitarum Sanctorum Apostolorum*? The "Collection of Pseudo-Abdias" Reconsidered," *Revue d'histoire des textes* VIII (2013): 227–268.

Rose, Els. "The Apocryphal Acts of the Apostles in the Latin Middle Ages: Contexts of Transmission and Use." In The Apocryphal Acts of the Apostles in Latin Christianity, Proceedings of the International Sumer School on Christian Apocryphal Literature (ISCAL), Strasbourg, 24–27 June 2012. Edited by Els Rose, 31–51. Turnhout: Brepols, 2014 [E-book Only].

Roughton, Philip G. "Stylistics and Sources of the Postola sögur in AM 645 4to and AM 652 4to." *Gripla* XVI (2005): 7–50.

Roughton, Philip G. "'Þa syndi hann þeim mikinn skugga': Unmasking the Fantastic in the *Postola Sögur*." In *The Fantastic in Old Norse/Icelandic Litearture. Sagas and the British Isles*. Edited by John McKinnel, David Ashurst, and Donata Kick, 846–855. Durham: The Centre for Medieval and Renaissance Studies, Durham University, 2006.

Said, Edward. *Orientalism*. New York: Vintage 1979 [1978].

Schieffer, Rudolf. "Motu Propriu. Über die Papstgeschichtliche Wende im 11. Jahrhundert." *Historisches Jahrbuch* 122 (2002): 27–42.

Schiewer, Regina D. "Predigten und Predigtsammlungen." In *Die deutsche Literatur des Mittelalters. Verfasserlexikon* 11. Col. 1264–1265. 2nd and rev. edition. Berlin and New York: Walter de Gruyter, 2004.

Schiewer, Regina D. *Die Deutsche Predigt um 1200: Ein Handbuch.* Berlin and New York: Walter de Gruyter, 2008.

Schrage, Eva-Maria. "Von Ketzern und Terroristen? Zum analytischen Nutzen eines interdisziplinären Feindbildbegriffs." In *Von Ketzern und Terroristen: Interdisziplinäre Studien zur Konstruktion und Rezeption von Feindbildern.* Edited by Alfons Fürst, Harutyun Harutynyan, Eva-Maria Schrage et al., 217–238. Münster: Aschendorff Verlag, 2012.

Schüssler Fiorenza, Elisabeth. *The Power of the Word: Scripture and the Rhetoric of Empire.* Minneapolis: Fortress, 2007.

Seelow, Hubert. Review of *Kristni á Íslandi*, by Hjalti Hugason et al. *Skandinavistik* 23 (2002): 57–58.

Segovia, Fernardo F. "Introduction: Configurations, Approaches, Findings, Stances." In *Postcolonial Commentary on the New Testament Writings.* Edited by Fernando F. Segovia and R. S. Sugirtharajah, 1–68. The Bible and Postcolonialism 13. London: T&T Clark, 2009.

Sigurdsson, Erika. *The Church in Fourteenth-Century Iceland: The Formation of an Elite Clerical Identity.* The Northern World 72. Leiden: Brill, 2016.

Sigurðardóttir, Sigríður. *Skagfirska kirkjurannsóknin: Miðaldakirkjur 1000–1318.* Rit Byggðasafns Skagfirðinga I. [s.n.]: Byggðasafn Skagfirðinga, 2012.

Sigurðsson, Gísli. *Túlkun Íslendingasagna í ljósi munnlegrar hefðar: Tilgáta um aðferð.* Reykjavík: Stofnun Árna Magnússonar á Íslandi, 2002.

Sigurðsson, Gísli. *The Medieval Icelandic Saga and Oral Tradition: A Discourse on Method.* Publications of the Milman Parry Collection of Oral Literature 2. Cambridge: Harvard University Press, 2004.

Sigurðsson, Jón Viðar. "Samskipti íslenskra biskupa við útlenda yfirboðara á öldum áður." In *Saga biskupsstólanna*, edited by Gunnar Kristjánsson, 491–515. [s.n]: Hólar, 2000.

Sigurðsson, Jón Viðar. *Kristninga i Norden 750–1200.* Oslo: Det Norske Samlaget, 2003.

Sigurðsson, Jón Viðar. "Allir sem sjá líta þó ekki jafnt á: sagnaritun um íslenskar miðaldir fram um 1300," in *Íslensk sagnfræði á 20. öld.* Edited by Guðmundur J. Guðmundsson, Guðmundur Jónsson and Sigurður Ragnarsson, 33–57. Reykjavík: Sögufélag, 2009.

Sigurðsson, Jón Viðar. *Det norrøne samfunnet: Vikingen, kongen, erkebiskopen og bonden.* Oslo: Pax, 2008.

Sigurðsson, Jón Viðar. *Viking Friendship: The Social Bond in Iceland and Norway, c. 900–1300.* Ithaca: Cornell, 2017.

Skórzewska, Joanna A. *Constructing a Cult: The Life and Veneration of Guðmundr Arason (1161–1237) in the Icelandic Written Sources.* Leiden: Brill, 2011.

Smith, Jonathan Z. "What a Difference a Difference Makes." In *Relating Religion: Essays in the Study of Religion*. 251–301. Chicago: University of Chicago Press, 2004.
Southern, Richard. *Western Society and the Church in the Middle Ages*. The Pelican History of the Church II. Harmondsworth: Penguin Books, 1970.
Spiegel, Gabrielle M. "Introduction." In *Practicing History: New Directions in Historical Writing after the Linguistic Turn*. Edited by Gabrielle M. Spiegel, 1–31. New York: Routledge, 2005.
Spivak, Gayatri Chakravorty. "Can the Subaltern Speak." In *Marxism and the Interpretation of Culture*. Edited by Cary Nelson and Lawrence Grossberg, 271–313. Champaign: University of Illinois Press, 1988 [1985].
Stefánsson, Magnús. "Kirkjuvald eflist." In *Saga Íslands* II. Edited by Sigurður Líndal, 57–144. Reykjavík: Hið íslenska bókmenntafélag, Sögufélagið, 1975.
Stefánsson, Magnús. "Kong Sverre – prest og sønn av Sigurd Munn?" In *Festskrift til Ludvig Holm-Olsen på hans 70-årsdag den 9. juni 1984*. 287–307. Øvre Ervik: Alvheim og Eide, 1984.
Stefánsson, Magnús. *Staðir og staðamál: Studier i islandske egenkirkelige og beneficialrettslige forhold i middelalderen* I. Bergen: Historisk institutt, Universitetet i Bergen, 2000.
Steffensen, Jón. "Ákvæði kristinna laga þáttar um beinafærslu." *Árbók hins íslenzka fornleifafélags* 63 (1966): 71–78.
Stock, Brian. *Implications of Literacy: Written Language and Models of Interpretation in the Eleventh and Twelfth Centuries*. Princeton: Princeton University Press, 1983.
Stollberg-Rilinger, Barbara. "Was heißt Kulturgeschichte des Politischen? Einleitung." In *Was heißt Kulturgeschichte des Politischen?* Edited by Barbara Stollberg-Rilinger, 9–24. Berlin: Duncker and Humblot, 2005.
Strömbäck, Dag. *The Conversion of Iceland: A Survey*. Text series/Viking Society for Northern Research 6. London: University College, 1975.
Sturlunga saga. 2 vols. Translated by Julia H. McGrew and R. George Thomas. New York: Twayne Publishers, 1970–1974.
Summerlin, Danica. "Papal Councils." In *A Companion to the Medieval Papacy: Growth of an Ideology and an Institution*. Edited by Keith Sisson and Atria A. Larson, 174–198. Brill's Companions to the Christian Tradition 70. Leiden and Boston: Brill, 2016.
Sveinsson, Einar Ólafur. *The Age of the Sturlungs: Icelandic Civilization in the Thirteenth Century*. Islandica XXXVI. Translated by Jóhann S. Hannesson. Ithaca: Cornell University Press, 1953.
Swanson, Robert N. "Manning the Church: Priests and Bishops." In *The Routledge History of Medieval Christianity 1050–1500*. Edited by Robert N. Swanson, 31–44. The Routledge Histories. London and New York, Routledge, 2015.

Taira, Teemu. "Discourse on 'Religion' in Organizing Social Practices: Theoretical and Practical Considerations," in *Making Religion: Theory and Practice in the Discursive Study of Religion*. Edited by Frans Wijsen and Kocku von Stuckrad, 125–146. Leiden: Brill, 2016.

Tellenbach, Gerd. *Die westliche Kirche vom 10. bis zum frühen 12. Jahrhundert*. Die Kirche in ihrer Geschichte 2, F1. Göttingen: Vandenhoeck & Ruprecht, 1988.

Tomasch, Sylvia. "Postcolonial Chaucer and the Virtual Jew." In *The Postcolonial Middle Ages*, edited by Jeffrey Jerome Cohen, 243–260. New York: St Martin's, 2000.

Tierney, Brian. *The Crisis of Church and State 1050–1300: With Selected Documents*. Englewood Cliffs: Prentice-Hall, 1964.

Tómasson, Sverrir. *Formálar íslenskra sagnaritara á miðöldum: Rannsókn bókmenntahefðar*. Stofnun Árna Magnússonar, Rit 33. Reykjavík: Stofnun Árna Magnússonar, 1988.

Tómasson, Sverrir. "Bergur Sokkason og íslenskar Nikulás sögur." In *Tækileg vitni: Greinar um bókmenntir*. 311–344. Reykjavík: Stofnun Árna Magnússonar í íslenskum fræðum and Hið íslenska bókmenntafélag, 2011.

Tucker, John. "Scribal Hands in AM 655 4to X," *Opuscula* 6 (1979): 108–125.

Turville-Petre, Gabriel. *Origins of Icelandic Literature*. Oxford: Clarendon Press, 1953.

Tulinius, Torfi H. *Skáldið í skriftinni: Snorri Sturluson og Egils saga*. Íslensk menning. Reykjavík: Hið íslenska bókmenntafélag and ReykjavíkurAkademían, 2004.

Tulinius, Torfi H. "The Self as Other: Iceland and the Culture of Southern Europe in the Middle Ages." *Gripla* XX (2009): 199–215.

Tulinius, Torfi H. *The Enigma of Egill: The Saga, the Viking Poet, and Snorri Sturluson*. Islandica LVII. Translated by Victoria Cribb. Ithaca: Cornell University Press, 2014.

Van Dijk, Teun A. "Discourse as Interaction in Society." In *Discourse as Social Interaction*. Vol. 2. *Discourse Studies: A Multidisciplinary Introduction*. Edited by Teun A. van Dijk, 1–37. London: Sage Publications, 1997.

Vandvik, Eirik, ed. *Latinske Dokument til Norsk Historie fram til år 1204*. Oslo: Det Norske Samlaget, 1959.

Vésteinsson, Orri. "Bókaeign íslenskra kirkna á miðöldum." BA thesis, University of Iceland, 1990.

Vésteinsson, Orri. *Christianization of Iceland: Priests, Power, and Social Change 1000–1300*. Oxford: Oxford University Press, 2000.

Vésteinsson, Orri. "Brotasaga." In *Kristni á Íslandi: Útgáfumálþing á Akureyri 15. apríl 2000 og í Reykjavík 23. október 2000*. Edited by Ágústa Þorbergsdóttir, 111–115. Reykjavík: Skrifstofa Alþingis, 2000.

Vésteinsson, Orri. "The Formative Phase of the Icelandic Church ca 990–1240 AD." In *Church Centres: Church Centres in Iceland from the 11th to the 13th Century and Their Parallels in Other Countries*. Edited by Helgi Þorláksson, 73–83. Snorrastofa: Rit 2. Reykholt: Snorrastofa, 2005.

Vídalín, Arngrímur. "Ný bókfestukenning? Spjall um aðferðir." *Saga* LIII/2 (2015): 124–138.

von Stuckrad, Kocku. "Discourse" in *Vocabulary for the Study of Religion* 1 *A-E*. Edited by Robert A. Segal and Kocku von Stuckrad, 429–438. Leiden, Brill: 2015.

von Stuckrad, Kocku. "Religion and Science in Transformation: On Discourse Communities, the Double-Bind of Discourse Research, and Theoretical Controversies." In *Making Religion: Theory and Practice in the Discursive Study of Religion*. Edited by Frans Wijsen and Kocku von Stuckrad, 203–224. Leiden, Boston: Brill, 2016.

Walter, Ernst. "Die lateinische Sprache und Literatur auf Island und in Norwegen bis zum Beginn des 13. Jahrhunderts: Ein Orientierungsversuch." *Nordeuropa* 4 (1971): 195–229.

Ward, Benedicta. *Miracles and the Medieval Mind: Theory, Record and Event 1000–1215*. London: Scholars Press, 1982.

Webber, Teresa. "Reading in the Refectory: Monastic Practice in England." London University Annual John Coffin Memorial Palaeography Lecture, February 2010. Revised 2013 version, accessed 22. May 2015, https://www.reading.ac.uk/nmsruntime/saveasdialog.aspx?lID=130218&sID=416690.

Weiter, Dennis. *Feindbildkonstruktionen im Nahostkonflik: Ursache für das Scheitern der Roadmap 2003?* Hamburg: Diplomica, 2012.

Wellendorf, Jonas. "Ecclesiastical Literature and Hagiography." In *The Routledge Research Companion to the Medieval Icelandic Sagas*. Edited by Ármann Jakobsson and Sverrir Jakobsson, 48–58. London and New York: Routledge, 2017.

Whaley, Diana, ed. *Poetry from the Kings' Sagas* 1, part 2. Vol. I of *Skaldic Poetry of the Scandinavian Middle Ages*. Turnhout: Brepols, 2012.

Williamson, Beth. "Material Culture and Medieval Christianity." In *The Oxford Handbook for Medieval Christianity*. Edited by John H. Arnold, 60–75. Oxford: Oxford University Press, 2014.

Widding, Ole. "Et fragment af Stephanus saga (AM 655, 4° XIV B), tekst og kommentar." *Acta Philologica Scandinavica* 21 (1952): 143–172.

Widding, Ole. "Håndskriftanalyser." *Bibliotheca Arnamagnæana* 1; *Opuscula* II (1961): 65–75.

Winroth, Anders. *Conversion of Scandinavia: Vikings, Merchants, and Missionaries in the Remaking of Northern Europe*. New Haven: Yale University Press, 2012.

Wolf, Kirsten. "Gregory's Influence on Old Norse-Icelandic Religious Literature." In *Rome and the North: The Early Reception of Gregory the Great in Germanic Europe*. Edited by Rolf H. Bremmer Jr., Kees Dekker and David F. Johnson, 255–274. Mediaevalia Groningiana New Series 4. Peeters: Paris, 2001.

Wolf, Kirsten. *The Legends of the Saints in Old Norse-Icelandic Prose*, TONIS. Toronto: Toronto University Press, 2013.

Zoëga, Guðný. "Early church organization in Skagafjörður, North Iceland. The results of the Skagafjörður Church Project." *Collegium Medievale* 27 (2014): 21–60.

Zoëga, Guðný. "A family revisited: The Medieval household cemetery of Keldudalur, North Iceland." *Norwegian Archaeological Review* 48 (2015): 105–28.

Zoëga, Guðný and Douglas Bolender. "An Archaeology of Moments: Christian Conversion and Practice in a Medieval Household Cemetery." *Journal of Social Archaeology* 17 (2017): 69–91.

Þorláksson, Helgi. *Gamlar götur og goðavald: Um fornar leiðir og völd Oddaverja í Rangárþingi.* Reykjavík: Sagnfræðistofnun Háskóli Íslands, 1989.

Þorláksson, Helgi. Review of *Ætt og saga: Um frásagnarfræði Sturlungu eða Íslendinga sögu hinnar miklu,* by Úlfar Bragason. *Saga* 49 (2011): 226–228.

Þorsteinsson, Björn. *Ný Íslandssaga.* Reykjavík: Heimskringla, 1966.

Þórarinsson, Jón. *Íslensk tónlistarsaga 1000–1800.* Reykjavík: Tónlistarsafn Íslands, 2012.

Index of Biblical References

Gen.
28:17 — 119n300

Exod.
4:10 — 101

Isa.
32:3-4 — 154

Jer.
1:7 — 101

Ps.
45:17 — 274
32 — 287
38 — 287
50 — 288

Matt.
4:1-11 — 211
4:19 — 146
4:21-22 — 146
5:44 — 173
9:9 — 148n58
10:2-4 — 146
10:8 — 154
11:5 — 154
12:22-28 — 287
12:30 — 197
16:13-19 — 146
16:16-19 — 160–161
16:18 — 162
17:1-8 — 146
18:15-17 — 162
18:21-22 — 162
26:69-75 — 146
28:16-20 — 146
28:19 — 137

Mark
2:14 — 148n58
3:16-19 — 145n50
3:24 — 287
5:1-13 — 157
9:50 — 198n233
14:66-72 — 146

Luke
4:1-13 — 212
5:27 — 148
6:14-16 — 145n50
6:28 — 173
7:21 — 154
10:5 — 198
10:16 — 274
22:32 — 161
22:56-62 — 146
23:33-43 — 225

John
1:1-18 — 148
1:42 — 162
1:43 — 148
18:25-27 — 146
21:15-17 — 161
21:15-19 — 146
20:22 — 146
20:28 — 146

Acts
1:12-23 — 148
1:13 — 145n50
2:1-13 — 146
5:1-11 — 157
5:12-42 — 165
8:9-24 — 175
14:4 — 145n50
14:14 — 145n50

1Cor.
3:11 — 161n93
3:17 — 119n300
10:4 — 161
11:20 — 119n300

Gal.
1:1   144n47

Rom.
16:7   145n50

1Pet.
2:15   119n300

Rev.
22:1-2   239

General Index

40 Homiliae in Evangelia   82, 286

Abdias, legendary bishop of Babylon   68, 70–71, 169
Absence, typology of   195
Acculturation   16
Acta Sebastiani   292
Adalbert, archbishop of
    Hamburg-Bremen   54
Adam of Bremen   51, 54, 56, 235
Age of Peace
    Gizurr's   232, 242–246
    Pax Romana   202
    Between Church and King in
        Norway   249
Aldhelm, abbot of Melmesbury and bishop of Sherborne   72n135
Allegory   81, 118, 126, 143, 281, 283
Alms   108
Alþingi   1n1, 53n64, 238, 244, 245
AM 645 4to   X, 67–69, 105, 189n206, 210, 216, 228, 285, 287n33, 289–291
AM 652/630 4to   X, 67–69, 105, 189n206, 228, 287, 290–291
Ambrose   161, 289
Ambrosiaster   161
Anastasius, pope   255
Andrew
    Apostle   72, 77, 114, 136, 141, 146n51, 155–157, 159, 169, 181, 211–212, 216
    Saga of (Icelandic)   69n123, 69n124, 135, 146, 162n97, 179, 180n165, 181, 183, 186, 189n206, 201, 285, 287
Anger of God   179, 214–217
Anger, capital sin   137, 176, 183–184, 194
Annanias   165
Ansgar, missionary   51
Antiquitates, by Josephus   292
Apocryphal Acts of the Apostles   77n158, 175
Apostolic Creed   see Creed
Architecture   41, 117
Ari Þorgilsson, *the wise*   32, 53, 63, 121, 231, 242
Arianism   175
Arngrímr Brandsson, monk   292

Arnór Tumason, chieftain   272–273, 275
Arrogance, capital sin   176
Auður Ketilsdóttir, *djúpúðga*   232
Augustine   99n234, 122, 161, 203, 205–206, 292
Augustinian canons   57, 251
Augustus, emperor   138, 202–203, 244
Authority
    Apostolic   45, 134, 144–145, 155, 159, 163, 168, 226–227
    Clerical   47, 101–103, 115, 135
    Discursive   133–134
    Episcopal   47, 83, 222, 245–246, 254–257, 259, 262–263, 268, 275
    Papal   26, 39–41, 43–46, 161, 237–238, 249, 267, 275, 279
    Of the Church   3, 61, 89, 209, 228, 235, 247
Axis mundi   119
Árni Magnússon, manuscript
    collector   282n1, 287–288
Árni Þorláksson, bishop   252

Bakhtin, Mikhail   18n47
Bamberg confession   141, n33
Bartholomew
    Apostle   69n123, 69n124, 136n15, 151, 154n77, 155n78, 159n87, 179, 184, 213
    Latin accounts of   69, 287, 291, 153n75, 287, 291
    Saga of (Icelandic)   151–152, 153n73, 153n75, 166n114, 179, 210, 213, 285, 291
Basil of Caesarea
    Saint   285
    Life of   284, 286n25
Baptism   52, 97, 130, 164n109, 173n134, 184, 202–203, 225, 231–232
Baptismal Fonts   84, 86–87
Battle of Fimreite   266
Becoming
    Christianization as a process of   59–60
    Opponents in a state of   195–196
Bede the Venerable   72n135, 121–122, 161
Beloved disciple   147
Bergen   52, 79, 250, 267
Bergr Sokkason   105–106

Bernard the Saxon 235
Bjarnastaðahlíð-panels 217–222, 225
Bjarnvarðr (Bjarnharðr), missionary 90
Blasius (Blaise)
　Saint 183
　Saga of (Icelandic) 183, 282
Blickling Homilies 77–79
Blót, blóta (sacrificial ceremonies) 174, 179, 182, 214
Blótmaðr (man of blót) 174, 181–182
Blótbiskup (heathen religious leader) 166n114, 181, 182n169, 208
Body
　and spiritual struggle 193–195, 196–197
Book of Icelanders 32, 54, 63, 121, 231, 242, 244
Book of Settlements 54, 59, 90, 91n198, 232
Bourdieu, Pierre 21, 102n241, 134
Brandr Sæmundarson, bishop 237, 254–255, 256n111, 263, 265
Breakspear, Nicholas (Hadrian IV) 57, 249
Bremen diocese 49
Brynjubítr 273
Bureaucracy 55, 97, 236
Burial practices 97, 233–234

Canon law 15, 38, 41–43, 46, 111, 259
Canons regular 251
Capitulary 143n41
Catholic Homilies 77–78
Cemetery 8, 234, 234n17
Charity 108
Charlemagne 40, 127, 198n235
Chieftain 1n1, 2, 11–12, 14, 17, 25, 31, 51, 55, 59, 89–90, 109, 111, 119, 231, 238, 242–243, 247–248, 251–252, 254, 257, 261–262, 264, 269–271, 273–279
　Apostle as 148–149, 160
　Bishop Gizurr as 246
　Christ as 138
　Devil as 214
　Ordained 91–95
Chieftain Church (goðakirkja) 12, 14, 246–247, 254, 263, 279
Chieftaincy (goðorð) 93
Christianization
　Of Iceland 3, 10, 30, 37–38, 53–59, 60, 88, 111

　Of Marriage 15
　Of Scandinavia 36, 48–50
Church bells 271
Church building 29, 34, 89, 114, 117–120, 234
　Allegorical interpretation of 141, 281
　As a location of discourse 117–120, 171
Church chieftains (kirkjugoðar) 12
City of God 203, 205n255
Clement
　Saint and bishop of Rome 167–168, 175, 187
　Saga of 166–167, 169, 175, 187, 285, 289
Cletus, (Anacletus) bishop of Rome 166–167
Cluny 39n10
Cnut the Great, king 241
Codex Scardensis (SÁM 1) 34n91, 69, 104, 162n97, 174, 288
Commandments 143, 167, 180, 184, 190–191, 201, 204–205, 209, 215, 223
Computus of Garland 121
Concubinage 253
Corpus permixtum 110
Coronation oath, of Magnús Erlingsson 250
Cosmic battle 193
Creed, apostolic 101, 139–141
Crozier
　In medieval Iceland 87, 268n148
　Of Páll Jónsson 220–222
Cultural history 7, 9, 15–17
Cultural memory 117

Day of Judgment 122, 124n321, 215, 217, 224
De XII abusivis saeculi 82, 286
Decretal, papal 43, 46
Decretum Gelasianum 162
Decretum Gratiani 42, 162
Deleuze, Gilles 195
Demoniac 157, 159n87
Demons 123, 151, 154, 156–157, 179–180, 182, 193, 210–212, 210n275, 210n276, 211–214, 218, 220–223, 257
Denmark 49–50, 50n55, 52, 55n71, 241
Descartes, René 18
Descensus Christi ad Inferos see *Niðrstigningar saga*
Devil, the 77, 110n271, 124, 136, 142, 149, 152–153, 159, 176, 190–191, 193, 197, 209, 210, 221–223, 257, 261
Dialogues of Gregory the Great 82, 103, 193, 286

Dictatus papae 40–42
Dionysius Exiguus 120–121
Discourse
   Concept of 18–23
   Ecclesiastical 17–18, 23, 29–31, 34, 89,
      109, 111, 114n285, 134, 142n39, 144, 146,
      151–152, 160, 163, 171–172, 175, 177, 181,
      197, 199, 207, 215, 225, 228, 244, 262,
      266–267, 278–279
Disobedience 183, 189, 191–192, 257, 262, 266
District priests (þingaprestar,
   leiguprestar) 92–93
Doctrine
   As Teaching (discursive) see Teaching
   Ecclesiastical 201, 262, 237
   Of Lay Patronage 252
   Of the Sacraments 125
Domitian, Roman emperor 184–185, 208
Door of Valþjófsstaður 83–84

Easter table (*tabula computistica*) 120–121
Ebo of Rheims, archbishop 50
Ecclesiastical imagination 120, 128
Ecclesiastical language 98, 101, 115, 116n288
Egeas, earl 159n87, 183
Egill Skallagrímsson 129
Egils saga 129, 131
Eilífr Goðrúnarson, skald 239
Einar Ólafur Sveinsson 11
Einar Þorvarðarson, chieftain 256
Eiríkr Ívarsson, archbishop 57, 89, 93, 251,
   254, 261–262, 267–268
Elite
   Imperial 29, 279
   Interpretative 29, 279
   Political 14, 29, 44, 54, 89, 93, 98, 236,
      247, 253–254, 276–277
   Religious 43, 94, 236, 264
Elmo see Erasmus of Antioch
Elucidarius 103, 195, 222
Empire
   As culture 29n80
   British 27
   Byzantine 91n197
   Carolingian 40
   Chines Han 28
   Concept of 21, 25, 27–30, 279
   Danish North Sea 241

   Of God 152
   Ottoman 28
   Persian 26
   Roman 26–27, 178
   Roman Church as 25–26, 25n69, 29,
      37–39, 46, 249, 264
Enemy image (*Feindbild*) 172
Envy
   Angel of 189–190
   Capital sin 176, 182–183, 188, 194, 266
Erasmus of Antioch (Elmo) 284
Erik the Victorious, king of Sweden 52
Erik Bloodaxe, king of Norway 129
Erlingr Ormsson, *Skakke* 249
Ermoginis 182
Eucharist 35, 77, 200
Eugene III, pope 57
Eustace see Placidus
Eutropus, disciple of Abdias 70
Evangeliary (*evangeliarium*) 143n41
Evangelical Lutheran Church of
   Iceland 6n9
Evangelists 88, 141
Excommunication 9n18, 269, 271
Eyjólfr Sæmundsson, chieftain 63, 251
Eyrbyggja saga 232n5
Eysteinn Erlendsson, archbishop 57, 248–
   254, 255n105, 256–257, 260–262

Færeyinga saga 232n5
Fall of man see original sin
Faroe Islands 26, 53
Feindbild see enemy-image
Figural interpretation see typology
Figuralism see typology
Filetus, opponent of James 182
Finnur Jónsson, church historian and
   bishop 6n10, 7n11, 256n107
First Grammatical Treatise 32, 80, 285
Flatatunga-panels 83n186, 85–86
Flóamanna saga 240
Forty Armenian Martyrs (*Passio quadraginta*
   militum) 291
Foucault, Michel 18–19, 59, 118, 134
Frederick I (Barbarossa), Holy Roman
   Emperor 267n146
Frederick II, Holy Roman Emperor 38
Friðrekr (Frederick), missionary 90

Garland   see *Computus* of Garland
Gelasius I, pope   161
Gemeinde-Symbol   140
Gemma animæ   142, 199
Gísli Finnason, priest   102, 109
Gizurr Hallsson, chieftain   253, 257, 261, 283
Gizurr Ísleifsson, bishop   12, 55, 87, 231, 242, 244
Goðorðsmaðr (owner of a chieftaincy)   93
Golden Age   see Age of Peace
Gospel of Nicodemus   77n158, 210, 289
Gospel of Pseudo-Matthew   77n158, 292
Gospels (canonical)   141–143, 146, 148, 154, 163–164, 180, 211, 292
Grágás   13, 14n34, 90, 91n197, 94
Gramsci, Antonio   21, 65n109
Great commission (Matt 28:19)   137, 146, 149
Gregory I (the Great), pope   82, 96, 103, 193, 242, 281, 284, 286–287, 292
Gregory VII, pope   40, 42, 45, 47, 192, 245, 249
Gregory of Tours   72
Grímr Hólmsteinsson, priest   106
Guðmundr Arason, bishop   87, 112, 233n14, 264–271, 273–276
Guðmundr Þorvaldsson, *dýri*   253
Gunnlaugr Leifsson, monk   99, 235

Hadrian IV, pope   see Nicholas Breakspear
Hagiography   8, 23, 29, 31–34, 66, 73, 69, 99–100, 103–105, 111, 128–131, 136, 139, 171–172, 188, 206, 234n21, 270, 288
Hafliði Másson, lawspeaker   111n275, 243
Hákon Sigurðarson, earl   239
Hákon Sverrisson, king of Norway   267
Hákon the Good, king of Norway   52
Hamar   26, 52
Hamburg-Bremen archbishopric   52–53, 235, 245, 246
Hannes Finnsson, bishop   256n107
Haraldr 'Bluetooth' Gormsson, king of Denmark and Norway   51
Haraldr Greycloak, king of Norway   52
Hartwig, archbishop of Salzburg   245
Haukadalur   33, 63, 93, 95, 231
Haukdælir   91, 121, 231, 232, 246
Heathens   169, 173, 174, 177, 178, 179, 180, 181, 182, 187, 188, 195

Heaven   118n299, 119, 160, 176, 187, 203, 205, 206n261, 209, 218, 225, 226, 227, 228, 232n5, 292
Hebionites   175
Hebrew Bible   128–129, 209
Hegel, Georg Wilhelm Friedrich   171n129
Hegemony
  Concept of   65n109
  Cultural   60–66
  Ideological   62n91
Heiðarvíga saga   128
Heimskringla   131, 240
Helgi Eyvindarson *magri*, settler   232
Hell   119, 123, 124n321, 160, 209, 210n275, 215, 217–218, 221–225, 292
Henry IV, Holy Roman Emperor   40, 245
Heresy   149, 165, 166, 169, 173n134, 174–176, 189, 190n209, 191–192, 207, 261
Heretic   123, 166, 171, 173–177, 187–189, 191–192, 195, 207–208, 262
Hermeneutical Jew   see Jews
Herod, king of Judea   208
Hierarchy
  Ecclesiastical   1, 40, 42, 46–48, 54, 59, 89, 134, 159–160, 166–170, 247, 251, 255, 278
  Imperial   26, 60
  Social   21, 172, 193
Hilary of Poitiers   161
Holy Spirit   136, 146, 148–150, 164n108, 170, 202, 212, 224, 238, 270n153
Hólar in Eyjafjörður   85
Hólar in Skagafjörður
  Battle of   272–273, 275
  Bishopric   1, 9n20, 26, 53, 55, 57, 121, 232, 235, 264, 292
  Cathedral   83, 88, 218
  Episcopal Seat   55–56, 63–64, 87, 109–112, 244, 254
Hólar, battle of   271–273, 275–276
Honorius Augustodunensis   122, 124, 126, 142, 199
Höskuldsstaðabók   292
Hrafnkels saga   13
Hróðólfr (Rudolf), missionary bishop   90, 235
Hugh of St. Victor   124
Humbert of Silva Candida, cardinal   40

Hungrvaka x, 63n94, 121, 234, 242–243, 245, 254, 256

Icelandic Homily Book 74n147, 75, 78–81, 88, 96, 101, 103–108, 110n271, 111n274, 121, 123, 140–142, 164, 173, 176, 184–188, 191, 193, 191, 199–202, 205–206, 207n263, 208, 215, 217, 223, 244, 263, 271, 281, 284–286, 290–291, 293
Icelandic School, the 11–12
Iconography 41, 85, 129, 145, 183, 221
Ideology
    Christianity as 62, 119, 198n235
    Of divine kingship 51, 250
    Imperial 29, 144n48, 199
    Myth as 132
Idolatry 149, 154, 174, 182, 184, 214
Idols 151, 159, 173, 179–180, 182, 190, 213
Illugi Bjarnarson, chieftain 93
Imperial hermeneutical framework 17, 20–21, 24–25, 37, 132–133, 197, 278
Imperial studies 20–21, 24–25, 132–133
Innocent III, pope 36, 161, 198n235, 237, 237n35
Innocent IV, pope 38
Inventories 34, 83, 86–87, 118, 286n32
Investiture Controversy 40, 245
Irenaeus of Lyon 175
Isidore of Seville 122, 283n13
Ísleifr Gizurarson 54, 56, 63, 91, 234–235, 242
Íslendingabók see *Book of Icelanders*

James the Greater, apostle
    Apostle 146–147, 168–169, 182, 200n240, 208
    Saga of (Icelandic) 69n123, 137n22, 146, 154, 189, 285, 287, 291
James the Less, apostle
    Apostle 146–148
    Saga of (Icelandic) 69n124, 136, 148n58, 153n74, 154n77, 175, 287
Jesus Christ 135–139, 141–142, 144–151, 153–154, 156, 158–162, 163n102, 164–165, 168, 173, 179, 185–186, 188, 197, 199, 212, 225, 228, 287
Jews 123, 137, 171, 173–174, 185–188
    hermeneutical 186
    virtual 186
John
    Apostle 69n124, 86, 136, 141, 146–147, 154n77, 155, 155n78, 168–170, 184–185, 192, 198, 224, 227
    Saga of (Icelandic) 146–147, 150, 158, 168, 170, 182, 184, 223, 227, 287, 290
John the Baptist
    Saint 130
    Saga of (Icelandic) 106
John Chrysostom 292
John XXII, pope 237n35
Jón Arason, bishop 87
Jón Ögmundarson, bishop 55, 57, 64, 87, 93, 102, 109, 121, 235, 245
Joseph of Arimathea 289
Judas Iscarioth 129, 148, 164
Jude, apostle
    Apostle 68, 70, 72, 146–147, 154, 158, 169, 182, 190n209, 287
    Saga of (Icelandic) 69n123, 155, 157, 166n114, 189, 191, 287, 291
Judges-delegate 43, 45
Judgment Day see Day of Judgment
Julius Africanus 70n129
Justin Martyr 175

Ketill Þorsteinsson, bishop 218
Kiss of peace (*osculum pacis*) 200
Kingship see Ideology
Klængr Þorsteinsson, bishop 254–256, 263
Knútsdrápa 241
Kojève, Alexandre 171n129
Kolbeinn Tumason, chieftain 264–265, 268, 270–271
Konráð Gíslason 282, 291
Konungs Skuggsjá 293
Kristni á Íslandi 6–7, 9n19
Kristni saga 242
Kulturhistorisk Leksikon for Nordisk Middelader 5n5, 6n7
Kygri-Björn Hjaltason 289, 292
Kyriarchy 144n48

Laity 31, 65–66, 78, 104, 107, 114, 131, 171, 210, 247, 252, 266
Landnámabók See *Book of Settlements*

Lateran Council
  2nd 57
  3rd 46
  4th 121, 237, 292
Latin
  Proficiency 96–101, 104, 143
  As an Ecclesiastical Language see Ecclesiastical Language
lay patronage (*ius patronatus*) 252
Lazius, Wolfgang 70
Lefebvre, Henri 118
Legenda aurea 71, 148n58
Letter of privilege, of Magnús Erlingsson 250
Leo I, pope 161
Leo IX, pope 40, 42, 47, 52
Lincoln, Bruce 4n4, 21, 22n61, 132n1, 132n2, 134
Linus, pope 166–167
Lipsius, Richard Adalbert 69, 70, 71n132
Literacy 61, 66, 95, 98, 98–99, 102, 114, 134, 236
Liturgical Clothing 87, 220
Liturgical Texts 23, 31, 61, 79, 81, 103
Liturgical Year 74–75, 78, 80, 82, 143n41, 145
Liturgy
  As a Package 22n63
  In monasteries 74
  Medieval Catholic 73, 97, 100, 117, 120, 139n26, 140n31, 159, 199–201, 171, 199
  Of the Eucharist 77
  Of the Office see Office Liturgy
  Of the Word 77
Ljúfini 94
Lord's Prayer (*Pater noster*) 76, 96, 123, 139–141
Luke, evangelist 141
Lund, archbishopric 47n42, 52–53, 56–57, 246, 249, 278

Mandate, apostolic 137, 144–150
Magnús Erlingsson, king 249–250, 266
Marianus Scotus of Mainz 121n306
Marital affairs 15, 40, 96, 107, 253–254, 258
Mark, evangelist 141
Martin of Tours
  Saint 175, 180, 211
  Saga of 69n125, 175, 180, 210, 285
Martyrdom 72n135, 155, 174, 181, 206, 279

Mary, mother of Jesus
  Annunciation 284
  Nativity 271
  Purification of 188, 217
  Saint 86, 145, 147n55, 218, 225, 283
  Saga of 289, 292
Mass 68, 76–79, 87, 95, 96–97, 106, 108–112, 142–143, 158, 170, 187, 194, 199–201, 222, 273, 285
Master-Slave Dialectic 171n129
Materiality 82–87
Matthew
  Apostle 135–136, 141, 148, 154, 157, 181–182, 189n206, 208, 216
  Saga of (Icelandic) 69, 135–136, 148–149, 216, 221, 228, 282, 285, 287, 291
Matthias
  Apostle 148, 155n78
  Saga of (Icelandic) 136, 145, 148, 155n78, 287
Memory studies 117
Mettener Collection I 76
Michael
  Archangel 105, 281
  Saga of 105
Miracles 66, 154–155, 164–165, 180, 215, 282, 285
Mission
  Missionary activity 50, 72, 137, 152, 154, 159, 164, 169, 178, 182, 179–180
  Missionary bishop 235
  Missionary king 49, 205–206, 231
Monastery 1, 2, 8–9, 16, 16n40, 23, 33, 55–58, 62, 64–65, 67, 73–74, 80–81, 90, 95, 99, 103, 105–108, 111, 158, 218, 235, 255, 285, 286n32, 292
  Augustinian 9, 57, 64, 73
  Benedictine 9, 33, 55n71, 57, 218, 80, 218, 235, 292
  Helgafell 57n77, 64
  Hítardalur 58
  Bær in Borgarfjörður 90, 235
  Munkaþverá 58
  St. Victor 57, 64, 73
  Þykkvibær 57n77, 58, 64, 73
  Þingeyrar 33, 55–58, 64, 80–81, 99, 105, 218, 235, 292, 292n65
Morkinskinna 246

GENERAL INDEX 325

Nero, Roman emperor 135n13, 175, 177, 184, 208
Nicholas of Myra, bishop 106, 282
Niðarós
  Archbishopric 26, 28, 52–53, 56–57, 95, 238, 248–249, 254, 255, 259, 263, 267–268, 273–276, 278–279
  Cathedral 221
Niðrstigningar saga 69n125, 285
Night Office (Matins) 73–74, 77
Nordic studies (Norræn fræði) 5
Norway 49, 52, 55n71, 76, 78, 81, 95, 97, 186, 205, 220n306, 221, 233, 235, 241, 247–251, 256n111, 266–268, 275
Norwegian Homily Book (AM 619 4to) 78–80, 118, 281, 286, 291n59

Office Liturgy 73–74, 96, 106, 111, 111n274, 200
Old Christian Laws section (*Kristinna laga þáttur*) 90, 91n197, 92, 94–95, 100, 102, 139, 234, 238, 238n38
Olof, King of Sweden 52
Origen of Alexandria 161
Ornamentation 23, 32, 34–35, 66, 76, 83, 85–86, 117–118, 218, 221, 278
Oslo 26, 49, 52
'Other' 171–173, 188, 192–193, 197, 207, 228
Ólafr Haraldsson, King of Norway 49, 52, 79, 130, 240
Ólafr Tryggvason, King of Norway 49, 52, 130, 231

paganism 6n8, 51, 128–129, 69, 178, 260
Páll Jónsson, bishop 63n94, 109, 121, 220–222, 237, 253, 270n156, 285
Panopticon 117, 118
papacy 40–48, 53, 56, 99, 119, 161n91, 166, 245, 299, 306, 307, 308, 310, 311, 313
Papal-historical turn (Papstgeschichtliche Wende) 39
Papal legates 43–46, 57, 249–250
Papal letters 41, 43–44, 48, 82, 162, 236n29, 237–239
Papal primacy 161n91
Paradise 222, 224–225, 228, 257
Paschal II, pope 53
Passion narratives
  Medieval (*passiones*) 69, 73, 153n73, 153n75, 174n136, 183, 186, 201, 216, 223, 291
  Of the Canonical Gospels 185
  Passio Domini, sermon 164, 173, 185n184
  Passionaries 68, 72
Pater noster see Lord's Prayer
Paul
  Apostle 39n10, 42, 87, 135n13, 141, 144, 145, 145n50, 148, 151n68, 159n87, 162n95, 166, 175–176, 178, 184, 198n233, 201, 210–211, 227, 288–289
  Saga of (Icelandic) 69n125, 136, 148, 154n76, 285, 287, 290
Peace
  Age of see Age of Peace
  Kiss of see Kiss of Peace
  Disturbers of 206, 208, 224
  Of the Cemetery 205
  Of the Church (discursive) 10, 198–209, 229, 244–246, 275
  Of God movement (*Pax Dei*) 258
Penance 77, 108, 114, 203
Pentecost 105, 146, 150, 164
Performance
  Performative texts 23, 158–159
  Performative context 72–73, 107
  Liturgical 107, 171, 199
Persecuting society 192
Peter
  Apostle 39n10, 41–2, 87, 119, 136, 137, 139n26, 141, 146, 147n57, 154n77, 160–169, 175–177, 198n233, 204, 207, 211, 225–227, 237–238, 241, 260, 262, 289
  Primatus Petri see Primacy
  Saga of (Icelandic) 69n125, 146, 151n68, 160, 162–167, 175–176, 184, 185n184, 201, 204, 207, 227, 260–261, 285, 287, 290–291
Peter Damian 40
Peter of Poitiers 287
Phenomenology of the Spirit, Hegel 171n129
Philip
  Apostle 105n251, 136, 147, 148n58, 153n74, 154n77, 169, 181
  Saga of (Icelandic) 69n124, 137n22, 147n55, 48n58, 153n74, 175, 287
Physiologus 81, 215, 283

Placidus (Eustace)
  Saint 290
  Saga of (Icelandic) 282, 289
Polimius, king 136n15, 151, 184
Polytheism 178
Possession, demonic 180, 213–214
Postcolonial
  Concept of 24, 59, 133
  Postcolonial historiography 59
  Postcolonial studies 24, 27, 133
  Postcolonial hermeneutics 20–21, 24
'Power over' 27, 30, 39, 132n3, 144n48, 152
Primacy
  Papal (Roman) 41, 43, 45, 161–162
  Primatus Petri 160–166
Proprietary church system 103, 247
Prosper's epigrams 82, 125, 286
Psalter 32, 96, 98, 288
Pseudo-Ambrose 223
Pseudo Clementine Corpus 175
Pseudo-Melito 224
Pseudo-Abdian Collection 68–72, 169
Purgatory 124n321

Ragnheiður Þórhallsdóttir 253
Rainbow allegory 81, 215, 283
Refectory 73, 105, 158
Reform
  Gregorian 39–43, 45–46, 57, 192n220, 237, 245, 247–249, 251–253, 256, 258–260, 264, 268
  Monastic 39n10
Reformation
  Of modern democracies 20n55
  Protestant 6n9, 78n163, 111
Regula Benedicti 73, 80
Relics 236, 270–271, 290
Religious specialist 102, 115, 209, 278
'Reluctant bishop' motive 266
Retributive dynamics (discursive) 133, 228, 278
Ringerike style 85–86
Romaldus 283
Roman Penitential 86
Roman rite 199
Rule of Benedict See *Regula Benedicti*
Rúðólfr (Rudolf), missionary bishop see Hróðólfr
Rúnólfr Sigmundarson, abbot 106

Sacrament 96n220, 108, 125
  Of penance 114
  Eucharistic See Eucharist
  Extreme Unction 97
  Of baptism See Baptism
Sacred language 99
Sæmundur Sigfússon, *the wise* 251
Saga of bishop Martin See Martin of Tours
Saga of Bishop Þorlákr See Þorlákr Þórhallsson, bishop
Saga of Blaise (Blasius) See Blasius (Blaise)
Saga of Clement See Clement
Saga of John the Baptist See John the Baptist
Saga of Mary of Egypt see 291
Saga of Nicholas 106, 282
Saga of Sebastian see Sebastian
Saga of the Apostle Andrew See Andrew
Saga of the Apostle Bartholomew See Bartholomew
Saga of the Apostle James See James the Greater
Saga of the Apostle John See John
Saga of the Apostle Paul See Paul
Saga of the Apostle Peter See Peter
Saga of the Apostle Thomas See Thomas
Saga of the Apostles Philip and James See James, Philip
Saga of the Apostles Simon and Jude See Jude, Simon
Salvation History (Heilsgeschichte) 187, 215, 236
Saphira 165
Satan See Devil
Saxony 49, 63, 90, 95, 245
Schüssler Fiorenza, Elisabeth 30, 134n9, 144, 155, 230, 230n1
Sebastian
  Saint 223
  Saga of (Icelandic) 181, 292–293
Second Council of Lyon 174n138
Second Lateran Council See Lateran Council
Selja, Norway 235
Senses of scripture 126–127
Septem artes liberales 95
Serenus, bishop of Marseilles 82
Sermo humilis 33
Sermon 2–3, 8, 23, 31–33, 66, 74–82, 88, 103–104, 107–108, 110n271, 118–121,

GENERAL INDEX

138, 160–164, 171, 178, 184–188, 191, 193, 198n233, 201–202, 205–206, 215, 217, 222–226, 244, 271, 273, 278, 281, 283–284, 290, 293.
  Concept 74n149
  Types of 75–76
Servile priests 92–95, 278
Sexual morality 255, 258–259
Sigurðr Ormsson, chieftain 270n156, 271, 273
Sigurður Nordal 11n25, 12, 108
Sigvatr Þórðarson, skald 241
Simon Magus 164–166, 175–177, 184, 188, 204, 207–208
Simon (the Zealot)
  Apostle 68, 72, 146–148, 154, 158, 169, 182, 189–190
  Saga of (Icelandic) 69n123, 70, 155n78, 157, 166n144, 189, 191, 287, 291
Simone de Beauvoir 171n129
Simony 175, 175n141
Skagerrak 49
Skaldic Poetry 239–242
Skálholt
  Bishopric 1, 26, 53, 55, 64, 67, 212, 232, 253, 292
  Cathedral 83, 87
  Episcopal Seat 63, 80, 109, 111, 121, 244, 254, 283, 285–286
Skapti Þóroddsson, lawspeaker and skald 240
Snorra Edda 131
Snorri Sturluson, chieftain, scholar 112n280, 131, 273
Sociology of knowledge 19–20
Soul 79, 122, 194–195, 197, 203, 214, 216–217, 221, 225, 228, 262, 274–275
Space of representation (Lefebvre) 118
Speech against the bishops 267
Spirit see Holy Spirit
St. Père de Chartres 79
St. Victor monastery 57, 64
Stactaeus 224, 227
Staðir-controversy 248, 258
Stavanger 26, 52
Stave Church Homily 117–118, 141, 271, 281
Stave church, building 221
Steindór Ormsson 287
Stephen martyr 186, 290
Stjórn (I, II, III) 100, 104

Stubbornness, capital sin 181, 258, 261, 271, 274–275
Sturla Þórðarson, saga writer and lawman 256, 271, 273
Sturlunga 91n198, 93–94, 103, 111, 231, 243, 255, 258, 264–265, 269
Sveinn Jónsson, follower of bishop Guðmundr 272
Sverrir Sigurðsson, king 266
Sweden 52, 55n71, 109
Syncretism 233, 239
Synod of Ingelheim 52

Teaching
  Correct 101, 201, 260
  Erroneous 177, 191
  Kenning, discursive theme 134–143, 171
  Of the Apostles 135–136, 139, 155–156, 164n109, 177, 191, 227
  Of Christ 135–136
  Of the Church 134–135, 139, 167, 170, 260, 262, 271, 274
  Of the Gospels 143
Teitr Ísleifsson 63, 93, 231
Tertullian 175
Textual community 114–115
Textus receptus (of the Apostle's Creed) 101, 141
Thecla 283
Theodwin, cardinal 57
Theophilus 285
Tithe 1, 7 14, 56, 244, 273
  Law 12, 57
Tranquility of order (*tranquillitas ordinis*) 203, 204
Transcultural history 16
Translatio Ecclesiae 114–116
Trinitarian faith 143, 225
Trinity 202, 212
Trinubium Annae 292
Typology see Figuralism

Ulrich Engelberti 96n220
University of Iceland 6n9
Uppsala-archdiocese 47n42, 53, 57
Urðar brunnr 239–240
Urnes style 221

Valþjófsstaður, door of see Door of Valþjófsstaður

Veldi (power, dominion)   151–153, 168, 191, 209–210, 216, 221–222
Venantius Fortunatus   71n135
Veraldar saga   122n309, 236, 282, 284
Vercelli Book   77–78
Víðines, battle of   271–273, 276
Villa (heresy)   173, 175, 187, 189, 191–192
violence   119, 137, 163n102, 175, 181, 184–185, 188, 198, 204–207, 243, 258–259, 264, 275
Virtutes Apostolorum   71–72, 190n209, 224
Vulgate   100, 162

Wessobrun confession   141n33
Wonders   see Miracles

Þangbrandr, missionary   90
Þingeyrar-monastery   55, 81, 99, 218, 235
Þingvellir   6n8, 53, 55

Þórðr Sölvason   91, 93
Þorgeirr Þorkelsson, lawspeaker   6n8, 244
Þorgils Oddason, chieftain   243
Þórir Guðmundsson, archbishop   274
Þorlákr Þórhallsson, bishop   8, 57, 63, 73, 87, 99, 130, 247, 251–254, 257–258, 260–261, 264, 268, 270
  Miracle book of   69n125, 285
  Penitential of   253
  Saga of   121, 252, 254
Þorvaldr Gizurarson, chieftain   275
Þrándur in Gata   232n5

Ælfric of Eynsham   77–78
Æthelweard   78

Ögmundr Þorvarðsson   266
Özurr, archbishop of Lund   56–57

Printed in the United States
by Baker & Taylor Publisher Services